国家双高"铁道机车专业群"系列　多语种教材
——铁道车辆技术专业

Control System of High-speed EMU
高速铁路动车组控制系统
（中英文对照版）

主　编　李向超　许卫红
副主编　冯　源　员珍珍　杨忻忻

西南交通大学出版社
·成　都·

图书在版编目（CIP）数据

高速铁路动车组控制系统：中英文对照版/李向超，许卫红主编. —成都：西南交通大学出版社，2024.3
ISBN 978-7-5643-9689-3

Ⅰ.①高… Ⅱ.①李… ②许… Ⅲ.①高速动车－控制系统－汉、英 Ⅳ.①U266

中国国家版本馆 CIP 数据核字（2024）第 009044 号

Control System of High-speed EMU

高速铁路动车组控制系统
（中英文对照版）

主　编　　李向超　　许卫红

责任编辑	张文越
封面设计	何东琳设计工作室
出版发行	西南交通大学出版社 （四川省成都市金牛区二环路北一段 111 号 西南交通大学创新大厦 21 楼）
邮政编码	610031
发行部电话	028-87600564　028-87600533
网址	http://www.xnjdcbs.com
印刷	四川森林印务有限责任公司
成品尺寸	185 mm×260 mm
印张	18.25
字数	488 千
版次	2024 年 3 月第 1 版
印次	2024 年 3 月第 1 次
定价	63.00 元
书号	ISBN 978-7-5643-9689-3

课件咨询电话：028-81435775
图书如有印装质量问题　本社负责退换
版权所有　盗版必究　举报电话：028-87600562

Brief Introduction

This book is one of the series of textbooks for college-enterprise cooperation in higher vocational education. In view of the characteristics of skilled talents training in higher vocational colleges, this book aims to cultivate students' practical ability for their future posts with its content structured around various tasks and projects of vehicle detection. The book is divided into two parts, including 7 chapters. The first part is about non-destructive testing, which includes magnetic particle testing and ultrasonic testing; the second part is about 5T detection system, which specifically includes Trace Hotbox Detection System (THDS), Trackside Acoustic Detection System (TADS), Truck Performance Detection System (TPDS), Trouble of Moving Freight Car Detection System (TFDS) and Train Coach Running Diagnosis System (TCDS) etc.

This book is a collection of theoretical and practical knowledge of railway vehicle detection and maintenance, which can be used as a book for students of railway vehicle major in higher vocational colleges, as well as a training textbook for relevant railway workers and a reference book for on-site operators.

内容简介

本书是高等职业教育校企合作系列教材之一，针对高等职业院校技能型人才培养的特点，以车辆检测的各项任务、项目过程为导向，培养学生面向岗位的实际能力。全书内容分为两部分，共 7 个项目。第一部分无损检测，具体内容包括磁粉探伤和超声波探伤；第二部分为 5T 检测系统，具体内容包括车辆轴温智能探测系统、车辆滚动轴承故障轨边声学诊断系统、车辆运行品质轨边动态监测系统、货车故障轨旁图像检测系统及客车运行状态安全检测系统等。

本书集铁道车辆检测理论知识和检修知识于一体，既可作为高等职业院校铁道车辆专业学生用书，又可做相关铁路职工培训教材以及现场岗位作业人员参考用书。

PREFACE

With the rapid development of high-speed railway in China, China has built the world's largest rail transit network. As an important carrier of the system, the performance of high-speed EMU directly affects the safety, speed and comfort of passengers' trip experience. Specific to the maintenance and inspection work, a large number of professional technicians for the inspection and maintenance of mechanical and electrical equipment are required to provide a solid and reliable talent guarantee to ensure the safe, sustainable and stable development of railway transportation. In addition, in the context of the "the Belt and Road" initiative, the pace of China's railway going global is accelerating, and the training of overseas railway talents is becoming more and more important. Under such a practical situation, we have compiled a bilingual textbook *Control System of High-speed EMU*.

This book introduces the basic knowledge of EMU control system, composition, principle, main circuit, control circuit, logic operation control circuit, composition of EMU auxiliary power supply system, power supply mode, DC/AC power supply circuit, etc., and explains the routine maintenance, troubleshooting and other procedures and standards, which is necessary for learning new technologies and new knowledge.

In the process of compiling this textbook, it was supported by the "Double High Construction Project" of Zhengzhou Railway Vocational and Technical College. The Locomotive and Rolling Stock College of Zhengzhou Railway Vocational and Technical College gave great support and help to the publication of this textbook. At the same time, the EMU Depot of China Railway Zhengzhou Group Co., Ltd. also provided a lot of help and guidance to the compilation of this textbook, and we would like to express our gratitude.

The chief editors of this book are Li Xiangchao and Xu Weihong from Zhengzhou Railway Vocational and Technical College. The associate editors are Feng Yuan, Yun Zhenzhen from Zhengzhou Railway Vocational and Technical college, Yang Xinxin from Chongqing Chemical Industry Vocational College. The compilation of the Chinese part of this textbook is divided as follows: Li Xiangchao wrote Project I, Project II, Project III, Project V, and Feng Yuan wrote Project IV. The English part of this textbook is divided as follows: Xu Weihong is responsible for translating Project 2 and 3, Yun Zhenzhen is responsible for translating Task 2 of Project 1, Project 4 and 5, and Yang Xinxin is responsible for translating Task 1 of Project 1. Li Jianhua, senior engineer of China Railway Zhengzhou Group Co., Ltd. is the chief reviewer of the book.

Due to the limitation of the author's level and the short time, it is inevitable that there are mistakes and inappropriateness, readers are kindly requested to give criticism and correction.

Editor
September 2023

前　言

随着我国高速铁路的快速发展，我国已经建成了世界上最大的轨道交通运输网。而高速动车组作为该系统的重要载体，其性能好坏直接影响旅客乘坐体验的安全性、快捷性和舒适性。具体到检修任务，需要大量的机电设备检修和维护专业技术人员。为确保铁路运输的安全持续稳定发展，提供坚实可靠的人才保障必不可少。另外，在"一带一路"倡议背景下，中国铁路走出去的步伐不断加快，海外铁路人才的培养也越发重要，在这样的实际形势下，我们编写了中英双语教材《高速铁路动车组控制系统》一书。

本书从动车组控制系统基础知识，动车组牵引、制动控制系统的组成、原理、主电路、控制电路，逻辑运行控制电路、动车组辅助供电系统组成、供电方式、直交流供电回路等的组成、工作原理等方面分别进行了介绍，对日常维护检修、故障处理等程序、标准也进行了讲解，是动车组新技术、新知识学习的必备用书。

本教材在编写过程中，得到了郑州铁路职业技术学院"双高建设项目"的支持，郑州铁路职业技术学院机车车辆学院为本教材的出版给予了大力的支持和帮助，同时，郑州铁路局动车段对本教材的编写也提供了很多的帮助和指导，在此一并表示感谢。

全书由郑州铁路职业技术学院李向超、许卫红担任主编，由郑州铁路职业技术学院冯源、员珍珍，重庆化工职业学院，杨忻忻担任主编。本教材中文部分编写分工如下：李向超编写项目一、项目二、项目三，冯源编写项目四冯继营编写项目五。英文部分翻译由许卫红负责翻译项目二和项目三，员珍珍负责翻译项目四和项目五以及项目一的任务二，杨忻忻负责翻译项目一的任务一。全书由中国铁路郑州局集团有限公司高级工程师李建华担任主审。

由于作者水平所限，加之时间仓促，难免有错误和不当之处，恳请读者给予批评指正。

编 者

2023 年 9 月

CONTENTS

Project 1　Understanding the Control System of EMU ·· 1

　　Task 1　Motor Train Set Electrical Schematic Diagram Mark ················ 1

　　Task 2　Overview of EMU Control System ···································· 23

Project 2　Analysis and Inspection of Traction Control Circuit of EMU ············· 30

　　Task 1　Main Circuit Analysis of EMU ·· 30

　　Task 2　Logic Operation Control ·· 37

　　Task 3　Control of Pantograph and Vacuum Circuit Breaker ··············· 46

　　Task 4　Traction Converter Control ··· 51

　　Task 5　CRH380B EMU Traction Control ····································· 55

　　Task 6　Failure Case Analysis ·· 60

Project 3　Analysis of Traction Control Circuit of Fuxing EMU ······················· 73

　　Task 1　Analysis of High-voltage and Traction Control Circuits
　　　　　　of CR400AF EMU ·· 73

　　Task 2　Analysis of CR400BF EMU Traction System ······················ 87

Project 4　Analysis of EMU Brake Control Circuit ·································· 94

　　Task 1　Understanding of the Composition of EMU Brake
　　　　　　Control System ·· 94

Task 2　Brake Control Circuit Analysis ·· 98

Project 5　Circuit Analysis of Auxiliary Power Supply System for EMU ·········· 117

    Task 1　Analysis of Auxiliary Converter ·· 117

    Task 2　Analysis of Auxiliary Power Supply Circuit ···················· 125

    Task 3　Other Control Circuits of Auxiliary Power Supply ··········· 132

    Task 4　Open and Close Control ··· 136

    Task 5　Fault Case Analysis ·· 141

目 录

项目一 动车组控制系统认识 ··· 148

    任务一 动车组电气原理图记号 ·· 148

    任务二 动车组控制系统概述 ··· 169

项目二 动车组牵引控制电路分析与检查 ···································· 175

    任务一 动车组主电路分析 ··· 175

    任务二 逻辑运行控制 ··· 180

    任务三 受电弓、真空断路器控制 ·· 188

    任务四 牵引变流器控制 ··· 193

    任务五 CRH380B 型动车组牵引控制 ···································· 197

    任务六 故障案例分析 ··· 201

项目三 复兴号动车组牵引控制电路分析 ···································· 212

    任务一 CR400AF 动车组高压、牵引控制电路分析 ················ 212

    任务二 CR400BF 动车组牵引系统分析 ································· 224

项目四 动车组制动控制电路分析 ··· 231

    任务一 认识动车组制动控制系统组成 ···································· 231

任务二　制动控制电路分析 ·· 234

项目五　动车组辅助供电系统电路分析 ······································ 251

任务一　浅析辅助变流器 ·· 251

任务二　辅助电源电路分析 ·· 258

任务三　辅助电源其他控制电路 ·· 264

任务四　开关门控制 ·· 267

任务五　故障案例分析 ·· 272

参考文献 ·· 279

Project 1

Understanding the Control System of EMU

【Project Description】

This project is an overall understanding of EMU control system. Through the study of this project, students can understand the symbols in the electrical schematic diagram of high-speed EMU, master the basic composition and working principle of the control system, and lay a foundation for the subsequent project study and future EMU operation and maintenance.

【Project Tasks】

(1) Marks of electric schematic diagram of EMU;
(2) Overview of EMU control system;

Task 1 Motor Train Set Electrical Schematic Diagram Mark

【Task Description】

Through the study of this task, we can understand the central line number of the electric schematic diagram of the EMU and the naming method of the electrical equipment, so as to be able to read and analyze the electrical schematic diagram, laying a foundation for the maintenance of the EMU and troubleshooting of the circuit.

【Background Knowledge】

1.1 Wire number

1.1.1 Definition of wire number

Define the wire number in the following direction (take "1234A1" as an example). Wire number format:

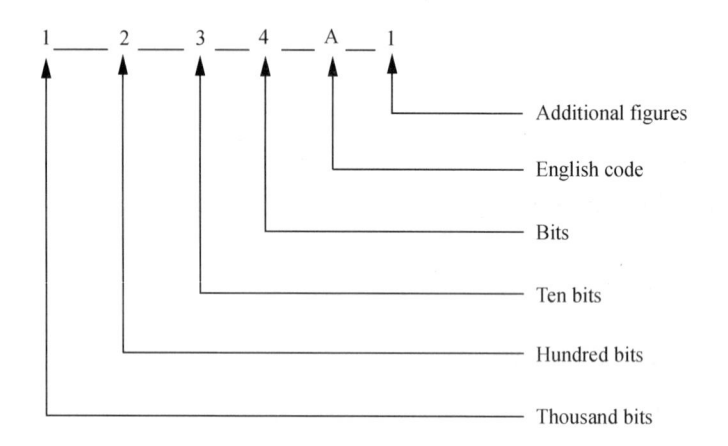

```
1 _ 2 _ 3 _ 4 _ A _ 1
                    └── Additional figures
                └────── English code
            └────────── Bits
        └────────────── Ten bits
    └────────────────── Hundred bits
└────────────────────── Thousand bits
```

Thousand bit and hundred bit: distinguish power supply system and signal type. 0 (zero) can be omitted.

Ten bit, one bit: used to distinguish circuits. 0 (zero) can be omitted. For example, when the wire number is 9: 009→9.

Additional English letters: In the same signal system, signals are associated, and English letters are used when they are separated on the circuit due to relay or switch.

Additional numbers: in the same signal system, when more detailed distinction is required on the basis of additional English letters, additional numbers can be added.

Some line numbers of CRH380A multiple units are classified in Table 1-1-1.

Table 1-1-1 Line number classification of CRH380A electric multiple unit

Wire number	Classification
1 ~ 99	Control command loop (DC 100 V)
100 ~ 199	DC 100 V system
200 ~ 249	AC 100 V system (stable output)
250 ~ 299	AC 100 V system (unstable)
300 ~ 399	AC 220 V system

Continue

Wire number	Classification
400～499	Auxiliary braking type, ATP signal, speed generator
500～599	Main conversion circuit
700～799	AC 400 V (single-phase) system
771、781、791	AC 400 V (three-phase) system
800～899	Air conditioning unit
900～906	Main circuit grounding and main circuit over-current detection
1100～1199	Broadcast loop
1400～1499	ATP antenna and radio service system
1500～1599	MTr2 secondary circuit (main circuit)
1600～1699	ATP device
2500～2502	UHV circuit (AC 25 kV system)

1.1.2 Special wire number

1) Wire number of vehicle information control device

For the output and input lines of the vehicle information control device, the following special line numbers can be used.

M+3-digit number: output and input line number of vehicle information control device.

MF + 3-digit number: cable number of optical cable.

1.2 Equipment code naming method

Mark the following basic methods for naming (take COMCORR1 as an example).

```
CM___CO__R__R__1
 │    │   │  │  │
 │    │   │  │  └─ Additional figures
 │    │   │  └──── Equipment code
 │    │   └─────── Function 2
 │    └─────────── Function 1
 └──────────────── Name
```

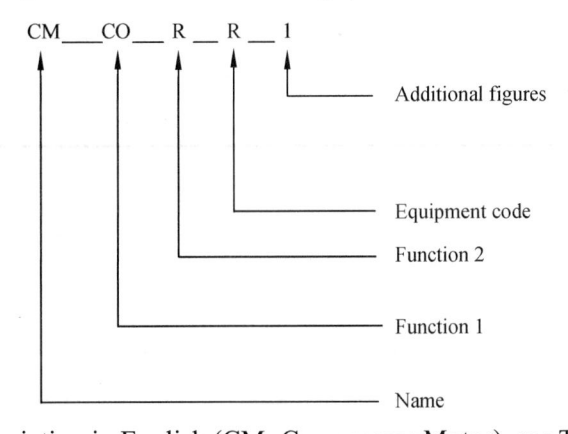

(1) Terms: abbreviation in English (CM=Compressor Motor), see Table 1-1-2.

Table 1-1-2　Equipment name and code

Code	Equipment
AC	Alternating Current
AP	Air Pressure
APU	Auxiliary Power Supply Unit
ATC	ATP Device
B	Brakes Gear
Bat	Battery
Bz	Buzzer
Cab	Drivers ' Cab
CI	Core Inverter
CM	Air Compressor
D	Side Sliding Door Device
EB	Emergency Braking
HMLp	Head Marker Lamp
MC	Main Controller
MLp	Marker Lamp
MM	Main Motor
MRr	Air Source
MT	Main Transformer
Pan	Pantograph
PrLp	Prepared Lamp
SB	Supplementary Brake
UB	Urgent Brake
VCB	Vacuum Circuit Breaker

(2) Function: indicates the action function (CO=Cut Off, R=Reserve). It can be omitted or repeated when unnecessary. The functions are shown in Table 1-1-3.

Table 1-1-3　Function code

Code	Function
C	Close
O	Open
CO	Cut Off
R	Reserve

(3) Equipment code: indicates the type of equipment with code (R=Relay). Equipment code is shown in Table 1-1-4.

Table 1-1-4 Equipment code

Code	Equipment
R	Relay
TR	Time Limit Relay
K	Knot
N	No Fuse Breaker
S	Switch
V	Valve
He	Heater
Th	Thermoneter
Lp	Lamp
T (Tr)	Transformer

(4) Additional numbers: When the same function is used for multiple devices, additional numbers can be used to distinguish.

1.3 Example of circuit analysis

Taking the operation command loop of the head car shown in Figure 1-1-9 as an example, the machine of the circuit corresponding to the label in the figure is shown as follows:

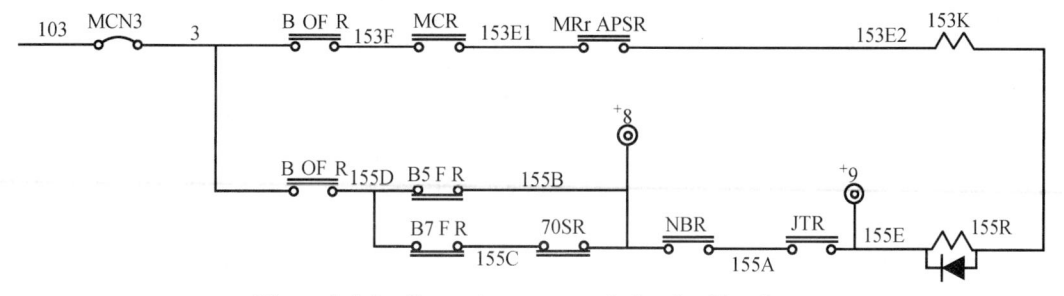

Figure 1-1-9 Operation command circuit of head car

① 103 line - DC 100 V power supply;

② MCN3 - circuit breaker for the third main controller (for operation command);

③ BOFR - relay magnetized by excitation when the braking command is in the running fast position;

④ 153F, 153E1, 153E2 -- lines associated with line 153;

⑤ MCR - relay for main controller (excitation at operation side);

⑥ MRrAPSR - relay for air pressure switch of main air reservoir (excitation under normal pressure);

⑦ 153K - contactor for emergency braking (contactor for supplying power to emergency braking solenoid valve);

Therefore, the following conditions are all conditions for emergency braking release. (Note: there are other conditions except 153K. Even if the circuit condition is established, the emergency braking will not be relieved.)

① The brake setter is in the running fast position;

② The head car is the main control operation;

③ The total air pressure is normal.

In addition, because the wire number is 153 system, it can be known that it is the circuit of emergency braking part.

1.4 Description of graphical symbols for electrical equipment

See Table 1-1-5 for electrical equipment codes.

Table 1-1-5 Code of Electrical Equipment

No.	Code	Equipment
1	153K	153 Wire Contactor
2	155R	155 Wire Relay
3	156R	156 Wire Relay
4	160SAR1, 2	Speed Auxiliary Relay (power loss above 160 km/h)
5	30DLR	30 km/h Door Lock Relay
6	30SR	30 km/h Speed Relay
7	33COR	Speed Condition Open Relay for Door Locking
8	5DLR	5 km/h Door Lock Relay
9	5SR	5 km/h Speed Relay
10	A5SR	5 km/h Auxiliary Speed Relay
11	70SR	70 km/H Speed Relay
12	ACK1	AC Knot 1
13	ACK1R	AC Knot 1 Relay

Continued

No.	Code	Equipment
14	ACK2	AC Knot 2
15	ACK2R	AC Knot 2 Relay
16	ACLN	Air Clean NFB
17	ACM	Auxiliary Compressor Motor
18	ACMGV	Auxiliary Compressor Motor Controller
19	ACMGVR1, 2	Auxiliary Compressor Motor Controller Relay 1 and 2
20	ACMHe	Auxiliary Compressor Motor Heater
21	ACMK	Auxiliary Compressor Motor Contactor
22	ACMN	Auxiliary Compressor Motor NEB
23	ACMR1, 2	Auxiliary Compressor Motor Relay 1, 2
24	ACMS	Auxiliary Compressor Motor Switch
25	ACOCR1, 2	AC Overcurrent Relay 1, 2
26	ACOCRR1, 2	AC Overcurrent Reserve Relay 1, 2
27	ACOSN	Alternating Car Other Supply NFB
28	ACVN1, 2	Alternating Current Voltage NFB 1, 2
29	ACVR1, 2	Alternating Current Voltage Relay 1, 2
30	ADCD1, 2	Automatic Door Control Device 1, 2
31	ADCOS11~12, 21~22	Automatic Door Control Equipment Open Switch 11~12, 21~22
32	ADN1, 2	Automatic Door Control Device NFB 1, 2
33	AHeK	Auxiliary Heater Contactor
34	AHeKN	Auxiliary Heater Contactor NFB
35	AHeS	Auxiliary Heater Switch
36	AHWN	Automatic Hand Wash Stand Basin NFB
37	AMLpR1~3	Automatic Mark Lamp Reserve Relay 1~3
38	AmpN1, 2	Amplifier NFB 1, 2
39	AOCN	Alternating Current Over Current NFB
40	APCR	Air Pipe Close Relay
41	APCS	Air Pipe Close Switch
42	APCV	Air Pipe Close Valve

Continued

No.	Code	Equipment
43	APOR	Air Pipe Open Relay
44	APOV	Air Pipe Opening Valve
45	APPS	Air Pipe Pressure Switch
46	APU	Auxiliary Power Unit
47	APUCN	Auxiliary Power Unit Control NFB
48	APUBMN	Auxiliary Power Unit Blower motor NFB
49	ARf	Auxiliary Rectifier
50	ARfK	Auxiliary Rectifier Knot
51	ARfKR	Auxiliary Rectifier Contactor Relay
52	ARfN2	Auxiliary Rectifier NFB 2
53	ARfRN	Auxiliary Rectifier Contactor NFB
54	Arr	Arrester
55	ASCN	Active Suspension Control NFB
56	ATCBR	ATC Brake Relay
57	ATCKB1R	ATC Release Braking (1N) relay
58	ATCKB4R	ATC Release Braking (4N) relay
59	ATN	Auxiliary Transformer NFB
60	ATPBTMN	ATP BTM Unit Power NFB
61	ATPCOR	ATP Cut-out Relay
62	ATPDMIN	ATP DMI Unit Power NFB
63	ATPDRUN	ATP DRU Unit Power NFB
64	ATPFN	ATP Fan Unit NFB
65	ATPN1	ATP NFB 1
66	ATPPK	ATP Main Power Knot
67	ATPSTMN	ATP STM NFB
68	ATPVCN	ATP Unit Voltage Controller NFB
69	ATr	Auxiliary Transformer
70	B OF R	Brake Control Handle "Operating" Positioning Relay
71	B1 F R	Brake Control Handle 「 1N fast 」 Positioning relay
72	B2 F R	Brake Control Handle 「 2N fast 」 Positioning relay

Continued

No.	Code	Equipment
73	B3 F R	Brake Control Handle 「3N fast」 Positioning Relay
74	B4 F R	Brake Control Handle 「4N fast」 Positioning Relay
75	B5 F R	Brake Control Handle 「5N fast」 Positioning Relay
76	B6 F R	Brake Control Handle 「6N fast」 Positioning Relay
77	B7 F R	Brake Control Handle 「7N fast」 Positioning Relay
78	B F R	Positioning Relay Brake Control Handle 「fast (running - 7N)」
79	B1~3K	Brake Control Handle 「1N-3N」 Positioning Knot
80	B4~5K	Brake Control Handle 「4N-5N」 Positioning Knot
81	B6~7K	Brake Control Handle 「6N-7N」 Positioning Knot
82	B非K	Brake Control Handle "Fast" Positioning Knot
83	Bat	Battery
84	BatK1,2	Battery Knot 1, 2
85	BatK2R	Battery Knot 2 Relay
86	BatKCN	Battery Knot Control NFB
87	BatKN	Battery Knot NFB
88	BatN1,2	Battery NFB 1, 2
89	BatVDN	Battery Voltage Detection NFB
90	BCCN	Braking Control Unit Controls NFB
91	BCU	Brake Control Unit
92	BCUHe	Brake Control Unit Heater
93	BCUN	Braking Control Unit NFB
94	BKK	Contactor for Auxiliary Power Supply Extension
95	BKKN	Contactor Circuit Breaker for Auxiliary Power Extension Supply
96	BKKONR	BKK Input Relay
97	BKKR	BKK Control Relay
98	BKKR-R	BKK Reset Relay
99	BMK	Blower Motor Contactor
100	BNPFsR	Internal Relay of Coupling and Decoupling Electrical Control nel
101	BNR	
102	BNS	
103	BNUBAR	
104	BNUBR	

009

Continued

No.	Code	Equipment
105	BR1	Brake Relay 1
106	BTRCN	Braking Transform Control Unit NFB
107	BV	Brake Valve
108	BVN	Brake Valve NFB
109	BVR	Brake Valve Relay
110	BVR1, 2	Brake Valve Relay 1, 2
111	BVTR	Brake Valve Time Limit Relay
112	BzS	Buzzer Switch
113	CabGS	Cab Grounding Switch
114	CabHe1, 2	Cab Heater 1, 2
115	CabHeN1, 2	Cab Heater NFB 1, 2
116	CabHeS1, 2	Cab Heater Switch 1, 2
117	CabLp	Cab Lamp
118	CabLpN	Cab Lamp NFB
119	CabLpS	Cab Lamp Switch
120	CabRLpConR	Cab Room Lamp Contactor Receptacle
121	CabRrLp	Cab Reserved Lamp
122	CabRrLpN 1, 2	Cab Reserved Lamp NFB 1, 2
123	CabTeLp	Cab Test Lamp
124	CabTeS	Cab Test Switch
125	CabUCN	Cab Unit Core NFB
126	CBCDN	Cab Blower Compressor Device NFB
127	CBCN	Cab Blower Control NFB
128	CBMN	Cab Blower Motor NFB
129	CBN	Cab Blower Motor NFB
130	CDR1, 2	Current Detection Relay 1, 2
131	CI	Converter Inverter
132	CIBM1~3	Converter Inverter Blower Motor 1~3
133	CIBMN1~3	Converter Inverter Blower Motor NFB 1 ~ 3
134	CIBMNR	Converter Inverter Blower Motor NFB Relay
135	CICN1, 2	Converter Inverter Control NFB 1, 2

Continued

No.	Code	Equipment
136	CIFR1, 2	Converter Inverter Fault Relay 1, 2
137	CIGRR1, 2	Converter Inverter Grounding Relay 1, 2
138	CM	Compressor Motor
139	CMCN	Compressor Motor Control NFB
140	CMCOR	Compressor Motor Cut-out Relay
141	CMCOR-R	Compressor Motor Cut-out Relay-Reset
142	CMCORR1, 2	Compressor Motor Cut-out Repeat Relay 1, 2
143	CMGV	Compressor Ground Controller
144	CMK	Compressor Motor Knot
145	CMN	Compressor Motor NFB
146	CMSN	Compressor Motor Synchronization NFB
147	CMV	Compressor Motor Valve
148	CMVTR	Compressor Motor Valve Time Limit Relay
149	CORR	Cut-out Repetitive Relay
150	COSN	Cut-out Switch NFB
151	COSN1	Cut-out Switch NFB
152	CrFM	Cab Room Fan Motor
153	CrFMN	Cab Room Fan Motor NFB
154	CrFMS	Cab Room Fan Motor Switch
155	CSR	Constant Speed Relay
156	CT1	Current Transformer 1
157	CT3	Current Transformer 3
158	CttCN	Contactor Control NFB
159	CUHCS	Coupler Unit Handle Closing Switch
160	CUHOS	Coupler Unit Handle Open Switch
161	CVT	Constant Voltage Transformer
162	DCR	DC Relay
163	DICOS1, 2	Door Interlock Cut-out switch 1, 2
164	DIR	Door Interlock Relay
165	DIRR11, 12	Door Interlock Reserve Relay 11, 12

Continued

No.	Code	Equipment
166	DIRR21, 22	Door Interlock Reserve Relay 21, 22
167	DIRR31, 32	Door Interlock Reserve Relay 31, 32
168	DIRR41, 42	Door Interlock Reserve Relay 41, 42
169	DIRS	Door Interlock Relay Switch
170	DLS	Door Lock Switch
171	DMS1~4	Door Microswitch 1~4
172	DN	Door NFB
173	DOCHN	Door Buzzer NFB
174	DPSR 1~4	Door Dress Sense Relay 1~4
175	DS1~4	Door Switch 1~4
176	DSN	Door Switch NFB
177	DV11, 12, 21, 22	Magnetic Valve 11, 12, 21, 22
178	DV31, 32, 41, 42	Magnetic Valve 31, 32, 41, 42
179	DVCN1, 2	Door Valve Control NFB 1, 2
180	DVCR1, 2	Door Magnetic Valve Close Relay 1, 2
181	DVN1, 2	Gate Valve NFB 1, 2
182	DVOR1, 2	Magnetic Valve Opening Relay 1, 2
183	DVR 11, 12, 13, 21, 22, 23	Door Magnetic Valve Relay 11, 12, 13, 21, 22, 23
184	DVS1, 2	Magnetic Valve Switch 1, 2
185	EBR	ATP Emergency Brake Relay
186	EBz	Emergency Buzzer
187	EBzCOS	Emergency Buzzer Cut-out switch
188	EBzR	Emergency Buzzer Relay
189	EBzRR	Emergency Buzzer Restart Relay
190	EBzRS	Emergency Buzzer Restart Switch
191	EBzS1, 2	Emergency Buzzer Switch 1, 2
192	ECgConR	Electronic Charger Contact Relay
193	ECgConV	Electronic Charger Contact Valve
194	ECgRIsR	Electronic Charger Contact Release Relay
195	ECgRIsV	Electronic Charger Contact Release Valve

Continued

No.	Code	Equipment
196	EGCN	Emergency Ground Switch Control NFB
197	EGCS1, 2	Emergency Ground Switch Close Switch 1, 2
198	EGCV	Emergency Ground Switch Close Valve
199	EGCVN	Emergency Ground switch Close Valve NFB
200	EGOCK	EGS Open and Close Valve
201	EGOS1, 2	Emergency Ground Switch Open Switch 1, 2
202	EGOV	Emergency Ground Switch Open Valve
203	EGOVN	Emergency Ground Switch Open Valve NFB
204	EGS	Emergency Ground Switch
205	EGSHe	Emergency Ground Switch Heater
206	EGSR	Emergency Ground Switch Relay
207	EL1, 2	Electronic Luminescence 1, 2
208	ELN	Electronic Luminescence NFB
209	EVBat	Emergency Ventilation Battery
210	EXConR	External Power Connector Receptacle
211	EXR1, 2	External Power Relay 1, 2
212	ExTh	External Thermometer
213	FDRR	Pass Neutral-section Detection Repetitive Relay
214	FiCN1 ~ 4	Toilet Control NFB
215	FiFR1 ~ 3	Toilet Fault Relay
216	FiHeN1	Dirt Box Heating NFB
217	FiLvN	Dirt Box Display Control Unit NFB
218	FiOS1, 2	Photoelectric Sensor
219	FiPB	Forced Flushing Switch
220	FiT80R	Dirt Box 80% Relay
221	FiT100R	Dirt Box 100% Relay
222	FrBz	Fire Buzzer
223	FrBzR	Fire Buzzer Relay
224	FrBzRS	Fire Buzzer Restart Switch
225	FrBzS1, 2	Fire Buzzer Switch 1, 2

Continued

No.	Code	Equipment
226	FrLP	Fireproof Lamp
227	FVSN	Instantaneous Valve Sensor NFB
228	GB11 ~ 14	Grounding Brush 11 ~ 14
229	GB21 ~ 24	Grounding Brush 21 ~ 24
230	GHe	Glass Heater
231	GHeN	Glass Heater NFB
232	GHeTh	Glass Heat Thermometer
233	GR3	Ground Relay 3
234	GRR3-1	Ground Reserve Relay 3
235	GRR3-2	Ground Reserve Relay 3
236	GRT	Grounding Relay Transformer
237	GS	Ground Switch
238	HELPS	Hang Switch
239	HGS	Coupling Start
240	HLp1 ~ 4	Head Lamp 1-4
241	HLp1 ~ 4 HR	Head Lamp 1-4 High Beam Relay
242	HLp1 ~ 4LR	Head Lamp 1-4 Low Beam Relay
243	HMLpDS	Head Marker Lamp Dimmer Switch
244	HMLpN	Head Marker Lamp NFB
245	HMLpS	Head Marker Switch
246	HmRS	Hourmeter Restart Switch
247	Innet1 ~ 2N	Internet Running NFB
248	IVK1	Inverter Cantactor 1
259	JAHeK	Joint Auxiliary Heater
250	JAHeR	Joint Auxiliary Heater Relay Knot
251	JaN1, 2, 3	Joint Sleeve NFB 1, 2, 3
252	JBVR	Joint Battery Relay
253	JCMR	Joint Compressor Motor Relay
254	JRrLpK	Joint Reserved Lamp Knot
255	JRrLpR	Joint Reserved Lamp Relay

Continued

No.	Code	Equipment
256	JTR	Emergency Brake Relay
257	KBA1R	Release Braking 「1N」 Auxiliary Relay
258	KBA4R	Release Braking 「4N」 Auxiliary Relay
259	KBA6R	Release Braking 「6N」 Auxiliary Relay
260	KBMg	Key Control Box Magnetic Coil
261	KBMgN	Key Control Box Magnetic Coil NFB
262	KBMgS	Key Control Box Magnetic Coil Switch
263	KHCR	Hood Close Relay
264	KHCS	Hood Close Switch
265	KHCV	Hood Command Solenoid Valve
266	KHOR	Hood Open Relay
267	KHOS	Hood Open Switch
268	KHOV	Hood Open Solenoid Valve
269	KRR	Contactor Reserve Relay
270	LKJCOR	LKJ Cut-out Relay
271	LKJN	LKJ NFB
272	LKJPK	LKJ Power Knot
273	LvADCD	Lavatory Automatic Door Control Device
274	LvADN	Lavatory Automatic Door NFB
275	LvDCS1,2	Lavatory Door Close Switch 1, 2
276	LvDOS1,2	Lavatory Door Open Switch 1, 2
277	LVHe1~4	Level Verify Heater 1~4
278	LvLp	Lavatory Lamp
279	LvLpN	Lavatory lamp NFB
280	LvLpS1,2	Lavatory Lamp Switch 1, 2
281	MaRConR1	Machine Room Contactor Receptacle 1
282	MaRLp1,2	Machine Room Lamp 1, 2
283	MaRLpN1,2	Machine Room Lamp NFB 1, 2
284	MC	Main Controller
285	MCN1~3	Main Controller NFB 1 ~ 3
286	MCPR	Main Controller Plug Relay

Continued

No.	Code	Equipment
287	MCR	Main Controller Relay
288	MCRR	Main Controller Reserved Relay
289	MCCUTR	Main Controller 「cut」 Positioning Relay
290	MDLN	Main Lock NFB
291	MDLR	Main Lock Relay
292	MGFR1, 2	APU Medial Fault Relay 1,2
293	MLpN	Mark Lamp NFB
294	MLpR1, 2	Mark Lamp Relay 1, 2
295	MLpS	Mark Lamp Switch
296	MMBM1, 2	Main Motor Blower Motor 1, 2
297	MMBMN1, 2	Main Motor Blower Motor NFB 1, 2
298	MMCOR	Main Motor Cut-out Relay
299	MMCOR-R	Main Motor Cut-out Relay-Reset
300	MONN1, 2	Monitor Device NFB 1, 2
301	MOTN1, 2	Monitor Terminal Device NFB 1, 2
302	MRHPS	Main Reservoir High Pressure Switch
303	MRLPS	Main Reservoir Low Pressure Switch
304	MRPSR	Main Reservoir Pressure Select Relay
305	MRrAPSR	Main Reservoir Air Pressure Switch Relay
306	MSP1, 2	Speaker Monitor 1, 2
307	MTBM	Main Transformer Blower Motor
308	MTBMN	Main Transformer Blower NFB
309	MTCOR	Main Transformer Cut-out Relay
310	MTCOR-R	Main Transformer Cut-out Relay - Reset
311	MTCORR	Main Transformer Cut-out Reserved Relay
312	MTOFR	Main Transformer Oil Flow Relay
313	MTOFRR	Main Transformer Oil Flow Reserve Relay
314	MTOPM	Main Transformer Oil Pump Motor
315	MTOPMN	Main Transformer Oil Pump Motor NFB
316	MTr	Main Transformer
317	MTThR	Main Transformer Thermal Relay

Continued

No.	Code	Equipment
318	MTThRR	Main Transformer Thermal Reserved Relay
319	MXR	Mix Relay
320	MXRN1, 2	Mix Relay NFB 1, 2
321	NBR	Normal Brake Relay
322	NBTR	Normal Braking Time Limit Relay
323	NRLpR	Number Restricted Lamp Relay
324	NVR	Voltage Free Relay
325	NVR1N	No Voltage Relay 1 NFB
326	NVR1 VD	No Voltage Relay 1 Voltage Detector
327	OCTN	Overcurrent Transformer NFB
328	PaConR1 ~ 4N	PC Contactor NFB
329	PaIvN	PC Inverter NFB
330	Pan	Pantograph
331	PanCGS	Pantograph Change Switch
332	PanCOR	Pantograph Cut-out Relay
333	PanCOR-R	Pantograph Cut-out Relay - Reset
334	PanDAR	Pantograph Down Auxiliary Relay
335	PanDRN	Pantograph Down Relay NFB
336	PanDS	Pantograph Down Switch
337	PanDWR	Pantograph Down Relay
338	PanIR	Pantograph Interlocking Relay
339	PanN	Pantograph NFB
340	PanUCV	Pantograph Up Contain Valve
341	PanUR	Pantograph Up Relay
342	PanUS	Pantograph Up Switch
343	PanUV	Pantograph Up Valve
344	PanUVN	Pantograph Up Valve NFB
345	PCON	Pressure Cut-out NFB
346	PCOR	ATP Power Supply Cut-out Relay
347	PCOV	Pressure Cut-out Valve

Continued

No.	Code	Equipment
348	PDN1	Destination Display Circuit Breaker Place Display NFB
349	PG1～4	Pulse Generator 1~4
350	PLpCOS1，2	Primary Lamp Cut-out Switch 1, 2
351	PLpN1，2	Primary Lamp NFB 1, 2
352	PR	Power Relay
353	PS1～4	Pressure Switch 1~4
354	RCAR	Traction Command Auxiliary Relay
355	RConN	Room Contactor NFB
356	RConR1，2	Indoor Contactor Receptacle 1, 2
357	RCS	Reservoir Close Switch
358	RLp	Room Lamp
359	RLpCAR	Room Lamp Control Auxiliary Relay
360	RLpConR	Room Lamp Contactor Receptacle
361	RLpK	Room Lamp Knot
362	RLpN1～3	Room Lamp NFB 1~3
363	ROR	Root Open Relay
364	ROS	Root Open Switch
365	ROV	Root Open Valve
366	RrLp	Reserved Lamp
367	RrLpCgK	Reserved Lamp Change Knot
368	RrLpCgN	Reserved Lamp Change NFB
369	RrLpCgN2	Reserved Lamp Change NFB 2
370	RrLpCgR	Reserve Lamp Change Relay
371	RrLpCgS	Reserved Lamp Change Switch
372	RrLpN	Reserved Lamp NFB
373	RS	Restart Switch
374	RSR1	Restart Switch Relay
375	SBN1，2	Sub Brake NFB 1, 2
376	SBNR	Sub Brake NFB Relay
377	SBN1R	Sub Brake NFB Relay 1

Continued

No.	Code	Equipment
378	SCNCRN1, 2	Section Control NFB MCR NFB 1, 2
379	SCN1 ~ 3	Section Control NFB 1~3
380	SCK	Section Control Contactors
381	SCR	Section Control Relay
382	SCTR1, 2	Section Control Time Limit Relay 1, 2
383	SGZR1, 2	Section Fault Relay 1, 2
384	SMCR1, 2	Section MCR1, 2
385	SVCBCR	Section VCB Close Relay
386	SVCBOR	Section VCB Open Relay
387	SConN1 ~ 4	Sport Contactor NFB 1-5
388	SePR	Sensor Power Relay
389	SePN	Sensor Power NFB
390	SG	Speed Generator
391	SIV	Static Inverter
392	SKG1 ~ 4	Skid Resistance Generator 1~4
393	SKN	Skip Resistance NFB
394	SKVR	Skid Resistance Valve Relay
395	SKVRR	Skid Valve Reserve Relay
396	SLR	Skid Resistance Detection Relay
397	SLRR	Slip Resistance Detection Reserved Relay
398	SP	Speaker
399	SPCOS	Speaker Control Open Switch
400	SqS	Sequence Switch
401	SRLpN1	Seat Represent Lamp NFB 1
402	SRLpN2	
403	SS1 ~ 4	Speed Sensor 1~4
404	SVCBCR	Section Vacuum Circuit Breaker Close Relay
405	SVCBOR	Section Vacuum Circuit Breaker Open Relay
406	SVCN	Emergency Brake Switching Control NBF
407	TAX2N	TAX2 NFB
408	TAX2PK	TAX2 Power Knot

019

Continued

No.	Code	Equipment
409	TeLp	Test Lamp
410	TInFN	Train Information Equipment NFB
412	ToBz	Toilet Buzzer
413	ToBzR	Toilet Buzzer Relay
414	ToBzS1 ~ 3	Toilet Buzzer Switch 1~3
415	ToConN	Toilet Connector NFB
416	ToConR1, 2	Toilet Connector Receptacle 1, 2
417	ToFM1, 2	Toilet Fan Motor 1, 2
418	ToFMN1, 2	Toilet Fan Motor NFB 1, 2
419	TSC1N	TSC1 NFB
420	TSC1PK	TSC1 Power Knot
421	TSHeN	Toilet Seat Heater NFB
422	TThRN	Train (Tyre) Thermal Relay NFB
423	TThRR	Train (Tyre) Thermal Reserve Relay
424	TWBat	Train Wireless Radio Battery
425	TWBatN	Train Wireless Radio Battery NFB
426	TWCN	Train Wireless Radio Control NFB
427	TWEmCgK	Train Wireless Radio Emergency Change Knot
428	TWEmCgS	Train Wireless Radio Emergency Change Switch
429	TWN	Train Wireless Radio NFB
430	TyClV	Tyre Clean Valve
431	TyClVN	Tyre Clean Valve NFB
432	UBR	Urgent Brake Relay
433	UBRS	Urgent Brake Restart Switch
434	UBRSR	Urgent Brake Restart Switch Relay
435	UBRSWR	Urgent Brake Restart Switch Relay
436	UBS1, 2	Urgent Brake Switch 1, 2
437	UBTR1, 2	Urgent Brake Time Limit Relay 1, 2
438	UN1	Power Supply (AC 400 V) NFB of air Conditioning Unit 1 in the Switchboard
439	UN2	Power Supply NFB of air Conditioning Unit 2 in Power Distribution Panel

Continued

No.	Code	Equipment
440	UN12	Air Conditioning Unit 1 Control Power Supply (AC 100 V) NFB
441	UN22	Air Conditioning Unit 2 Control Power Supply (AC 100 V) NFB
442	UCN3	Air Conditioning Display Setter Power NFB
443	UCN11	Power Supply of Internal Contactor Panel of Air Conditioning Unit 1
444	UCN21	Power Supply of Internal Contactor Panel of Air Conditioning unit 2
445	UR0	Urgent Command Relay
446	UVN	Urgent Magnetic Valve NFB
447	UVR	Urgent Magnetic Valve Relay
448	UVR1, 2, 3	Urgent Magnetic Valve Relay 1, 2, 3
449	UVRS	Urgent Magnetic Valve Relay Short Circuit Switch
450	V1	Voltmeter 1
451	V3	Voltmeter 3
452	V4	Voltmeter 4
453	VCB	Vacuum Circuit Breaker
454	VCBARN	Vacuum Circuit Breaker Auxiliary Relay NFB
455	VCBA1R	Vacuum Circuit Breaker Auxiliary Relay
456	VCBCOR	Vacuum Circuit Breaker Cut-out Relay
457	VCBCOR-R	Vacuum Circuit Breaker Cut-out Relay - Restart
458	VCBCR1, 2	Vacuum Circuit Breaker Close Relay 1, 2
459	VCBCS	Vacuum Circuit Breaker Close Switch
460	VCBHe	Vacuum Circuit Breaker Heater
461	VCBN	Vacuum Circuit Breaker NFB
462	VCBOAR	Vacuum Circuit Breaker Opening Auxiliary Relay
463	VCBOR1, 2	Vacuum Circuit Breaker Open Relay 1, 2
464	VCBOS	Vacuum Circuit Breaker Open Switch
465	VCBRR	Vacuum Circuit Breaker Reserve Relay
466	VCgS	Voltmeter Change Switch
467	VDTN	Voltage Detection Transformer NFB
468	VeFM	Ventilation Fan Motor
469	VeFMCN1, 2	Ventilation Fan Motor Control NFB 1, 2

Continued

No.	Code	Equipment
470	VeFMN	Ventilation Fan Motor NFB
471	VN1	Voltmeter NFB 1
472	VN3	Voltmeter NFB 3
473	VN4	Voltmeter NFB 4
474	WaPFS	Water Pump Float Switch
475	WaPHe	Water Pump Heater
476	WaPHm	Water Pump Hour Meter
477	WaPMV1	Water Pump Magnetic Valve 1
478	WaPMV2	Water Pump Magnetic Valve 2
479	WaP	Water Pump
480	WaPN	Water Pump NFB
481	WaPR	Water Pump Relay
482	WaPTh	Water Pump Thermostat
483	WhDR	Whistle Down Relay
484	WhDV	Whistle Down Valve
485	WHeN1, 2	Water Heater NFB 1, 2
486	WLMN	Water Level Meter NFB
487	WLMR	Water Level Meter Relay
488	WPN	Wiper NFB
489	WVCN	Water Voltage Control NFB
490	24 V Power N	24 V Power Supply N
491	Forward R	Reversing Switch "Forward" Positioning Relay
492	Backward R	Reversing Switch 「Backward」 Positioning Relay
493	Traction Command R	Traction Command Relay
494	Constant Speed SW	Constant Speed Switch
495	Constant Speed Cut SW	Constant Speed Cut Switch
496	Reset SW	Reset Switch
497	Start Test SW	Start Test Switch
498	Onboard Test SW	Onboard Test Switch
499	Snow Resistance SW	Snow Resistant Switch
500		

Task 2 Overview of EMU Control System

【Task Description】

This task mainly introduces the composition of the EMU control system, the concept of the control circuit and the working principle of the control system. After learning this task, you should have a preliminary understanding of EMU traction, braking conditions and other knowledge.

【Background Knowledge】

1.1 Technical characteristics of electric traction control

The electric traction control system takes the traction motor as the research object. Because of the high requirements for the traction power level, the voltage level and current level of the traction motor are generally large and cannot be directly controlled. Therefore, at present, the power electronic converter is basically used to control the traction motor. Figure 1-2-1 shows the composition of general electric traction control system.

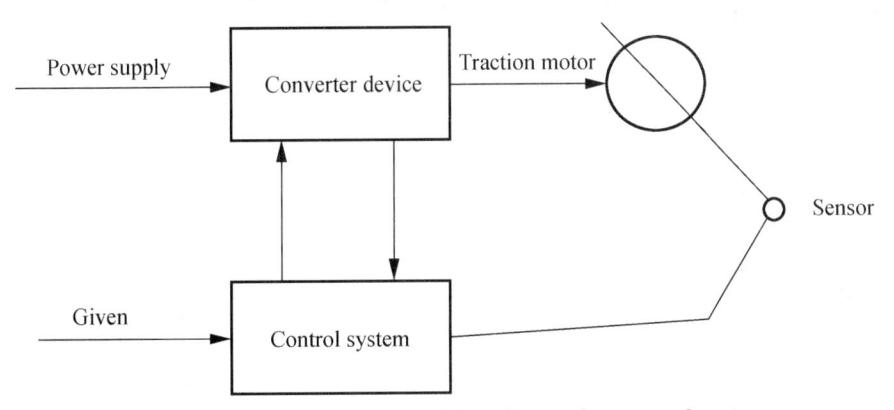

Figure 1-2-1 Composition of electric traction control system

Compare the driver's given quantity with the detected controlled quantity to form a deviation control signal, and control the output signal of the power electronic converter through the control system, that is, control the input signal of the traction motor, so as to achieve the purpose of controlling the controlled quantity. In order to achieve speed regulation and improve traction performance, the controlled quantities of traction motor mainly include motor speed, motor voltage, motor current, motor power and motor excitation current.

In the electric traction system, the traction motor supplies power through the converter, which is actually the electric energy conversion circuit of the whole system. Electric traction control system has experienced three stages of development history. The early electric traction control system was relay control system, which mainly executed the starting, stopping and speed regulation of the locomotive with the help of switch appliances such as relays and contactors. With the development of power electronics technology, analog control systems composed of integrated circuits, especially operational amplifiers, have emerged. However, the correction parameters of the regulator composed of analog circuits are not easy to adjust and change once determined, so the analog control system is not suitable for different types of locomotives, and the control system must be redesigned for one type of locomotive. Modern electronic technology tends to mature, especially the emergence of microprocessors, and computers are gradually applied to locomotive control systems. At present, with the development of high-speed railway, there are more and more microprocessors in the locomotive in high-speed EMU, which are used to realize the control, fault detection, protection, recording and display of traction braking characteristics during locomotive operation, and complete the control functions at different levels to form a train control network.

1.2 Basic principle of EMU control system

The control circuit of EMU is to connect the control appliances, signal devices and control power supply that control the traction converter, traction transformer, braking device and auxiliary devices into an electrical control system, receive and transmit the instructions and status information of the train network information control device, and realize the operation and control of EMU.

CRH380A multiple unit is a 6M2T formation with the speed of 300 km/h. Each motor car has 1 traction converter and 4 traction motors controlled by a computer controller. The braking device of each vehicle is controlled by a braking control unit (BCU). In order to convey information and complete coordinated and unified control, a distributed control system based on train information network is formed.

The traction command, braking command and other commands from the cab are conveyed to the computer controller or BCU of each vehicle through the train information network to executed the operation control of train traction and braking. It also detects the status of each equipment, protects and records the fault once it occurs, and feeds back the fault information to the cab through the train information network in time to provide the driver with fault handling measures.

1.3 Control process of EMU traction and braking

1.3.1 Traction command

The driver operates the driver's main controller to issue traction commands, which mainly include:

(1) Direction command: forward/backward, controlling the rotation direction of traction motor.

(2) Traction working condition command: traction motor operates under motor working condition.

(3) Traction level command: 1~10 levels, corresponding to traction characteristics of different power levels.

(4) Constant speed command: control the constant speed operation of the train.

1.3.2 Braking command

The driver operates the driver's brake controller. The brake command mainly includes:

(1) Regenerative braking command: give priority to regenerative braking, and the traction motor operates under the generator working condition.

(2) Service braking level command: level 1~7, corresponding to braking characteristics of different deceleration levels.

(3) Fast braking command: sent through the through line, operable, or acting during protection.

(4) Emergency braking command: it is sent through the through line and can be operated or acted during protection.

1.3.3 Relevant links of vehicle information terminal device and transmission of instructions

The traction and braking of the whole train are realized by each vehicle unit. Take one motor train as an example, as shown in Figure 1-2-2.

The cab sends out traction commands (direction, traction working condition, traction level) and conveys them to the train level network through the central device. The vehicle terminal device receives the commands from the train network and then transmits them to the computer controller of the traction converter of the vehicle to control the traction converter and traction motor.

The braking command (regenerative braking condition, braking level) sent by the cab is conveyed to the terminal device through the central device, and the terminal device transmits the braking command to the braking control unit (BCU) of the vehicle. The BCU sends the regenerative braking mode command to the traction converter, giving priority to the implementation of regenerative braking. At this time, the traction motor operates in the generator state, and feeds the braking energy back to the grid while braking the train. At the same time, the traction converter feeds back the regeneration information to the BCU. When the BCU detects that the regenerative braking force is insufficient, it sends a command to the air braking system to supplement the air braking.

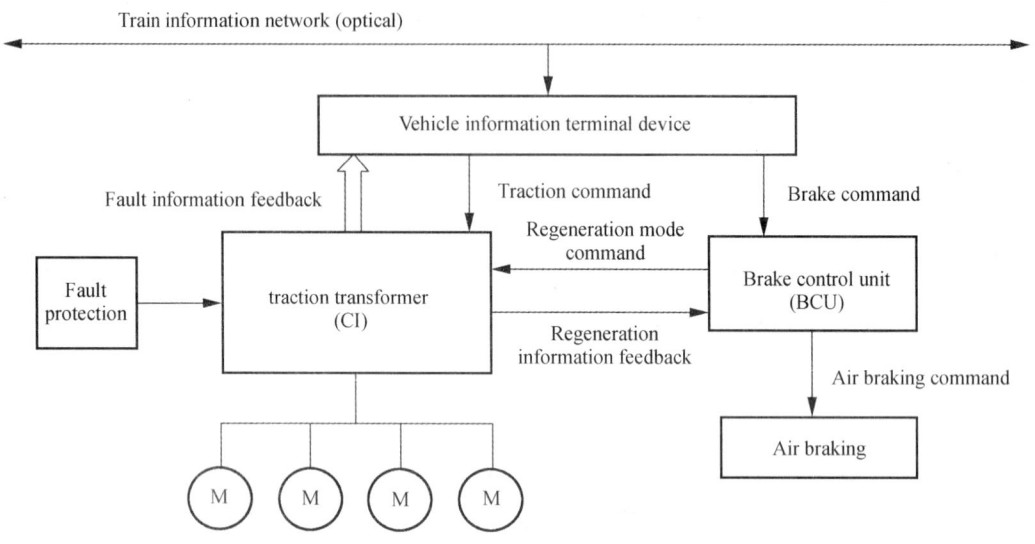

Figure 1-2-2 Command transmission diagram of vehicle information terminal device

At the same time, it is also necessary to detect faults and conduct fault protection, feed back the fault information to the terminal, and then feed back to the central device in the cab through the train level network, and display and guide the handling of faults on the display screen.

1.4 Composition of train information network system

1.4.1 Train level network structure

The train level network is composed of central device, terminal device, train information display, display control device, IC card read-write device, passenger information display and other equipment. The configuration of network equipment on the train is shown in Table 1-2-1. There are generally two types of EMU train level network. The first is optical fiber ring network, which connects all central devices and terminal devices using ANSI/ATA-878.1 (ARCNET) protocol. The second is self diagnostic transmission network, which connects central devices and terminal devices in bus mode, using HDLC as the data exchange protocol. The train information network structure is shown in Figure 1-2-3.

Table 1-2-1 Configuration of train level network equipment

Vehicle No.	T1c-1	M2-2	M1-3	T2-4	T1K-5	M2-6	M1S-7	T2C-8
Central unit	1							1
Terminal unit	1	1	1	1	1	1	1	1
Train information display	2						1	2
Display control device	2						1	2
IC card read-write device	2							2

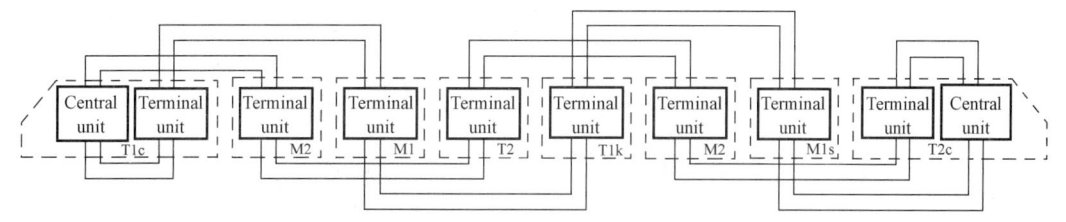

Figure 1-2-3 Train information network structure

1.4.2 Vehicle level network structure

The vehicle level network refers to the information exchange channel between the central device/terminal device and the equipment in the compartment. Point to point communication mode is adopted between central device/terminal device and equipment, optical fiber connection is adopted between traction converter (CI), brake control unit (BCU) and terminal device, and current loop mode is adopted between other equipment and central device and terminal device. See Table 1-2-2 for BCU/CI device configuration.

Table 1-2-2 BCU/CI Device configuration

	T1c-1		M2-2	M1-3	T2-4	T1K-5	M2-6	M1S-7	T2C-8
	Central Unit	Terminal Unit	Terminal Unit	Terminal Unit	Terminal Unit	Terminal Unit	Terminal Unit	Terminal Unit	Central Unit
BCU		○	○	○	○	○	○	○	
CI			○	○			○	○	

1.5 Control of traction converter

One traction converter of each vehicle of CRH380A multiple unit is controlled by a computer controller, as shown in Figure 1-2-4.

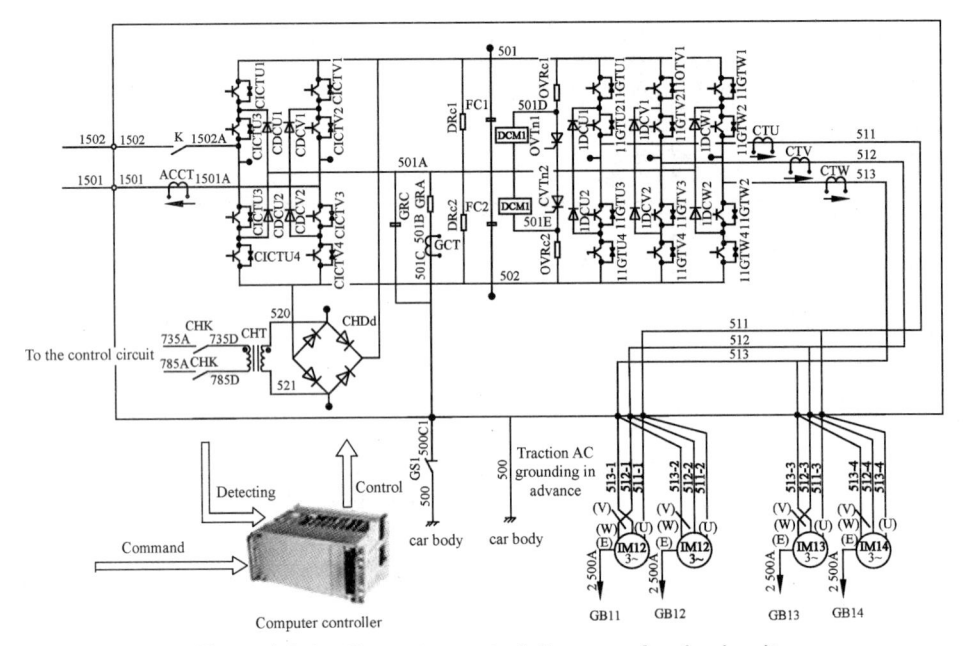

Figure 1-2-4　Computer control diagram of main circuit

In addition to the CPU and memory of the general purpose computer, the control computer should solve the problem of signal input and output through relevant interfaces to achieve target control.

1.5.1　Detection

To control, the computer controller must be detected by various sensors to form a closed loop control to achieve the best control accuracy; monitoring and protection shall be carried out at the same time.

Detection links mainly include:

(1) Single phase AC current detection: current sensor ACCT.

(2) Intermediate DC voltage detection: DCPT1, DCPT2.

(3) Ground fault current detection: GCT.

(4) Three phase current detection: CTU, CTV, CTW.

(5) Traction motor speed detection: speed sensor on each traction motor shaft.

1.5.2　Control

The computer controller controls the pulse rectifier and traction inverter of the traction converter, and protects them quickly in case of failure.

Control links mainly include:

(1) Pulse rectifier control: complete four quadrant converter control of rectification/regeneration.

(2) Traction inverter control: complete the control of variable frequency and voltage.

(3) Overvoltage protection control: when DC voltage is overvoltage, trigger thyristor to discharge.

(4) Overcurrent, overvoltage/undervoltage and grounding protection control: when overcurrent, overvoltage/undervoltage and grounding occur, lockout pulse and shutdown protection will be performed.

【Project Testing】

1. Please describe the classification of CRH380A EMU line numbers.
2. Try to describe the naming method of equipment marks.
3. Analyze the concept of EMU control circuit.
4. Draw the schematic diagram of relevant command transmission of vehicle information terminal device and analyze the working principle of traction and braking control.
5. Analyze the basic composition of CRH380A EMU control system.

Project 2

Analysis and Inspection of Traction Control Circuit of EMU

【Project Description】

This project is an overall understanding of EMU traction control system. The main circuit, logic operation control circuit, pantograph, vacuum circuit breaker and other control circuits of CRH2/CRH380A and CRH3/CRH380B multiple units are mainly introduced. Through the study of traction control principle, students are required to analyze the main circuit and logic operation circuit diagram, and be able to eliminate the faults according to the EMU maintenance operation standards and common fault handling methods.

【Project Tasks】

(1) Main circuit analysis of EMU;
(2) Logic operation control circuit;
(3) Control of pantograph and vacuum circuit breaker;
(4) Traction converter control;
(5) Traction control of CRH380B EMU.

Task 1 Main Circuit Analysis of EMU

【Task Description】

This task mainly analyzes the main circuit of CRH380A EMU, so that students can master the composition and working principle of CRH2/CRH380A EMU traction drive system. After learning this task, students should be able to analyze the working process of the main circuit.

【Background Knowledge】

1.1 Composition of main circuit system

The traction circuit system takes M1 Car and M2 Car as one unit. The power supply is obtained from the catenary through the pantograph from the single-phase AC 25 kV, 50 Hz catenary voltage, and is connected to the primary side winding of the traction transformer through VCB. The traction circuit is opened and closed by VCB. Two coils are set at the secondary winding side of the traction transformer, which are connected to one traction converter respectively. When the voltage at the primary side winding is 25 kV, the voltage at the secondary side winding is 1500 V. The third winding of the traction transformer is connected to the auxiliary converter to provide power to the auxiliary equipment.

The basic unit device of the main circuit is composed of one traction transformer, two main converter devices and eight traction motors. Four traction motors are controlled by one main converter, power is supplied to the traction motors during traction, and regenerative control is performed during braking. In addition, it has protection function. The composition of a power unit traction system is shown in Figure 2-1-1.

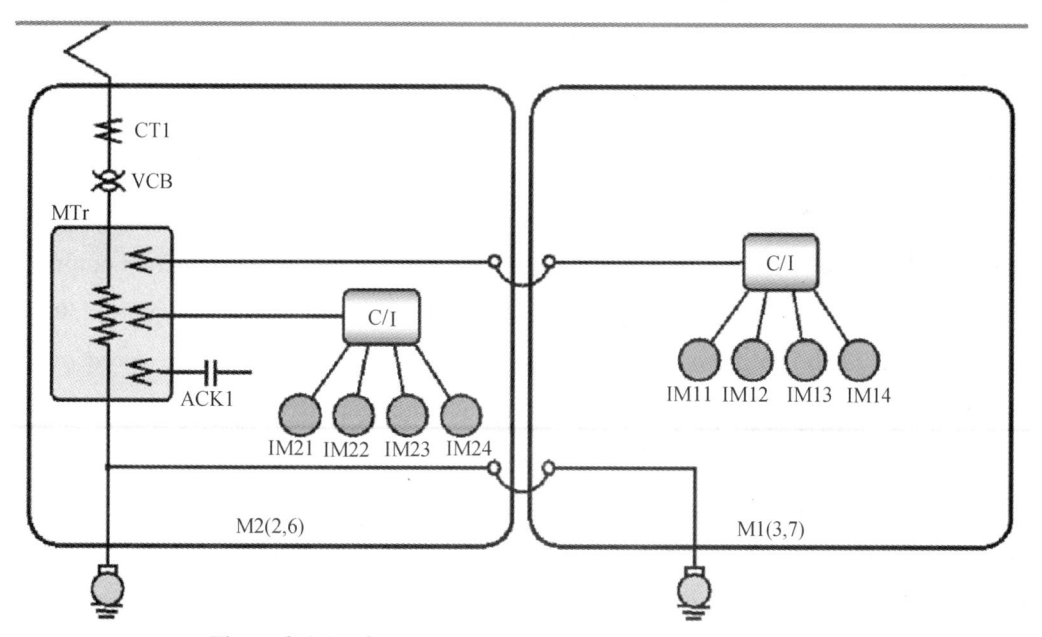

Figure 2-1-1　Composition diagram of traction drive system

1.2　Principle of traction drive system

The principle of traction drive system is shown in Figure 2-1-2.

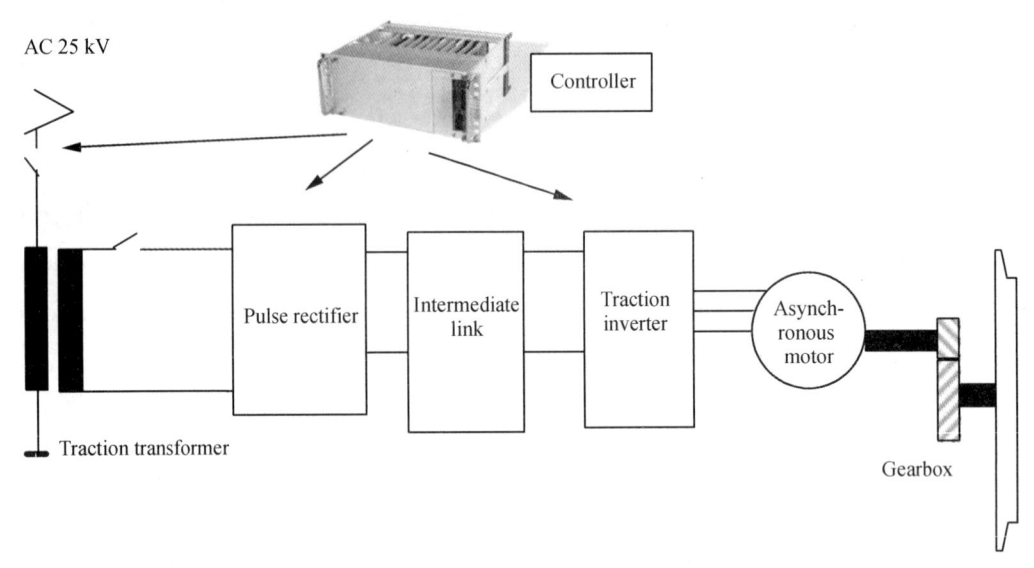

Figure 2-1-2　Schematic diagram of traction transmission system

　　Traction condition: the pantograph transmits AC 25 kV single-phase power- frequency alternating current of the catenary to the traction transformer through relevant high-voltage electrical equipment. The traction transformer steps down and outputs 1500 V single-phase alternating current to supply the traction converter. The pulse rectifier converts the single-phase alternating current into direct current. The DC 2600-3000 V is output to the traction inverter through the intermediate DC circuit, and the traction inverter outputs a three-phase AC power supply with adjustable voltage/frequency (voltage: 0-2300 V; frequency: 0-220 Hz) to drive the traction motor. The torque and rotational speed of the traction motor are transmitted to the wheelset through the gear box to drive the train.

　　Regenerative braking: it is called electric braking. During electric braking, on the one hand, the traction inverter is controlled to make the traction motor in the power generation state, and the traction inverter works in the rectification state, the three-phase AC power generated by the traction motor is set to DC power and the intermediate DC link is charged to make the voltage of the intermediate DC link rise; on the other hand, the pulse rectifier works in the inverter state, and the DC power supply of the intermediate DC circuit is inverted into single-phase AC, which is fed back to the catenary through high-voltage equipment such as vacuum circuit breaker and pantograph, so as to realize energy regeneration.

1.3 Main circuit of traction drive system

1.3.1 25 kV ultra-high voltage circuit

The main circuit diagram of traction drive system is shown in Figure 2-1-3.

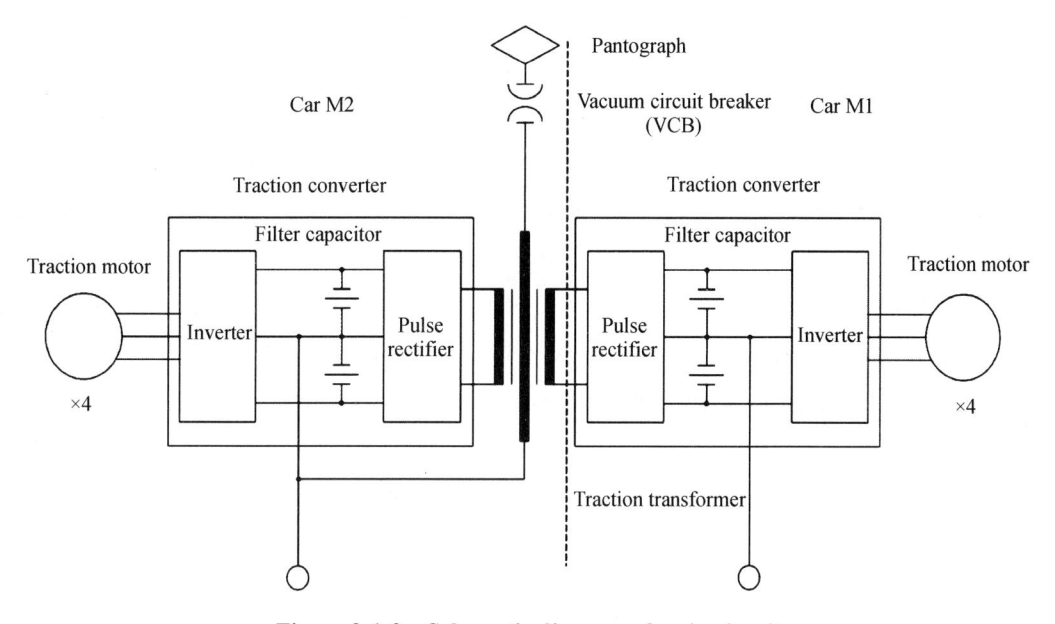

Figure 2-1-3　Schematic diagram of main circuit

The power supply is 25 kV, 50 Hz single-phase alternating current, using one of the pantographs installed on cars No. 4 and No. 6 (one of the two pantographs is usually in the folded state of the bow) to receive power from the catenary. Car No. 2 and Car No. 6 are connected through a 25 kV UHV cable. The M1/M3/M5 cars are equipped with traction transformers, which are connected to the 25 kV UHV power supply of each car through UHV cables, and connected to the primary winding of the traction transformer through the UHV connectors and the vacuum circuit breaker VCB of each car.

1.3.2 Secondary circuit of traction transformer

The low-voltage side of the traction transformer (MTr) is composed of three windings, two of which are secondary windings that supply power to the train drive circuit (traction converter), and the rest is the third winding that supply power to the lighting, air conditioning and other auxiliary circuits, control circuits, communication circuits, etc. of the EMU.

1.3.3 Traction converter

One of the secondary windings is connected to the traction converter of M1/M3/M5 cars, and the other winding is connected to the traction converter of M2/M4/M6 cars through the connector between M1/M3/M5 cars and M2/M4/M6 cars. In addition to providing power to traction motor during power operation and feedback regenerative power from motor during braking to catenary, traction converter also has the protection function.

The traction converter consists of a pulse rectifier part that converts single-phase AC power into DC intermediate power, an inverter part that converts the converted DC intermediate power into three-phase AC power with variable voltage and variable frequency, and a DC smoothing circuit (filter capacitor) that obtains constant DC voltage. In addition, an overvoltage protection circuit composed of a resistor and a semiconductor switch is arranged on the intermediate DC circuit. As shown in Figures 2-1-4 and 2-1-5. The pulse rectifier controls the basic wave power factor at the power input side to close to 1 through PWM control. Thereby, fluctuations in catenary voltage can be reduced, equipment can be miniaturized, and power consumption can be reduced. During power operation, the inverter converts the input DC intermediate voltage into three-phase AC power with variable voltage and frequency according to the control command, and then uniformly supplies power to the four parallel induction motors to control the speed and torque of the induction motors. During regenerative braking, the inverter functionally becomes a power commutation rectifier. The induction motor inputs the induced three-phase AC power to the inverter, and then the inverter outputs DC power to the DC intermediate circuit side. In order to control the speed and torque of induction motor, the inverter is controlled by vector control. Through vector control, the current components related to the torque of the motor (torque current) and the current components related to the magnetic field of the motor (excitation current) are independently controlled. Through vector control of inverter, high-precision torque control and high-speed torque control can be expected.

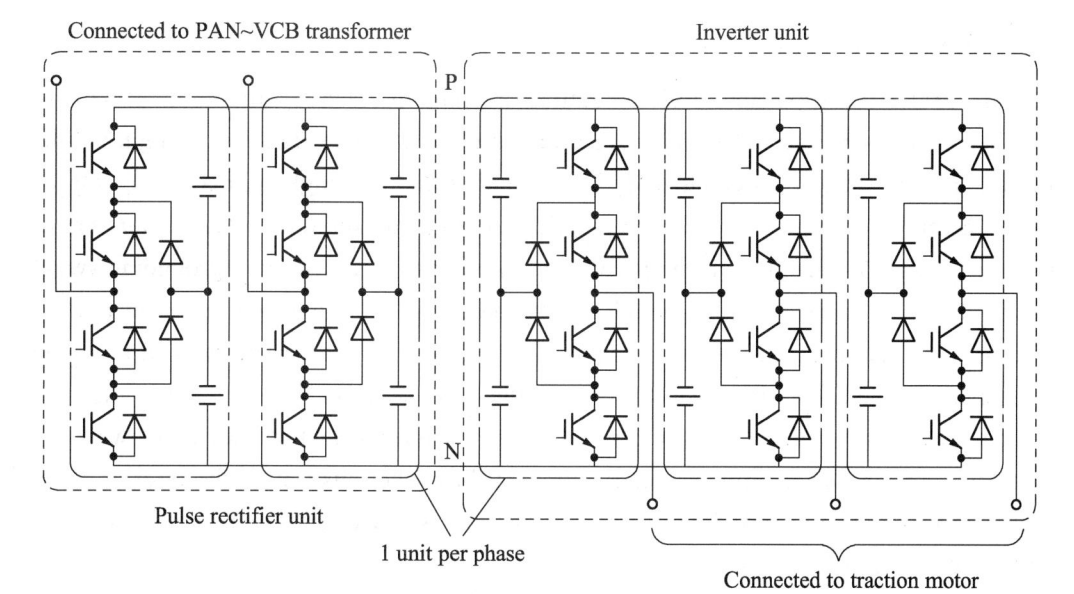

Figure 2-1-4　Power module connection

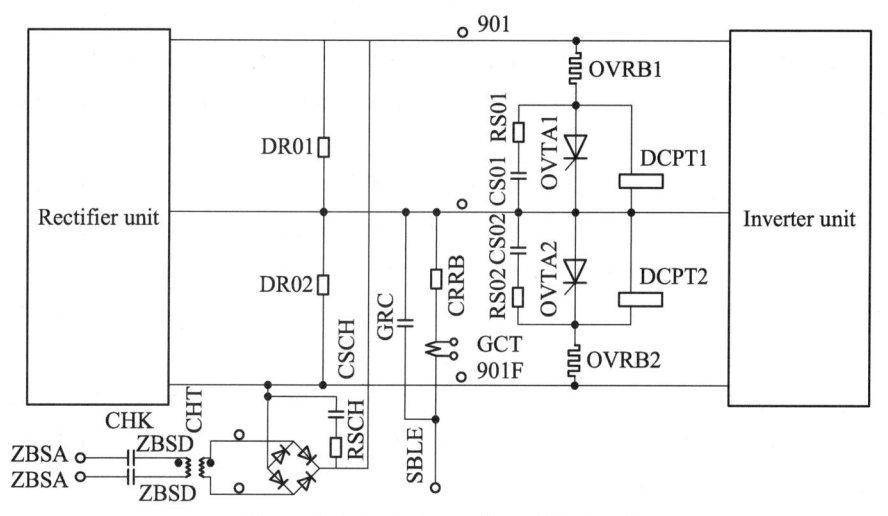

Figure 2-1-5　Intermediate DC circuit

1.3.4　Traction motor

Two traction motors are installed on each bogie of M1, M2, M3, M4, M5 and M6 cars. The motor is a three-phase squirrel cage induction motor, and a speed sensor is installed on the reverse drive side. The speed sensor detects the speed (rotation number) of the traction motor, that is, the train speed, and sends the speed information to the inverter. This speed information (speed feedback signal) is used for speed control, torque control and braking control of the motor.

1.3.5　Protection circuit

(1) Protective grounding switch. Pantograph and protective grounding switch are installed on the same car. The protective grounding switch prevents the ultra-high voltage from being applied to the vehicle body by grounding the ultra-high voltage power supply. When the accident current of the main circuit cannot be blocked due to the vacuum circuit breaker (VCB), or when the catenary voltage is abnormal, the protective grounding switch (EGS) is forced to operate to ground the catenary, the grounding current flows to the catenary, and the disconnector of the substation trips, so that the catenary is in a voltage free state. In addition, in order to ensure the safety of maintenance personnel, the pantograph is grounded in advance by protecting the linkage locking device between the grounding switch and the high-voltage equipment box when inspecting the interior of the high-voltage equipment box. Even if the pantograph rises, electric shock accidents can be prevented.

(2) The vacuum circuit breaker. VCB is installed for the purpose of quickly, safely and reliably blocking the overcurrent when the circuit behind the secondary side of the traction transformer fails. In normal conditions, the vacuum circuit breaker VCB is also a switch that operates the opening and closing of the main circuit. It has two functions: circuit breaker and switch.

(3) AC lightning arrester. Due to the lightning surge from the catenary and the switching surge caused by the load break, the AC arrester can be shunted by the AC arrester (Arr) in parallel with the traction transformer and limited to the voltage value determined by the voltage limiting characteristics of the AC arrester. Therefore, the use of AC lightning arrester can prevent high voltage from being applied to various equipment.

(4) The converter and overcurrent relay. The converter (CT1) is inserted at the input side of 25 kV (ultra-high voltage). The AC over-current relay (ACOCR1 and ACOCR2) is connected to the secondary side of the converter. The current of the 25 kV circuit is monitored through the converter. When the current of the converter exceeds the set value of the AC over-current relay, it can send out a tripping signal to make VCB trip.

1.3.6　Grounding device

The main circuit grounding device is installed on the non wheel side of the drive shaft gear unit of M1, M2, M3, M4, M5 and M6 cars. Through the grounding device, the return line current of the traction transformer directly flows to the axle to prevent bearing damage caused by the return line current flowing to the bogie bearing. The traction transformer grounding wire is connected to the transfer terminal board corresponding to each drive shaft of M1/M3/M5 cars. In addition, M2/M4/M6 cars are connected to the transfer terminal board corresponding to each drive shaft through the connector between M1/M3/M5 cars and M2/M4/M6 cars, which is the same as M1/M3/M5 cars, and then connected to the grounding brush of each shaft.

Task 2 Logic Operation Control

【Task Description】

Through the study of this task, students can master the function of the main controller and the principle of traction command transmission, analyze the logic operation control circuit, inspect and maintain the main controller according to the maintenance operation standards, and test the action of the main circuit and the main circuit contactor.

【Background Knowledge】

2.1 Overview

The driver controller is in the cab, and there is one set in T1c-1 or T2c-8 respectively. The driver controller is composed of direction controller, traction controller and driver brake controller to complete the setting of EMU traction direction, traction control command and braking command, as shown in Figure 2-2-1. The driver controller shall cooperate with the constant speed switch and start test switch in the cab at the same time to realize the constant speed control command and the test after converter failure.

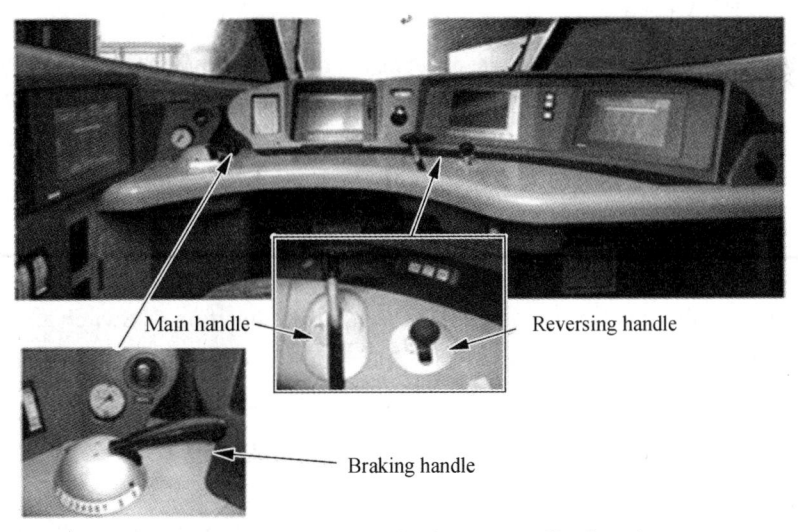

Figure 2-2-1 Layout of driver controller in cab

The commands for traction control of EMU mainly include: forward, backward, traction, level and other commands, which are operated by the driver through the main controller (main handle and reversing handle). The transmission principle diagram of traction control command is shown in Figure 2-2-2. Each command line of the main controller's forward (Line 4) or backward (Line 5), traction command (Line 9), and level 1~10 command (Line 11, 12, 13, 15, 17, 19) is input to the central device of vehicle information control, and the traction operation control is carried out by transmitting commands to the traction converter through control transmission. In order to ensure that the control circuit acts correctly according to the instructions, certain logic conditions must be met in the control process.

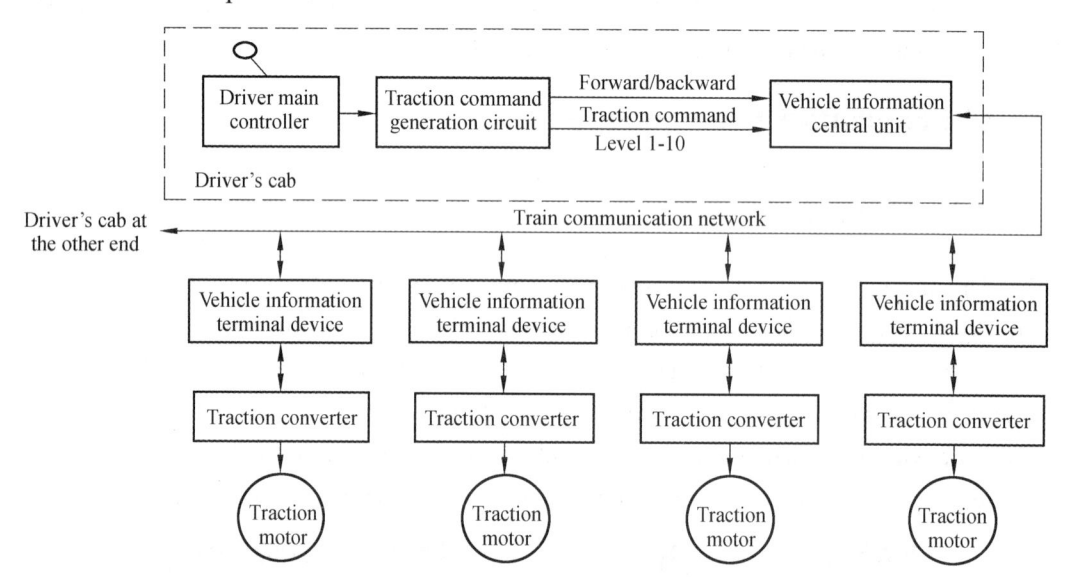

Figure 2-2-2 Schematic diagram of command transmission of traction controller

2.2 Principle of traction controller

2.2.1 Direction controller

The direction controller is also called the direction handle. As shown in Figure 2-2-3, the direction handle has three positions: "Forward" position, "Switch" position and "Backward" position. In the "Forward" position, the forward relay is energized; in the "Backward" position, the rear relay is energized; in the "Switching" position, both relays do not act. The direction controller controls the generation of traction direction (forward or backward) command conditions and traction command relay conditions.

Note: All control powers come from DC 100 V auxiliary power Line 103. 103-1, 103-2, and 103-3 in the figure in this section represent the 1st to 3rd branches associated with Line

103 respectively.

In the "Forward" position of the reversing switch, R in front of the reversing switch is energized (forward mode).

When the reversing switch is in the "Backward" position, R behind the reversing switch is energized (backward mode).

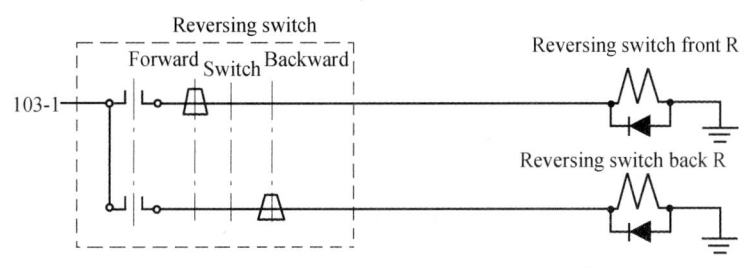

Figure 2-2-3　Direction controller control

1. Direction command generation conditions

As shown in Figure 2-2-4 and Figure 2-2-5, when the main control relay MCR is energized and the direction handle is in the "Forward" position, Line 4 is pressurized to transmit the forward command to the monitor; When the direction handle is in the "Backward" position, Line 5 is pressurized to transmit the backward command to the monitoring central device.

Figure 2-2-4　Command conditions before direction switch

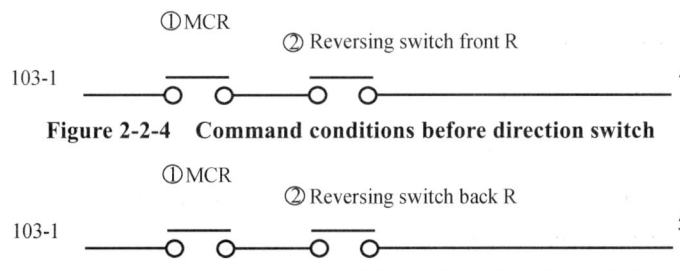

Figure 2-2-5　Command conditions after direction switch

2. Generation conditions of traction command R

As shown in Figure 2-2-6, when other conditions are met, the direction control handle will leave the "Switch" position.

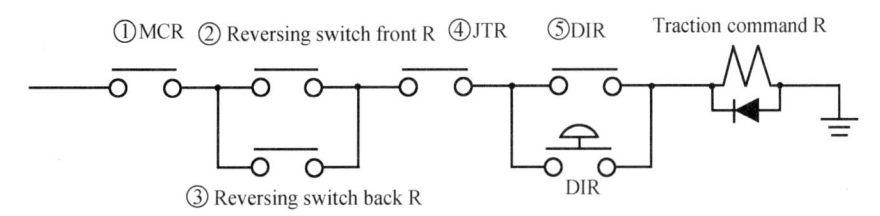

Figure 2-2-6　Traction command R condition

When in the "Forward" or "Backward" position, the front R or rear R of the reversing switch is energized, the corresponding normally open contact is closed, and the traction command R is energized. The traction command can only be issued after the traction command R acts. It can be seen that when the direction handle is in the "Off" position, no traction command can be issued. Power on conditions of traction command R includes:

① Operating terminal: MCR excitation;

② The reversing handle leaves the "Switching" position: R in front of the reversing switch or R behind the reversing switch is excited;

③ No quick braking and emergency braking: JTR excitation;

④ The side sliding door is closed or the door closing interlock switch is ON: DIR excitation or DIRS ON.

The traction command relay can only be energized when the above conditions are met at the same time. These conditions indicate that only under safe conditions, the operation of the direction controller can generate the traction command R action condition.

2.2.2 Traction controller

Traction controller, also known as main controller (MC), is mainly used to generate 10 level commands of traction commands, and generate traction command conditions and constant speed operation command conditions at the same time.

1. Traction command level

As shown in Figure 2-2-7, when the traction direction handle is in the "Forward" or "Backward" position, the traction command relay R is powered on. When the traction controller is operated, Lines 11, 12, 13, 15, 17 and 19 are pressurized respectively, and each line is input to the monitoring central device to transmit the traction command to the traction converter through the network. Each line is input to the central device of the monitor for power operation control.

According to different positions of traction controller handles and different line pressurization, 10 levels of traction commands are formed. The corresponding relationship between level and line pressurization is shown in Table 2-2-1.

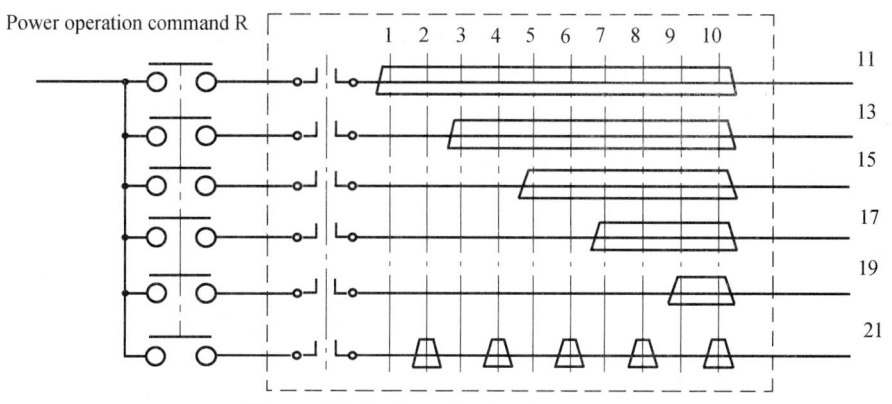

Figure 2-2-7 Traction level command

Table 2-2-1 Corresponding level of traction controller to command line

		\multicolumn{10}{c}{Master controller level instruction}
		1	2	3	4	5	6	7	8	9	10
Pressurization line	11	○	○	○	○	○	○	○	○	○	○
	13			○	○	○	○	○	○	○	○
	15					○	○	○	○	○	○
	17								○	○	○
	19									○	○
	12		○		○		○		○		○

○ = 「Pressurized」, blank space = 「No pressurization」

2. Traction command conditions

The traction command condition is to notify the monitoring central unit and send out the traction control command.

Put MC at the "Switching" position, and switch MC to R for excitation. Therefore, MCPR can be excited to make traction command conditions (Line 9) effective. The logic relationship is shown in Figure 2-2-8.

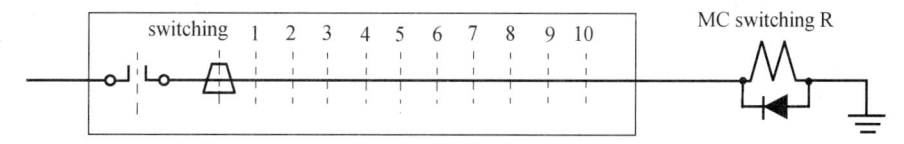

Figure 2-2-8 MC switching R conditions

MCPR conditions are as follows, and the logic diagram is shown in Figure 2-2-9.
MCPR is excited when the following conditions are met.
(Condition) ①∩② (∩ means and, ∪ means or):

① Traction command R excitation: refers to Figure 2-2-6.

② MC disconnects R excitation: (MC neutral state) see Figure 2-2-8.

※ Once the MCPR is excited, the power operation command R is self maintained until it is not excited.

After MCPR gets excitation, the main controller command can be input into the monitor through Line 9.

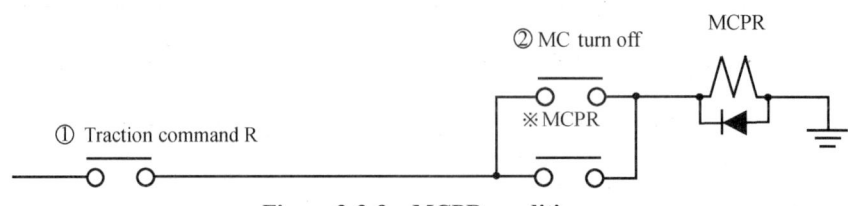

Figure 2-2-9 MCPR conditions

In Figure 2-2-8, MC is in the "Switch" (neutral) position, and MC switches to R for excitation. The normally open contact of MC R switch is closed. When the direction handle is not in the "OFF" position, the main control handle turns on the relay MCPR and is powered on, and the state remains unchanged through the auxiliary contact when the main controller operates at other levels. The normally open contact of MCPR in Figure 2-2-9 is closed. When other conditions are met, Line 9 is energized and the relay PR point is closed. Line 9 is connected to the monitoring central device, indicating that the traction command is valid. The PR is connected to the brake controller through the contact signal, indicating that the traction command is valid.

In items ① to ⑩, if the following conditions are met, the traction command line (Line 9) will be pressurized and PR excited. The contact signal of PR is input to the braking device to enable the braking device to identify the traction operation mode, as shown in Figure 2-2-10.

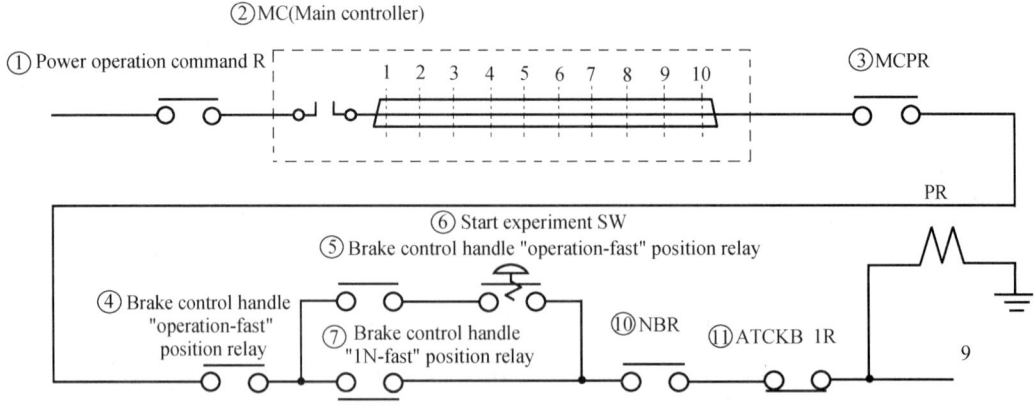

Figure 2-2-10 Traction command conditions

(Conditions) ① ∩ ② ∩ ③ ∩ ④ ∩ {(⑤ ∩ ⑥) ∩ ⑦} ∩⑧ ∩⑨:

① Traction command R excitation: refer to Figure 2-2-7.
② MC level is 1-10.
③ MCPR excites: refer to Figure 2-2-9.
④ Brake control handle "Operating fast" position relay excites.
⑤ B7 Brake control handle "7N fast" position relay excites.
⑥ Start test SW is ON.
⑦ Brake control handle "1N fast" position relay non-excited.
⑧ NBR excites: slow down ATP service braking.
⑨ ATCKB1R is non-excited: ATP relaxation braking B1.

When the above conditions are met at the same time, the traction command is valid. The above conditions indicate that once there is a braking command, regardless of whether it comes from the brake handle or ATP, the traction command condition cannot be generated. Therefore, braking has higher priority than traction, so as to ensure driving safety.

3. Constant speed switch circuit (constant speed driving)

The output conditions of constant speed control command are: under the basic conditions of ATPCOS normal position (ATP is valid, no Cut out), LKJCOS normal position (existing signal equipment is valid, no Cut out), and power operation above gear 2, the constant speed relay (CSR) is energized by operating the constant speed switch (constant speed SW) on the driver's console (see Figure 2-2-11), and the NO contact of CSR is closed, which is input to the central device of vehicle information control (Line 23).

In the project of ①~⑪, if the following conditions are met, CSR will be excited.

(Conditions) ① ∩② ∩ ③ ∩ ④ ∩ ⑤ ∩ ⑥ ∩ ⑦ ∩⑧ ∩⑨ ∩ ⑩ ∩⑪:

① Traction command R excites
② ATPCOR is excitation: ATP is normal.
③ LKJCOR is excitation: LKJ is normal.
④ Brake control handle "Operating fast" position relay excites.
⑤ Brake control handle "1N fast" position relay doesn't excite.
⑥ NBR excites: release ATP service braking.
⑦ ATCKB1R is non-excited.
⑧ EBR excites: release ATP emergency braking.
⑨ Constant speed closing SW is OFF.
⑩ MC block is fixed at any one of 5~10.
⑪ Constant speed SW is ON.

※ The constant speed SW changes to ON. When the CSR is excited, even if the constant speed SW is opened, it will maintain itself.

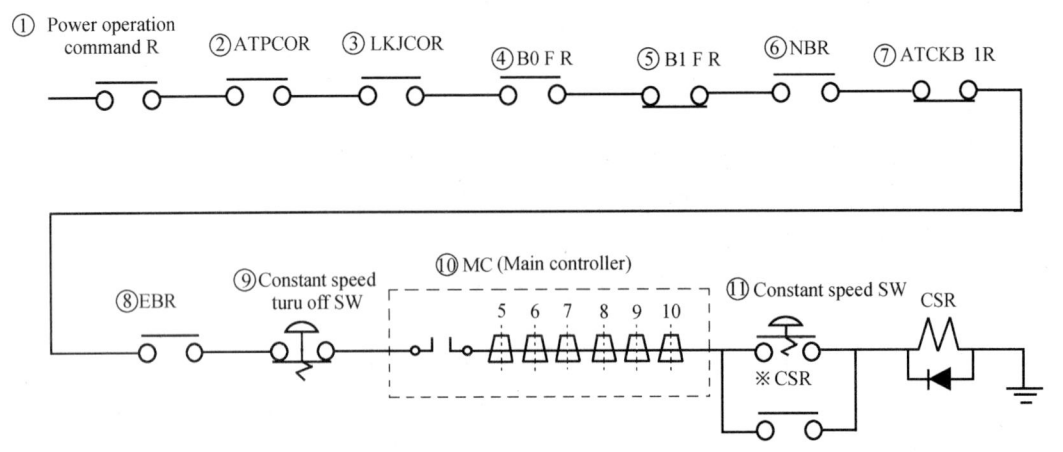

Figure 2-2-11　CSR excitation conditions

4. Constant speed control conditions (Line 23)

In items ① and ②, if the following conditions are met, the constant speed control conditions (see Figure 2-2-12) (Line 23) are pressurized (constant speed control command).

(Conditions) ① ∩ ②:

① Traction power operation command R excites.

② CSR excites.

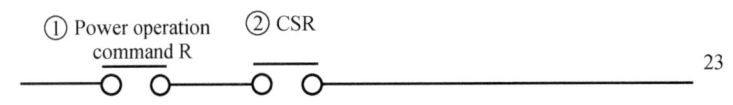

Figure 2-2-12　Constant speed control conditions

2.2.3 Other circuits related to control

The driver controller operation and directly related traction control circuits are introduced in the previous section. In order to facilitate the understanding of the system, some control circuits related to the driver controller are also described here.

1. Main control relay MCR

The main control relay determines whether the driver's operation is effective. There is a main control relay in the cabs at each end, and its operation is effective only when the main control relay is closed. When the main control operation is performed in the cab at one end of the EMU, the operation in the cab at the other end is invalid through interlocking control. The operation and interlocking of the main controller relay are shown in Figure 2-2-13 and Figure 2-2-14.

The following are the control conditions of the main control relay. Under the following conditions, the main control relay MCR is closed:

① The brake controller is not in "Pull-out" position: brake control handle "Operating fast" position relay excites.

② MCRR is non-excited: the MCR of the head car on the opposite side is non-excited.

③ MXR is non-excited: no coupling with other marshalling.

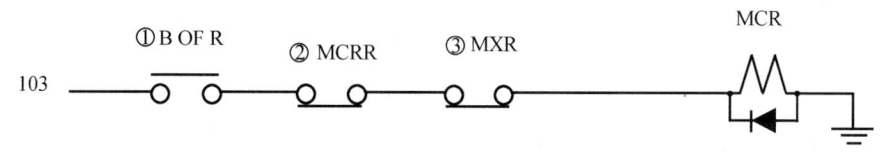

Figure 2-2-13 MCR conditions

Car T1c-1's main controller relay MCR uses Line 3 (Line 103) as the power supply, and acts under the condition that the brake setter handle position (Operating fast) (the brake setter handle is not unplugged and effective) makes the brake control handle "Operating fast" position relay contact closed and the main controller auxiliary relay MCRR normally closed contact NC is closed (the main controller on the other side of the driver's desk is not effective).

In order to ensure that the driver can only drive in the cab on one side, that is, when T1c-1 is driving, the operation of T2c-8 is invalid (or vice versa), MCR and MCRR perform interlocking control.

The auxiliary relay MCRR of the main controller is controlled by the state of the main control relay in the cab on the other side. When the main control relay on the other side is closed, the MCRR is energized, and the main control relay MCR on this side cannot be energized. The interlocking relationship of main control relay of T1c-1 and T2c-8 cars is shown in Figure 2-2-14, and the interlocking signal is transmitted by 3X (3Z) and 3Y (3W) through lines. This interlocking relationship enables the driver to drive only at one end.

If there is a coupling relationship with other marshalling, the main control relay at the coupling position cannot be powered on, that is, the intermediate driver cannot be the operating end.

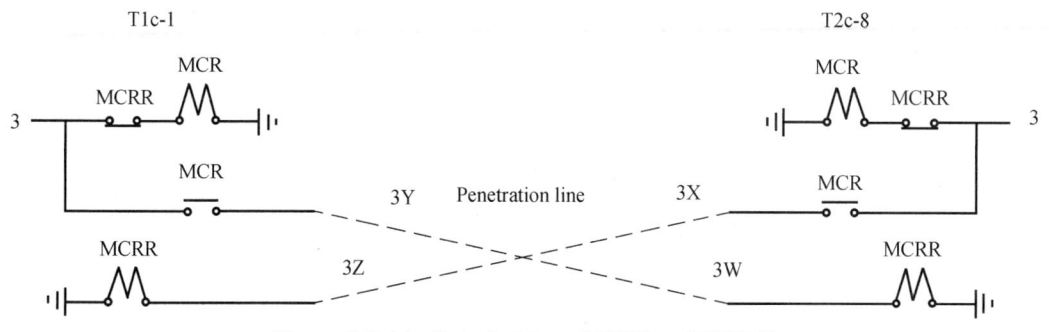

Figure 2-2-14 Interlocking of MCR and MCRR

Task 3 Control of Pantograph and Vacuum Circuit Breaker

【Task Description】

This task mainly introduces the working principles of the control circuit of pantograph and vacuum circuit breaker. The students are required to be able to analyze the working process of pantograph interlocking control, pantograph lifting and vacuum circuit breaker.

【Background Knowledge】

3.1 Pantograph management

Pantographs of CRH2 EMU are set on T2-4 and M2-6 cars, and the pantographs of CRH380A EMU are set on M3-4 and M5-6 cars. Under normal conditions, only single pantograph can be raised. Therefore, when the pantograph rising interlocking relay (PanIR) selects the pantograph on one side, the rising command of the pantograph on the other side cannot be input. The lifting command of the pantograph can be sent out through the operating switch set on the driver's console or the display of the monitor.

3.1.1 Interlock device of MCR and MCRR

For the interlocking relationship between the main controller relay MCR and the auxiliary relay MCRR of the main controller of cars T1c-1 and T2c-8, refer to the operation command logic part.

If the MCRR of T2c-8 car is excited, the penetration line 110 (emergency grounding switch EGS condition) and 111 (VCB condition) are pressurized (DC 100 V) from the MCRR contact of T2c-8 car, the coils of VCB auxiliary relay (VCBRR) and ground protection switch relay (EGSR) are excited, and the contact of each relay is closed.

3.1.2 Interlocking device on Car T2-4 and Car M2-6 or Car M3-4 and Car M5-6

PanIR and pantograph up relay (PanUR) of M3-4 and M5-6 are shown in Figure 2-3-1. After inputting the rising command of pantograph to Car M3-4, the PanIR of Car M5-6 of Line 106G is excited. As the PanIR of Car M5-6 is excited, the normally closed contact of the PanIR of Car M5-6 is open, so the PanUR is not excited. When Car M5-6 is input with pantograph rising command, PanUR of M3-4 train cannot be excited according to the same logic. This ensures that the single pantograph is raised.

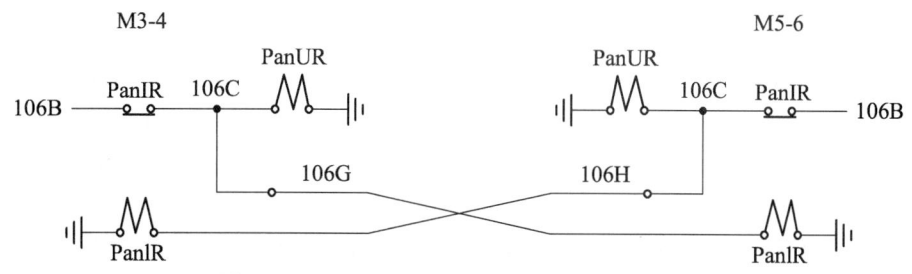

Figure 2-3-1 Pantograph interlocking control

3.1.3 Command to raise the pantograph

When the EGSR and VCBRR are not excited, after operating the pantograph raising switch (PanUS), the command to raise the pantograph is pressurized by selecting Line 106 X (Car M2-6) or Line 106Y (Car T2-4) through the pantograph change switch (PanCGS) (note: CRH380A is Car M5-6 or Car M3-4). After Line 106 is pressurized, the pantograph up relay PanUR is energized, and contact "a" of PanUR is closed. If no command to lower the pantograph is input (PanDWR is not excited), the pantograph up valve PanUV is energized, and the pantograph rises, as shown in Figure 2-3-2.

The monitor display inputs the command to raise the pantograph, and the equipment command relay (URO1) or (URO4) switches to one side of the monitor terminal device to excite the PanUR of the unit.

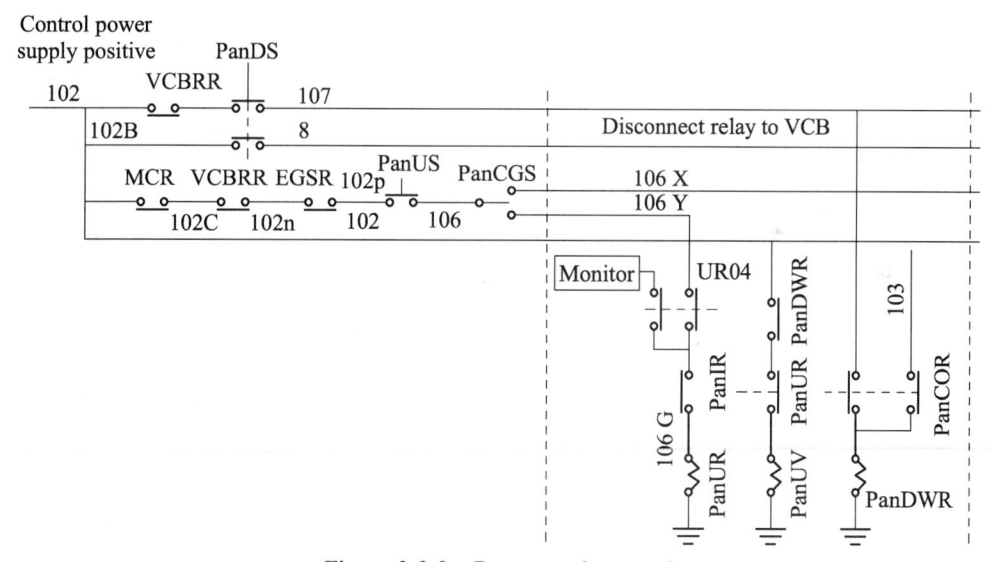

Figure 2-3-2 Pantograph control

3.1.4 Command to lower the pantograph

Press the pantograph down switch (PanDS), Line 107 is pressurized under the pantograph lowering command. At the same time, Line 8 is pressurized under the VCB

047

disconnect command (refer to the auxiliary circuit connection). Line 107 is pressurized, the pantograph downward relay (PanDWR) is excited, and its normally closed contact disconnects the excitation of PanUV; At the same time, the parallel pantograph downward auxiliary relay (PanDWAR) is also excited, and its normally closed contact disconnects the excitation of PanUR to ensure reliable pantograph lowering.

The monitor display inputs the command to lower the pantograph, and the pantograph cut-out relay (PanCOR) is excited, so that PanDWR works.

3.2 Vacuum circuit breaker control circuit

In normal operation, the vacuum circuit breaker VCB connects or disconnects the connection between the 25 kV high-voltage circuit and the traction transformer; In case of fault, VCB can quickly, safely and reliably cut off the current, protect the circuit and ensure the safety of the train. It has both the functions of a circuit breaker and a switch.

3.2.1 VCB input control

VCB input refers to the operation of VCB close switch (VCBCS) after confirming that the pantograph of Car 4 or 6 is raised. Line 7 which is inputted VCB command is energized and VCBCR1 is excited. When VCB of each car is put into operation, its protective device does not act. At this time, VCBOR2 is excited. After both VCBCR1 and VCBOR2 are excited, VCB-M is excited and VCB is put into operation when the contactor of traction converter of M1/M3/M5 and M2/M4/M6 cars is in the open state (KRR demagnetization) and NFB (MTOPMN) for oil pump of main transformer is put into operation.

1. VCB input control command

As shown in Figure 2-3-3, when the main control relay MCR is excited, the VCB close switch (VCBCS) is closed, or the VCB command of automatic passing neutral-section sent by the information control terminal device is closed, SVCBCR is closed, and VCB input command line 7 is energized.

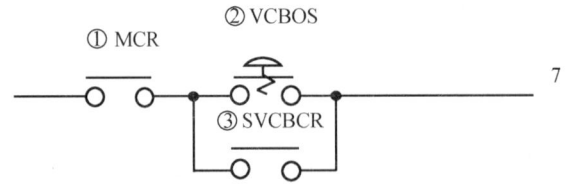

Figure 2-3-3 VCB input conditions

2. VCBCR1 conditions

As shown in Figure 2-3-4, when MCR is excited, VCBCS is closed, and the information display does not send out the unit selection command, and UR0 is not excited,

VCBCR1 is excited.

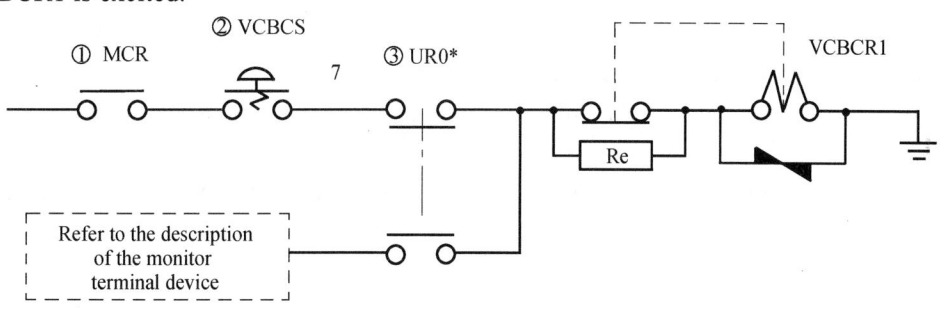

Figure 2-3-4　VCBCR1 conditions

3. VCBOR2 conditions

As shown in Figure 2-3-5, VCBOR2 can be energized under two types of interlocking conditions and system normal conditions. When all conditions are met, VCBOR2 can be excited. That is, in the following conditions, when ① ∩ ② ∩ ③ ∩ ④ ∩ ⑤ ∩ ⑥ ∩ (⑦ ∩⑧) ∩ ⑨ ∩ (⑩ ∩ ⑪) is valid, VCBOR2 is closed.

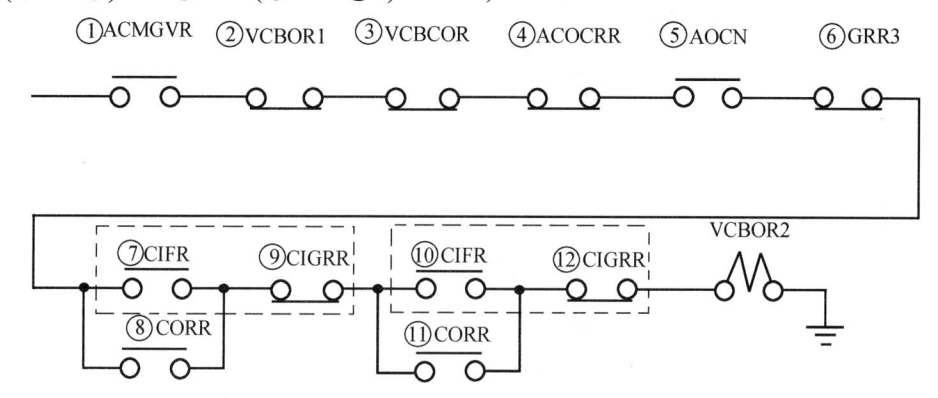

Figure 2-3-5　VCBOR2 conditions

(1) ACMGVR is excited: the auxiliary air pressure is normal.

(2) VCBOR1 is non-excited: there is no VCB disconnection command.

(3) VCBCOR is non-excited: the monitor display does not send the command to disconnect VCB.

(4) ACOCRR non-excited: it is not primary overcurrent.

(5) AOCN is excited: it is not tertiary overcurrent.

(6) GRR3 is non-excited: the third circuit is not grounded.

(7) CIFR is excited: the traction converter device is normal.

(8) CORR is excited: the traction motor is switched off.

(9) CIGRR is non-excited: the traction converter device is grounded normally.

4. VCB-M conditions

As shown in Figure 2-3-6, VCB closes after VCB-M is powered on. VCB-M under the

049

following conditions:

① When ∩ {(② ∩ ③ ∩ ④ ∩ ⑤)∪ ⑦} ∩ ⑥ is valid, it is closed.

(1) OCTN (transformer overcurrent NFB) is not excited.

(2) MTOPMN is excited: the circuit breaker of oil pump of traction transformer is put into operation.

(3) KRR is non-excited: the contactor of traction converter device is disconnected (M1/M3 car).

(4) KRR is non-excited: the contactor of traction converter device is disconnected (M2/M4 car).

(5) VCBCR1 is excited.

(6) VCBOR2 is excited.

(7) The VCB is in the "ON" position.

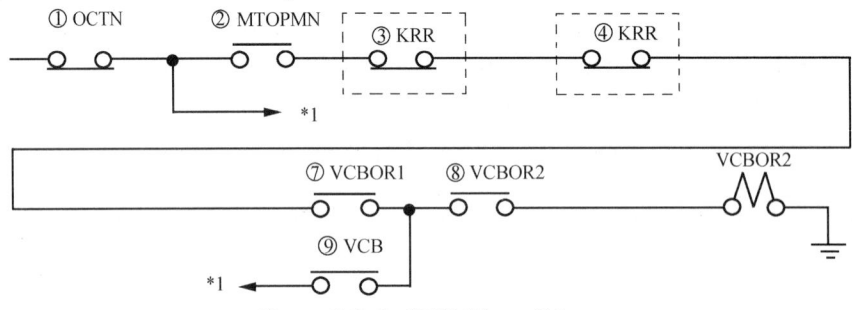

Figure 2-3-6   VCB-M conditions

3.2.2 VCB disconnection control

The common VCB circuit breaker is to operate the VCB open switch (VCBOS), Line 8 of VCB circuit breaker command is pressurized, VCBOR1 works, VCB-M becomes non pressurized, and all VCBs of the train are open. In addition, when lowering the pantograph switch (PanDS), in order to prevent the current break caused by the pantograph, pressurize Line 8 and use VCB to break the current. As an abnormal open circuit, VCBOR2 is not pressurized due to any of the following actions, and VCB of the unit is disconnected.

1. VCB disconnection command condition

As shown in Figure 2-3-7, after the VCB disconnection command sent by the breaker VCBOS or the over-current phase breaker, SVCBOR is closed, VCB disconnection command (Line 8) is pressurized, and VCBOR1 is excited.

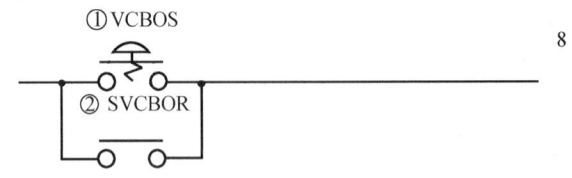

Figure 2-3-7   VCB disconnection command

2. VCB is disconnected in case of abnormality

As an abnormal open circuit, VCBOR2 has no voltage due to any of the following actions, and VCB of the unit is disconnected.

① ACMGVR (relay for small air compressor regulator): OFF (low auxiliary air pressure);

② VCBCOR (VCB open relay): ON (disconnection remotely controlled by the device);

③ ACOCCR (AC current auxiliary relay): ON [primary overcurrent detection];

④ AOCN (auxiliary circuit overcurrent NFB): OFF (tertiary overcurrent detection);

⑤ GRR3 (third stage circuit grounding relay): ON (third circuit grounding detection);

⑥ CIFR (traction converter fault detection relay): OFF (traction converter circuit fault detection);

⑦ GRR (primary circuit grounding relay): ON (primary circuit grounding detection).

Task 4 Traction Converter Control

【Task Description】

This task mainly introduces the interface of control and status information between equipment related to traction converter. In addition to completing the traction control, the traction controller also exchanges information with the monitoring device terminal and the control interface of the main circuit breaker to control the pre-charging of the filter capacitor.

【Background Knowledge】

4.1 Interface between traction converter and vehicle information control terminal device

The data transmission between the traction converter and the terminal device is carried out through optical cables, transmitting and receiving control command information and fault signals. In addition to the control command information transmitted by optical cable, as a backup, hard wires are used to input the following signals to the traction converter:

- Forward (Line 4);
- Backward (Line 5);
- Reset (Line 6);
- Traction level A (Line 9A);

- Traction level B (Line 9B).

In addition, hard wires are used to input the following fault and status signals from the traction converter to the terminal device:
- Relay for normal diagnosis of control unit (WDTR);
- Relay for fault detection of traction converter (CIFR2);
- Relay for traction converter grounding detection (CIGRR2);
- Relay for traction converter control power supply (DCR);
- Relay for main circuit current detection device (CDR2).

4.2 Interface between traction converter and braking control device

Signal transmitted from traction converter to braking control device: regenerative feedback; regenerate valid signal.

Signal transmitted from braking control device to traction converter: regenerative braking mode.

The traction converter controls the electric braking according to the regenerative braking mode signal from the braking control device. The traction converter calculates the braking torque according to the output current of the inverter and the speed of the traction motor, and transmits it to the braking control device as a regenerative feedback signal. The braking control device operates the necessary braking force. When the braking force of the electric braking is insufficient, the air braking shall be used to supplement it.

The insufficient electric braking force is detected through the traction converter. If the insufficient electric braking force is detected, the UBCDR (regenerative effective signal) contact is open and transfers to the air braking. The UBCDR contact is in the open state. At the side of the braking control device, when the speed is above 160 km/h, the pressure switch BCS2 (detection pressure, low pressure) for braking control is OFF, or when the speed is below 160 km/h, the pressure switch BCS1 (detection pressure, high pressure) for braking control is OFF; if the timing relay UBTR for insufficient braking detection is OFF, the excitation of UV (emergency brake valve) is disconnected, and the emergency braking acts.

4.3 Relevant interfaces between traction converter and VCB circuit of vacuum circuit breaker

4.3.1 Conditions for VCB input

In order to prevent the impact current on the traction converter when VCB is put into operation, the power contactor (K) at the primary side of the traction converter shall not be put into operation first, and the relay (KRR) shall be put into degaussing state. After the VCB input status is input to the traction converter, the filter capacitor can be pre-charged (CHK), and the traction converter primary power contactor (K) can be put into operation.

4.3.2 VCB disconnection conditions

When the VCB is in the input state and the traction converter fails, the fault detection relay (CIFR1) is used for demagnetization; or if the traction converter grounding is abnormal and the grounding detection relay (CIGRR1) is excited, VCB will be disconnected.

4.4 Filter capacitor pre-charging

In order to prevent the excessive impact current when the contactor (K) for input of the primary side power supply of the traction converter is put into operation, the filter capacitor shall be charged before the input of K. The time to start charging is when the signal of the inverter is input from the terminal device. The following shows the process from charging to K input. The pre-charging circuit is shown in Figure 2-4-1 and Figure 2-4-2.

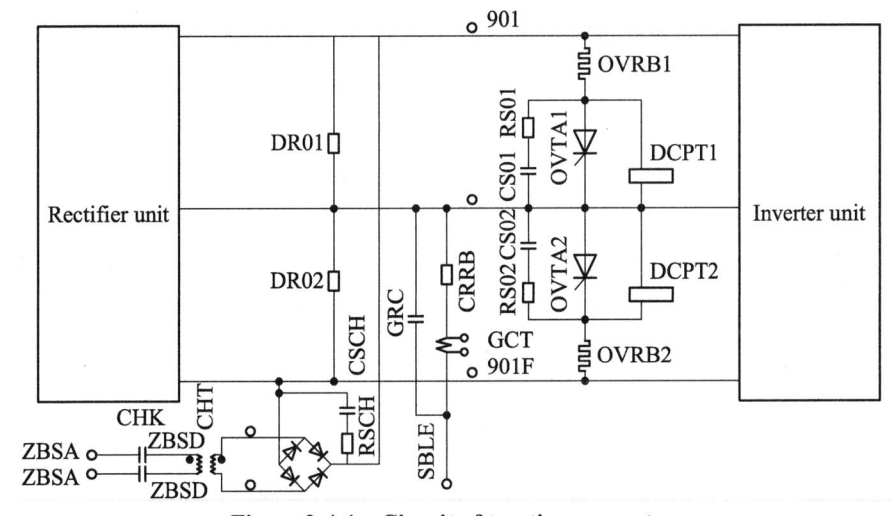

Figure 2-4-1   Circuit of traction converter

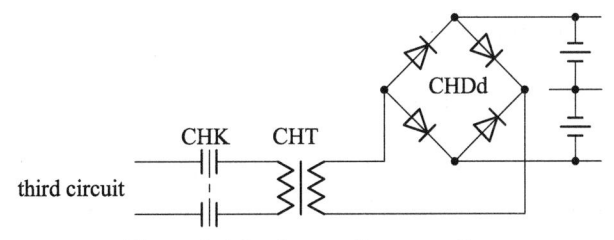

Figure 2-4-2   Supporting capacitor

Reverser input

Input of contactor (CHK) for output charging

Charging of filter capacitor

Charging contactor (CHK) disconnected

K input, composition of preparatory charging circuit

4.5 Fault protection action

4.5.1 AC overcurrent of primary circuit and abnormal grounding of secondary circuit

When AC overcurrent (ACOCR) of the primary circuit and abnormal grounding of the tertiary circuit (GR3) are detected, VCB trips and the power contactor (K) at the primary side of the traction converter is disconnected. In addition, this information (ACOCRR1, GRR3-1) is also input to the terminal unit.

4.5.2 The ventilator stops when the traction transformer is abnormal

When the traction transformer temperature anomaly (MTThRR) and the traction transformer oil pressure pump anomaly (MTOFRR) are detected, the traction transformer anomaly information is input to the traction converter. In addition, when the power supply of the traction converter blower (CIBM), traction motor blower (MMBM) and the blower are cut off (BMK), fan stop information is input to the traction converter. When inputting the information of traction transformer abnormality and ventilator stop, disconnect the pulse rectifier inverter gate off and disconnect the power contactor (K) at the primary side of traction converter. This information is also input to the terminal device.

4.5.3 ACCT

The secondary current of traction transformer is detected through ACCT. When the secondary overcurrent of traction transformer is detected, the gate-off of pulse rectifier and inverter and the power contactor (K) at the primary side of traction converter are disconnected through the current value.

4.5.4 CTU、CTV、CTW

Detect U, V, and W three-phase current of traction motor. Once overcurrent or current imbalance is detected, the gate-off of the pulse rectifier and inverter and the power contactor (K) at the primary side of the traction converter will be disconnected.

In the case of non-overcurrent, when the current value is below the set value, the gate-on of the pulse rectifier and inverter is turned on.

4.5.5 GCT

Detect the grounding current at secondary side of traction transformer. According to the setting value, OVTH is on, the gate-off of the pulse rectifier and inverter and the power contactor (K) at the primary side of the traction converter are disconnected.

4.5.6 Overvoltage suppression thyristor unit (OVTH unit)

As shown in Figure 2-4-1, OVTH unit is composed of silicon controlled rectifier, snubber resistor (OVRe1, OVRe2), buffer capacitor (FC), gate level drive substrate, DC voltage detector (DCPT1, DCPT2), etc.

When the over-voltage of filter capacitor is detected and the control power supply is turned off, the silicon controlled rectifier is on, enabling the filter capacitor to discharge.

DCPT is assembled in OVTH unit to detect DC voltage. When the OVTH false firing, DC over-voltage, DC low voltage, abnormal voltage, etc. are detected, the gate off of pulse rectifier and inverter traction converter primary power contactor (K), etc. are disconnected according to the conditions.

4.5.7 Over temperature in cooling unit and mechanical room

Detect the U and V phase temperature (THCU, THCV) of the pulse rectifier, U, V, and W phase temperature (THIU, THIV, THIW) of the inverter, and the temperature in the mechanical room (CITHR1 ~ 5). When the overtemperature is detected, protective measures such as gate-off of pulse rectifier and inverter and disconnection of power contactor (K) at primary side of traction converter shall be taken.

Task 5 CRH380B EMU Traction Control

【Task Description】

This task is an overall understanding of CRH380B EMU traction system. Through the study of this task, the students are required to master its working principles, and be able to analyze the working process of the main circuit.

【Background Knowledge】

5.1 High voltage power supply

5.1.1 Pantograph

The catenary provides AC 25 kV voltage, which is collected by the pantograph. Each CRH380B multiple unit is equipped with two pantographs, which are connected to two traction units of a high-voltage system through high-voltage cables on the roof. During normal operation, each high-voltage system only needs to raise one pantograph to collect current.

5.1.2 Vacuum circuit breaker (Figure 2-5-1)

Each independent high voltage system is equipped with two main circuit breakers, which are installed at the ends of 02 and 07 car roofs respectively. The main circuit breaker is not only used to switch the operating current of the traction unit, but also used to interrupt the overcurrent and short-circuit current under fault conditions. In order to maintain and repair high-voltage equipment, a double pole grounding switch is installed on the main circuit breaker. The grounding switch connects both ends of the main circuit breaker with the working grounding. The grounding switch has the function of preventing short circuit.

Figure 2-5-1　Vacuum circuit breaker

5.1.3 Grounding switch (Figure 2-5-2)

Once the grounding switch is connected, the traction device and the grounding circuit can be connected together to realize grounding through the knife switch. The grounding switch is composed of upper housing and lower housing. The upper housing is mounted on the roof of the towing vehicle with 4 M10 bolts and contains a shaft with two movable blades mounted on the end of the shaft. The lower housing is installed under the roof and contains a control lever for manually operating the grounding switch to move two knife switches from the balanced position to the relevant grounding contact of the main circuit breaker.

Figure 2-5-2　Structure of grounding switch

5.1.4　Lightning arrester (Figure 2-5-3)

Each transformer car of the EMU is equipped with two lightning arresters: one is installed at the right rear of each pantograph to protect the train and the electrical system at the rear section from overvoltage (such as lightning overvoltage). The other lightning arrester is located at the front end of the primary side of the transformer, which is used to prevent the voltage generated by the switch that cannot bear in the main transformer.

Figure 2-5-3　Lightning arrester

5.1.5　Voltage and current transformers (Figure 2-5-4, 2-5-5)

The network terminal detection device is composed of current transformer and voltage transformer. The voltage transformer is used to measure and monitor the voltage of the contact line of the power grid. The current transformer is connected to the lower port of each main circuit breaker to measure the current of the EMU. The other two transformers are used to monitor the main transformer. These two transformers are used to measure the line current and return current of the traction unit.

Figure 2-5-4　Voltage transformer 　　　Figure 2-5-5 Current transformer

5.1.6　High voltage disconnector

There are two roof disconnectors in the whole train, which are located on the top of the transformer and are normally closed. In case of failure, the disconnector will disconnect the roof cable. If the main circuit system of one traction unit fails, the train control system can isolate the roof line so that another traction unit can be operated.

5.1.7　High voltage jumper (Figure 2-5-6)

The high-voltage line on the roof must go beyond the connection part between cars. This is realized by the support insulator at the car end and the support insulator jumper cable. The design of jumper cable is applicable to the maximum relative motion between car bodies. The rewind design can meet the maximum relative motion between car bodies. The size of each single winding can meet the maximum operating current requirements. If one winding is broken, the current will be maintained by the other winding and can be easily checked by visual inspection.

Figure 2-5-6　High voltage jumper

5.1.8 Traction transformer

The CRH380B EMU traction transformer is located in the equipment compartment under the train TC02/TC07 of EMU, and the transformer and cooling unit are integrated in one frame. The transformer is a single-phase transformer. The main transformer reduces the primary voltage of 25 kV/50 Hz to the secondary voltage of 1,850 V/50 Hz for four traction windings. Its secondary windings provide electric energy for the traction converter.

5.2 Traction system

The traction system is mainly used to provide traction power for multiple units, and the main equipment includes traction converter, overvoltage limiting resistor, traction motor, and traction motor cooling fan. Schematic diagram of traction system is shown in Figure 2-5-7.

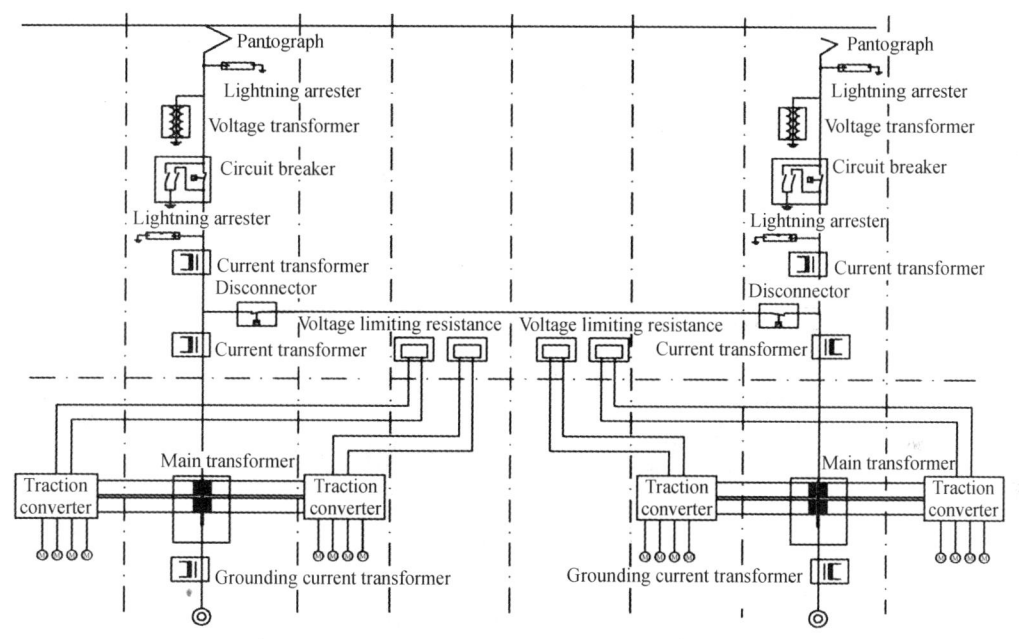

Figure 2-5-7 Schematic diagram of traction system

CRH380B EMU are equipped with four identical and independent power units. Each power unit has a traction converter with traction control unit and four parallel traction motors. Each traction converter basically consists of two 4-quadrant choppers (4QC), an intermediate voltage circuit with resonant circuit, a brake chopper BC, and an input line contactor of a pulse width modulation inverter (PWMI) traction converter. The train control unit TCU controls two sets of 4-quadrant choppers (4QC), one set of inverter, one set of traction control device, cooling system and intermediate DC link. Each group of inverters controls four traction motors. The main function of the converter is to obtain the intermediate DC voltage of 3200-3600V from the 1AC 1850V/50Hz output by the traction transformer through four quadrant rectification, and then supply power to the traction motor through the three-phase AC voltage with adjustable voltage and frequency output by the inverter.

The EMU are equipped with 4 voltage limiters. Each power unit contains a voltage limiter. The voltage limiter is located at the end of the 04/05 intermediate car. The upper limit voltage resistor on the roof is used to prevent overvoltage of traction converter. In case of converter failure, the voltage limiting resistor can ensure a limited and safe discharge intermediate circuit. When the energy generated by electric braking cannot be absorbed by the pantograph and catenary, the overvoltage limiting resistor will timely convert this energy into heat energy.

The EMU has 16 traction motors, which are installed on the following power bogies: Car 01, Car 03, Car 06, and Car 08. It is a four pole three-phase asynchronous traction motor. Forced air cooling is adopted. Temperature monitoring is adopted to protect the traction motor from overheating. The mechanical force transmission system is used to transfer the driving torque of the traction motor to the wheel set. This set of system is mainly composed of axial and radial flexible couplings and gear transmission devices on wheel sets. The design of coupling can compensate the relative movement between motor and wheel during driving.

Task 6 Failure Case Analysis

【Task Description】

This task mainly introduces the main circuit fault protection and fault cases. Through the learning of this task, the students are required to analyze the causes of the failure and the troubleshooting methods.

【Background Knowledge】

6.1 Main circuit fault

The main circuit fault protection is shown in Table 2-6-1.

Table 2-6-1 Fault handling of main circuit

Fault type	Protection action: VCB trip	Protection action: K OFF	Protection action: Converter without output	Fault indicator	Display screen: Fault code	Display screen: Other displays	Reset method and steps
Transformer primary overcurrent	√	√	√	VCB	162	Panel information	Press the reset switch first; then switch on OCTN; close VCB again
Transformer oil pump stops running	√	√	√	—	165	Panel information	Close the oil pump circuit breaker
Transformer insulation oil circulation stops	—	√	√	Electrical equipment	132	Panel information	Automatic reset after status removal
Transformer temperature rises	—	√	√	Electrical equipment	133	Panel information	Automatic reset after status removal
Tertiary overcurrent of transformer	√	√	√	VCB	163	Panel information	Switch on ACON again; switch on VCB
The third side of transformer is grounded	√	√	√	VCB	164	Panel information	Press the reset switch; close the VCB again
Abnormal synchronous power supply (overvoltage)	—	—	√	—	—	Converter (each vehicle)	Automatic reset after fault 1 second and state removal
Abnormal synchronous power supply (undervoltage)	—	—	√	—	—	Converter (each vehicle)	Automatic reset after fault 1 second and state removal
Abnormal synchronous power supply (frequency)	—	—	√	—	—	—	Automatic reset after fault 1 second and state removal
Transformer secondary overcurrent 1	—	—	√	—	—	Converter (each vehicle)	Automatic reset after fault 1 second and state removal
Transformer secondary overcurrent 2	√	√	√	Electrical equipment VCB	141 005	Converter (each vehicle) Panel information	Switch on the circuit breaker of traction converter 1 of operating distribution panel again
DC overvoltage 1	—	—	√	—	—	—	Automatic reset after fault 1 second and state removal
DC overvoltage 2	—	—	√	—	—	—	Automatic reset after fault 1 second and state removal
DC overvoltage 3	—	√	√	—	004	Converter (each vehicle)	Operate reset switch
DC undervoltage 1	—	—	√	—	—	—	Automatic reset after fault 1 second and state removal
DC undervoltage 2	—	√	√	—	—	Converter (each vehicle)	Automatic reset after fault 1 second and state removal

Continued

Fault type	Protection action			Display				Reset method and steps
	VCB trip	K OFF	Converter without output	Fault indicator	Display screen		
					Fault code	Other displays	
Abnormal DC voltage	—	—	√	—	—	—	Automatic reset after fault 1 second and state removal
Abnormal main circuit components	√	√	√	VCB Electrical equipment VCB	141 005	Converter (each vehicle) Panel information	Switch on the circuit breaker of traction converter 1 of operating distribution panel again
DC 100 V abnormal	—	√	√	—	004	Converter (each vehicle)	Operate reset switch
Abnormal control power supply	—	√	√	—	004	Converter (each vehicle)	Operate reset switch
Abnormal gate control power supply	—	√	√	—	004	Converter (each vehicle)	Operate reset switch
Microcomputer abnormality	—	√	√	Electrical equipment	139	Panel information	Operate reset switch
Traction motor overcurrent 1	—	—	√	—	004	Converter (each vehicle)	Automatic reset after fault 1 s and state removal; operate the reset switch when detecting twice within 10 seconds interval
Traction motor overcurrent 2	—	√	√	—	004	Converter (each vehicle)	Operate reset switch
Traction motor current imbalance	—	√	√	—	004	Converter (each vehicle)	Operate the reset switch for 3 seconds
Abnormal pulse generator	—	√	√	—	004	Converter (each vehicle)	Operate reset switch
Excessive braking force	—		√	—	—	Converter (each vehicle)	Reset after brake disconnection
The temperature of cooling device is too high	—	√	√	—	—	Converter (each vehicle)	Automatic reset after status removal
The temperature in the equipment room is too high	—	√	√	—	—	Converter (each vehicle)	Automatic reset after status removal
MM and CI fans stop running	—	√	√	Electrical equipment	137 138 134	Converter (each vehicle) Panel information	Automatic reset after status removal (Each fan circuit breaker is connected again)

Continued

Fault type	Protection action			Display			Reset method and steps
	VCB trip	K OFF	Converter without output	Fault indicator	Display screen		
					Fault code	Other displays	
OVTh Misplaced arc	—	√	√	—	004	Converter (each vehicle)	Automatic reset 5 seconds after the fault occurs and after the fault is removed; K is disconnected and reset switch is operated when detecting three times within 30 seconds interval
					Fault code	Other displays	
Poor charging	—	—	—	—	005	Converter (each vehicle)	Close traction converter 1 again
Main transformer secondary side grounding 1	—	√	√	—	004	Converter (each vehicle)	Operate reset switch
Main transformer secondary side grounding 2	√	—	—	Electrical equipment VCB	142 004	Converter (each vehicle) Panel information	Switch on VCB again Operate reset switch
Regenerative braking failure	—	—	—	—	—	—	Brake release
Traction does not work	—	—	—	—	—	Converter (each vehicle)	Automatic reset after fault 1 second and state removal

6.2 Example of fault handling process

6.2.1 Pantograph cannot be raised

Handling process when pantograph cannot be raised is show in Table 2-6-2.

063

Table 2-6-2 Handling process when pantograph cannot be raised

Phenomenon	MON indicates that the pantograph is not raised, and the network voltage meter does not display.
Vehicle type	CRH380A、CRH380AL
Causes	① The [Pantograph · VCB] circuit breaker in the cab distribution panels at both ends is in "OFF" position. ② The pressure of auxiliary air cylinder is too low. ③ EGS is closed. ④ VCB is closed. ⑤ The [pantograph raising] circuit breaker in the combined switchboard of Cars 04 and 06 (CRH380A)]/[Cars 05 and 13 (CRH380AL)] is in "OFF" position. ⑥ [Valve plate power supply 1 and 2] circuit breakers in the combined distribution panel of Cars 05 and 13 of CRH380AL EMU are in "OFF" position.
Train working	Normal operation after troubleshooting
Steps	Processing
1	1.1 Confirm whether the circuit breaker [Pantograph VCB] of the cab distribution panel at the main control end is closed. If it is disconnected, it will be closed. 1.2 Confirm whether the "Incomplete preparation" indicator is off. If the indicator is on, turn the [Auxiliary Air Compressor Control] knob right and hold it for 3 seconds. Start the auxiliary air compressor to blow air until the "Incomplete preparation" indicator is off.

Continued

Phenomenon		MON indicates that the pantograph is not raised, and the network voltage meter does not display.
1		1.3 Confirm whether EGS is in the disconnected state. If it is closed, close the circuit breaker [protective grounding] in the cab at the main control end, turn the [protective grounding removal] knob switch right and hold it for 3 seconds. After disconnecting EGS, disconnect the circuit breaker [protective grounding]. 1.4 Confirm whether VCB is disconnected. If it is closed, press the [VCB OFF] button to disconnect VCB. 1.5 If the pantograph still cannot be raised, notify the onboard mechanic.
2		2.1 Immediately confirm whether the circuit breaker [Pantograph VCB] in the distribution panel in the other cab is closed. If it is disconnected, it will be closed.
2		2.2 Confirm whether the circuit breaker [Pantograph · VCB] in the combined switchboard of [Cars 04 and 06 (CRH380A)]/ [Cars 05 and 13 (CRH380AL)] is closed. If it is disconnected, it will be closed. 2.3 Confirm whether the circuit breakers of [Valve plate power supply 1 and 2] in the combined distribution of [Cars 05 and 13 (CRH380AL)] are closed. If they are disconnected, they will be closed. 2.4 After confirmation, notify the driver.
3		3.1 Raise the pantograph again. If the pantograph still cannot be raised, change the pantograph. 3.2 If the pantograph for pantograph change operation cannot be raised, all pantographs shall be removed remotely, and pantograph lifting shall be operated remotely one by one, but two near pantographs (reconnection, CRH380AL) shall not be raised. 3.3 If all the pantographs of the EMU cannot be raised, the mechanic shall notify the driver to apply for rescue.

6.2.2 VCB of the whole train cannot be closed

Handling process when VCB of the whole train cannot be closed is shown in Table 2-6-3.

065

Table 2-6-3 VCB of the whole train cannot be closed

Phenomenon	After pressing the [VCB closing] button or passing the phase, the VCB of the whole train cannot be closed.
Vehicle type	CRH380A、CRH380AL
Causes	① The VCBOR3 relay is normally open, and the electric shock is stuck, which results in the electrification of Line 8. ② The normally open contact of EXR1 relay is stuck, resulting in the power supply of Line 8.
Train working	First deal with the emergency, and then stop the vehicle if it is invalid
Steps	Processing
1	1.1 Without stopping, press the [VCB Close] button. If it is closed, continue to operate; 1.2 If it is not closed, confirm whether the circuit breaker [Pantograph · VCB] of the cab distribution panel at the main control end is closed. If it is disconnected, it will be closed.
1	1.3 Confirm whether the "Incomplete preparation" indicator is off. If the indicator is on, turn the [Auxiliary Air Compressor Control] knob right and hold it for 3 seconds. Start the auxiliary air compressor to blow air until the "Incomplete preparation" indicator is off. 1.4 Turn the direction handle to "OFF" position. 1.5 Press the [VCB closing] button, and if the VCB of the whole train still cannot be closed, notify the onboard mechanic.

Continued

Phenomenon	After pressing the [VCB closing] button or passing the phase, the VCB of the whole train cannot be closed.	
2		2.1 Immediately disconnect the circuit breaker of [Pantograph circuit breaker] in the combined switchboard of [Cars 2, 6 (CRH380A)]/[Cars 02, 08, 10, 14 (CRH380AL)]. 2.2 Confirm whether the [pantograph raising] circuit breaker in the combined switchboard of [Cars 04 and 06 , (CRH380A)]/[Cars 05 and 13, (CRH380AL)] is closed. If it is disconnected, it will be closed.
3		3.1 Confirm whether the circuit breakers of [Valve plate power supply 1 and 2] in the combined distribution of [Cars 05 and 13 (CRH380AL)] are closed. If they are disconnected, they will be closed. 3.2 After confirmation, notify the driver.
	3.3 The onboard machinist shall close the circuit breakers [Vacuum Circuit Breaker] one by one, notify the driver to reset RS in turn and press the [VCB Close] button, and judge the fault unit that causes the VCB of the whole train to fail to close through this operation. 3.4 After finding the fault unit, the onboard mechanic shall disconnect the circuit breaker [vacuum circuit breaker] in the corresponding combined distribution panel of the unit. 3.5 The driver remotely removes the faulty VCB unit and closes ACK2 for extended power supply.	
4		If the VCB of the whole train cannot be closed automatically after the EMU pass neural-section, the following procedures shall be followed: 4.1 If the driver finds that the VCB of the whole train cannot be closed automatically after passing neural-section, he shall notify the onboard mechanic. 4.2 The onboard mechanic shall immediately confirm that [Passing neural-section VCB control 1], [Passing neural-section VCB control 2], [Phase transition device power supply] Whether the circuit breakers of [Passing neural-section control 1] and [Passing neural-section control 2] are closed. If they are open, they will be closed. 4.3 After confirmation, notify the driver. 4.4 If the VCB of the whole train still cannot be automatically closed after the EMU pass neural-section, the driver shall manually pass neural-section.

6.2.3 The protective grounding switch cannot be disconnected after being closed

Handling process when the protective grounding switch cannot be disconnected after being closed is shown in Table 2-6-4.

Table 2-6-4 Handling process when the protective grounding switch cannot be disconnected after being closed

Phenomenon	EGS is closed and cannot be disconnected.
Vehicle type	CRH380A、CRH380AL
Causes	① The circuit breaker [protective grounding] in the cab distribution panel is in the "Open" position. ② The [Protection grounding closing] button or knob in the cab is in the "Close" position. ③ The air pressure of auxiliary air cylinder is too low. ④ The circuit breaker of [protective grounding break] in the combined switchboard is in the "Open" position.
Train working	Parking treatment
Steps	Processing
1	1.1 Confirm whether the circuit breaker [protective grounding] in the cab distribution panel at the main control end is closed. If it is disconnected, it will be closed. 1.2 Confirm whether the [Protective grounding switch] knob in the cab is in "Close" position. If it is in "Open" position, turn it to "Close" position. 1.3 Confirm whether the "Incomplete Preparation" indicator is off. If the indicator is on, turn the [Auxiliary air compressor control] knob right and hold it for 3 seconds. Start the auxiliary air compressor to blow air until the "Incomplete Preparation" indicator is off. 1.4 The [Protective grounding cut-off] knob switch in the right-handed cab power distribution panel shall be switched for 3 seconds. If the protective grounding switch still cannot be switched off, notify the onboard mechanic.

Continued

Phenomenon	EGS is closed and cannot be disconnected.	
2		2.1 Immediately confirm whether the circuit breaker [protective grounding break] in the power distribution panel of [Cars 04 and 06 (CRH380A)]/[Cars 05 and 13 (CRH380AL)] is closed. If it is open, it will be closed. 2.2 After confirmation, notify the driver.
3		3.1 Rotate the 【protective grounding cut-off】knob switch in the cab power distribution panel for 3 seconds again. 3.2 If the protective grounding switch is disconnected, place the [protective grounding] circuit breaker in the cab distribution panel at the disconnection position to maintain operation. 3.3 If the protective grounding switch still cannot be disconnected, notify the onboard mechanic.
4		4.1 Climb on the roof according to the specified procedure and manually disconnect the protective grounding switch. 4.2 Notify the driver after handling.
5		5.1 Confirm that the protective grounding switch is disconnected through the MON screen. 5.2 Set the [protective grounding] circuit breaker in the cab distribution panel at the break position to maintain operation.

6.2.4 Traction converter fault (004)

Handling Process of traction converter fault (004) is shown in Table 2-6-5.

Table 2-6-5　Handling process of traction converter fault (004)

Phenomenon	K is disconnected, and the motor car cannot be towed and regenerative braking.
Vehicle type	CRH380A、CRH380AL
Causes	DC overvoltage; control power supply is abnormal; traction motor overcurrent; the current of traction motor is unbalanced; PG abnormality; the secondary side of the main transformer is grounded.
Train working	Continue running
Steps	Processing

Continued

Phenomenon		K is disconnected, and the motor car cannot be towed and regenerative braking.
1		When the "Fault occurrence information" prompt flashes on the main menu page of the MON screen, accompanied by an audible alarm, the driver presses the [Fault Details] button at the bottom left to confirm the fault condition and notify the onboard mechanic.
2		The MON screen switches to the fault information page of "Traction converter fault (1004)".
3		3.1 Confirm the fault details through the "Traction converter information (Editing)" page on the MON screen.
		3.2 Check the fault cause through the "Traction converter information (car)" page on the MON screen.
4		4.1 RS reset. 4.2 If the fault is eliminated, it can operate normally. 4.3 If the fault is not eliminated after 3 resets (the interval between resets shall not be less than 3 seconds), the corresponding M train shall be cut off remotely to maintain operation.

6.2.5 Traction converter fault 2 (005)

Handling process of traction converter fault 2 (005) is shown in Table 2-6-6.

Table 2-6-2 Handling process of traction converter fault 2 (005)

Name	2.3 Traction converter fault 2 (005)
Phenomenon	VCB or K is disconnected; when VCB is disconnected, the fault display lamp "VCB" on the driver's console is on, and the VCB is not allowed to be closed again before the fault is handled (if the fault is only secondary side overcurrent 2, the VCB can be put into operation after the fault M is removed remotely); reduced traction and regenerative braking force.
Vehicle type	CRH380A、CRH380AL
Causes	Overcurrent at secondary side of traction transformer 2; abnormal main circuit components; poor charging of intermediate circuit of traction converter.
Train working	Continue running
Steps	Processing
1	When the "Fault occurrence information" prompt flashes on the main menu page of the MON screen, accompanied by an audible alarm, the driver presses the [Fault details] button at the bottom left to confirm the fault condition and notify the onboard mechanic.
2	The MON screen switches to the fault information page of "Traction converter fault 2 (005)".

Continued

Name	2.3 Traction converter fault 2 (005)
3	3.1 Confirm the cause through the "Traction converter (car)" page on the MON screen. 3.2 Remove the faulty vehicle remotely and notify the mechanic.
4	4.1 Immediately disconnect the circuit breaker of [Traction converter 1] in the power distribution panel of the corresponding car for 15 seconds and then put it into operation. 4.2 Notify the driver after handling.
5	5.1 If the fault is eliminated, reset vehicle M remotely and operate normally. 5.2 If the fault is not eliminated, the M train shall be cut off remotely to maintain operation.

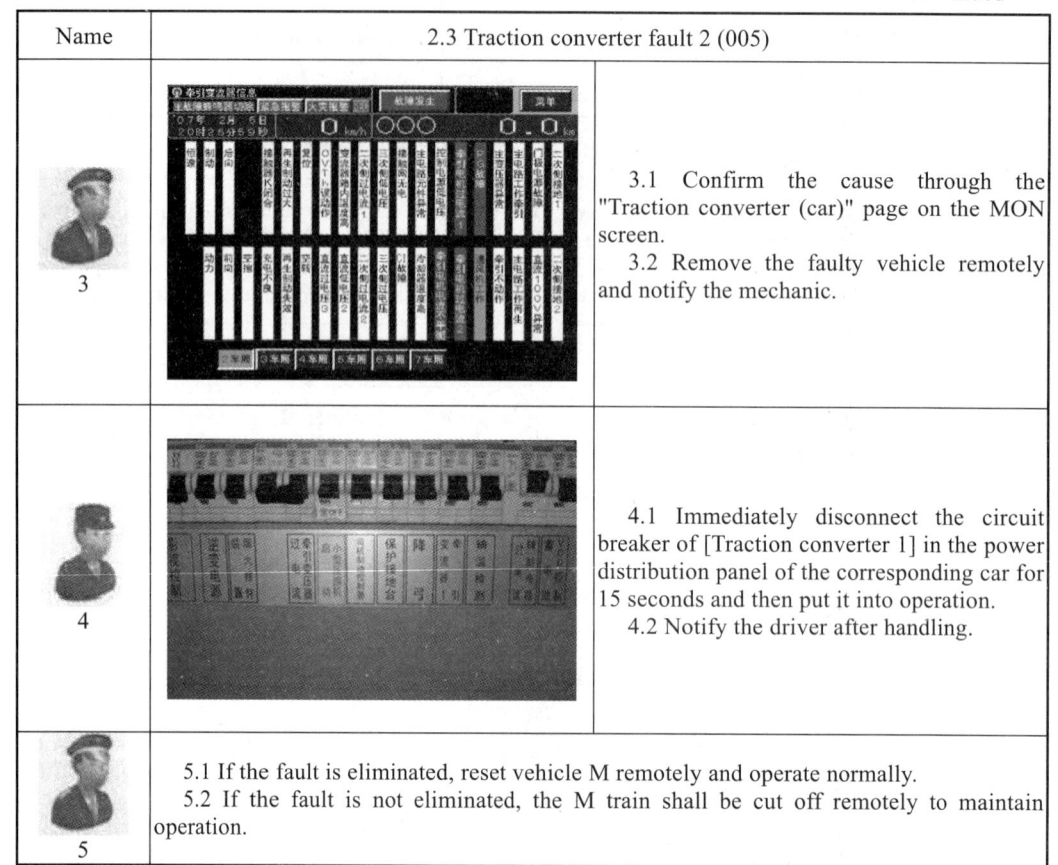

【Project Testing】

1. Analyze the composition of traction drive system.

2. Analyze the main circuit structure of CRH380A EMU.

3. Draw a diagram to analyze the working process of traction control.

4. Analyze the working principle of the logic operation command circuit of the direction controller.

5. Analyze the working principle of the traction controller logic operation command circuit.

6. Please draw the relay interlocking control circuit of the main controller and analyze its working process.

7. Try to analyze the working principle of VCB control circuit of vacuum circuit breaker.

8. Analyze the control process of traction converter and regenerative braking.

9. Try to analyze the working process of raising and lowering pantograph.

Project 3

Analysis of Traction Control Circuit of Fuxing EMU

【Project Description】

This project is an overall understanding of the traction control systems of Fuxing EMU CR400AF and CR400BF. The students are required to master the composition and working principle of the traction system of Fuxing EMU, and analyze the working process and fault protection of the main circuit and control circuit.

【Project Tasks】

(1) Be able to analyze high voltage and traction control circuit of CR400AF EMU;

(2) Be able to analyze CR400BF EMU traction system.

Task 1 Analysis of High-voltage and Traction Control Circuits of CR400AF EMU

【Task Description】

This task mainly introduces the high voltage and traction control system of CR400AF EMU. After learning this task, the students should master the composition and function of the whole system and be able to analyze the circuit.

【Background Knowledge】

1.1 High voltage system

1.1.1 High voltage system performance

The high-voltage system has the functions of supplying power for the whole train, electrical protection, monitoring network voltage and working current. Each of the 3rd and 6th cars is equipped with a basic high-voltage unit, which consists of a pantograph, a high-voltage isolation switch, a vacuum circuit breaker, a lightning arrester, a voltage transformer, current transformer, high voltage connector, high voltage cable, and grounding device.

1.1.2 Technical characteristics

(1) The high-voltage equipment box is integrated with low resistance and does not protrude from the outer contour of the car body, which is beneficial to reduce the running resistance of the car.

(2) Miniaturized high-voltage system adopts the design method that high-voltage components are integrated in the high-voltage box to save installation space, as shown in Figure 3-1-1.

(3) The high-voltage system is energy-saving and environmentally friendly, and the maintenance amount is reduced. The high-voltage components are integrated in the high-voltage box, which is less affected by environmental pollution. It can reduce the number of times to wipe the high-voltage components and save labor and water.

(4) The active pantograph can control the air circuit control unit according to the speed, pantograph position, different line information, etc. to realize active control, as shown in Figure 3-1-2.

Figure 3-1-1 Integrated high-voltage equipment box   Figure 3-1-2 Active control of pantograph

1.1.3 High voltage system principle

One basic high-voltage unit is set for TP03 car and TP06 car respectively, and the setting of each high-voltage unit is the same; the disconnector can isolate the corresponding high-voltage unit; the vacuum circuit breaker can isolate the fault pantograph, voltage transformer, current transformer, etc.; each high-voltage unit shall be detected through current and voltage transformers to implement overvoltage and overcurrent protection; each high voltage unit is equipped with 2 lightning arresters to realize two-level protection of high voltage circuit overvoltage, as shown in Figure 3-1-3.

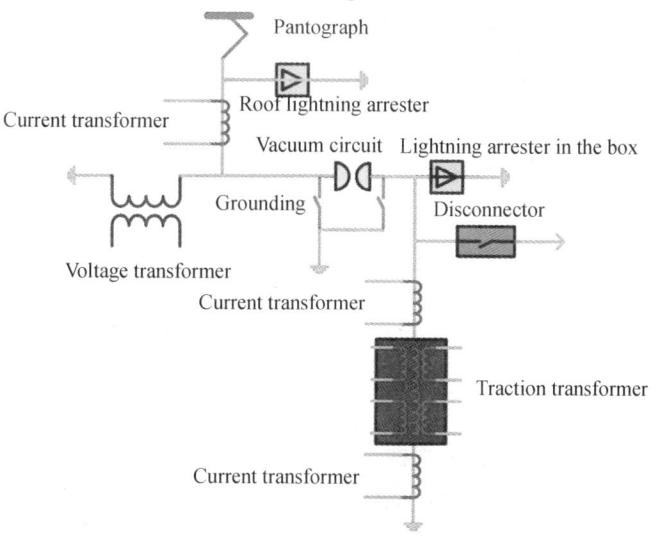

Figure 3-1-3　High voltage system diagram

1.1.4　Pantograph control

Pantograph raising and lowering control is divided into TCMS control and hard wire control, including normal pantograph raising and pantograph lowering under emergency traction mode, as shown in Figure 3-1-4.

1.1.5　VCB control

VCB closing and disconnecting control is divided into TCMS control and hard wire control, and the VCB is controlled under normal control and emergency traction mode, as shown in Figure 3-1-5.

1.1.6　Emergency power-off control

During normal operation, the emergency power-off loop is established without triggering the disconnection of the emergency power-off loop. When the loop loses power, the emergency power-off will be triggered. The EMU will trigger the VCB disconnection through the hard wire command, and the pantograph will be lowered.

When the emergency power-off loop is disconnected and cannot be recovered due to some interlocking condition fault during operation, the loop bypass function can be realized by operating the emergency power-off bypass switch in the cab of the pantograph raising unit, so as to avoid that the pantograph cannot be raised due to a single point fault, as shown in Figure 3-1-6.

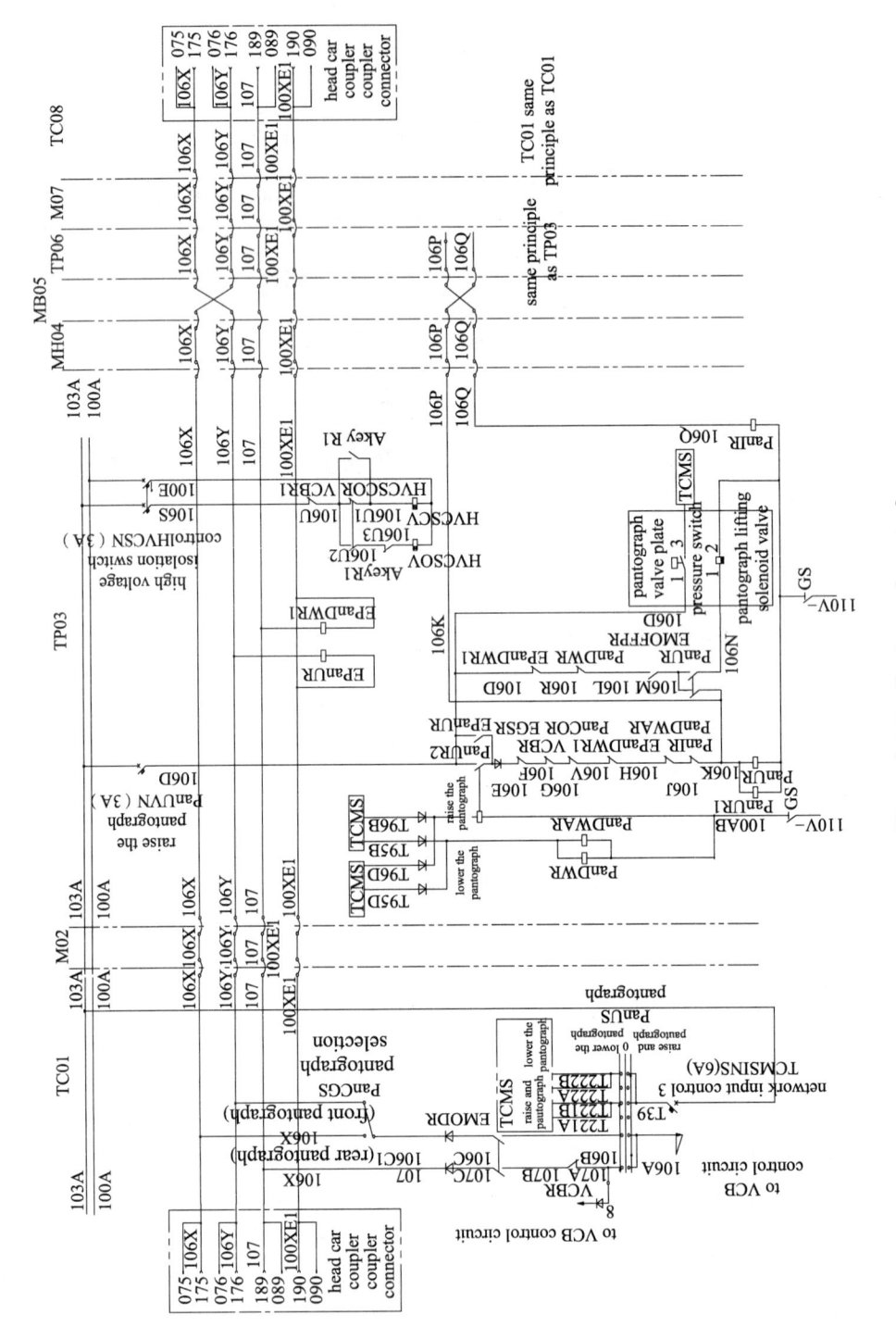

Figure 3-1-4　Pantograph control

Figure 3-1-5 VCB Control

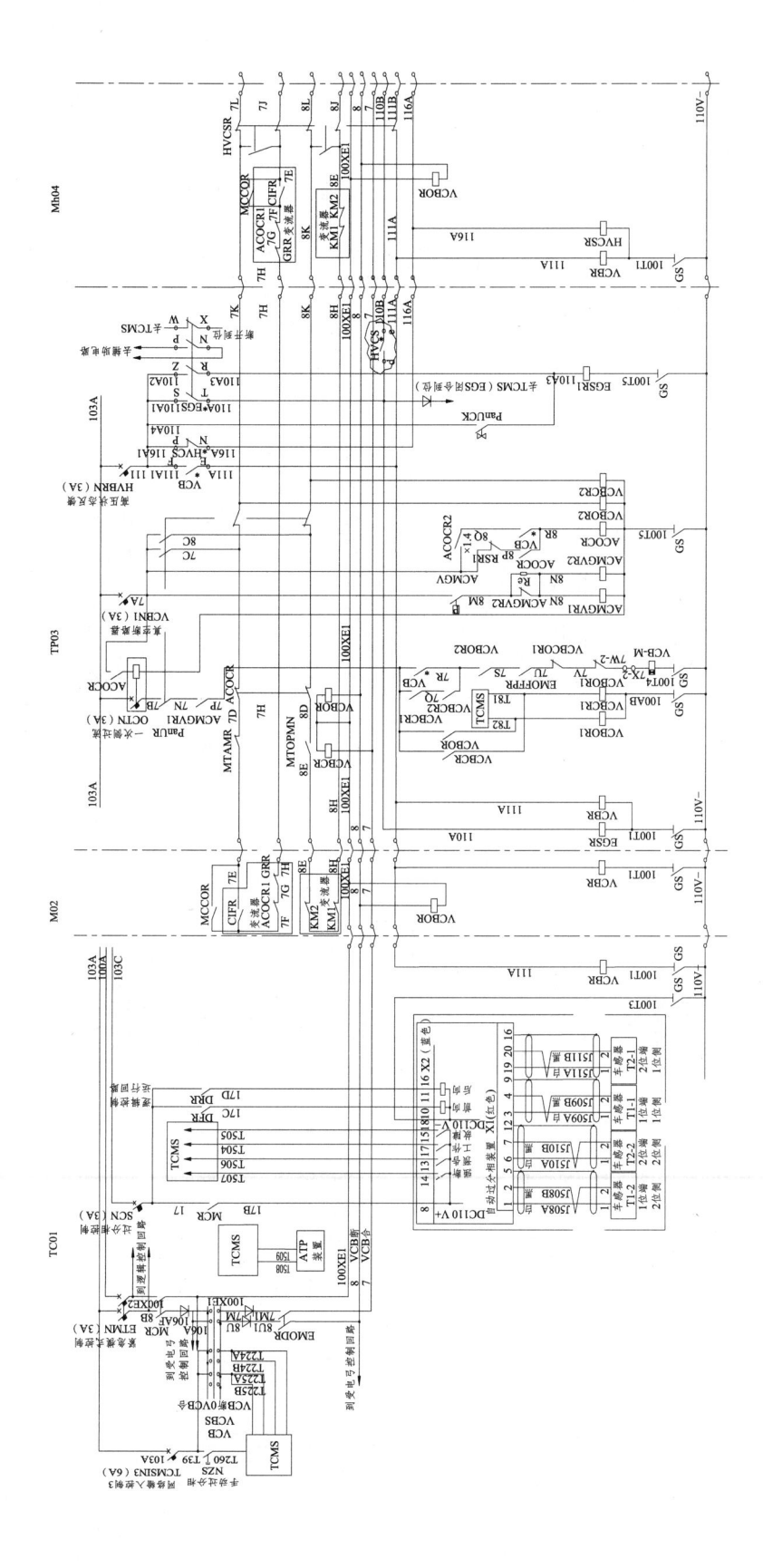

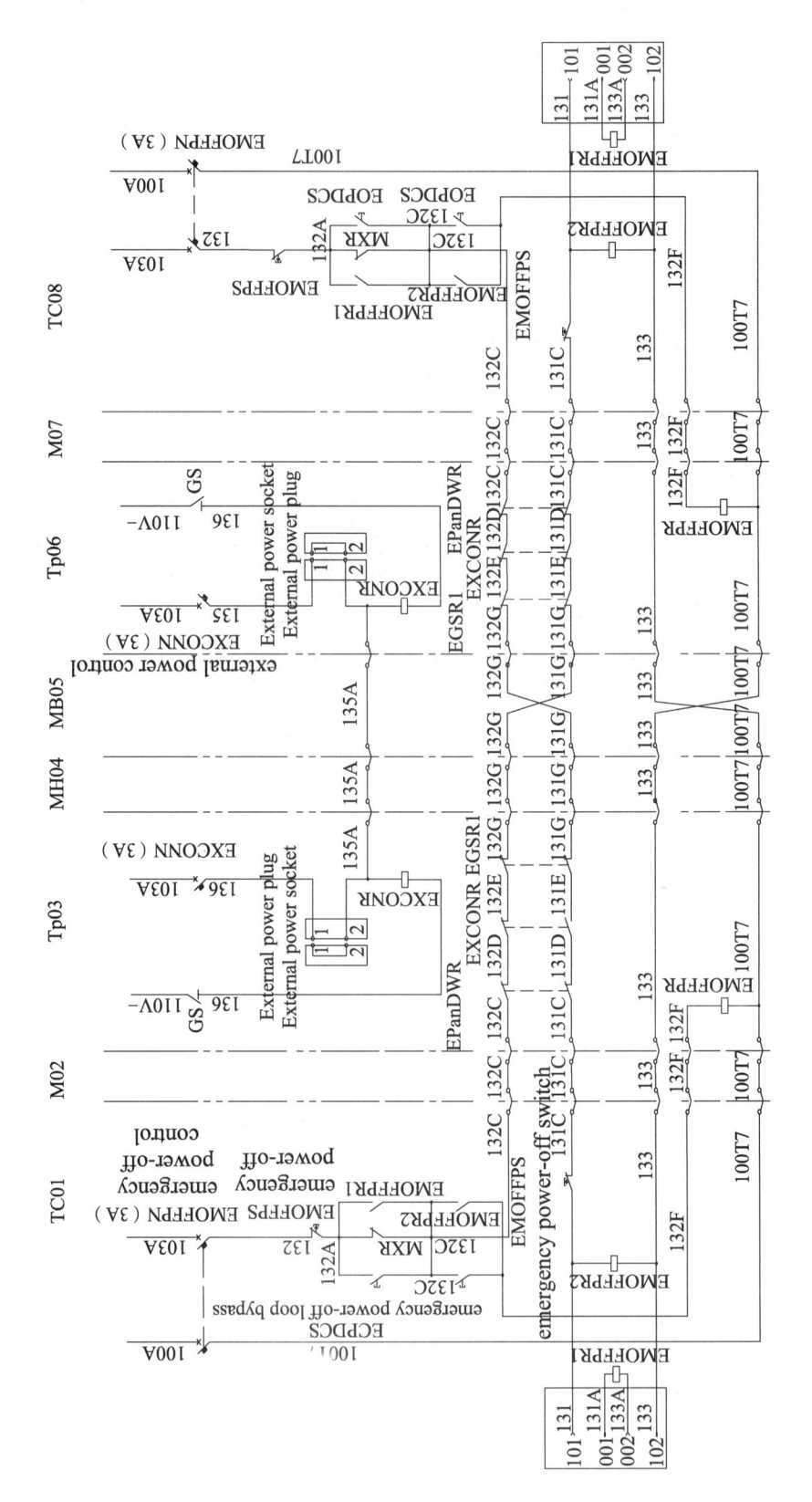

Figure 3-1-6　Emergency power off control

1.1.7 Control circuit of high-voltage disconnector

When the EMU operate normally, the high-voltage disconnector is closed. When the unit needs to cut off the high-voltage bus due to grounding or over-current fault, the high-voltage disconnector of TP03 car or TP06 car can be selectively disconnected by operating the remote cut button on the HMI display. When the cut command is effective, the HVCSCOR relay is powered on, making the HVCSOV valve powered on, driving the high voltage isolation switch to open. When it is necessary to reset again, it can only be completed through remote reset on the HMI display, as shown in Figure 3-1-7 and 3-1-8.

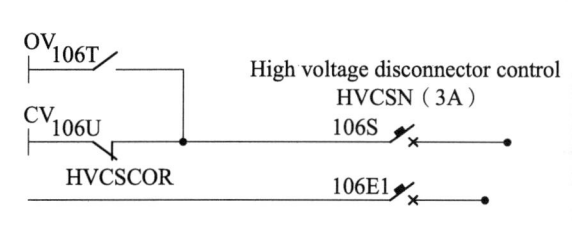

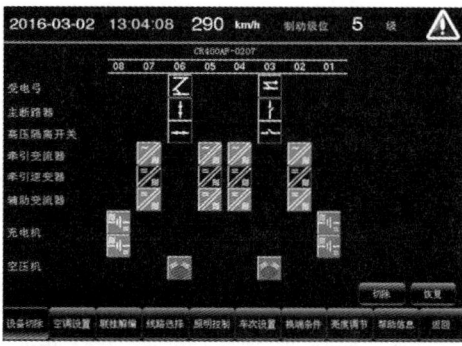

Figure 3-1-7 Disconnector control

Figure 3-1-8 HMI display screen

1.1.8 Network side overcurrent control circuit

When the network side current sensor detects that the network side current is greater than 1,200 A, the overcurrent relay of the pantograph raising unit acts, the fault group VCB trips, and the [primary side overcurrent] circuit breaker trips and cannot be closed; by operating RS reset, TCMS outputs that RSR1 relay is powered on, RSR1 normally closed contact is disconnected, which causes ACOCR relay to lose power, and the primary over-current circuit breaker can be put into operation, as shown in Figure 3-1-9.

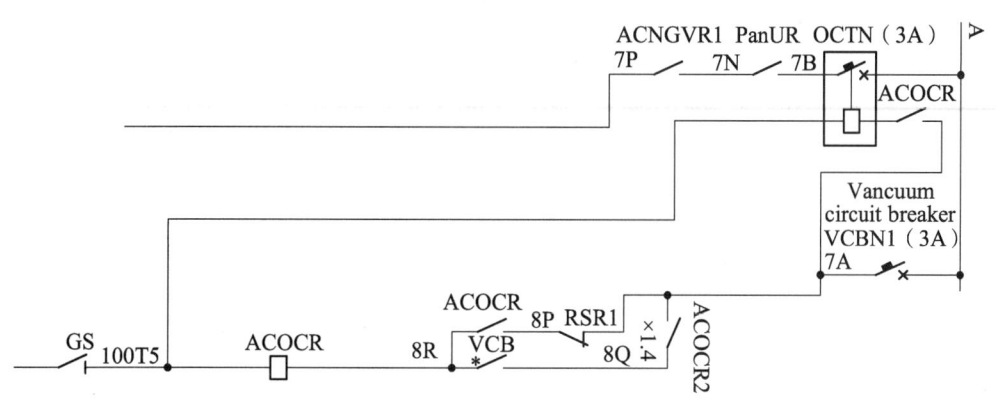

Figure 3-1-9 Network side overcurrent control

1.1.9 High voltage interlock control (EGS control)

The air circuit control interlocking box is added to the action air circuit of the protective grounding switch (EGS) of CR400AF EMU, as shown in Figure 3-1-10.

EGS closing condition: EGCV solenoid valve is powered on to control EGS closing.

EGS disconnection condition: EGOV solenoid valve is energized to control EGS disconnection.

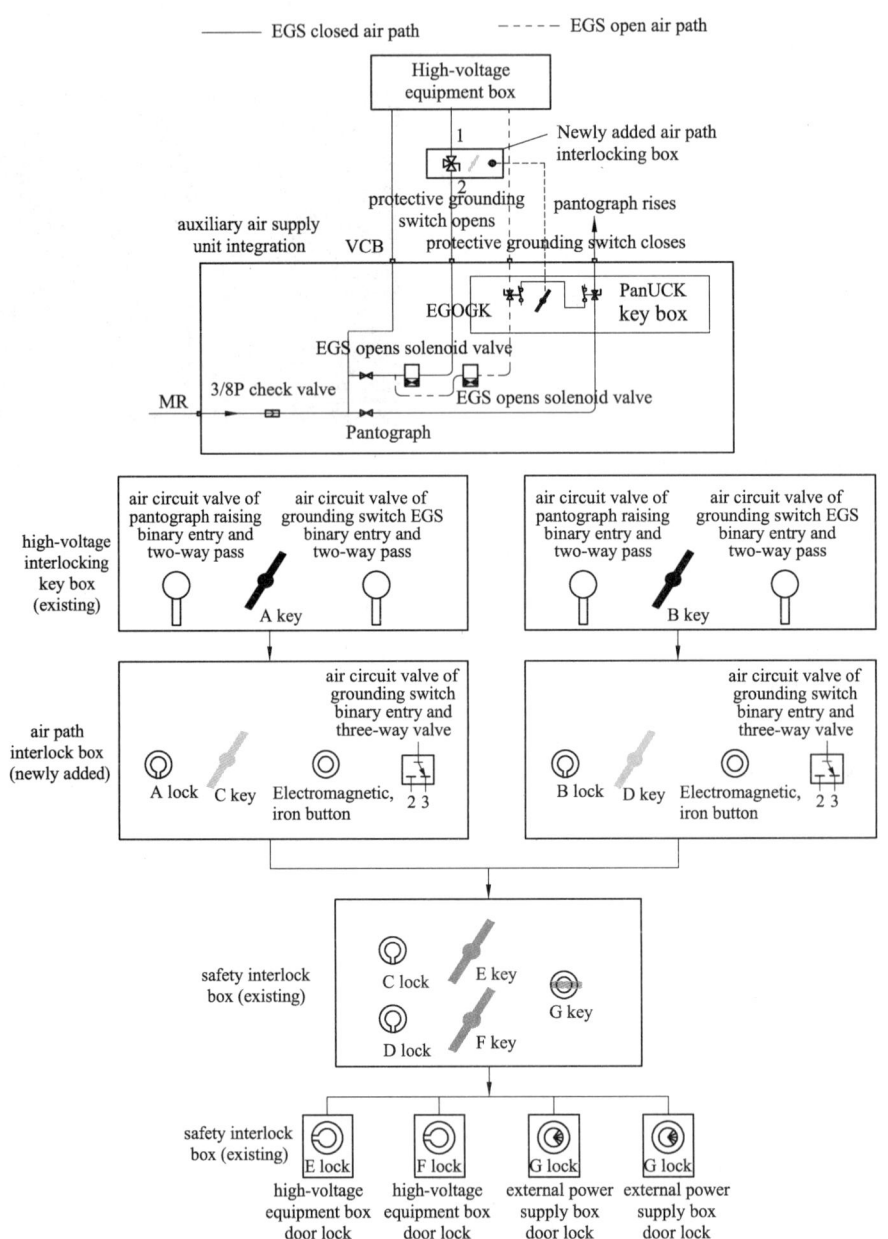

Figure 3-1-10 High voltage interlock control

The operation method of high-voltage interlocking control is as follows.

During maintenance:

(1) Put the main control into operation, and operate the protective grounding control switch in the cab to the red point position.

(2) Set the EGOGK and PanUCK handles in the key box of the auxiliary air compressor in cars 3 and 6 horizontally, pull out the outer box, and press the black (unlock) button to take out the key (blue) to open the air circuit interlock box.

(3) Insert the blue keys of Car 3 and Car 6 into the air circuit interlock box of the car and rotate it 60° anticlockwise to confirm that the EGS is closed in place.

(4) Press and hold the blue buttons of the air circuit interlocking boxes of Car 3 and Car 6 respectively, turn the yellow key clockwise for 60° and take it out;

(5) Insert the yellow key of Car 3 and Car 6 into the safety interlock box of Car 4, and take out the green key of the high-voltage equipment box and the green key of the external power connector box of Car 3 and Car 6 according to the operating instructions. You can open the high-voltage equipment box of Car 3 and Car 6 and the external power connector box of Car 3 and Car 6 respectively.

After maintenance:

(1) Return all the green keys of the high-voltage equipment box and the external power connector box of Car 3 and Car 6 to the safety interlock box of Car 4, and take out the yellow keys of the air circuit interlock box of Car 3 and Car 6.

(2) Press and hold the blue button at the air circuit interlocking box of Car 3 and Car 6 respectively, insert the corresponding yellow key of the car and turn it counterclockwise by 60°, release the button, turn the blue key clockwise by 60° and take it out.

(3) At the key boxes of the auxiliary air compressor of vehicles 3 and 6, press and hold the [black (unlock)] button, return the blue key to the key box and release the [black (unlock)] button.

(4) Set the EGOGK and PanUCK handles in the key box of the auxiliary air compressor in Car 3 and Car 6 to the vertical position.

(5) Operate the protective grounding control switch to the non red point position in the cab, and confirm that the whole train EGS has been disconnected in place through the HMI screen.

1.2 Traction system

1.2.1 Traction system framework

The frame of traction system is shown in Figure 3-1-11. The whole train is composed of two symmetrical power units (4M4T). Each power unit depressurizes the 25 kV network voltage through one main transformer and sends it to two traction converters. The converters supply power to four three-phase asynchronous traction motors of the vehicle through AC-DC-AC conversion. The auxiliary converter provides AC 380 V auxiliary power for the vehicle. The structural features are as follows:

(1) Main and auxiliary integrated structure-high integration;

(2) Rack control mode - high power redundancy;

(3) Direct torque control - excellent control performance;

(4) Double four quadrant and carrier phase-shifting control - effectively suppress grid side harmonics.

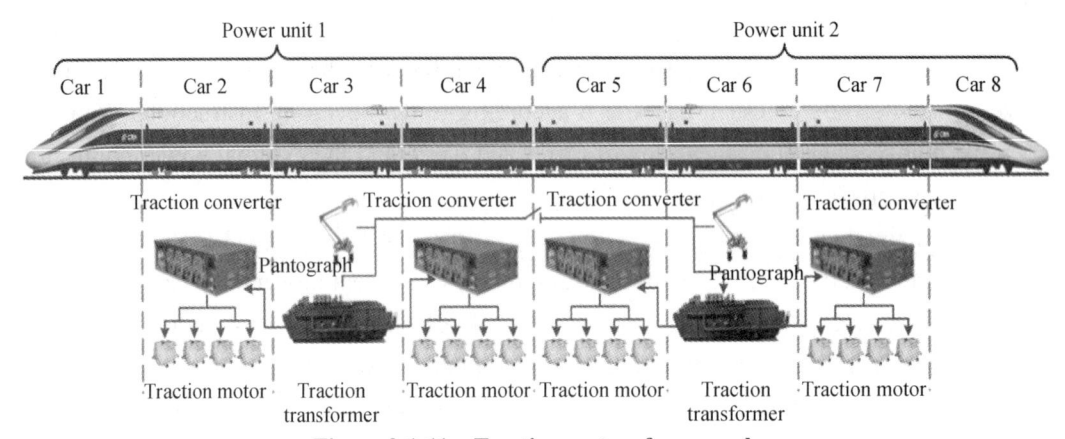

Figure 3-1-11　Traction system framework

1.2.2　Main functions and features

Main functions: traction, regenerative braking, auxiliary power generation, passing through the phase without power off, fire-free return power generation, etc

Main features: the integration of main and auxiliary parts can realize the functions of passing phase and returning power generation with high integration; frame control mode, high power redundancy; double four quadrants can effectively suppress grid side harmonics.

Other control functions of the traction system include:

(1) Execute TCMS fault degradation mode and speed limit command;

(2) Execute TCMS instructions related to auxiliary converter power supply;

(3) Internal speed limit management of traction system;

(4) Emergency traction;

(5) Charging of intermediate DC circuit;

(6) Startup of converter;

(7) Intermediate DC circuit voltage monitoring;

(8) Four quadrant phase-shift control;

(9) Ground fault monitoring;

(10) Traction safety interlock;

(11) Wheel diameter correction;

(12) Converter cooling monitoring;

(13) Traction motor cooling monitoring;

(14) Anti idling/electric sliding control;

(15) Network voltage/power limit.

1.2.3 Traction braking characteristics

Three operation modes of vehicle traction: level mode, speed mode and emergency traction mode.

(1) Level mode: the network system generates the traction force percentage according to the level information, and sends it to each car's traction converter to achieve traction control. There are 8 traction levels.

(2) Speed mode: the network system generates the percentage of traction force or regenerative braking force according to the target speed, and sends it to each car's traction converter for constant speed control.

(3) Emergency traction mode: when working under the emergency traction mode, the traction handle is placed in the traction area, and the traction converters of each car receive the traction command signal and exert 50% power.

1.2.4 Traction system performance

(1) The rated traction power is 10,000 kW, and the regenerative braking is not less than 1.3 times of the traction power;

(2) It has the function of over phase power generation (>78 km/h power generation,<55 km/h exit); CR300AF generates electricity for >70 km/h, and exits for <55 km/h.

(3) The system has complete system functions such as traction, regenerative braking and auxiliary power generation;

(4) The system has a complete protection scheme for overvoltage, overload, overtemperature, overspeed, idling, and various components.

(5) Rescue return (>55 km/h power generation, <35 km/h exit) self generating function.

CR300AF generates electricity for >50 km/h, and exits for <30 km/h.

DC/DC modules are added to the traction converter. When the traction converter is switched to the loopback mode, the output voltage after DC110 V voltage inversion will charge the intermediate DC voltage, establish the excitation current required by the traction motor, and the motor will be switched to the power generation working condition to provide working power for the auxiliary converter through the intermediate DC link. As shown in Figure 3-1-12.

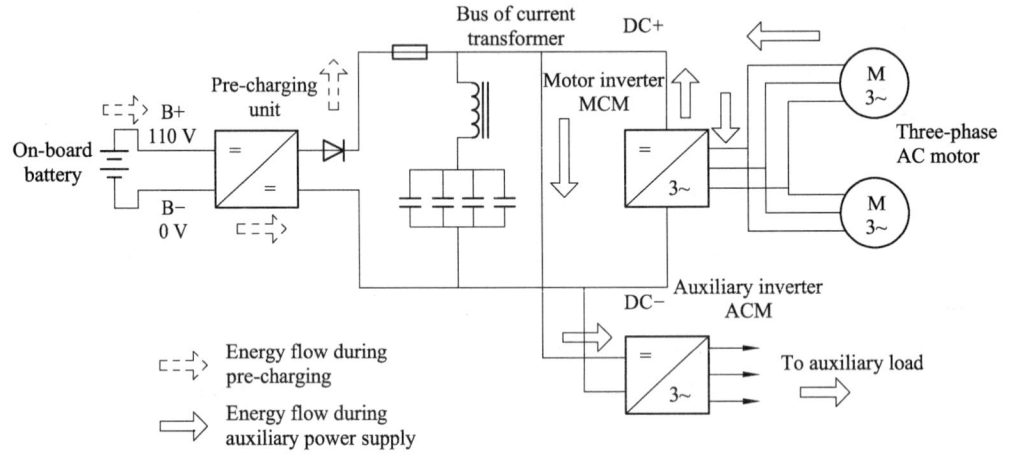

Figure 3-1-12   DC/DC module

1.3   Control circuit

The traction control unit (TCU) is the core control part of the electric drive system. It is powered by external DC 110 V. Through detecting the voltage, current, speed, temperature, pressure, etc., it completes the real-time closed-loop control of the traction converter and realizes the traction function required by the train. MVB communication interface and Ethernet vehicle level communication protocol conforming to train communication network standard shall be provided to form control and communication system with central control unit, etc. At the same time, when the train control and diagnosis system fails, the emergency traction function can be realized by hard wire.

1.3.1   Control function of passing neutral-section

The traction converter performs passing neutral-section control according to the neutral-section passing command sent by the network. When receiving the neutral-section passing command, if the train speed is greater than 80 km/h, the micro braking power generation will be carried out; if the train speed is less than 55 km/h, the micro braking power generation will be exited.

Under emergency conditions, the traction converter stops when passing neutral-section.

The control process of passing neutral-section is as follows:

(1) After receiving the neutral-section passing command, unload the traction torque or braking torque within 0.8 seconds, control the traction inverter to the micro braking power generation state, and then block the four quadrants;

(2) After the VCB is disconnected, disconnect the shorting contactor.

The control process of passing neutral-section is as follows:

(1) After the neutral-section passing command is canceled and VCB is closed, the converter will perform charging short circuit action;

(2) After the short circuit is closed, close the short circuit contactor with a delay of 1 second, and then start the four quadrants with a delay of 1 second;

(3) The traction inverter exits the micro braking power generation state and enters the normal traction and braking response state.

1.3.2 Description of rescue return power generation control function

The traction converter performs rescue loopback control according to the rescue loopback command sent by the network. The rescue loopback power generation requires that the train speed is more than 55 km/h, and when the train speed is less than 35 km/h, the rescue loopback power generation will exit.

The control process of rescue and return power generation is as follows:

(1) Before the train starts (train speed=0), direction command, rescue return command and DC110 V power input are valid;

(2) The traction converter has no fault;

(3) When the train speed is more than 55 km/h, start the chopper boost module to charge the intermediate circuit. After the charging is completed, the chopper boost module will quit the work, and then start the traction inverter to establish the intermediate voltage (3,000 V);

(4) The auxiliary inverter is started when the intermediate voltage is established;

(5) When the train speed is less than 35 km/h, the rescue loopback power generation will be stopped.

1.3.3 Description of emergency traction control function

When the hard line emergency traction command is valid, the train is considered to be in emergency traction condition. Under emergency traction conditions, only hard wire commands are trusted. When all the following conditions are met, start the traction converter to output 50% traction force:

(1) The emergency traction mode is valid;

(2) The emergency traction command is valid;

(3) The traction handle status bit signal is valid;

(4) The direction command is valid.

1.3.4 Traction enabling and zero position loading

1. Traction enabling circuit

After confirming that the main control signal is valid, the direction signal is valid (forward or backward), the car has no emergency braking, the car has no service braking, the traction handle traction sector, the doors of the whole train are closed, the ATP does not output emergency braking, service braking, and the traction cutoff signal, the traction enable relay PCR acts, and the PCR collects through TCMS and forwards the enable signal to TCU, as shown in Figure 3-1-13.

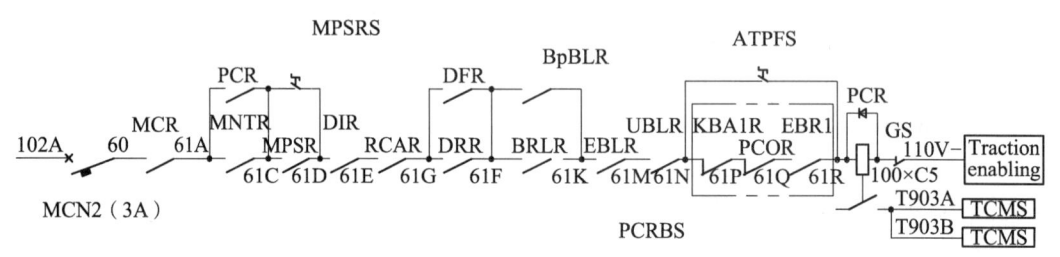

Figure 3-1-13 Traction enabling circuit

2. Zero position loading circuit of driver controller handle

To ensure driving safety, when the traction is lost due to emergency braking and other conditions, the traction handle must be returned to "OFF" position first and then to a certain traction gear when the traction is applied again to effectively prevent abnormal traction application after the problem is eliminated, as shown in Figure 3-1-4.

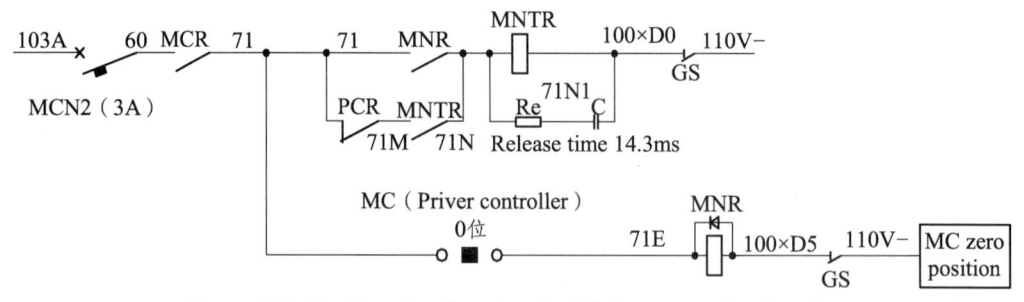

Figure 3-1-14 Zero loading circuit of driver controller handle

0 位: Zero position

Task 2 Analysis of CR400BF EMU Traction System

【Task Description】

This task is an overall understanding of CR400BF EMU traction system. After learning this task, the students are required to master the composition of the system, the structure of the main circuit and fault protection.

【Background Knowledge】

2.1 System structure

2.1.1 System composition

The traction system is composed of two symmetrical traction units, and each traction unit is composed of two motor cars and two trailers. The traction transformer depressurizes the 25 kV catenary voltage through four secondary windings and then sends it to two traction converters respectively. The traction converter supplies power to the four three-phase asynchronous traction motors of the car through AC-DC-AC conversion, while providing power to the auxiliary converter through the intermediate DC link, as shown in Figure 3-2-1.

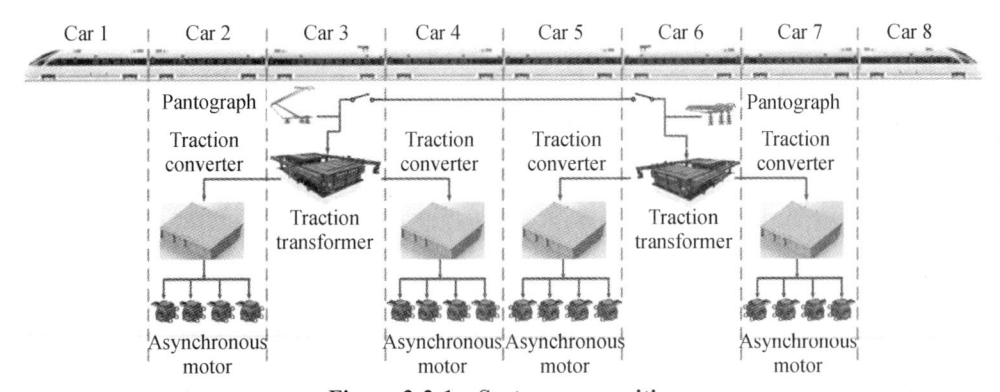

Figure 3-2-1 System composition

2.1.2 Main circuit

One main circuit is the main circuit of auxiliary separated traction system, and the other is the main circuit of auxiliary integrated traction system, as shown in Figure 3-2-2 and 3-2-3.

Figure 3-2-2　Main circuit of auxiliary main separation traction system

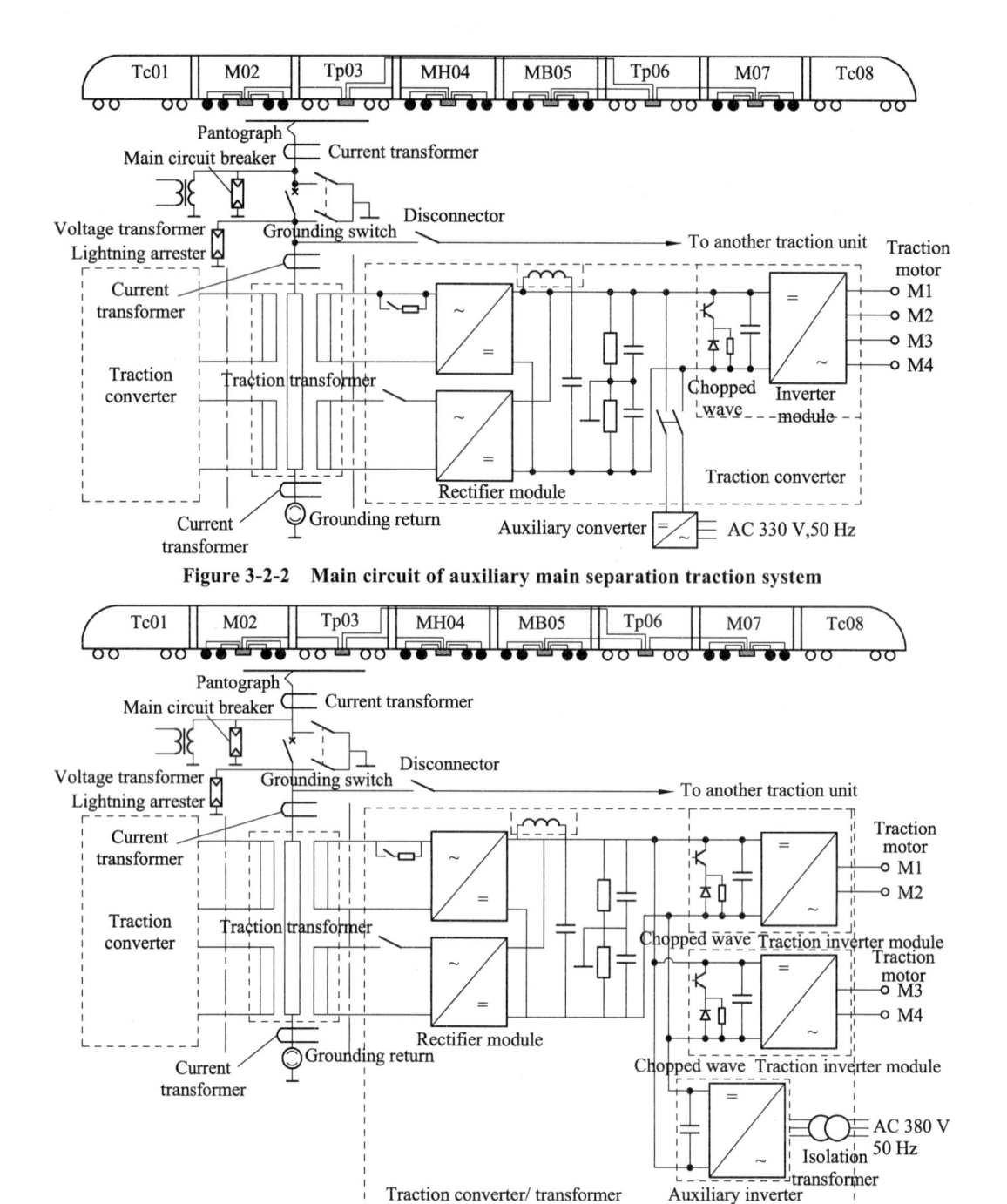

Figure 3-2-3　Main circuit of auxiliary main integrated traction system

　　The traction converter is installed in the traction equipment box under the power car of the EMU. Each traction converter basically consists of two 4-quadrant choppers (4QC), intermediate voltage circuit with resonant circuit, one brake chopper BC and two input line

contactors of pulse width modulation inverter (PWMI) traction converter, which are controlled by train control unit TCU.

2.2 Traction performance

The development of traction transmission technology aims to improve the traction and braking performance of rail vehicles, improve the reliability and energy efficiency of the entire vehicle system, reduce energy consumption, avoid pollution to the power grid as far as possible, effectively reduce operating costs, and meet operational requirements.

The EMU traction system is mainly used to convert electric energy into mechanical energy during traction operation (the path of energy transformation and transmission is shown by the blue arrow in the figure); during the operation of regenerative braking, mechanical energy is converted into electrical energy (the path of energy transformation and transmission is shown by the white arrow in Figure 3-2-4).

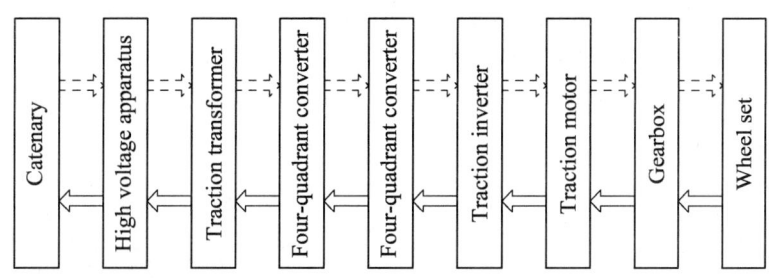

Figure 3-2-4　Energy transfer diagram

2.3 System functions

1. Running direction selection

After the cab is activated, raise the pantograph, close the VCB, set the direction switch to the "Forward" position, and close the door loop. After the brake is released, operate the traction handle to apply traction to make the car run.

2. Operation mode selection

The driver controller handle is equipped with a control mode selection button, which can select the current traction mode as level mode or speed mode, as shown in Figure 3-2-5.

The switching of operation mode shall be carried out when the handle is in "Zero" position.

When changing from level mode to speed mode, the set initial speed value is the actual speed of the current train.

When the speed mode is changed to stage mode, the initial stage value set is 0.

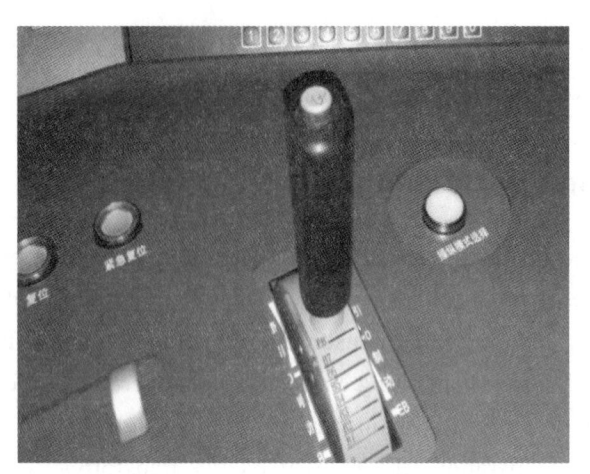

Figure 3-2-5 Driver controller handle

3) Self generating function

The EMU has the function of automatically passing neutral-section. When the speed is greater than 78 km/h, the DC link voltage in the middle of the traction converter can be maintained, and the auxiliary system maintains normal operation through the electric energy generated by the regenerative braking of the traction motor, as shown in Figure 3-2-6.

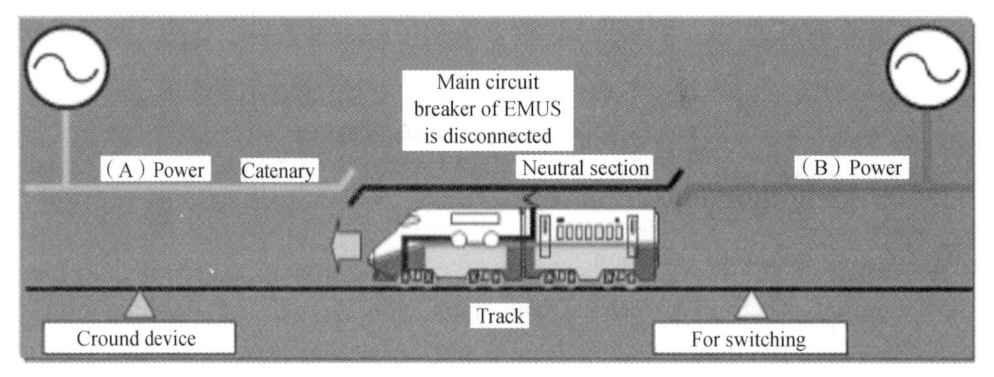

Figure 3-2-6 Automatic passing neutral-section

When the speed is greater than 55 km/h, start the fire-free loopback mode, add inverter modules to the traction converter; when the speed is less than 35 km/h, exit the loopback mode. After DC 110 V voltage inversion, the output voltage will charge the intermediate DC voltage, establish the excitation current required by the traction motor, convert the motor to the power generation condition, and continuously provide working power for the auxiliary converter through the intermediate DC link, as shown in Figure 3-2-7.

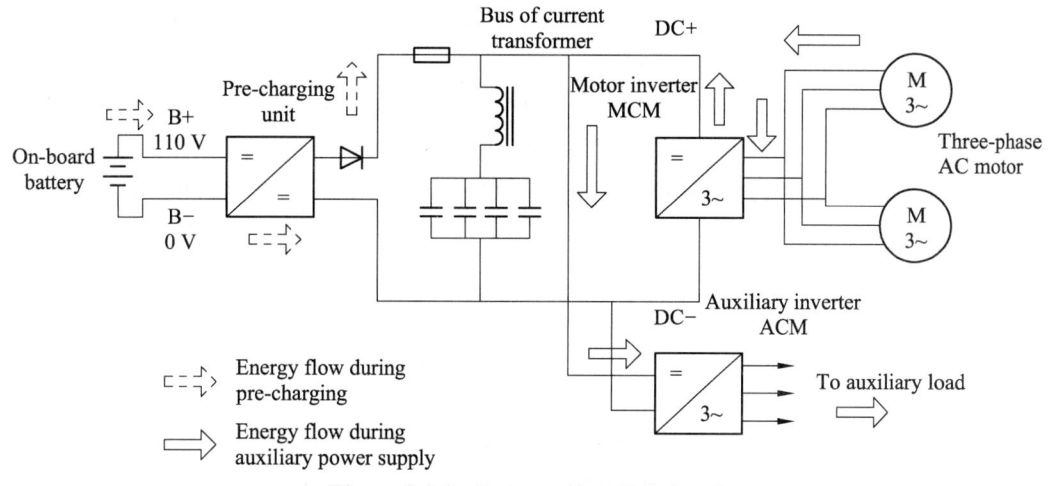

Figure 3-2-7　Intermediate DC circuit

2.4　Fault protection

1. Network voltage limit

When TCU detects that the network voltage is too low or too high, TCU will immediately block the four quadrants and inverter pulse, automatically trip the main breaker or main contactor, and restart after the network voltage returns to normal.

2. Converter cooling unit overtemperature or abnormal pressure

When the TCU detects that the cooling water temperature of the converter exceeds the set threshold, it blocks all converter pulses, and automatically resets the fault after the cooling water temperature returns to the normal value.

When TCU detects that the pressure of the converter cooling system exceeds the set threshold, it will block the converter pulse. After the pressure returns to the normal value, it will automatically reset the fault.

3. Traction transformer protection

Traction transformer primary side overcurrent protection: when TCU detects that the instantaneous peak value of traction transformer primary side current exceeds the set threshold value or the effective value exceeds the set threshold value, TCU blocks the pulse and trips VCB.

Traction transformer primary side grounding protection: when TCU detects that the current difference between the primary high-voltage side and the return side of the traction transformer exceeds the set threshold, TCU blocks all pulses and trips VCB.

Oil flow protection: when the oil flow speed is too low, the oil flow relay will act. The onboard electrical system will detect that the oil flow is too low for 10 seconds, block the pulse and disconnect the VCB.

Oil temperature protection: the inlet/outlet oil temperature of transformer is detected by PT100 temperature sensor. The alarm is divided into three levels. When the first and second level temperature protection is reached, only the traction power is limited. When the third level temperature protection is reached, TCU pulse will be blocked and the main breaker will be automatically tripped.

Oil pressure protection: when the internal pressure of the transformer is too high, its pressure relief valve will act. After the onboard electrical system detects this action, it will block the pulse and disconnect the VCB.

Oil level protection: when the oil level is low, the transformer low level alarm relay will act, and the onboard electrical system will give an alarm prompt after detecting this action; When the oil level is lower, the transformer low liquid level cut-off relay will act. After the onboard electrical system detects this action, it will block the pulse and disconnect VCB.

When TCMS detects that the motor temperature exceeds the set threshold, the corresponding inverter pulse is blocked. When the motor temperature returns to the normal value, the software will reset the fault automatically.

4. Traction motor protection

The detection device informs TCMS of the motor temperature, and TCMS will compare the motor temperature with the ambient temperature to generate two-stage over temperature protection. The overtemperature of stator does not limit the train speed. When the drive end and non drive end are overtemperature, the train speed will be limited, and TCU will be notified to block the corresponding inverter pulse. When the motor temperature returns to the normal value, the software will reset the fault automatically.

5. Other protection

DC circuit overvoltage: when the intermediate DC circuit voltage exceeds the set threshold, TCU blocks all pulses and disconnects the short circuit contactor. When the intermediate DC voltage returns to the normal value, the software will reset the fault automatically.

Abnormal DC circuit charging: when the charging cannot reach the specified voltage setting threshold within the predetermined time, all converter pulses are blocked and the main breaker is disconnected.

Traction system grounding protection: through the grounding voltage of the intermediate circuit of the traction converter, grounding detection can be carried out on the secondary side of the traction transformer, the intermediate DC link, the AC side of the traction inverter, and the high-voltage side of the auxiliary converter. When the intermediate DC grounding detection voltage of the traction converter is abnormal, the grounding fault will be reported, and the main circuit will be disconnected or the traction protection will be blocked.

Short circuit and over-current protection of traction system: input/output short circuit and over-current faults of all components of traction system can be detected through primary side current of traction transformer, four quadrant input current, inverter output current, intermediate DC link current and intermediate DC link voltage sensor. IGBT pulse will be blocked in case of overcurrent fault of converter output current; when the transformer input has overcurrent, the main breaker will be disconnected; in case of short circuit fault, the main breaker will be disconnected or the faulty traction unit will be blocked.

Differential protection of high-voltage system: TCMS will automatically trip the main breaker to protect the high-voltage traction system when the difference between the primary side current of traction transformer and the grounding return current transformer exceeds the threshold value.

【Project Testing】

1. Analyze the over-current control circuit at the network side of CR400AF EMU.
2. Briefly describe the operation method of CR400AF EMU high-voltage interlocking control.
3. Analyze the rescue return function of CR400AF EMU.
4. Analyze the working principle of main circuit of CR400BF EMU.
5. Briefly describe the fault protection of traction system of CR400BF EMU.

Project 4

Analysis of EMU Brake Control Circuit

【Project Description】

This project is the overall understanding and learning of EMU braking control system. By learning the composition of brake control system, classification of brake mode, brake control principle and other relevant knowledge, students are required to analyze the brake control logic operation circuit diagram. Be able to check and remove faults according to the maintenance standard of EMU.

【Project Tasks】

(1) Understand the composition of EMU brake control system;
(2) Brake control circuit analysis

Task 1 Understanding of the Composition of EMU Brake Control System

【Task Description】

This part introduces the basic composition, braking mode and function of EMU brake control system. After learning this task, students should master the arrangement of brake control device on the train, and be able to draw and analyze the schematic diagram of brake instruction transmission.

【Background Knowledge】

1.1 Composition of EMU brake control system

CRH2 EMU brake system adopts compound brake mode, namely regenerative brake+ electric command air brake. The electric command air brake is a direct electric air brake controlled by microcomputer. Brake control system includes: brake signal generating device, brake signal transmission device, brake control device. The brake signal generator, namely the driver's brake controller, is located at the control console in the cab of car No. 1 and No. 8 (T1c, T2c). Brake signal transmission device by means of train information control system includes the central device, vehicle terminal device, collect and transmit the brake instruction, while receiving the brake state instruction. The brake control device is hoisted under the floor of each vehicle as a centralized control device that receives brake instructions and implements brake force control. It is integrated with the brake control unit (BCU), air valve assembly, air reservoir, etc.

The main composition and distribution of brake control equipment are shown in Table 4-1-1.

Table 4-1-1 Main composition and distribution of brake control equipment

Grouping Status / Equipment Distribution	1	2	3	4	5	6	7	8
	T1c	M2	M1	T2	T1 k	M2	M1 s	T2c
Driver's brake controller	√							√
Brake command transmission device — Central processing unit for command transmission	√							√
Brake command transmission device — Command transmission network	Train Information Control Network							
Brake command transmission device — Transmission terminal unit	√	√	√	√	√	√	√	√
Brake control unit	√	√	√	√	√	√	√	√
Basic brake device	√	√	√	√	√	√	√	√

The conversion action of regenerative brake and air brake is determined by the microcomputer according to the amount of braking force generated. If regenerative brake force is insufficient, it is supplemented by air brake.

At the same time, a brake command conversion device is installed in the driver room of each of the two head cars. The device can convert the air pressure change signal of the train tube connected to the locomotive into an electrical signal, which can be used for braking when being rescued.

1.2 The function of EMU brake control system

The EMU brake command mode adopts manual brake mode and automatic brake mode controlled by ATP/LKJ. The action mode adopts the control mode of electric-air coordinated brake which combines the electrical regenerative brake mode and the electrical command air brake mode. The brake force control is carried out according to the speed-adhesion curve mode. It also has the function of sliding detection and load bearing function. The use of electric brake is preferred. When the electric brake force is insufficient, air brake is added. According to different instruction types, brake control can be divided into five modes: Service Brake, fast brake, emergency brake, auxiliary brake and snow resistant brake. The corresponding control line is as follows:

(1) Service brake (Lines 61 ~ 67 and Line 10 are pressurized,).

(2) Fast brake (Line 152 is not pressurized, Line 10 is pressurized).

(3) Emergency brake (Line 153 and Line 154 are not pressurized).

(4) Auxiliary brake (Pressurize between Line 411 and Line 461).

(5) Snow resistant brake (Line 157 is pressurized).

CRH2 brake system has the functions of service brake, fast brake, emergency brake, auxiliary brake and snow resistant brake.

1.2.1 Service brake

Service brake levels are set at 1-7 levels (recorded as 1N ~ 7N), and 1M1T is used as a unit to coordinate control the regenerative brake force and air brake force (including the train and trailer) of the train to delay the input of air brake.

CRH2 brake system adopts digital command type and consists of 7 brake command lines with number 61 ~ 67, which can form 7 service brake levels. The brake system will automatically delay inflation control. In the case of delay, the excess regenerative brake force generated on the M train is transferred to the T train to maintain the brake force required on the marshalling train. The service brake also has the function of load adjustment between the empty train and heavy train, and the brake force can be changed according to the need, so that the EMU can maintain a certain reduction speed.

1.2.2 Fast brake

The fast brake adopts the same compound brake mode as the service brake, and has the brake force of 1.5 times of the maximum service brake(7 level). When the brake handle is operated or the brake fails to slow down to the speed set in the blocked interval, it takes effect according to the instructions issued by ATP or LKJ2000.

1.2.3 Emergency brake

It is set according to the brake mode started when the safety loop is out of power. Any of the following situations can lead to the loss of power in the whole loop and cause the emergency brake instructions:

(1) The total wind pressure drops below the specified value;
(2) Train separation;
(3) Insufficient brake force is detected;
(4) Operate the emergency brake button to make the electromagnetic valve lose power;
(5) Change the end of the operation, the handle is placed in the (key) pick position.

The above emergency brake makes each train produce pure air brake according to different speed ranges, and a relatively low reduction speed is adopted when the train speed is in the range of 160—200 km/h. A relatively high reduction speed is adopted in the speed range below 160 km/h; The emergency brake does not have the function of load adjustment between the empty train and heavy train.

1.2.4 Auxiliary brake

When the brake device is abnormal, the brake instruction line is broken and the transmission is abnormal, the electrical instruction auxiliary brake can be enabled, which can produce the air brake equivalent to the service brake of level 3, level 5, level 7 and fast brake.

The auxiliary brake can be generated by operating the auxiliary brake pattern generator (SBT) switch on the driver's console and the auxiliary brake pattern generator (ASBT) switch in the lead unit distribution panel. However, the auxiliary brake has nothing to do with the speed of the train, that is, the amount of the brake force emitted does not change with the speed change and the train weight , and only the predetermined brake force is emitted. This is different from service brake and fast brake.

In addition, it should be noted that the brake control device also controls the speed of the main air compressor and the opening and closing of the door. Therefore, the power supply of the brake control device should not be disconnected when the auxiliary brake is used.

1.2.5 Snow resistant brake

The purpose of snow resistant brake is to prevent snow from falling between the brake disc and the brake pad. When the snow resistant brake is in operation, the brake cylinder will gently push out the brake pad to block the gap between the brake pad and the brake disc surface to prevent the entry of snow. when the train is running at a speed below 110 km/h, the snow resistant brake switch is in action and the brake handle is operated. The brake cylinder (BC) pressure set value corresponding to snow resistance brake is (60 ± 20) kPa, which is the pre-charging pressure of the brake cylinder when the brake conditions are met. When the actual air brake control signal is output by BCU, the brake cylinder is still inflated to the corresponding pressure according to the required air brake force. The brake cylinder (BC) pressure setting corresponding to snow resistance brake can be changed by adjusting the switch on the BCU panel.

Task 2 Brake Control Circuit Analysis

【Task Description】

This part introduces the function, working principle and brake control circuit of EMU brake controller. After learning this task, the students should analyze the brake control circuit, troubleshoot and handle faults according to inspection and maintenance standards.

【Background Knowledge】

2.1 Introduction to Brake Control

2.1.1 Brake control principle

The EMU brake control system can realize the issuance and transmission of brake instructions, the control of service brake and fast brake, the control of emergency brake, the control of auxiliary brake, the control of snow resistant brake, and the coordination control of air brake and regenerative brake. The brake instructions of EMU are issued by the driver's brake controller and transmitted to the brake control device of each vehicle through the train information control system. The BCU of the brake control device is used to calculate and implement regenerative brake and air brake according to the brake control law (reduction speed changes with speed). The air brake controls the current of the electro-pneumatic valve (EP valve), sends the corresponding air pressure signal to the relay valve, and the relay valve sends the compressed air to the bogie foundation brake gear. The pressurized cylinder is transformed into oil pressure through the air-oil conversion. Finally, the hydraulic cylinder of the brake disc hydraulic caliper pushes the brake pad to press the moving disc surface to complete the brake function. In order to ensure the correct action of the control circuit according to the instructions, certain logic conditions must be satisfied during the control process. The transfer diagram of the brake control instruction of a power unit is shown in Figure 4-2-1.

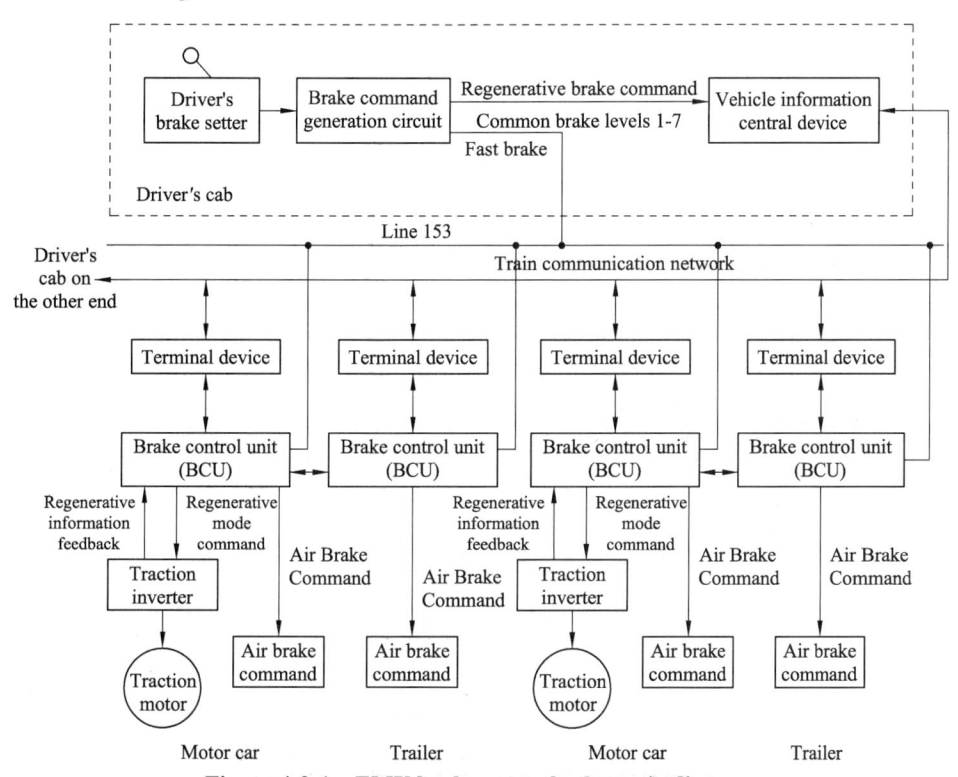

Figure 4-2-1   EMU brake control schematic diagram

Figure 4-2-2   Brake handle

2.1.2 Function of brake controller

The operating surface appearance of the driver's brake controller of CRH_2 EMU CMC100 is shown in Figure 4-2-2, including 10 positions of "Operation", "Level 1-7", "Fast" and "Pull out". The driver's brake controller has four functions: first, in the "Operation" position, it is interlocked with the traction control signal to generate traction instruction conditions, and the traction instruction is effective; second, in the brake level, issued "1 ~ 7" service brake; Third, in the "Fast" position, the command of fast brake is issued; Fourth, in the "Pull out" position, in an emergency situation to stimulate fast brake. In addition, regenerative electrical brake commands are generated.

2.2 The brake controller electrical instruction circuit

Figure 4-2-3 is the logic control schematic diagram of brake stage switches and relays. There should be 9 pairs of contact switches and 9 relays. The corresponding relationship between each position and relay is shown in Table 4-2-1.

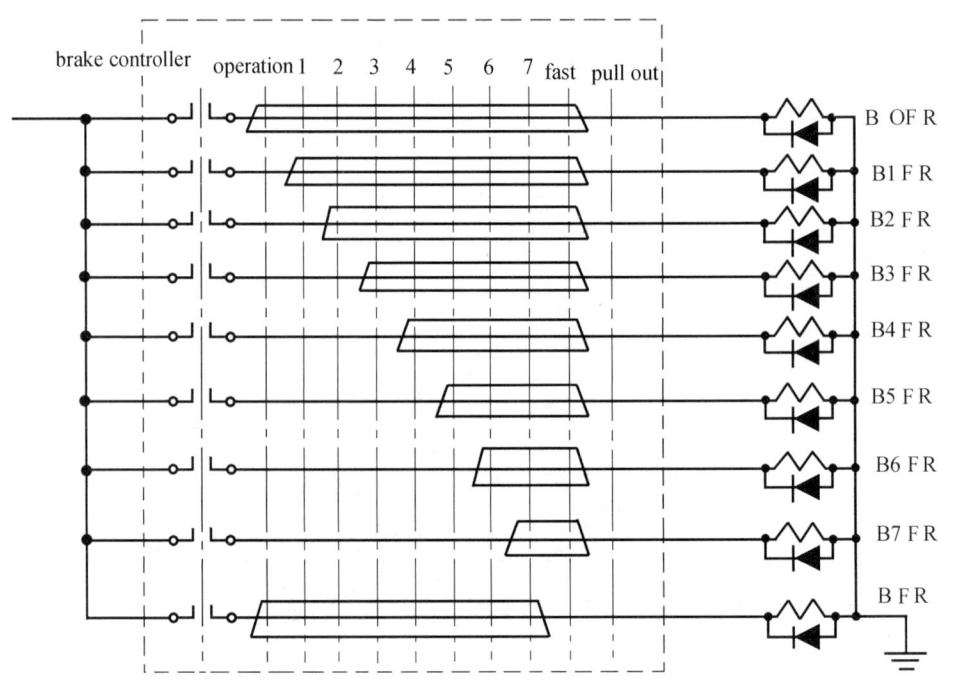

Figure 4-2-3 Division control brake level and relay control schematic diagram

Table 4-2-1 Correspondence between brake controller and excitation relay

		Brake controller instruction								
		Operation	1	2	3	4	5	6	7	Emergency
Relay	B OF R	○	○	○	○	○	○	○	○	○
	B1 OF R		○	○	○	○	○	○	○	○
	B2 OF R			○	○	○	○	○	○	○
	B3 OF R				○	○	○	○	○	○
	B4 OF R					○	○	○	○	○
	B5 OF R						○	○	○	○
	B6 OF R							○	○	○
	B7 OF R								○	○
	B OF R	○	○	○	○	○	○	○	○	

○ = Excitation、Blank = Not excitation

2.2.1 Analysis of service brake instruction circuit

The brake force instruction of service brake is sent to BCU by the brake instruction line (61 ~ 67 lines) through the central device and terminal device. And through the 10 line, issue a command to determine whether the regenerative brake is available. In order to improve the safety of the brake instructions, the 67 line (the maximum service brake) is connected to the BCU by a hard wire running through.

The service brake instruction generation devices are driver's brake controller, ATP and brake instruction converter. According to the operating position of the driver's brake controller, B1FR~ B7FR excitation, through its normally open contact to power 61 ~ 67 lines. After the speed limit is exceeded, the service brake is performed by ATP, releasing the NBR, and the ATCBR is excited by the normally closed contacts of the NBR. As a result, the normally open contact of the ATCBR is closed, and the 61, 66 and 67 lines are powered, and the maximum service brake command is issued. If the brake force of B1 or B4 is sufficient according to ATP, ATCKB1R or ATCKB1R and ATCKB4R are excited separately, so that line 61 or 64 can be powered and B1 or B4 instruction can be issued.

During EMU rescue and return, the brake instruction converter is connected with the BP tube of the locomotive, and the BP pressure signal is supplied to the brake instruction converter. The brake instruction converter will power X61 ~ X67 lines according to BP pressure signal, and excitation B1 not R ~ B7 not R. When receiving the rescue of the same type of EMU, directly supply power to the through line (line 61 ~ 67).

When regenerative brake instructions are available, the electric-air coordination control will be carried out by the following steps: the BCU of each train recognizes the brake instructions, calculates according to the speed and train weight, and outputs the required brake force. If the regenerative brake instruction line (line 10) gets power, the traction control unit will control the regenerative brake force according to the regenerative brake mode voltage (brake force construction value) of BCU, and the result of the regenerative brake force obtained will be fed back to the BCU. The BCU receives the regenerative brake force from the traction control unit feedback (regenerative feedback voltage and current detection signal CDR), and the insufficient brake force is made up by the air brake.

Line 10 is powered when any one of B1FR, ATCBR, ATCKB1R excites, and sends out the instruction that regenerative brake conditions are valid. However, when the speed is less than 5 km/h, the auxiliary brake is selected, and the power brake SW is open, the command will not be sent to Line 10.

2.2.2 Fast brake instruction electrical circuit

Usually, the fast brake through line (Line 152) transmits electrical signals to the BCU to keep the fast brake off. That is, when Line 152 loses power, the BCU starts the fast brake.

The fast brake action is issued under the following conditions:

① Driver brake controller operation (on "Fast" position);
② ATP gives fast brake instruction (EBR loss of power);
③ The JTR is powered off.

1) Driver brake controller operation

The "Fast" position is set through the driver's brake controller, and the "Fast" position relay (B not R) loses magnetism, its normally open contact opens, and Line 152 loses power.

2) Fast brake through ATP (EBR loss of power)

By the action of ATP, the relay (EBR) for ATP fast brake of the main switchboard lose power, and therefore, its normally open contact is opened, causing Line 152 to lose power. However, if the ATPCOS is in the disconnected position (ATPCOR excitation), the ATP fast brake relay (EBR) does not work.

3) Fast brake caused by JTR loss of power

JTRTD falls when line 154D loses power, and then JTR loses magnetism.

Line 154D changes from normal power to power loss under the following conditions:

① The pressure of MR Is too low.

Main duct pressure switch (MRHPS) → Main duct pressure switch relay off (MRrAPSR) → Disconnect between 154B1-154B2.

②Train separation.

Electrical connector is disconnected → Line 154 is powered off.

③ Detection of insufficient brake force.

The time relay (UBTR), which is used to detect the insufficient brake force of the train loses magnetism→the emergency brake relay (UVR) loses magnetism→154A-154K disconnection→Line 154 loses power.

④The driver's brake controller is on "Pull out" position

B transport FR normally open contact disconnect→MCR loss of magnetism→154M line loss of power.

⑤ train attendants operate the emergency brake switch.

⑥ Start the emergency brake switch (UBS1 or UBS2)→154A power loss.

4) The relationship between fast brake mode air brake and regenerative brake

If the driver's brake controller is placed in the fast position, because B1FR is in the excitation state, Line 10 is also in the power state. When the EMU is in the fast brake state caused by ATP, the ATCBR excites because the NBR loses power at the same time as the EBR loses power. The ATCBR also excites when the JTR is out of power. Due to the ATCBR excitation, the normally open contact of the ATCBR becomes closed, and Line 10 gets power. Therefore, when the fast brake instruction is issued, the regenerative brake instruction line leading to the traction converter is powered by Line 10; at the same time, depending on the regenerative brake mode voltage sent from the BCU, the regenerative brake control unit (operated by a traction converter) performs braking in the same manner as it would normally do.

2.2.3 Emergency brake instruction circuit

The through line (Line 153) is powered through the normally open contact of the head car at 153K. The through line (Line 154) is powered from Line 153 through the normally closed contact of the MCR at the rear driver's desk.

Emergency brake works when:

① Train separation.

② The total air duct pressure is too low.

③ Insufficient brake force is detected.

④ Emergency solenoid valve lose power.

⑤ The driver's brake controller handle is on "Pull out" position.

1) Train separation

When the vehicles at the front end of the train separation lost power on Line 154, JTR lost magnetism, the fast brake came into play. The vehicles at the rear end of the train separation, the system of Line 153 and Line 154 becomes a state of loss of power, the emergency brake electromagnetic valve(UV) loses magnetism and the emergency brake function, the JTR loses magnetism → leads to the loss of power of Line 152, and the fast brake instruction is issued. The brake cylinder BC pressure will obtain the highest pressure value produced by both emergency brake and fast brake.

2) The total air duct pressure is too low

The total air duct pressure in the hood of the rear vehicle of the two ends is detected by the main air duct pressure switch (MRHPS). When the pressure is lower than the set value (590 ± 10) kPa, the contact is disconnected. Due to the disconnection of the MRHPS contact, the main duct pressure switch relay (MRrAPSR) becomes magnetically deactivated. Thus, the normally open contact of MRrAPSR becomes disconnected, and the 153K relay is opened, Line 153 loses power. At the same time, other contacts make Line 154D lose power and JTR lose magnetism. Thus, UV loses magnetism, at the same time the emergency brake plays a role, issued a fast brake instruction.

3) Insufficient brake force is detected

When insufficient brake force is detected, the UBTR loses magnetism. When UBTR loses magnetism, the power supply circuit of UV and UVR is disconnected between 153B-153C. After UV lose magnetic, the car's emergency brake start ; At the same time, due to the normally open contact UVR, between 154A-154K is disconnected, so the JTR loses magnetism, Line 152 loses power, fast brake work.

(1) Conditions for Insufficient brake force detection.

When the relay (UBR) used to detect the insufficient brake force of each vehicle is in the state of loss of magnetism, the insufficient brake force detection function starts (see Figure 4-2-4). When Line 155 is powered on, the normally open contact of 155R closes and the UBR excites. If the following conditions are established, the contact becomes loss of excitation.

Condition: ①∩{②∪(③∩④)}∩⑤∩⑥

① B is not R is the loss of magnctism: the driver's brake controller is positioned;

② B5FR excitation: the driver's brake controller is placed in the "B5-fast" position;
③ 70SR excitation: the speed is below 70 km/h;
④ B7FR magnetic: the driver's brake controller is placed in the "B7-fast" position;
⑤ NBR is lost: start ATP braking (commonly used);
⑥ JTR for magnetic loss: start fast brake.

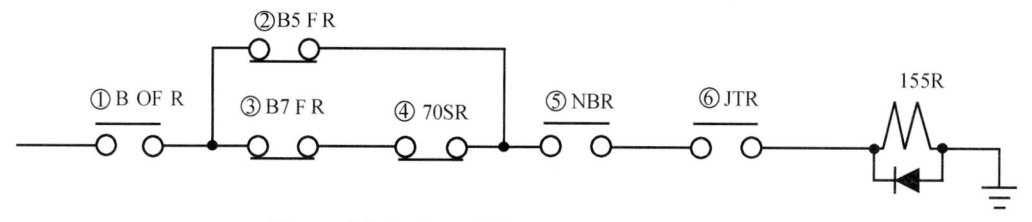

Figure 4-2-4 Insufficient brake force detection

When the UBR is demagnetized, the normally open contact of the UBR is open, and the UBTR is self-protected in the following circuit. In this state, the insufficient brake force detection function work (see Figure 4-2-5).

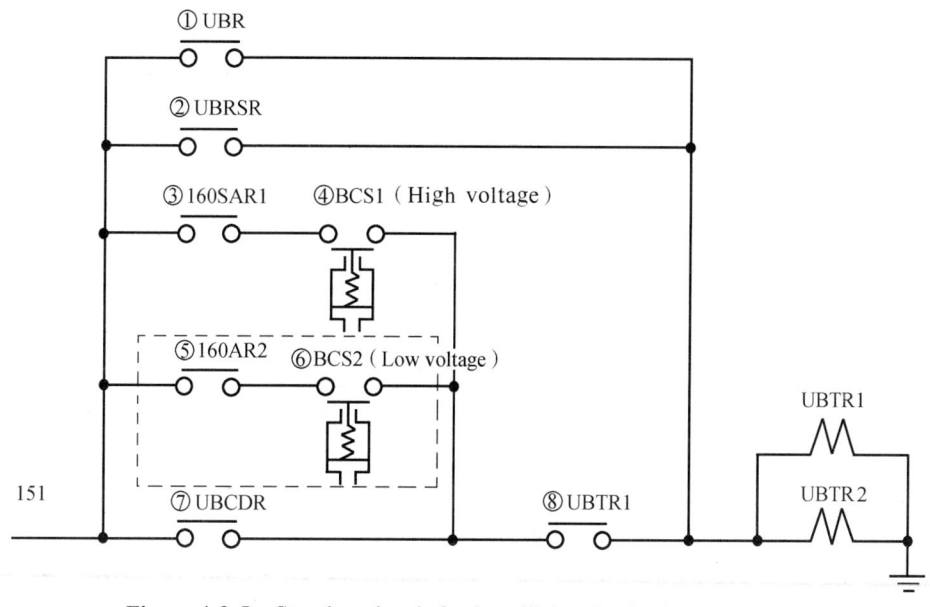

Figure 4-2-5 Starting circuit for insufficient brake force detection

When the speed is above 160 km/h, BCS2 (low voltage) will turn OFF, or when the speed is below 160 km/h, BCS1 (high voltage) will turn OFF. At the same time, if the traction converter detects insufficient regenerative brake force (UBCDR OFF), UBTR will disconnect the self-protection circuit and lose power. When the UBTR is OFF, the UV (emergency brake valve) loses magnetism and the emergency brake comes into play. When the UBR is OFF, the UBTR is still in a power-off state even after the brake pressure (brake force) detection is restored.

Reset the circuit of insufficient brake force detection: when the function of insufficient brake force detection is not started, UBR excites again and UBTR excites again; If the condition of detecting insufficient brake force is not true, UBR and UBTR also constitute self-protection circuit. The URTR performs the same reset when the UBRSR (relay for the urgency brake reset switch) excites.

（2）Emergency brake reset method.

After the emergency brake starts, the EMU will slow down until it stops, which cannot be relieved midway and must be reset.

The relay (156R) excites when the following conditions are true.

Condition: ①∩②∩③ ④

① B not R is loss of magnetism: the driver's brake controller is set to the "Fast" position;

② B7FR excitation: the driver's brake controller is placed in the "7-fast" position;

③ UBRSWR excitation: Reset according to emergency brake reset switch (UBRS);

④ MCR excitation: the driver's brake controller at the control end is set to the "Operation-fast" position.

After the relay (156R) is ON, Line 156 (emergency reset throughline) gets power, and the UBRSR (relay used for emergency brake reset switch) of each vehicle excites. The normally open contact in the UBSR excites the UBTR, and the emergency brake can be reset and released as soon as the power is restored to Line 153 and the UV and UVR are re-excited (see Figure 4-2-6).

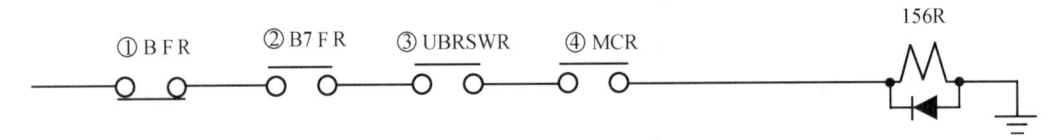

Figure 4-2-6 Emergency brake reset

2.2.4 Auxiliary brake instruction circuit

When the auxiliary brake is used, the auxiliary brake circuit breakers SBN1 (driver's station) and SBN2 (switchboard) which are normally opened are closed, and the auxiliary brake relay (SBNR) excites. When the driver's brake controller is used at the control end, one among B1-3K, B4-5K, B6-7K, B not K gets power according to the position of the handle, the AC voltage is output from the auxiliary brake pattern generator (used by the driver's station) to the through line (Line 411, Line 461). The auxiliary brake pattern generator (for each vehicle) will supply the voltage of Line 411 and Line 461to BCU after voltage change and rectification, and directly control the EP valve. The brake control path which does not pass through the train information control device is constituted. As the normally closed contact of SBNR becomes disconnected and the command line (Line 10) becomes disconnected, regenerative brake will not work.

2.2.5 Snow resistant brake instruction circuit

The purpose of the snow resistant brake is to prevent snow from entering between the brake disc and the brake pad during snow. To this end, it is necessary to push the brake pad out and block the gap between the brake pad and the brake disc surface. This function can operate the snow resistant brake switch (snow resistant SW) in the driver's console to power Line 157, through the train information control device, the instruction is transmitted to the BCU of each train. The BCU is issued by identifying the speed (under 110 km/h).

2.3 Description of connection conditions of schematic diagram

2.3.1 Brake instruction condition (Line 61) (1 gear)

In the ① ~ ③ project, the brake instruction (Line 61) is pressurized if the following conditions are met.

(Condition): ①∪②∪③
① B1FR excitation (see Figure 4-2-7);
② ATCBR excitation (ATP maximum service brake);
③ ATCKB1R excitation (ATP mitigating brake 1N).

Figure 4-2-7　Brake instruction condition 1 gear

2.3.2 Conditions of brake instruction (Line 62) (2 gear)

The brake instruction (Line 62) is pressurized if the following conditions are met.
B2FR excitation (see Figure 4-2-8).

Figure 4-2-8　Brake instruction condition 2 gear

2.3.3 Conditions of brake instruction (Line 63) (3 gear)

The brake instruction (Line 63) is pressurized if the following conditions are met. B3FR excitation (see Figure 4-2-9).

①$\overline{B3FR}$
———o o——————————————— 63

Figure 4-2-9 Brake instruction condition 3 gear

2.3.4 Conditions of brake instruction (Line 64) (4 gear)

In the project of ① and ②, the brake instruction (Line 64) is pressurized if the following conditions are met.

(Condition): ①∪②

① B4FR excitation (see Figure 4-2-10);
② ATCKB4R excitation (ATP mitigating brake 4N).

Figure 4-2-10 Brake instruction condition 4 gear

2.3.5 Conditions of brake instruction (Line 65) (5 gear)

The brake instruction (Line 65) is pressurized if the following conditions are met. B5FR excitation (see Figure 4-2-11).

①$\overline{B5FR}$
———o o——————————————— 65

Figure 4-2-11 Brake command condition 5 gear

2.3.6 Conditions of brake instruction (Line 66) (6 gear)

In the ① ~ ② project, the brake instruction (Line 66) line is pressurized if the following conditions are met.

(Condition): ①∪②

① B6FR excitation (see Figure 4-2-12);
② ATCBR excitation (ATP maximum service brake).

Figure 4-2-12 Brake instruction Condition 6 gear

2.3.7 Conditions of brake instruction (Line 67) (7 gear)

In the ① ~ ② project, the brake instruction (Line 67) line is pressurized if the following conditions are met.

(Condition): ①∪②

① B7FR excitation (see Figure 4-2-13);

② ATCBR excitation.

Figure 4-2-13   Brake instruction Condition 7 gear

2.3.8 Fast brake

A pressurized signal is sent to the brake controller composed of the fast brake throughline (Line 152) to keep the fast brake off.

In the ① ~ ③ project, Line 152 is pressurized if the following conditions are met.

(Condition): ①∩②∩③ (see Figure 4-2-14)

① JTR excitation (not emergency brake);

② EBR excitation (not ATP very brake);

③ BFR excitation (not in the fast brake position).

Fast brake instruction condition -- When Line 152 is not pressurized (loss of power), the brake control unit (BCU) recognizes the fast brake instruction and immediately initiates fast brake.

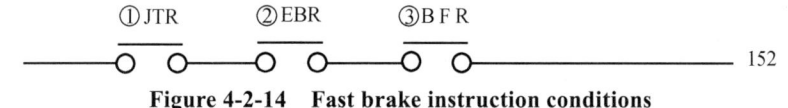

Figure 4-2-14   Fast brake instruction conditions

Fast brake is effective when:

① Brake setter operation (brake setter handle "Fast" position);

② Fast brake according to ATP (release EBR);

③ fast brake according to the release of JTR (controlled by a variety of factors).

1) Brake setter operation

Set the brake setter to [Fast] position, and [Fast] position relay "B non R" becomes non-excitation, and its a contact is opened to turn off the voltage transmitted to Line 152.

2) Fast brake through ATP (release EBR)

By the action of ATP, the relay (EBR) used for ATP fast brake on the main switchboard is released, thereby disconnecting its a contact and shutting off the voltage to Line 152.

However, if the ATPCOS is in the disconnected position (ATPCOR excitation), the relay (EBR) for ATP fast brake does not work.

3) Fast brake by releasing the JTR

When Line 154D is out of power, JTRTD is disconnected and JTR's excitation stops. Line 154D becomes disconnected under the following conditions:

① MR (main air cylinder) pressure reduction: main air duct high pressure switch off (MRHPS) →main air duct pressure switch relay off (MRrAPSR) →153K power off → 154B1-154B2 disconnection;

② Train separation: electrical connector disconnect → no voltage in Line 154;

③ Detection of insufficient brake force: Time limit relay (UBTR)on the vehicle for detecting insufficient braking force degaussing → Emergency brake valve relay (UVR) degaussing →154A-154K disconnection → no voltage in Line 154 (4) Select the brake setting device: B transport FR a contact disconnect →MCR degaussing → Line 154M degaussing;

④ Pull out the brake setting device: a contact in B transport FR disconnects →MCR degaussing→ Line 154M degaussing;

⑤ Train attendant switch treatment: start emergency brake switch (UBS1 or UBS2) →154A no voltage.

Conditions of JTR:

In the ①~④ project, if the following conditions are met, JTRTD and JTR (1P191608-14F) are used for excitation, and fast brake is not implemented.

(Condition): ①∩②∩③ ④ (see Figure 4-2-15)

① MCR excitation;

② BFR is non-excitation;

③ B7FR excitation;

④ UBRSWR (emergency brake restart) excitation.

※ Once JTR excites, carry on self-holding (self-locking) until Line 154 becomes unpressurized, JTR will not be excited.

When JTRTD changes from excitation to non-excitation, release after delay of 0.2 seconds →JTR non-excitation → fast brake action.

4) Correlation with regenerative brake

①If the brake setter is placed in the "Fast" position, because "B1FR" is in the excitation state, so Line 10 is also in the state of pressure;

②The fast brake caused by ATP release both EBR and NBR, so the ATCBR is excited, a contact of ATCBR becomes closed, and Line 10 is pressurized;

③When JTR is not excited, ATCBR will also be excited and Line 10 will be pressurized.

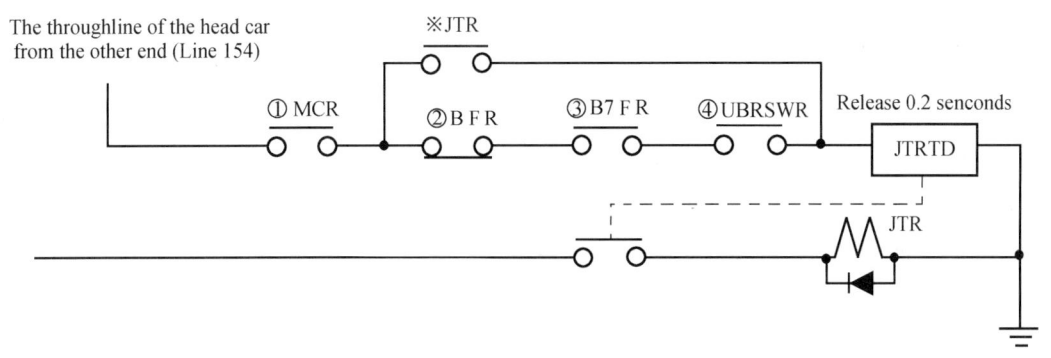

Figure 4-2-15 Conditions of JTR

Therefore, when the fast brake instruction is issued, the traction converter inputs the Line 10 pressure instruction, meanwhile, the regenerative brake mode signal is inputed from the brake control unit (BCU). The regenerative brake control acts as the service brake.

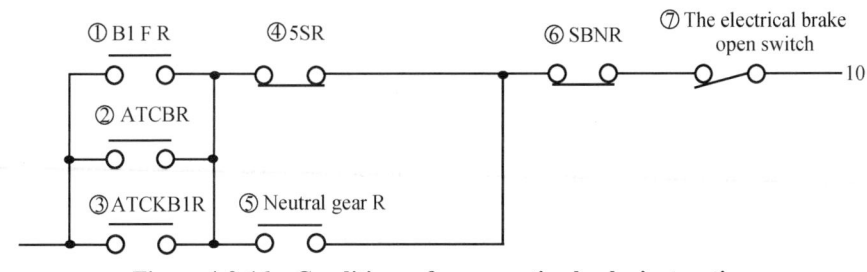

Conditions of regenerative brake instruction (Line 10) :

the regenerative brake instruction line (Line 10) is pressurized if the following conditions are met.

(Condition): (①∪②∪③)∩(④∪⑤)∩⑥∩⑦ (see Figure 4-2-16)

① B1FR excitation;

② ATCBR excitation;

③ ATCKB1R excitation;

④ 5SR is unexcited: the speed is above 5 km/h;

⑤ neutral gear R excitation;

⑥ SBNR is non-excitation: (brake device is normal, not auxiliary brake mode);

⑦ The electrical brake open switch SW is OFF (off) (regenerative brake is not cut off).

Figure 4-2-16 Conditions of regenerative brake instruction

2.3.9 Emergency brake

It is pressurized via a contact at 153K of the head car and through line (Line 153). The throughline (Line 154) is pressurized from Line 153 through the b contact of the MCR at the rear driver's desk without emergency brake. In case of loss of power on Line 153, emergency brake work.

Emergency brake works in the following situations.

① Train separation;

② The main duct pressure is reduced;

③ Detection of insufficient brake force;

④ When the emergency solenoid valve is closed;

⑤ When the brake setter handle is pulled out.

Conditions for 153K:

153K is excited if the following conditions are met. When 153K is excited, Line 153 (the through-line that is pressurized during normal operation) is pressurized to form an emergency brake circuit. When the circuit is not pressurized, emergency brake and fast brake work.

(Condition): ①∩②∩③ (see Figure 4-2-17)

① B transport FR excitation;

② MCR excitation;

③ MRrAPSR excitation: the air pressure switch of the total air cylinder is ON (switched on).

Figure 4-2-17 Conditions for 153K

1) Train separation

On the front side of the train separation only Line 154 system is not pressurized, the JTR is demagnetized, and the fast brake is working.

In the rear side of the train separation, the systems of Line 153 and Line 154 are turned into no voltage, when the emergency brake electromagnetic valve (UV) is degaussing, emergency brake is working, meanwhile, JTR is degaussing → because Line 152 did not add voltage, fast brake is also ordered. BCU (Brake control Unit) will be treated with high priority for emergency brake and fast brake.

2) When the pressure of the total air duct decreases

The total air duct pressure in the hood of the two head cars is detected by the high pressure switch of the main air duct (MRHPS). If it is lower than the set value (590 ± 10) kPa, disconnect the contact. As the MRHPS contact is opened, the pneumatic switching relay (MRrAPSR) of the main duct becomes unexcited, and its a contact becomes open, disconnecting the excitation of the 153K relay. While making Line 153 unpressurized, other contacts make line 154D unpressurized to degausse JTR. Thus, UV (emergency electromagnetic valve) degaussing, when the emergency brake plays a role, fast brake is also ordered.

3) When insufficient brake force is detected

When insufficient brake force is detected, the UBTR (urgency brake Limited time relay) is demagnetized. When the UBTR is turned off, the UV (urgency magnetic valve) and UVR (urgency magnetic valve relay) pressurized circuits are blocked between 153B-153C. After the UV is demagnetized, start the emergency brake of the vehicle. At the same time, due to the a contact of the UVR, between 154A-154K is blocked, so the JTR is demagnetized and loses the pressurization of Line 152, fast brake takes action.

4) Composition of insufficient brake detection

5) Conditions for 156R (emergency reset)

156R (1P191608-15D) is excited if the following conditions are met. When the 156R is excited, the throughline 156 is pressurized. When line 156 becomes unpressurized, start the emergency brake.

(Condition): ①∩②∩③ ④ (see Figure 4-2-18)

① BFR is non-excitation;
② B7FR excitation;
③ UBRSWR (emergency brake restart switch relay) excitation;
④ MCR excitation.

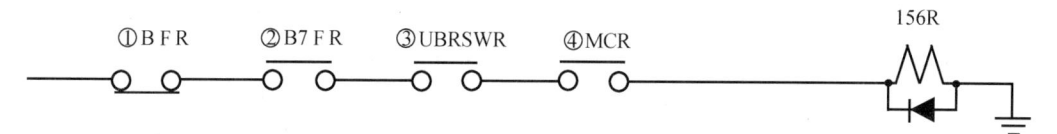

Figure 4-2-18　Conditions for 156R

conditions for UBRSWR　(emergency brake reset):

UBRSWR excites if the following conditions are met (see Figure 4-2-19).

UBRS is ON: emergency brake reset switch is ON (closed)

Figure 4-2-19　conditions for UBRSWR

After the relay (156R) is ON, Line 156 (emergency reset throughline) is pressurized and the UBRSR (relay for emergency brake reset switch) of each vehicle is excited. After the UBTR is excited at the a contact of the UBRSR, the emergency brake is reset and relieved as soon as the pressure of Line 153 is restored and the excitation circuits of the UV and UVR are constructed.

2.3.10 Snow resistant brake

The purpose of snow resistant brake is to close the gap between the brake pad and brake disc by gently pressing the brake shoe to prevent snow from entering between the brake disc and brake shoe when it snows. As the snow resistant brake switch (snow resistant SW) and Line 157 of the operator platform are pressurized, the instructions are transmitted to the BCU of each vehicle through the vehicle information control device. BCU works by identifying speeds (below 110 km/h).

Conditions for Snow resistant brake instruction (Line 157) :

The snow resistant brake instruction (Line 157) is pressurized if the following conditions are met.

(Condition): ①∩② (see Figure 4-2-20)

① Snow resistant SW is ON;

② MXR is not excited: it is not connected to other marshalling.

Figure 4-2-20　Conditions for Snow resistant brake instruction

2.3.11 Auxiliary brake

When the auxiliary brake is used, the auxiliary brake relay (SBNR) is excited when the auxiliary brake circuit breakers SBN1 (driver's station) and SBN2 (switchboard) which are normally disconnected are put into operation. When brake setters are used in the selected driver's station, according to the position of the handle, BFK, B1-3K, B4-5K, B6-7K start to work, and output AC voltage from the auxiliary brake mode generator (used in the driver's station) to the throughline (Line 411, Line 461). The auxiliary brake mode generator (for all vehicles) will supply the voltage of Line 411 and Line 461 to the brake control device to directly control the EP valve after voltage change and rectification. Therefore, the brake control path which does not pass through the vehicle information control device is constituted. Regenerative brake does not work because the b contact of the SBNR is turned on and the command line (Line 10) is unpressurized.

1) Conditions of SBNR (auxiliary brake)

SBNR excites if the following conditions are met.

After the excitation of SBNR, the stage signal output relays of auxiliary brake, such as B6-7K, B4-5K, B1-3K and BFK become excitable, and it becomes possible to issue the auxiliary brake force instruction from the auxiliary brake mode generator.

The auxiliary contact of SBN1 is ON: the auxiliary contact of the circuit breaker for auxiliary brake is ON (see Figure 4-2-21).

①The auxiliary contactor of SBN1

Figure 4-2-21　Conditions of SBNR

2) Conditions of B6 ~ 7K (auxiliary brake mode)

In the projects of ①~③, if the following conditions are met, B6 ~ 7K becomes excitation.

(Condition): ①∩②∩③ (see Figure 4-2-22)

① SBNR excitation;

② B6FR excitation;

③ BFR excitation.

Figure 4-2-22　Conditions of B6 ~ 7K

3) Conditions of B4 ~ 5K (auxiliary brake mode)

In the projects of ① ~ ③, if the following conditions are met, B4 ~ 5K becomes excitation.

(Condition): ①∩②∩③ (see Figure 4-2-23)

① SBNR excitation;

② B4FR excitation;

③ B6FR is non-excitation.

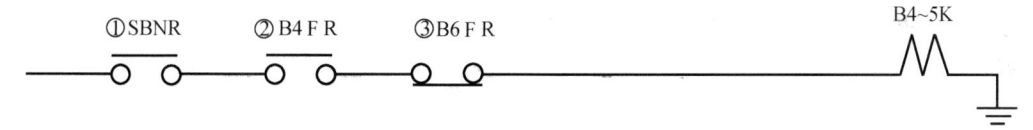

Figure 4-2-23　Conditions of B4 ~ 5K

4) Conditions of B1 ~ 3K (auxiliary brake mode)

In the projects of ① ~ ③, if the following conditions are met, B1 ~ 3K becomes excitation.

(Condition): ①∩②∩③ (see Figure 4-2-24)

① SBNR excitation;

② B1FR excitation;

③ B4FR is non-excitation.

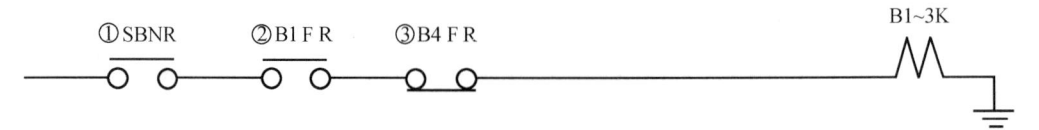

Figure 4-2-24　Conditions of B1 ~ 3K

5）Conditions of BFK (auxiliary brake mode)

If the following conditions are met, BFK becomes excitation.

(Condition): ①∩②∩（③∪④）(see Figure 4-2-25)

① SBNR excitation;

② MCR excitation;

③ BFR is non-excitation.

④ JTR is non-excitation.

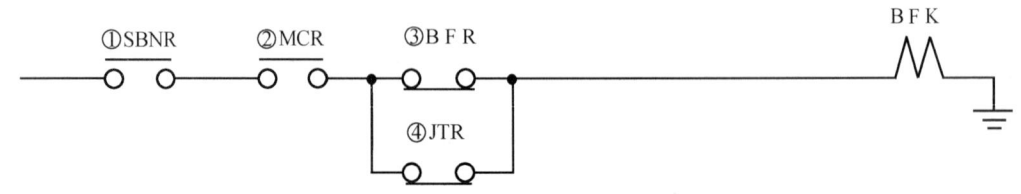

Figure 4-2-25　Conditions of BFK

【Project Testing】

1. Analyze the basic composition of EMU brake control system.

2. Briefly describe the five brake modes and their corresponding instruction lines.

3. Analyze under what circumstances fast brake occurs.

4. Analyze JTR excitation conditions.

5. Briefly describe the functions of the brake controller.

Project 5

Circuit Analysis of Auxiliary Power Supply System for EMU

【Project Description】

This project mainly introduces the structure of the auxiliary power supply system, power supply mode, AC/DC power supply circuit, extended power supply, open/close control and other aspects. Students are required to be able to analyze the circuit of the auxiliary power supply system, and to check and deal with faults according to the maintenance standards.

【Project Tasks】

(1) Analysis of the auxiliary converter;
(2) Analysis of auxiliary power supply circuit;
(3) Auxiliary power supply and other control circuits;
(4) Opening and closing control;
(5) Fault case analysis

Task 1 Analysis of the Auxiliary Converter

【Task Description】

This task is to learn the knowledge of auxiliary converters for EMU. The main circuit structure of AC and DC, working principle and typical EMU application of auxiliary converters are introduced.

【Background Knowledge】

1.1 Auxiliary Converter

In order to ensure the normal operation of the train, the train is equipped with three-phase AC auxiliary circuit and auxiliary mechanical devices. Because the main transformer, traction converter device, traction motor etc emit a lot of heat during operation, the ventilator is needed for forced air cooling. The brake of the train, the pantograph and all kinds of pneumatic machinery on the train must be equipped with compressors to provide air source, etc. All these auxiliary devices must be driven by three-phase squirrel-cage asynchronous motors. To do this, a three-phase AC power supply is required on the train, which is done by an auxiliary converter. The train control system, as well as the lighting system, requires DC power, which is done by auxiliary rectifiers. Before hoisting the bow or when the high voltage equipment or main transformer fails, the related system is powered by the battery. Therefore, the DC part of the train auxiliary power supply system includes the auxiliary rectifier device and the storage battery.

Train auxiliary power supply system is mainly composed of auxiliary converter, auxiliary rectifier and related components. The auxiliary converter is used to provide three-phase AC 400 V power supply by the static converter, and the auxiliary rectifier is used to provide DC power supply by the rectifier unit.

In order to prevent the failure of auxiliary power supply equipment from affecting the normal operation of the locomotive, the auxiliary power supply system requires a high degree of redundancy. Therefore, the train generally uses multiple auxiliary converters with independent power supply at the same time, and some auxiliary converters can also be converted and connected.

The output voltage of the auxiliary converter is PWM wave, which has a very high value du/dt. In order to reduce the adverse impact of the high value du/dt on the auxiliary machine, it is generally required to add an EMC filter to the output end of the inverter, so as to make the voltage rise slope (du/dt value) of the output voltage $\leqslant 500$ V/μs、and the maximum peak voltage $U_{pk} \leqslant 1,000$ V.

1.1.1 Structure and characteristics of auxiliary converter

According to the different input side of the auxiliary converter, the main circuit of the auxiliary converter can be divided into two types: one, the input side is AC, which is called AC-DC-AC type; the other, the input side is DC, which is called DC -AC type. Now they are introduced separately.

1) AC-DC-AC auxiliary converter

The AC-DC-AC auxiliary converter is powered by the auxiliary winding of the locomotive traction transformer and consists of three parts: pulse rectifier, intermediate DC circuit and inverter. Its structure is shown in Figure 5-1-1. The circuit principle of AC-DC-AC auxiliary converter is shown in Figure 5-1-2. The functions of each part are as follows:

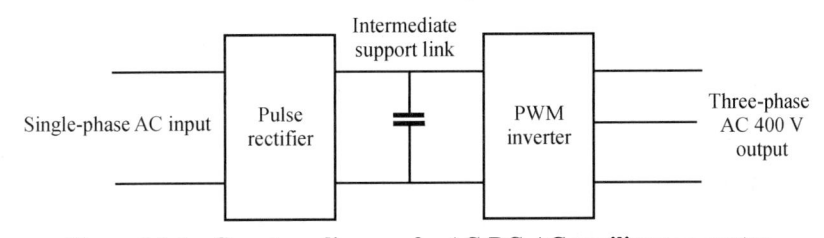

Figure 5-1-1　Structure diagram for AC-DC-AC auxiliary converter

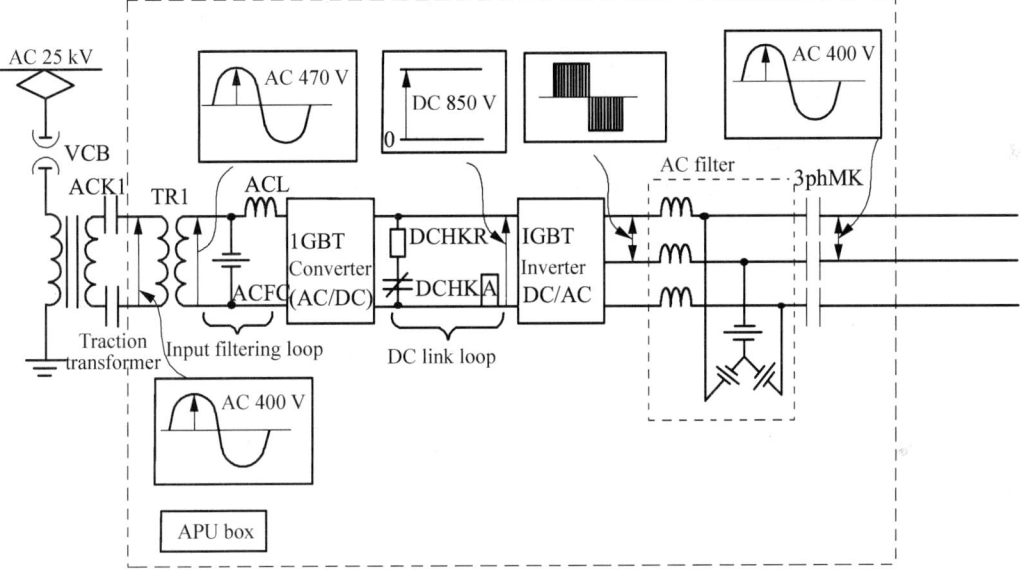

Figure 5-1-2　AC-DC-AC auxiliary converter circuit schematic

① Pulse rectifier: The pulse rectifier converts the single-phase AC voltage input by the traction transformer into a constant DC voltage, using pulse width modulation.

② Intermediate DC circuit: The filter capacitor will supply stabilized DC voltage to the inverter in the back section.

③ Inverter: Inverter converts DC voltage into three-phase AC voltage.

In order to reduce the high harmonic interference, it is necessary to add a filtering link between the traction transformer and the pulse rectifier to suppress the harmonic current.

The auxiliary converter with AC-DC-AC structure has the following characteristics:

① The traction transformer needs to provide auxiliary windings to supply power to the auxiliary converter.

② The pulse rectifier can ensure a higher power factor on the input side.

③ The starting mode of the converter is soft starting, which can effectively reduce the starting current of the motor.

④ It can work in a large range of network pressure.

⑤ The output voltage is stabilized and the three-phase output voltage is balanced.

2) DC-AC auxiliary converter

The DC-AC auxiliary converter takes the current directly from the intermediate DC link of the traction converter, so it only needs the inverter to realize the conversion from DC to three-phase AC. However, in order to ensure the sine of the output voltage and the voltage value of 400 V, additional step-down equipment must be added. Generally, there are two combinations: one is chopper step-down converter + inverter, as shown in Figure 5-1-3 (a), and the typical circuit principle is shown in Figure 5-1-4. The other is inverter + three-phase step-down transformer, as shown in Figure 5-1-3 (b). The typical circuit principle is shown in Figure 5-1-5. In order to ensure the sine of the output voltage waveform, the output duty cycle of the inverter must be ensured, which makes the input DC voltage of the inverter is high, the output AC voltage value is also high, so the step-down transformer must be used.

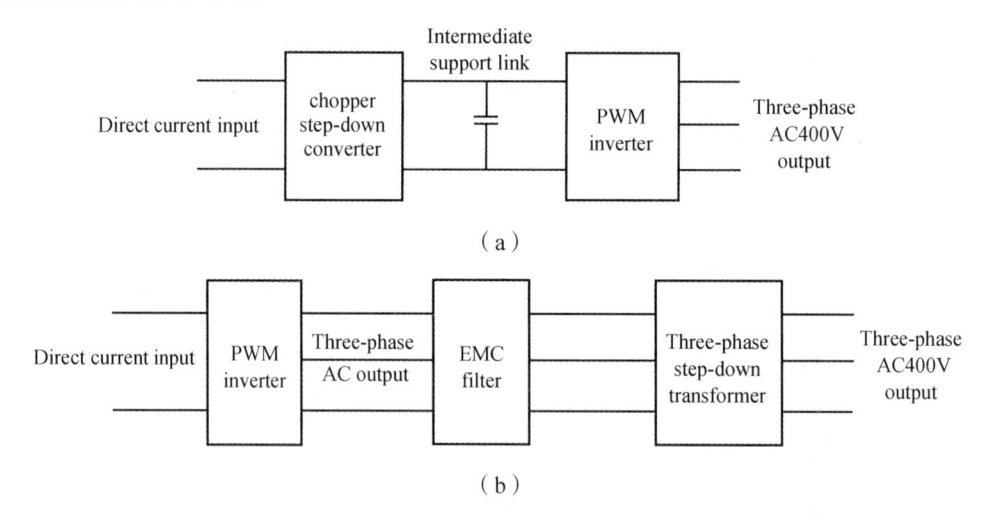

Figure 5-1-3　Structure diagram for DC-AC auxiliary converter

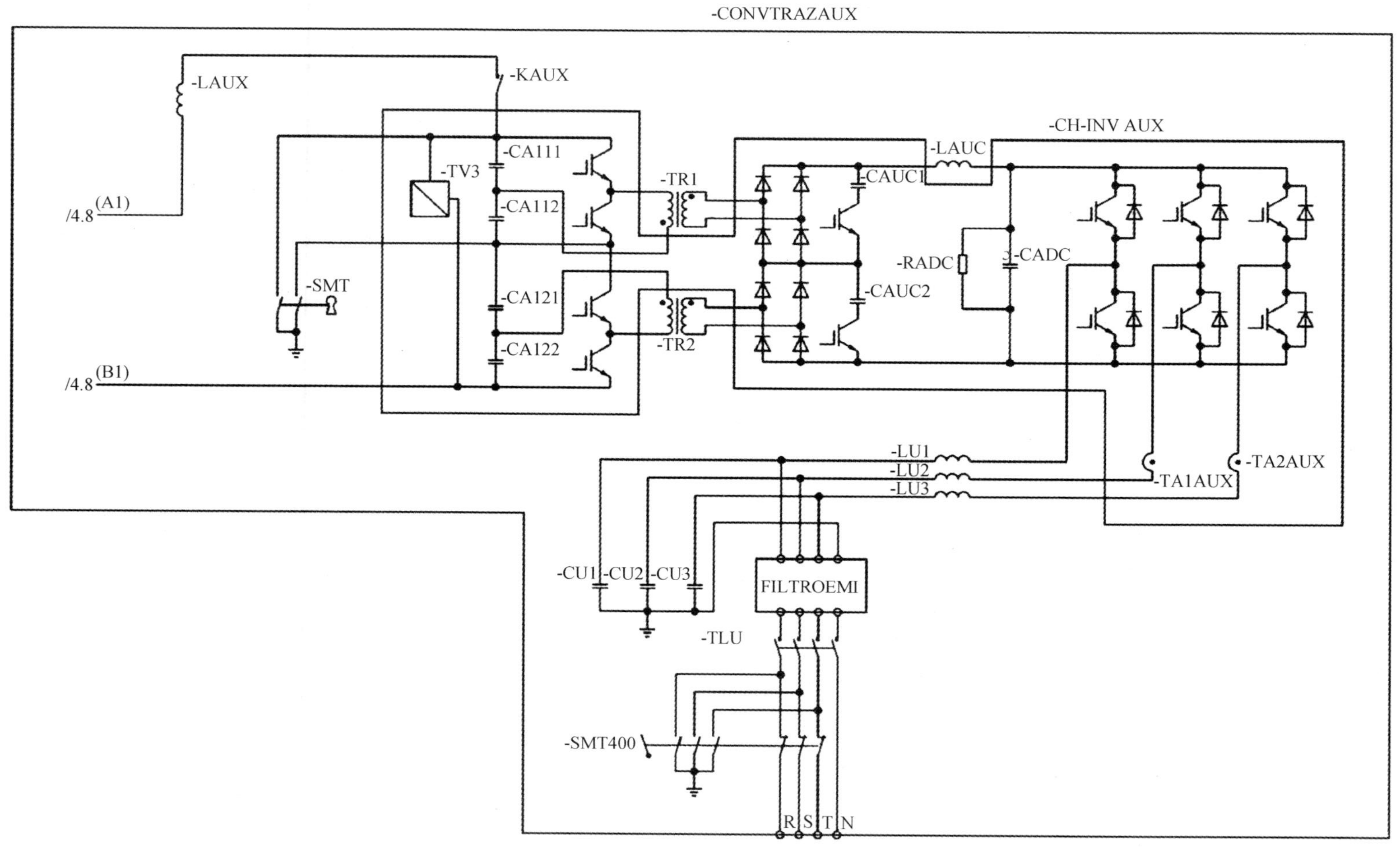

Figure 5-1-4 Circuit schematic diagram of DC -AC auxiliary converter using chopper step-down converter

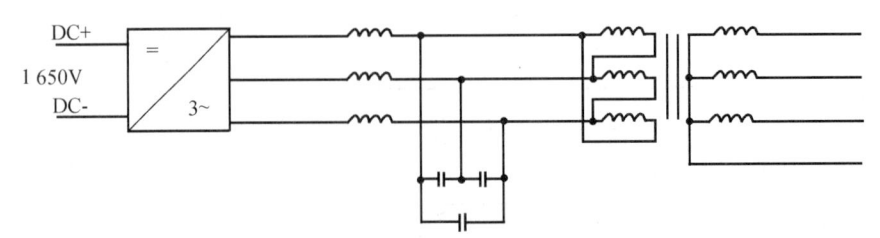

Figure 5-1-5　Circuit schematic diagram of DC-AC auxiliary converter with step-down transformer

① Chopper step-down converter [corresponding to the structure of 5-1-3 (a)] : the intermediate DC voltage of the traction converter is reduced to an appropriate value to ensure that the output voltage of the inverter is 400 V.

② Three-phase step-down transformer [corresponding to the structure of 5-1-3 (b)] : using the principle of electromagnetic induction, the inverter output higher AC voltage falls down to 400 V.

③ Inverter: inverter converts DC voltage into three-phase AC voltage.

Compared with AC-DC-AC auxiliary converters, DC-AC auxiliary converters have two distinct characteristics:

① There is no need for traction transformer to provide auxiliary windings, take current directly from the intermediate DC link of traction converter.

② Voltage reduction measures must be taken to ensure the amplitude of the output voltage.

1.1.2 Working principle of auxiliary converter

Auxiliary converter will use pulse rectifier, chopper, step-down inverter, three-phase step-down transformer.

1) Working principle of pulse rectifier

The structure, function and working principle of the pulse rectifier used in the auxiliary converter are the same as that of the train traction four quadrant pulse rectifier, so it will not be described again. Moreover, since the auxiliary converter does not need energy feedback, the pulse rectifier does not need to reverse the flow of energy. Therefore, the control of pulse rectifier of the auxiliary converter is simpler than that of the traction pulse rectifier.

2) Working principle of inverter

The inverter used by the auxiliary converter and the two-level PWM inverter used by the train traction drive system are the same in structure, function and working principle, which will not be repeated here. Because electrical equipment does not require precise control of speed, nor does it require energy feedback, its control is relatively simple.

3) Working principle of three-phase step-down transformer

There is no difference between three-phase step-down transformer and ordinary power transformer, which will not be repeated here.

4) Working principle of step-down chopper

Chopper is the use of self-shutdown device to achieve on-off control, the DC power supply voltage intermittently added to the load, through the change of on and off time to change the average load voltage, also known as DC-DC converter. It has the advantages of high efficiency, small size, light weight and low cost. The emergence of fast power electronics devices creates conditions for the improvement of chopper frequency, which can reduce the low-frequency harmonic components, reduce the requirements for filtering components, and reduce the volume and quality.

1.2 DC power supply system

Dc power supply system is mainly composed of rectifier and storage battery.

The main functions of the train rectifier are as follows: to provide power for the train DC electrical equipment such as control system and lighting system; charge the battery.

The rectifier usually uses a pulse rectifier or chopper to obtain the required DC voltage. The circuit schematic diagram of rectifier device is shown in Figure 5-1-6.

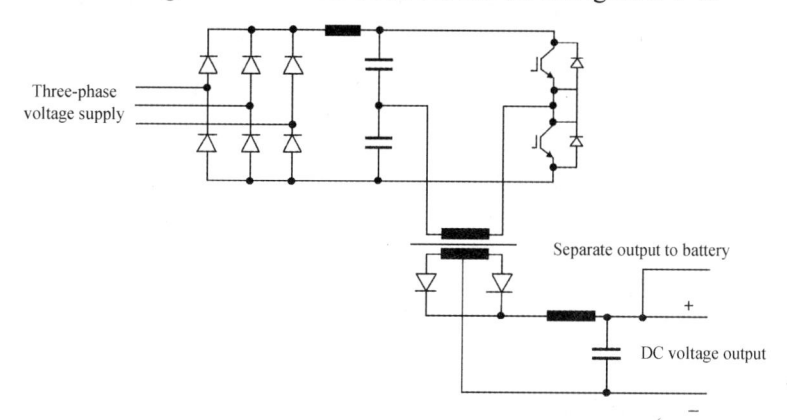

Figure 5-1-6　Circuit schematic diagram of rectifier device

The storage battery is designed to provide power for the related equipment when the rectifier cannot provide DC power supply (such as the failure of the related equipment of EMU or the fail to lift pantograph in EMU or the rectifier is unable to supply power), and it also plays a role of filtering and regulating the DC voltage out of the rectifier.

1.3 Schematic diagram of typical EMU auxiliary power supply system

The auxiliary power supply system of high-speed trains in our country has different characteristics: Figure 5-1-7 shows CRH1 auxiliary power supply structure, Figure 5-1-8 shows CRH2 auxiliary power supply structure, and Figure 5-1-9 shows CRH3 auxiliary power supply structure.

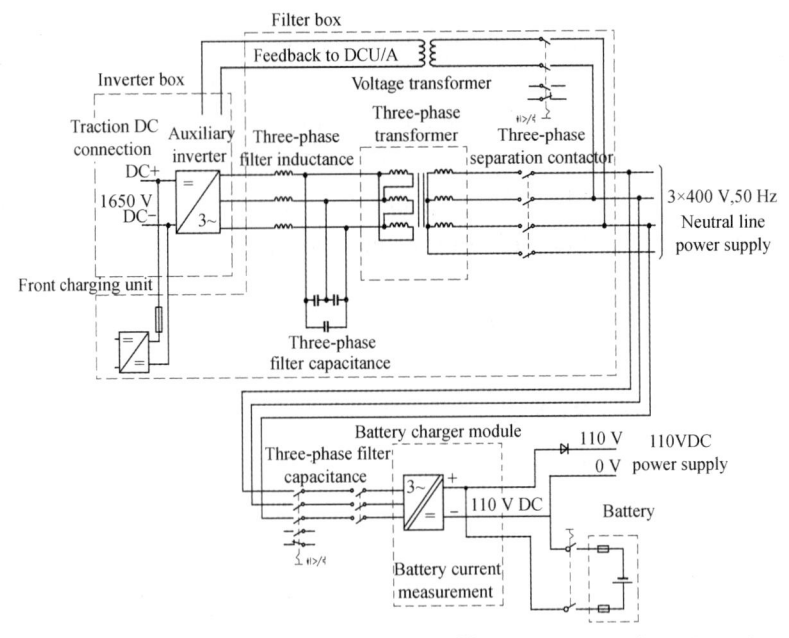

Figure 5-1-7 Schematic diagram of CRH1 auxiliary power supply system structure

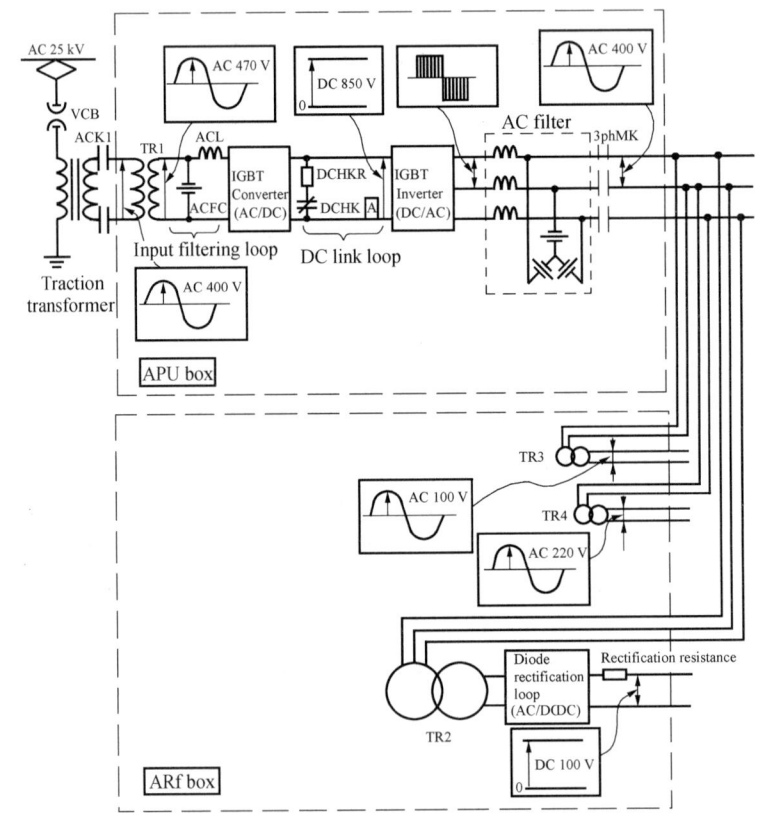

Figure 5-1-8 Schematic diagram of CRH2 auxiliary power supply system structure

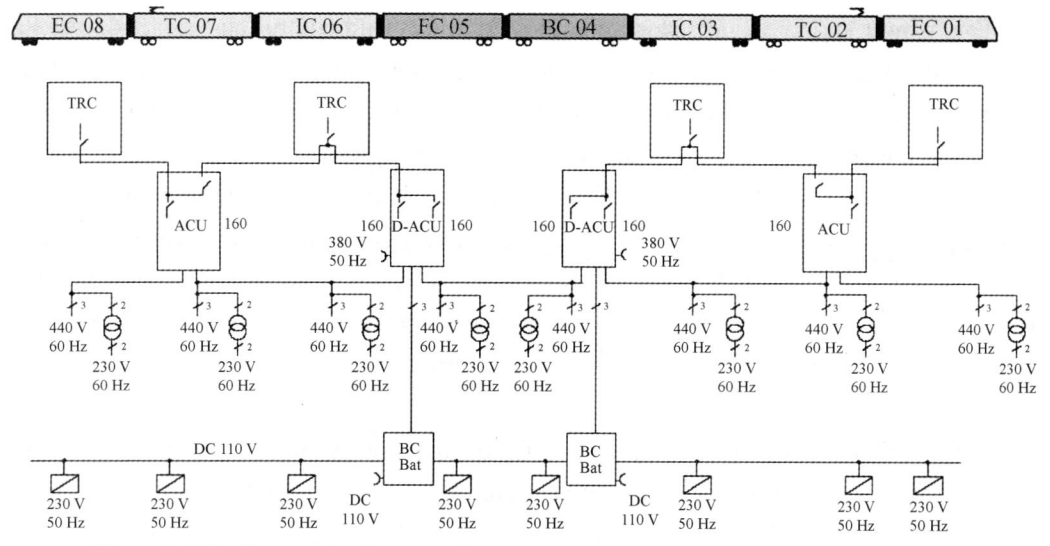

Figure 5-1-9   Schematic diagram of CRH3 auxiliary power supply system structure

Task 2 Analysis of auxiliary power supply circuit

【Task Description】

This task mainly analyzes the auxiliary power circuit of CRH2 and CRH380A EMU. Students are required to master the main circuit structure of auxiliary power supply of EMU and analyze the principle of AC and DC power supply, which will lay a foundation for future EMU maintenance work.

【Background Knowledge】

2.1 Overview of auxiliary power supply system

The CRH2 EMU consists of 8 cars, including 4 bullet cars and 4 trailers. The first and last cars are equipped with driver cabs for two-way driving. The configuration of the EMU is shown in Figure 5-2-1.

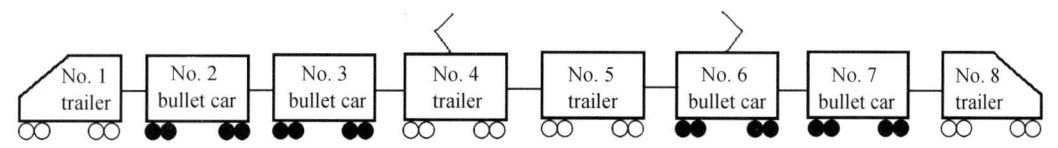

Figure 5-2-1   Formation configuration of CRH2 EMU

The auxiliary power supply system consists of traction transformer auxiliary winding,

125

auxiliary power supply device, storage battery, auxiliary and control electrical equipment, ground power supply and so on. An auxiliary power supply device consists of an auxiliary power unit (APU) and an auxiliary rectifier box (ARF). The auxiliary and control electrical equipment includes a variety of AC and DC electrical equipment.

Cars M1-2, M3-4 and M5-6 of the EMU are respectively equipped with one traction transformer MTr. Cars T1c-1 and T2c-8 are respectively equipped with a set of auxiliary power supply devices. No. 2, No. 4 and No. 6 cars are respectively installed with a battery set; an external power socket is installed on the side of the car body of No. M2-2 and M2-6 respectively; all carriages are equipped with various auxiliary and control electrical equipment.

The auxiliary power supply system of CRH2 train set is supplied by three auxiliary windings of traction transformer, adopting trunk power supply mode, according to each power system through the whole train.In the system directly connected with the traction transformer 3 coil, the air conditioning device, air exchange device and ATP master power supply are connected. The input of the auxiliary power supply unit (APU) is AC 400 V. The APU serves as the power supply to 5 systems, which are unstabilized single-phase AC 100 V system, stabilized single-phase AC 100 V system; stabilized single-phase AC 220 V system; stabilized three-phase AC 400 V system; DC 100 V system.

The auxiliary power supply system adopts redundancy design. Two traction transformers are installed on the EMU, and the AC 400 V voltage output from the auxiliary winding to the auxiliary power supply unit (APU) is supplied to the 4 carriages respectively. When one traction transformer fails, in order to make the other one operate normally, the traction transformer can supply power to the 8 carriages through the auxiliary winding, and the auxiliary winding power supply induction loop is set for switching. When the auxiliary winding power switch, the air conditioning unit runs with half power. The adjacent units have the function of mutual support. Two auxiliary power devices are installed on the EMU, and one auxiliary power device supplies the auxiliary power required by the four carriages. When an auxiliary power supply fails, an extended power supply loop is provided for switching in order to enable a functioning auxiliary power supply unit to supply power to the 8 carriages. The output capacity of the auxiliary power supply unit is designed to supply power to the entire train with a functioning auxiliary power supply unit in case of failure. Therefore, there is no need to reduce the load when an auxiliary power supply unit fails.

The auxiliary system is equipped with perfect safety grounding measures, self-diagnosis function and fault protection function. The interface of self-diagnosis function is set between the train information control system and the auxiliary power supply device, which is implemented by the train information control system.

A socket (AC 400 V, single-phase, 50 Hz) connected to the external power supply is installed on the side of the external vehicle body of the EMU, and there is one on each M2 car (No. 2 and No. 6). The vehicle maintenance base is equipped with an external power supply to assist the work of the auxiliary circuit.

2.2 Main circuit structure of auxiliary power supply

The auxiliary power supply is composed of the auxiliary power supply unit (APU) and the auxiliary rectifier (ARF), as shown in Figure 5-2-2. The functional block diagram of the auxiliary power supply unit is in the upper dotted line box, and the functional block diagram of the auxiliary rectifier is in the lower dotted line box.

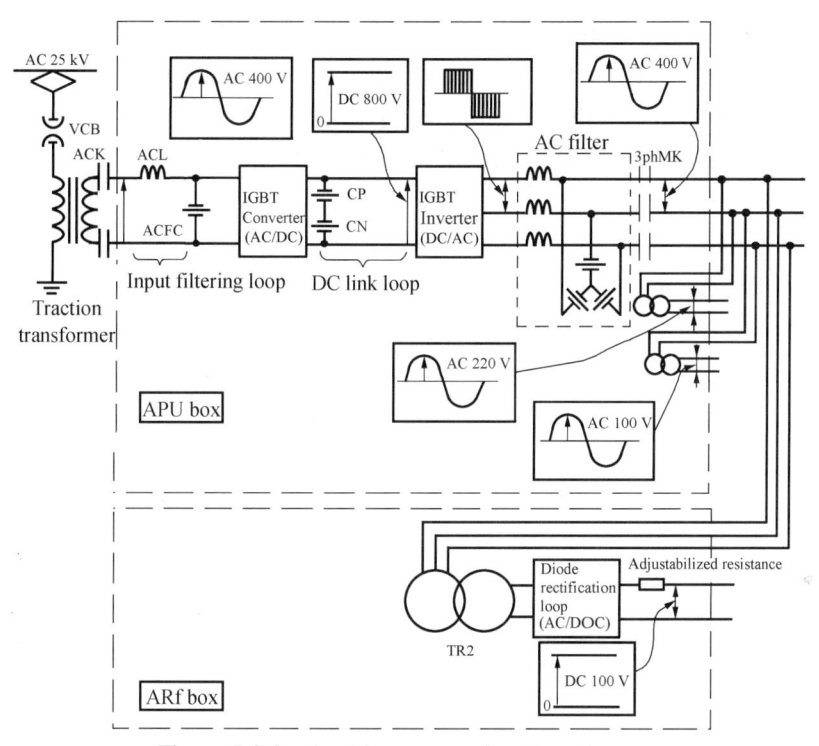

Figure 5-2-2　Auxiliary power function diagram

Main functions of APU:

① Input filter circuit: The input filter circuit reduces the high-frequency current component input from the power grid to the pulse rectifier and inverter.

② IGBT pulse rectifier: The pulse rectifier will convert the single-phase AC voltage input by the traction transformer into a stabilized DC voltage, and the control mode is pulse width modulation.

③ DC intermediate circuit: The filter capacitor supplies stabilized DC voltage to the inverter at the back end. When the APU stops, the discharge of the filter capacitor is completed by DCHK and DCHKR (discharge contactor and discharge resistor).

④ IGBT inverter: The inverter converts the DC voltage into the three-phase AC voltage of constant voltage and constant frequency (CVCF).

⑤ Output LC filter circuit: LC filter circuit reduces the high-frequency voltage component generated by the on-off of the power device in the output voltage of the inverter, making it output the sine wave voltage with less distortion.

⑥ Output contactor: Output contactor 3phMK plays the role of connecting and cutting off load.

ARF is mainly composed of three-phase transformer (TR2, 400 V/78 V), three-phase diode rectifier bridge module, single-phase transformer (TR3) and single-phase transformer (TR4). The input voltage of the Arf is provided by the three-phase voltage regulator output of the auxiliary APU. TR2 and three-phase diode rectifier module output stabilized DC 100 V voltage, TR3 output voltage regulated single-phase AC 100 V/50 Hz power supply, TR4 output voltage regulated single-phase AC 220 V/50 Hz power supply.

APU consists of APU input auxiliary rectifier, PWM three-phase output inverter, inverter output transformer, CVCF output transformer, auxiliary transformer and so on. The auxiliary rectifier cabinet is composed of a rectifier transformer and an auxiliary rectifier. The internal circuit structure is shown in Figure 5-2-3.

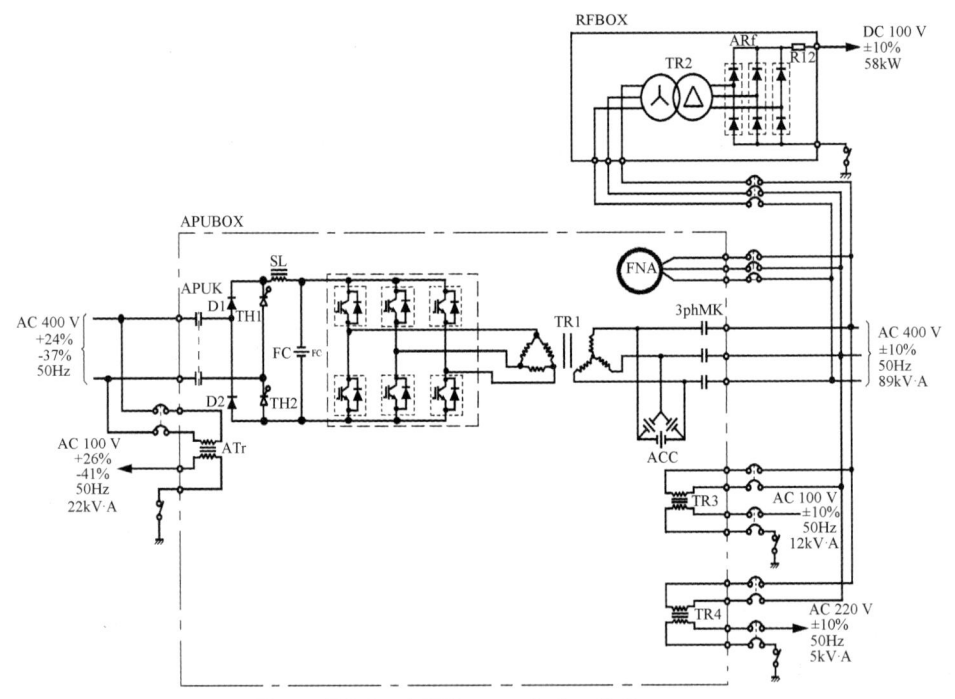

Figure 5-2-3　APU internal circuit diagram

2.3 Principle analysis of AC and DC power supply

2.3.1 Outline

The auxiliary circuit power supply of CRH380A EMU is obtained from the three winding of traction transformer MTr installed in M1-2, M3-4 and M5-6. The three winding power sources AC400 V、50 Hz of traction transformers of M1-2, M3-4 and M5-6 are connected to the through-line 704 and 754 systems through the electromagnetic contactor ACK1 respectively. The electromagnetic contactor ACK2 for extended power supply is normally disconnected in M4-5 to prevent the mixing of the power supply from the two systems of M1-2 and M5-6. One auxiliary power supply unit (APU) is installed on each of the two leading vehicles T1-1 and T2-8, and two APU is installed on the eight vehicles in total to obtain power from the above through-line 704 and 754 systems. The 772, 782 and 792 of the M4-5 APU3 form power supply trunk independently in the M3-4 and M4-5.

2.3.2 AC circuit

Table 5-2-1 is a summary of power supply, voltage and load of each vehicle according to different power supply systems. Auxiliary power supply unit (APU) includes inverter (SIV) which supplies three-phase (400 ± 10%) V, 50 Hz stabilized power supply and auxiliary transformer (ATR) which only depresses the traction transformer's three-winding voltage. In addition, the ARf Box is equipped with a constant voltage transformer (CVT) that accepts the output power of SIV and provides single-phase 220 V and 100 V ± 10% 50 Hz stabilized power supply to line 302 and line 202. The auxiliary power supply unit (APU3) only provides the inverse transformer (SIV) of the 3-phase (400 ± 10%) V, 50 Hz stabilized power supply.

Table 5-2-1   summary table of all kinds of power supply, vehicle electrical equipment in AC power system

Power supply system	Power supply	Voltage	Vehicles	Load
Lines 704 and 754	Traction transformer Auxiliary winding	Single phase 400 V, 50 Hz	Each car	Air conditioning unit、Air exchange unit
			T1-1,T2-8 M4-5	Auxiliary power supply unit (APU) Auxiliary power supply unit(APU3)
			T1-1,M1-2, M2-3,M3-4, M4-5,M5-6, M6-7,T2-8	Electric tea stove

Continued

Power supply system	Power supply	Voltage	Vehicles	Load
Lines 771, 781, 791	T1c-1,T2c-8 APU-SIV	Three-phase 400 V ±10%、50 Hz	M1-2,M5-6 M1-2,M2-3, M5-6,M6-7	Transformer oil circulating pump (MTOPM) Transformer electric blower (MTrBM) Traction converter electric blower Traction motor electric blower
			M2-3,M6-7	Air compressor
			T1-1,T2-8	Auxiliary rectifier (ARF)
Line 302	T1-1,T2-8 APU-CVT	Single-phase 220 V ±10%、50 Hz	M4-5(Dining car)	Kitchen equipment
			Each car	The socket
Line 202	T1-1,T2c-8 APU-ARf-CVT	Single phase 100 V ±10%、50 Hz	Each car	Air conditioning control、Display setting device
			T1-1,M1-2, M2-3,M3-4, M4-5,M5-6, M6-7,T2-8	Water supply unit
			T1-1,T2-8	Auxiliary brake
Line 251	T1-1,T2-8 APU-ATr	single-phase100 V+26%, -41%、50 Hz	Each car	Electric heating

In the above contents, for Line 704 and 754 system, Line 771, 781, 791 three-phase power supply system and Line 302 system, in order to realize extended power supply when one side power supply fails, electromagnetic contact ACK2 is set in M4-5 car and BKK is set in Car M3-4. In order to avoid mixing with the power supply from M1-2 and M5-6, these electromagnetic contactors are normally in the off position.

2.3.2 DC power supply loop

Table 5-2-2 is a summary of various power supplies and various vehicle electrical equipment in the DC power supply system.

Table 5-2-2 Summary table of all kinds of power supply, vehicle electrical equipment in DC power system

Power supply system	Power supply	Voltage	Vehicles	Load
Line 102	M1-2,M4-5, M6-7 Battery (Bat), Line 103 (BatK1, ON)	DC 100 (1 ± 10%)V	T1-1,T2-8	Operation control (including pantograph raising the bow, VCB control)
			M3-4, M5-6	Auxiliary air compressor Storage battery
Line 103	T1-1,T2-8 ARf	DC 100(1±10%)V	Each car	Auxiliary circuit, monitoring and control device, brake device, door closing device
			M1-2,M2-3, M3-4,M4-5, M5-6,M6-7	Traction converter control
			T1c-1,T2c-8	ATP
			T2c-8	Special storage battery for wireless train
Line 103 B	Line 102 (RrLpCgK, ON) Line 103 (RrLpCgK, OFF)	DC 100(1±10%)V	Each vehicle	Radio, emergency light
			T1-1,M1-2, M2-3,M3-4, M5-6,M6-7, T2-8	Sewage disposal unit
			M4-5	Automatic broadcast
			T1-1,T2-8	Sign light, lifting device, wiper device
Line 115	Line 103 (BatK2 ON)	DC 100(1±10%)V	Each car	Air conditioning control, automatic door device, guest room lighting, guest room (air conditioning), electric blower

1) Line 102 system

Line 102 system is powered directly from the battery, which is usually pressurized. It is connected with Line 103 and BatK1 ON, and the battery is floating charged from the auxiliary rectifier ARf. When the battery voltage drops abnormally, it is detected by the voltage detection circuit and the BatN2 becomes OFF to prevent the overdischarge of the battery. Using [T1-1, M1-2], [M2-3, M3-4], [M4-5, M5-6], [M6-7, T2-8] as units, there is no marshalling throughout.

2) Line 103 system

Line 103 runs through the entire marshalling. When the EMU is initially powered on, the pantograph is not raised, and the APU is not started and the DC 100 V voltage is output, the battery power supply contactor BatK1 connects Line 102 with Line 103, and Line 103 is provided by the battery with the DC 90 V battery voltage through Line 102. After raising the pantograph, closing the VCB and starting the APU, the auxiliary rectifier (ARf) provides 100 V DC voltage to Line 103 through the contactor ArfK.

3) Line 103B system

Normally, the power supply is from Line 103, and the emergency light switching contactor RrLpCgK is normally not excited, and the power supply is from 103 to 103B through its normally closed contact. When the OCS is out of power, the emergency light is switched and connected, and the power supply is from Line 103 through the normally open contact of RrLpCgK. On a per-car basis, there is no marshalling through.

4) Line 115 system

After the battery charging circuit is established, through ArfK, Line 103 is pressurized; Line 115 is then pressurized via BatK2. Line 115 is the same as Line 102 without marshalling through. It goes through the battery.

Task 3 Other Control Circuits of Auxiliary Power Supply

【Task Description】

This task describes the DC power system, the power expansion control, the BKK switch on control, and the APU device control.

【Background Knowledge】

3.1 DC power supply system

3.1.1 Battery contactor (BatK1, BatK2)

Brake setter BV(Run-Fast) is put in to pressurize 105 line of control BatK1. Then the brake setter is put in and pressurizes the relay (BVR1). Since the contact of BVR1 is closed, Line 102 pressurizes the contactor (BatK1) coil used in the storage battery. An auxiliary contact of VCB is connected in parallel with the contact of BVR1. If the VCB is put in, the BatK1 coil will continue to pressurize even if the brake setting handle is removed.

Due to the closure of the BatK1 contact, the battery Bat is connected to Line 103, and the battery is floating charged by the auxiliary rectifier ARf connected to Line 103.

A normally closed contact of auxiliary contactor BatN2 for storage equipment is inserted between the battery and Line 102. Another parallel with the battery, connected with the battery voltage monitoring voltmeter V1 and voltage detection circuit. When the battery voltage is lower than the specified value, the voltage detector will close the internal contact and pressurize the BatVDR coil relay of the auxiliary contactor for the battery.By closing the BatVDR contact, the BatN2 coil of the auxiliary contactor for the battery will be pressurized. The BatN2 contact will be disconnected and the battery Bat will be separated to prevent overdischarge. After establishing the output of the auxiliary rectifier, the 114 line is pressurized, and the BatK2R coil of the battery contactor is pressurized. Due to the closing of the BatK2R contact, pressure is applied to the BatK2 coil from Line 102, and the closing of the BatK2 contact enables the connection of Lines 103 and 115.

3.1.2 Emergency light switching circuit

Press the emergency light switch RrLpCgS, issue the emergency light input command, Line 170 is pressurized, and RrLpCgK coil of emergency light switching contactor is pressurized. After the RrLpCgK is put in, the power supply of the load connected to Line 103B is switched from Line 102 to Line 103.

3.1.3 Auxiliary power supply device

After the voltage is established (101-line pressurization), relay ARfKR for DC power contactor of auxiliary rectifier rectifier device and ARfK for DC power contactor of auxiliary rectifier rectifier device will operate and pressurize Line 103 DC100 V ±10%. Moreover, the normally open contact of ARfKR pressurizes Line 114 of BatK2 control instruction via the normally closed contact of parked relay MLpR1.

3.2 Three power supply extension power supply control

3.2.1 Outline

M1-2, M5-6 car traction transformer auxiliary winding power supply AC 400 V, 50 Hz through the AC circuit with contact 1(ACK1),connect Lines 704 and 754. The contactor 2(ACK2) for the AC circuit set on the M3-4 is kept open continuously in order to prevent the chaotic contact of the power supply from the M1-2 and M5-6 systems. When the traction transformer of one party is stopped, input three power induction commands through the monitor display, and run Lines 704 and 754 through the marshalling. The power supply can be supplied through the other party's transformer windings for three times. The auxiliary winding power supply AC400 V and 50 Hz of the M3-4 car traction transformer is connected to Lines 704Z and 754Z through the AC circuit with contactor 1(ACK1). Only supply power to the APU3 of Car 5.

3.2.2 Auxiliary winding power supply induction disconnect instruction

The auxiliary winding power supply induction disconnection command is transmitted from the monitor to the terminal device, through which the auxiliary winding extended power supply reset instruction relay (MTCOR-R) of Car M2 is excited. After MTCOR-R is excited, the contactor input relay (ACK2R) of the AC circuit is demagnetized, so ACK2 is demagnetized, and the auxiliary winding power supply induction circuit is disconnected. As the auxiliary winding power supply induction circuit is disconnected, the AC circuit contactor input relay 1(ACK1R)is excited , so ACK1 is input.However, when the external power supply is used, the normally closed contact of EXR2 is in the open state, so ACK1 cannot be put in. Induction power disconnect instruction (Monitor display)→MTCOR-R excitation→ACK2R demagnetization→ACK2 open (auxiliary power induction release)→ACK1R excitation→ACK1 input

3.2.3 Induction instruction of auxiliary winding power supply

The auxiliary winding power supply induction instruction is transmitted from the monitor to the terminal device, which will excite the auxiliary winding extended power supply command relay (MTCOR) of Car M2. After the action information of the MTCOR and ACK1, the external power relay (EXR) and VCB is input to the terminal device, according to the logic structure, ACK2R of Car 4 is excited , and ACK2 is input.

Induction power command (monitor display) → MTCOR excitation → ACK1R demagnetization→ACK1 disconnect →ACK2R excitation →ACK2 input→auxiliary power induction complete.

3.3 BKK switch on control

3.3.1 Outline

It is set in the auxiliary power supply device (APU) of the two head cars. When one of them fails, the BKK of Car M3-4 is put into use, thus the circuit of Lines 771, 781 and 791 is changed from the normal unit to the abnormal unit. When the auxiliary power supply device (APU3) of Car M4-5 fails, the BKK2 input in the APU3 is put into use, and the APU of Car T2-8 implements extended power supply to APU3.

3.3.2 BKK input instruction

After either of the APUs of the two head cars outputs the BKK input signal, MGFR1 or MGFR2 is demagnetized, and the normally closed contact of MGFR1 or MGFR2 is closed. In this state, after the BKK input instruction is transmitted to the terminal device, the terminal device excites the BKK input relay (BKKR) of the M3-4 vehicle. The normally open contact of BKKR is closed and BKK is put in. When the auxiliary power supply device (APU3) of Car M4-5 fails, BKK2 input signal is output, BKK2AR loses power, and the normally closed contact of BKK2AR is closed. In this state, after the input instruction of BKK2 is transmitted to the terminal device, the terminal device generates electricity to the BKK2R input relay (BKK2RR) of Car M4-5, and then the BKK2R is generated electricity. At this time, if the APU of the two head cars are working normally, the normally open contacts of MGFR3 and MGFR4 are in closed state, so that BKK2 is put in.

3.4 APU device control

3.4.1 Outline

The basic unit of the auxiliary power supply unit (APU) is composed of the inverter box and the auxiliary rectifier box. The device is installed under the body of T1-1 and T2-8. APU is the three-phase AC output that provides power to traction converter ventilator, traction motor ventilator, traction transformer ventilator, compressor, etc., and APU is also the single-phase DC output that provides power to auxiliary circuit, monitoring device, braking device, closing device, traction converter control, etc. APU is also a single-phase AC output power supply unit that provides power to air conditioning controls, displays, water pump units, auxiliary braking, etc.

3.4.2 Inverter box

The inverter is composed of the following parts: the converter part converts the single-phase AC power provided by the auxiliary (3rd) winding of the traction converter into intermediate DC power, the converter forms the three-phase AC power after waveform shaping of the converted intermediate DC power, and the DC smoothing circuit (filter capacitor) part absorbs the voltage ripple of the intermediate DC power to obtain constant voltage. In addition, the transformer (TR1) is placed on the input side of the converter in order to insulate the auxiliary (3rd) side of the traction converter from the inverter part. In addition, an auxiliary transformer (ATR) is set up in the inverter box. The single-phase AC power provided by the auxiliary (3 times) windings of the traction converter is step-down to AC 100 V in the ATR and provided to each car through Line 251.

3.3.3 Auxiliary rectifier box

The auxiliary rectifier box is composed of a frequency converter that converts three-phase AC power supplied by the inverter box into single-phase DC power and a voltage ripple that absorbs the converted DC power. It is composed of an auxiliary rectifier device formed by a DC smoothing circuit and a transformer that provides single-phase AC power after step-down. The auxiliary rectifier provides DC100 V to each vehicle through Line 103, and TR3 and TR4 provide single-phase AC100 V and AC220 V to each car through Line 202 and Line 302 respectively.

Task 4 Open and Close Control

【Task Description】

This task mainly analyzes three kinds of door circuit: the side door circuit, the inner door circuit and the disabled toilet automatic door circuit. The students can analyze the working process of the circuit.

【Background Knowledge】

4.1 Side door circuit

4.1.1 The close action

According to the closing instruction of the attendant switch, the 142Z line (one side) or 143Z line (two sides) is pressurized through Line 103, thus the closing instruction relay (DVCR1: one side, DVCR2: two sides) for the closing solenoid valve is excited. After the DVCR is excited, the relays for the closing solenoid valve (DVR11, 12, 13: one side, DVR21, 22, 23: two sides) are not excited. Thus, the contacts of DVR11, 31(one side) or DVR21, 41 are opened, the closing solenoid valve DV11, 31(one side) or DV21, 41(two sides) becomes unexcited, and the door is closed. In the closed state (DIRR excitation), when the speed reaches more than 30 km/h, press the solenoid valve DV12, 32(one side) or DV22, 42(two sides) to be excited, press the cylinder to press the door to keep the air tight.

4.1.2 The open action

Line 142 (one side) or 143 (two sides) is pressurized according to the closing command of the attendant switch, thus the open command relay for the closing solenoid valve (DVOR1: one side, DVOR2: two sides) is excited. After the DVOR is excited, the relays for the closing solenoid valve (DVR11, 12, 13: one side, DVR2122, 23: two sides) are excited. The close door pressing detection relay (DPSR1, 3: one side, DPSR2, 4: one side) becomes unexcited. When the speed is below 30 km/h (30DLR excitation), the pressing solenoid valve becomes unexcited, the oil pressure is released, and the cylinder is relaxed by the spring installed inside. As the oil pressure of the pressing device decreases, the contacts of the pressure switch PS1, 3 (one side) or PS3, 4 (two sides) are connected, and the closing solenoid valve changes to ON, completing the opening action. In addition, the speed 5 km/h is the condition of safe closing, and the speed 30 km/h is the condition of pressing action.

4.1.3 Side lights

According to the door closing switch (DS1, 3: one side, DS2, 4: two sides), the switching state of the door is detected. Since the contact of the door closing switch is off (closed state), the closing connecting auxiliary relay (DIRR11, 12, 31, 32: one side, DIRR21, 22, 41, 42: two sides) is excited. After the closing and connecting auxiliary relay is excited, the DIRR contact, which is the condition of the side light, turns on and the side light turns off.

4.1.4 Get-on-and-off voice control device

With the action of the closing solenoid valve relay, a sound is emitted from the speaker when the side door is opened and closed. Loudspeakers are arranged on one side and two sides respectively, and the switching side can be automatically identified.

4.1.5 Inner door circuit

From the side of the room, through the light induction switch on the side of the platform, the signal is input in automatic door switch device (ADCD), the inner end of the door conduct the open and close action.

4.2 Toilet automatic door circuit used by the disabled

The toilet automatic door device for the disabled is set in M3-4, and the toilet automatic door can be opened and closed by operating the toilet automatic door switch (LvDOS/ LvDCS).

4.3 Description of each condition of the connection diagram (side door circuit)

4.3.1 DVOR and DVCR conditions

At the DVS * switch "ON" position, if the following conditions are met, each relay will excite, as shown in Figure 5-4-1.

If the opening switch of DVS * is changed to ON, DVOR * excites.

If the closing switch of DVS * is turned ON, the DVCR * excites.

(* =1: one side, * =2: two sides)

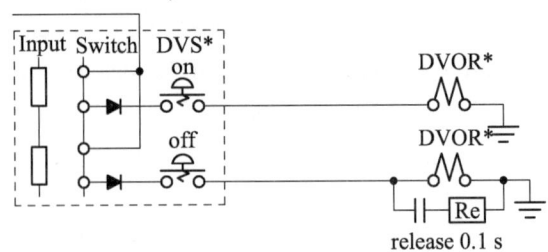

Figure 5-4-1　DVOR and DVCR conditions

4.3.2　DVR condition

If the following conditions are met, each relay of the DVR will excite, as shown in Figure 5-4-2.

(Condition)　①∩②∩③∩④

① DVCR * is non-excited: refer to 4.3.1 Dvor and DVCR Conditions;

② DVOR * excitation: refer to 4.3.1 Dvor and DVCR Conditions;

③ 5DLR is non-excited: the speed is less than 5 km/h;

④ DICOS * is OFF.

(* =1: one side, * =2: two sides)

※ After the excitation of DVR * 1, ①, ③ and ④ will be self-protected until any one of them opens

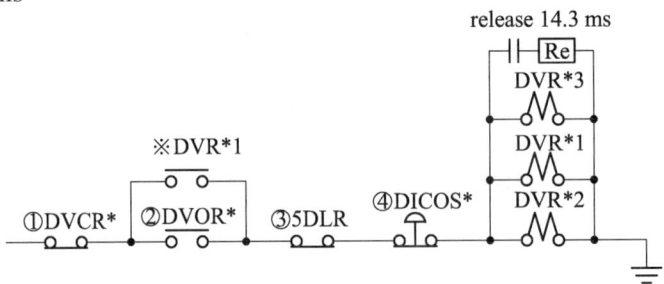

Figure 5-4-2　DVR condition

4.3.3　DPSR conditions

DPSR# will excite if the following conditions are met in the project of ① and ②, as shown in Figure 5-4-3.

(Condition)　①∩②

① DVR * 2 is unexcited: see (2);

② The normally closed contact of PS# is in the connected position.

(* =1: one side, * =2: two sides, # = 1-4: Door 1-4)

Figure 5-4-3　DPSR conditions

4.3.4　Dv#1 condition (solenoid valve for closing door)

if the following conditions are met, DV# 1 will act (excitation), as shown in Figure 5-4-4.

(Condition) ①∩②

① DVR * 1 excitation: refer to 4.3.2 DVR condition

② ② PS# normally open contact in the connected position (* =1: one side, * =2: two sides, # = 1-4: Door 1-4).

Figure 5-4-4　Dv # 1 condition

4.3.5　DV# 2 condition (Door compression solenoid)

if the following conditions are met, DV# 2 will act (excitation), as shown in Figure 5-4-5.

(Condition) ①∪(②∩③)

① DPSR# excitation: refer to 4.3.3 DPSR Condicions;

② 30DLR is not excited: the speed is above 30 km/h;

③ DIRR# 1 excitation: refer to 4.3.6 DiRR Condition (# = 1-4: Door 1-4).

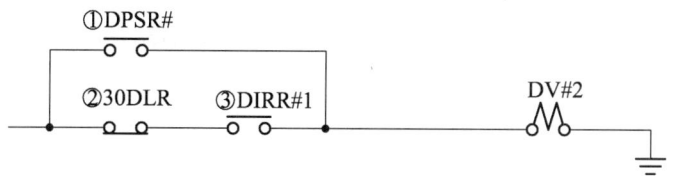

Figure 5-4-5　DV# 2 condition

4.3.6　DIRR condition

DIRR excites if the following conditions are met, as shown in Figure 5-4-6.

DS# is ON: Door # is closed (# =1 ~ 4: Door 1 ~ 4).

Figure 5-4-6　DIRR condition

4.3.7 Side light conditions

In the project (1) and (2) if the following conditions are met, the side light * will be on, as shown in Figure 5-4-7.

(Condition) ①∪②

① DIRR * 2 is unexcited: see 4.3.6 DIRR condition;

② DIRR&2 is unexcited: refer to 4.3.6 DIRR condition.

Figure 5-4-7   Side light conditions

4.3.8 33COR condition

If the following conditions are met, the 33X line will be pressurized and 33COR will be excited, as shown in Figure 5-4-8.

(Condition)

①DLS is ON.

Figure 5-4-8   33COR condition

4.3.9 30DLR conditions

If the following conditions are met, Line 33 is pressurized and 30DLR will excite, as shown in Figure 5-4-9.

(Condition) ①∩②

①30SR excitation: the speed is less than 30 km/h;

②33COR is unexcited: refer to 4.3.8 COR condition.

Figure 5-4-9   30DLR conditions

4.3.10 5DLR conditions

If the following conditions are met, Line 146 is pressurized and 5DLR excites.

5SR is not excited: the speed is above 5 km/h;

①5SR　　　　　　　　　　　　5DLR
　　　　　　　　　　　　　　　　146

Figure 5-4-10　5DLR conditions

4.3.11　DIR condition

If the following conditions are met, Line 144 is pressurized, DIR will excites, as shown in Figure 5-4-11.

※ Power supply will be run through from the side of the head car where the MCR is non-excited.

(Condition) {①∪(②∩③)}∩{④∪(⑤∩⑥)}∩⑦　(Middle car has no ⑦)

① DICOS2 is ON

② DIRR41 excitation: refer to 4.3.6 DIRR Condition;

③ DIRR21 excitation: refer to 4.3.6 DIRR Condition;

④ DICOS2 is ON;

⑤ DIRR31 excitation: refer to 4.3.6 DIRR Condition;

⑥ DIRR11 excitation: refer to 4.3.6 DIRR Condition.

⑦ MCR excitation: refer to the logic part of the operation instruction

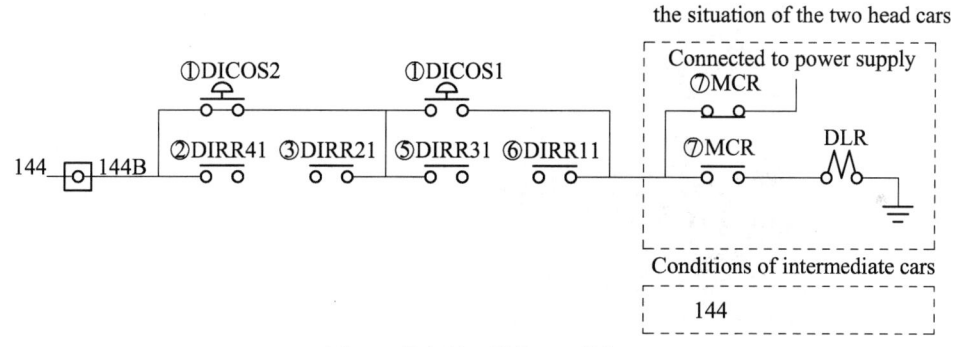

Figure 5-4-11　DIR condition

Task 5　Fault Case Analysis

【Task Description】

Through the study of this task, based on the accumulation of theoretical knowledge previously learned, the students can analyze the causes and handling process of fault cases, which lays a foundation for the maintenance of EMU and troubleshooting of circuit faults.

【Background Knowledge】

5.1 Auxiliary power supply device fault (135)

Auxiliary power supply device fault(135) and its handling process is shown in Table 5-5-1.

Table 5-5-1 Auxiliary power supply device fault (135) and its handling process

Phenomenon	The APU of this unit stops, and all auxiliary power supplies of this power unit lose power.
Car type	CRH380A、CRH380AL
Causes	① The load device is faulty, resulting in low output power of the APU. ② The load device leakage current fault causes the imbalance of APU three-phase output ③ The APU three-phase voltage AC400 V is grounded ④ The APU is faulty.
Train operation	Continues to run
Procedure	Handling process
1	When the "Fault occurrence information" prompt appears on the main menu page of the MON screen, accompanied by a sound alarm, the driver will press the "Fault details" button on the lower left to confirm the fault situation and notify the onboard mechanic.
2	The MON screen switches to "Auxiliary power supply is faulty(135)" fault information page. 2.1 Reset RS. 2.2 If the fault is rectified, the device runs normally. 2.3 If the fault is not eliminated, inform the onboard mechanic.
3	3.1 Immediately disconnect the [auxiliary power device control] circuit breaker in the corresponding distribution board of the damaged vehicle, and then put it into operation 15 seconds later. 3.2 Notify the driver after the processing is complete.

5.2 Auxiliary power device ventilator stop (143)

Auxiliary power device ventilator stop (143) and its handling process is shown in Table 5-5-2.

Table 5-5-2 Auxiliary power device ventilator stop (143) and its hand ling process

Phenomenon	This APU is down and all auxiliary power supplies to this power unit are lost.
Car type	CRH380A、CRH380AL
Causes	① The power cable is faulty or the ventilator inner is faulty. ② [Auxiliary power supply device] circuit breaker is faulty.
Train operation	Continues to run
Procedure	Handling process
1	When the "Fault occurrence information" prompt appears on the main menu page of the MON screen, accompanied by a sound alarm, touch the lower left [Fault details] button to confirm the fault situation and notify the onboard mechanic.
2	The MON screen switches to the "Auxiliary power device ventilator stop (143)" fault information page.
3	3.1 Immediately disconnect the [Auxiliary power device] circuit breaker in the corresponding distribution board of the damaged vehicle for 15 seconds and then put it into operation. 3.2 Notify the driver after the processing is complete.
4	4. Check whether the fault is rectified on the MON page. 4.1 If the fault is rectified, the device runs normally. 4.2 If the fault is not eliminated, turn on the BKK or BKK2 for extended power supply to maintain the running.

5.3 Auxiliary power supply device ACVN1 trip (146)

Auxiliary power supply device ACVN1 trip (146) and its handling process is shown in Table 5-5-3.

Table 5-5-3　Auxiliary power supply device ACVN1 trip (146) and its handling process

Phenomenon	The loss of AC 100 V regulated power supply circuit results in the failure of air conditioning, water supply control failure and radio out of operation.
Car type	CRH380A、CRH380AL
Causes	① The TR3 transformer is faulty. ② The load device is faulty. ③ [Auxiliary power device AC power supply 1] The circuit breaker is faulty.
Train operation	Continues to run
Procedure	Handling process
1	When the "Fault occurrence information" prompt appears on the main menu page of the MON screen, accompanied by a sound alarm, touch the lower left [Fault details] button to confirm the fault situation and notify the onboard mechanic.
2	The MON screen switches to the fault information page of "Auxiliary power device ACVN1 trip 146."
3	3.1 Immediately disconnect the circuit breaker of [auxiliary power device AC power supply 1] in the corresponding distribution board for 15 seconds and then put it into operation. 3.2 After the processing is complete, notify the driver for confirmation.

Continued

Phenomenon	The loss of AC 100 V regulated power supply circuit results in the failure of air conditioning, water supply control failure and radio out of operation.	
4		4. Check whether the fault is rectified on the MON screen. 4.1 If the fault is rectified, the device runs normally. 4.2 If the fault is not eliminated, maintain the operation and notify the onboard mechanic.
5		5.1 Disconnect the following electrical equipment circuit breakers for each vehicle in the control unit: air conditioning control, information display setting, water supply device, radio, auxiliary brake, etc. 5.2 Close the circuit breakers of [auxiliary power device AC power supply 1] first, and then close the circuit breakers of electrical equipment one by one. 5.3 During the process of closing the circuit breaker of the electrical equipment, if the fault of "Auxiliary power device ACVN1 trip" occurs again, disconnect the circuit breaker of the faulty equipment. 5.4 Repeat steps 5.2 and 5.3 until all electrical equipment circuit breakers are closed. 5.5 Remove the circuit breaker of the faulty device, close the circuit breaker of [the AC power supply of auxiliary power device 1], and maintain the operation.

5.4 Auxiliary power supply device ACVN2 trip (147)

Auxiliary power supply device ACVN2 trip (147) and its handling process is shown in Table 5-5-6.

Table 5-5-6 Auxiliary power supply device ACVN2 trip (147) and its handling process

Phenomenon	The AC 220 V power supply circuit is disconnected, causing the kitchen devices and power sockets to lose power.
Car type	CRH380A、CRH380AL
Causes	① The TR4 transformer is faulty. ② The load device is faulty. ③ The circuit breaker is faulty.
Train operation	Continues to run
Procedure	Handling process

145

Continued

Phenomenon	The AC 220 V power supply circuit is disconnected, causing the kitchen devices and power sockets to lose power.	
1		When the "Fault occurrence information" prompt appears on the main menu page of the MON screen, accompanied by a sound alarm, touch the lower left [Fault details] button to confirm the fault situation and notify the onboard mechanic.
2		The MON screen switches to the fault information page of "Auxiliary power device ACVN2 trip 147."
3		3.1 The onboard mechanic confirms the status of the circuit breaker. If it is in the off position, perform step 5; If it is in the closed position, immediately disconnect the circuit breaker of [Auxiliary power device AC power 2] in the distribution board of the damaged vehicle for 15 seconds before putting into operation. 3.2 After the processing is complete, notify the driver for confirmation.
4		4. Check whether the fault is rectified on the MON screen. 4.1 If the fault is rectified, the device runs normally. 4.2 If the fault is not eliminated, maintain the operation and notify the onboard mechanic.
5		5.1 Disconnect the following electrical equipment circuit breakers for each vehicle in the control unit: Car 05 (CRH380A) /Car 09 (CRH380AL) single-door display cabinet, disinfection cabinet, cooling fan, single-door freezer and microwave oven sockets; microwave oven socket of Cars 01, 03, 00 (CRH380AL), etc. 5.2 Close the circuit breakers of [auxiliary power device AC power supply 2] first, and then close the circuit breakers of electrical equipment one by one. 5.3 During the process of closing the circuit breaker of the electrical equipment, if the fault of "Auxiliary power device ACVN2 trip" occurs again, disconnect the circuit breaker of the faulty electrical equipment. 5.4 Repeat steps of 5.2 and 5.3 until all electrical equipment circuit breakers are closed. 5.5 Remove the circuit breaker of the faulty device, close the circuit breaker of the "AC power supply of auxiliary power device 2", and maintain the operation.

【Project Testing】

1. Briefly describe the composition of the auxiliary power supply system of the EMU.

2. Analyze the redundancy characteristics of traction transformer and auxiliary power supply of CRH2 EMU.

3. Analyze each power system of CRH_2/CRH380A EMU and the corresponding load.

4. Analyze the AC/DC power supply principle of CRH380A EMU.

5. Briefly describe the working principle of BKK extended power supply.

6. Try to describe how the CRH380A EMU five channel power supply is converted?

7. Try to describe the working principle of AC power supply circuit of CRH380B EMU.

项目一　动车组控制系统认识

【项目描述】

本项目是对动车组控制系统的整体认识。通过本项目的学习，学生应认识高速动车组电气原理图中的符号，掌握控制系统的基本组成和工作原理，为后续项目学习以及以后从事动车组运用、检修工作打下基础。

【项目任务】

（1）动车组电气原理图记号；
（2）动车组控制系统概述；

任务一　动车组电气原理图记号

【任务描述】

通过对本任务的学习，学生应认识动车组电气原理图中线号、电气设备的命名方法，从而能够识读、分析电气原理图，为从事动车组检修工作、排查电路故障打下基础。

【背景知识】

一、线　号

1. 线号的定义

按照下述方向定义线号（以"1234A1"为例）。
线号格式：

```
1 ── 2 ── 3 ── 4 ── A ── 1
│     │    │    │    │    │
│     │    │    │    │    └─ 附加数字
│     │    │    │    └────── 英文记号
│     │    │    └─────────── 个位
│     │    └──────────────── 十位
│     └───────────────────── 百位
└─────────────────────────── 千位
```

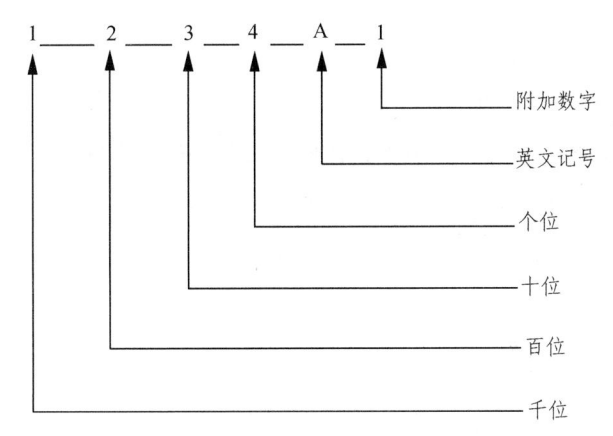

千位、百位：区别电源系统、信号种类。0（零）时可以省略。

十位、个位：用于区别回路。0（零）时可以省略。例，线号为9的时候：009→9。

附加英文字母：在相同信号系统中信号是相关联的，因为继电器或开关等原因在回路上被分离时采用英文字母。

附加数字：在相同信号系统中，需要在附加英文字母的基础上进行更详细的区分时，可再附加数字。

CRH380A型动车组部分线号分类见表1-1-1。

表1-1-1　CRH380A型动车组线号分类

线　号	分　类
1～99	控制指令回路（DC 100 V）
100～199	DC 100 V系统
200～249	AC 100 V系统（稳定输出）
250～299	AC 100 V系统系统（非稳定）
300～399	AC 220 V系统
400～499	辅助制动型、ATP信号、速度发电机
500～599	主变换回路
700～799	AC 400 V（单相）系统
771、781、791	AC 400 V（三相）系统
800～899	空调装置
900～906	主回路接地、主回路过电流检测
1100～1199	广播回路
1400～1499	ATP天线、无线电服务系统
1500～1599	MTr2次回路（主回路）
1600～1699	ATP装置
2500～2502	特高压回路（AC 25 kV系统）

2. 特殊线号

1）车辆信息控制装置的线号

关于车辆信息控制装置的输出输入线，可采用如下特殊线号：

M＋3位号码：车辆信息控制装置的输出输入线号；

MF＋3位号码：光缆的线号。

二、设备记号命名方法

记号以下述基本方法进行命名（以 COMCORR1 为例）。

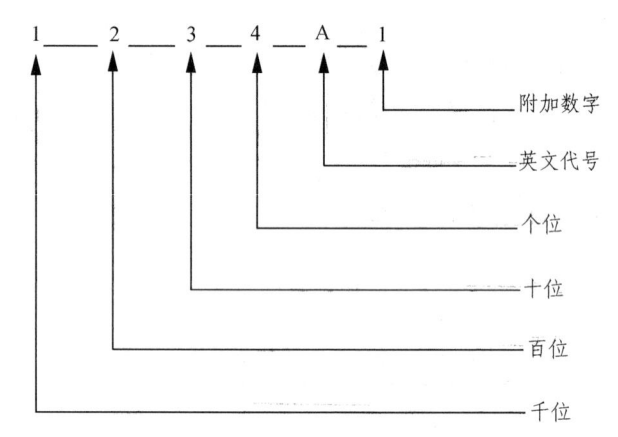

```
1___ 2___ 3___ 4___ A___ 1
                        ↑   ↑
                        │   └── 附加数字
                        └────── 英文代号
                    └────────── 个位
                └──────────── 十位
            └──────────── 百位
        └──────────── 千位
```

（1）名称：用英文的简称（CM = Compresser Motor），见表 1-1-2。

表 1-1-2 设备名称代号

记　号	机　器
AC	交流
AP	空气压力
APU	辅助电源装置
ATC	ATP 装置
B	制动挡
Bat	蓄电池
Bz	蜂鸣器
Cab	司机室
CI	主变换装置
CM	空气压缩机
D	侧拉门装置
EB	快速制动

续表

记号	机器
HMLp	前部标识灯
MC	主控制器
MLp	后部标识灯
MM	主电动机
MRr	气源
MT	主变压器
Pan	受电弓
PrLp	备用灯
SB	辅助制动开关
UB	紧急制动开关
VCB	真空断路开关

（2）功能：表示动作的功能（CO = Cut Off，R = Reserve）。不必要时可以省略，也可以重复。功能如表1-1-3所示。

表1-1-3 功能代号

记号	功能
C	关
O	开
CO	断开
R	辅助

（3）设备代号：表示有代号设备的种类（R = Relay）。

设备代号如表1-1-4所示。

表1-1-4 设备代号

记号	机器
R	继电器
TR	时限继电器
K	接触器
N	断路开关
S	开关
V	电磁阀
He	加热器
Th	温度检测器
Lp	指示灯
T（Tr）	变压器

（4）附加数字：相同的功能用于多个设备时，可用附加数字区别。

三、电路分析举例

以图 1-1-9 所示的头车的运转指令回路为例，图中标号对应电路的机器的表示如下：

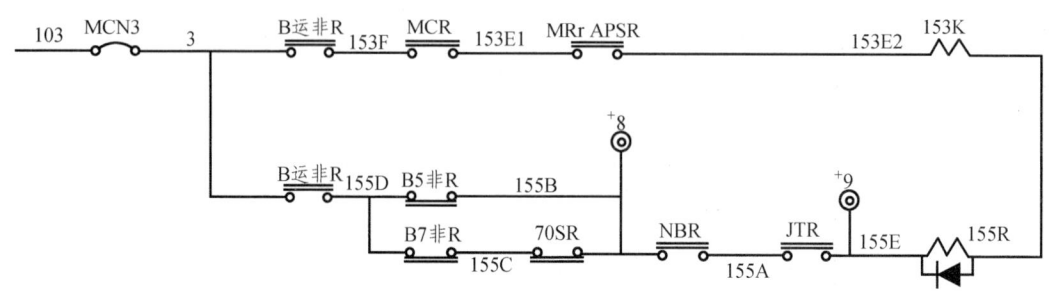

图 1-1-9 头车的运转指令回路

① 103 线——DC 100 V 电源；
② MCN3——第 3 个主控制器用（运转指令用）的断路开关；
③ B 运非 R（BOFR）——制动指令在运转~快速位置时被励磁化的继电器；
④ 153F、153E1、153E2——表示与 153 线有关联的线；
⑤ MCR——主控制器用继电器（操作侧时为励磁）；
⑥ MRrAPSR——总风缸空气压力开关用继电器（正常压力时为励磁）；
⑦ 153K——紧急制动用接触器（向紧急制动电磁阀供电用的接触器）；

因此下述条件均为紧急制动缓解的条件。（注意：除 153K 以外还有其他条件，即使该回路条件成立，紧急制动也不一定缓解。）

① 制动设定器为运转~快速位置；
② 本头车为主控操作；
③ 总风压力为正常值。

另外，因为线号为 153 系统，因此可得知是紧急制动部分的回路。

四、电气设备图形符号的说明

电气设备代号见表 1-1-5 所示。

表 1-1-5　电气设备代号

序 号	符 号	设备名称
1	153K	153 线接触器
2	155R	155 线继电器
3	156R	156 线继电器
4	160SAR1, 2	速度辅助继电器（160 km/h 以上失电）
5	30DLR	30 km/h 门锁继电器
6	30SR	30 km/h 速度继电器
7	33COR	门锁紧用速度条件开放继电器
8	5DLR	5 km/h 门锁继电器
9	5SR	5 km/h 速度继电器
10	A5SR	5 km/h 速度继电器辅助继电器
11	70SR	70 km/h 速度继电器
12	ACK1	交流电接触器 1
13	ACK1R	交流电接触器 1 继电器
14	ACK2	交流电接触器 2
15	ACK2R	交流电接触器 2 继电器
16	ACLN	滤清器 NFB
17	ACM	辅助压缩电机
18	ACMGV	辅助压缩电机控制器
19	ACMGVR1, 2	辅助压缩电机控制器继电器 1, 2
20	ACMHe	辅助压缩电机加热器
21	ACMK	辅助压缩电机接触器
22	ACMN	辅助压缩电机 NEB
23	ACMR1, 2	辅助压缩电机继电器 1, 2
24	ACMS	辅助压缩电机开关
25	ACOCR1, 2	交流电过继继电器 1, 2
26	ACOCRR1, 2	交流电过流预留继电器 1, 2
27	ACOSN	他车供电用断路器
28	ACVN1, 2	转换电源 NFB 1, 2
29	ACVR1, 2	交流定电压继电器
30	ADCD1, 2	自动门控设备 1, 2

续表

序 号	符 号	设备名称
31	ADCOS11~12、21~22	自动门控设备切断开关 11~12，21~22
32	ADN1，2	自动门控设备 NFB 1，2
33	AHeK	辅助加热器接触器
34	AHeKN	辅助加热器接触器 NFB
35	AHeS	辅助加热器开关
36	AHWN	自动洗手盆 NFB
37	AMLpR1~3	标志灯预留继电器 1~3
38	AmpN1，2	放大器 NFB 1，2
39	AOCN	交流电过流 NFB
40	APCR	空气管路关闭继电器
41	APCS	空气管路关闭开关
42	APCV	空气管路关闭阀
43	APOR	空气管路开启继电器
44	APOV	空气管路开启阀
45	APPS	空气管路压力开关
46	APU	辅助电源装置
47	APUCN	辅助电源装置控制 NFB
48	APUBMN	辅助电源装置风机电机 NFB
49	ARf	辅助整流器
50	ARfK	辅助整流器接触器
51	ARfKR	辅助整流器接触器继电器
52	ARfN2	辅助整流器 NFB 2
53	ARfRN	辅助整流器接触器 NFB
54	Arr	避雷器
55	ASCN	激活的悬挂控制 NFB
56	ATCBR	ATC 制动继电器
57	ATCKB1R	ATC 缓和制动（1N）继电器
58	ATCKB4R	ATC 缓和制动（4N）继电器
59	ATN	辅助变压器 NFB
60	ATPBTMN	ATP BTM 装置电源 NFB

续表

序 号	符 号	设备名称
61	ATPCOR	ATP 切断继电器
62	ATPDMIN	ATP DMI 装置电源 NFB
63	ATPDRUN	ATP DRU 装置电源 NFB
64	ATPFN	ATP 风扇电源 NFB
65	ATPN1	ATP 主电源 NFB 1
66	ATPPK	ATP 主电源接触器
67	ATPSTMN	ATP STM 装置电源 NFB
68	ATPVCN	ATP 装置电压控制器 NFB
69	ATr	辅助变压器
70	B 运非 R	制动控制手柄「运转-快速」定位继电器
71	B1 非 R	制动控制手柄「1N-快速」定位继电器
72	B2 非 R	制动控制手柄「2N-快速」定位继电器
73	B3 非 R	制动控制手柄「3N-快速」定位继电器
74	B4 非 R	制动控制手柄「4N-快速」定位继电器
75	B5 非 R	制动控制手柄「5N-快速」定位继电器
76	B6 非 R	制动控制手柄「6N-快速」定位继电器
77	B7 非 R	制动控制手柄「7N-快速」定位继电器
78	B 非 R	制动控制手柄「快速（运转-7N）」定位继电器
79	B1～3K	制动控制手柄「1N-3N」定位接触器
80	B4～5K	制动控制手柄「4N-5N」定位接触器
81	B6～7K	制动控制手柄「6N-7N」定位接触器
82	B 非 K	制动控制手柄「非常」定位接触器
83	Bat	蓄电池
84	BatK1,2	蓄电池接触器 1,2
85	BatK2R	蓄电池接触器 2 继电器
86	BatKCN	蓄电池接触器控制 NFB
87	BatKN	蓄电池接触器 NFB
88	BatN1,2	蓄电池 NFB 1,2
89	BatVDN	蓄电池电压检测 NFB
90	BCCN	制动控制单元控制 NFB

续表

序　号	符　号	设备名称
91	BCU	制动控制单元
92	BCUHe	制动控制单元加热器
93	BCUN	制动控制单元NFB
94	BKK	辅助电源扩展供电用接触器
95	BKKN	辅助电源扩展供电用接触器断路器
96	BKKONR	BKK投入继电器
97	BKKR	BKK控制继电器
98	BKKR-R	BKK复位继电器
99	BMK	风机电机接触器
100	BNPFsR	连挂解联电气控制盘内部继电器
101	BNR	连挂解联电气控制盘内部继电器
102	BNS	连挂解联电气控制盘内部继电器
103	BNUBAR	连挂解联电气控制盘内部继电器
104	BNUBR	连挂解联电气控制盘内部继电器
105	BR1	制动继电器1
106	BTRCN	制动命令转换控制单元NFB
107	BV	制动阀
108	BVN	制动阀NFB
109	BVR	制动阀继电器
110	BVR1，2	制动阀继电器1，2
111	BVTR	制动阀限时继电器
112	BzS	蜂鸣器开关
113	CabGS	司机室接地开关
114	CabHe1，2	司机室加热器1，2
115	CabHeN1，2	司机室加热器NFB 1，2
116	CabHeS1，2	司机室加热器开关1，2
117	CabLp	司机室照明灯
118	CabLpN	司机室照明灯NFB
119	CabLpS	司机室照明灯开关
120	CabRLpConR	司机室室内照明灯接触器插座

续表

序号	符号	设备名称
121	CabRrLp	司机室预留灯
122	CabRrLpN1，2	司机室预留灯 NFB
123	CabTeLp	中间司机室测试灯
124	CabTeS	中间司机室测试开关
125	CabUCN	司机室空调主断路器
126	CBCDN	司机室空调压缩机断路器
127	CBCN	司机室空调控制断路器
128	CBMN	司机室空调送风机断路器
129	CBN	司机室空调电机断路器
130	CDR1，2	电流检测继电器1，2
131	CI	变流器逆变器
132	CIBM1～3	变流器逆变器风机电机1～3
133	CIBMN1～3	变流器逆变器风机电机 NFB 1～3
134	CIBMNR	变流器逆变器风机电机 NFB 继电器
135	CICN1，2	变流器逆变器控制 NFB 1，2
136	CIFR1，2	变流器逆变器故障继电器1，2
137	CIGRR1，2	变流器逆变器接地继电器1，2
138	CM	压缩机电机
139	CMCN	压缩机电机控制 NFB
140	CMCOR	压缩机电机切断继电器
141	CMCOR-R	压缩机电机切断继电器-重新设置
142	CMCORR1，2	压缩机电机切断重复继电器1，2
143	CMGV	压缩机电机控制器
144	CMK	压缩机电机接触器
145	CMN	压缩机电机 NFB
146	CMSN	压缩机电机同步 NFB
147	CMV	压缩机电机阀
148	CMVTR	压缩机电机阀限时继电器
149	CORR	切断重复继电器
150	COSN	切断开关 NFB

续表

序号	符号	设备名称
151	COSN1	切断开关 NFB 1
152	CrFM	乘务员室风扇电机
153	CrFMN	乘务员室风扇电机 NFB
154	CrFMS	乘务员室风扇电机开关
155	CSR	恒速继电器
156	CT1	电流变压器 1
157	CT3	电流变压器 3
158	C t t CN	接触器控制 NFB
159	CUHCS	车钩手柄关闭开关
160	CUHOS	车钩手柄开启开关
161	CVT	恒压变压器
162	DCR	直流电源继电器
163	DICOS1, 2	门互锁切断开关 1, 2
164	DIR	门互锁继电器
165	DIRR11, 12	门互锁预留继电器 11, 12
166	DIRR21, 22	门互锁预留继电器 21, 22
167	DIRR31, 32	门互锁预留继电器 31, 32
168	DIRR41, 42	门互锁预留继电器 41, 42
169	DIRS	门互锁继电器开关
170	DLS	门锁开关
171	DMS1～4	门微型开关 1～4
172	DN	门 NFB
173	DOCHN	门鸣叫 NFB
174	DPSR 1～4	门按钮传感继电器 1～4
175	DS1～4	门开关 1～4
176	DSN	门开关 NFB
177	DV11, 12, 21, 22	门磁阀 11, 12, 21, 22
178	DV31, 32, 41, 42	门磁阀 31, 32, 41, 42
179	DVCN1, 2	门上阀门控制 NFB 1, 2
180	DVCR1, 2	门磁阀关闭继电器 1, 2

续表

序 号	符 号	设备名称
181	DVN1，2	门阀 NFB 1，2
182	DVOR1，2	门磁阀开启继电器1，2
183	DVR 11，12，13，21，22，23	门磁阀继电器11，12，13，21，22，23
184	DVS1，2	门磁阀开关1，2
185	EBR	ATP 紧急制动继电器
186	EBz	紧急蜂鸣器
187	EBzCOS	紧急蜂鸣器切断开关
188	EBzR	紧急蜂鸣器继电器
189	EBzRR	紧急蜂鸣器重启继电器
190	EBzRS	紧急蜂鸣器重启开关
191	EBzS1，2	紧急蜂鸣器开关1，2
192	EC g ConR	电子转换器接触继电器
193	EC g ConV	电子转换器接触阀
194	ECgRIsR	电子转换器接触缓解继电器
195	ECgRIsV	电子转换器接触缓解阀
196	EGCN	紧急接地开关控制 NFB
197	EGCS1，2	紧急接地开关关闭转换器1，2
198	EGCV	紧急接地开关关闭阀
199	EGCVN	紧急接地开关关闭阀 NFB
200	EGOCK	EGS 开启和关闭阀
201	EGOS1，2	紧急接地开关开启开关1，2
202	EGOV	紧急接地开关开启阀
203	EGOVN	紧急接地开关开启阀 NFB
204	EGS	紧急接地开关
205	EGSHe	紧急接地开关加热器
206	EGSR	紧急接地开关继电器
207	EL1，2	电子照明1，2
208	ELN	电子照明 NFB
209	EVBat	紧急通风蓄电池
210	EXConR	外部电源连接器插座

续表

序号	符号	设备名称
211	EXR1,2	外部电源继电器1,2
212	ExTh	外部热量
213	FDRR	过分相检测重复继电器
214	FiCN1~4	卫生间控制NFB
215	FiFR1~3	厕所故障继电器
216	FiHeN1	污物箱加热NFB
217	FiLvN	污物箱显示控制单元NFB
218	FiOS1,2	光电传感器
219	FiPB	强制冲洗开关
220	FiT80R	污物箱80%继电器
221	FiT100R	污物箱100%继电器
222	FrBz	防火蜂鸣器
223	FrBzR	防火蜂鸣器继电器
224	FrBzRS	防火蜂鸣器重启开关
225	FrBzS1,2	防火蜂鸣器开关1,2
226	FrLP	防火灯
227	FVSN	瞬时阀传感器NFB
228	GB11~14	接地刷11~14
229	GB21~24	接地刷21~24
230	GHe	玻璃加热器
231	GHeN	玻璃加热器FB
232	GHeTh	玻璃加热器热量
233	GR3	接地继电器3
234	GRR3-1	接地预留继电器3
235	GRR3-2	接地预留继电器3
236	GRT	接地继电器变压器
237	GS	接地开关
238	HELPS	救助开关
239	HGS	连挂开始
240	HLp1~4	头灯1~4

续表

序 号	符 号	设备名称
241	HLp1～4 HR	头灯 1～4 远光灯继电器
242	HLp1～4LR	头灯 1～4 近光灯继电器
243	HMLpDS	头部标志灯变光开关
244	HMLpN	头部标志灯 NFB
245	HMLpS	头部标志灯开关
246	HmRS	小时计重启开关
247	Innet1～2N	Internet 运行 NFB
248	IVK1	逆变器接触器 1
259	JAHeK	连接辅助加热器接触器
250	JAHeR	连接辅助加热器继电器
251	JaN1，2，3	机套 NFB 1，2，3
252	JBVR	连接蓄电池继电器
253	JCMR	连接压缩机电机继电器
254	JRrLpK	连接预留灯接触器
255	JRrLpR	连接预留灯继电器
256	JTR	紧急制动继电器
257	KBA1R	缓解制动「1N」辅助继电器
258	KBA4R	缓解制动「4N」辅助继电器
259	KBA6R	缓解制动「6N」辅助继电器
260	KBMg	主控制箱磁性线圈
261	KBMgN	主控制箱磁性线圈 NFB
262	KBMgS	主控制箱磁性线圈开关
263	KHCR	关闭头罩继电器
264	KHCS	头罩关
265	KHCV	打开头罩指令电磁阀
266	KHOR	打开头罩继电器
267	KHOS	头罩开
268	KHOV	打开头罩指令电磁阀
269	KRR	接触器预留继电器
270	LKJCOR	LKJ 切断继电器

续表

序 号	符 号	设备名称
271	LKJN	LKJ NFB
272	LKJPK	LKJ 电源接触器
273	LvADCD	盥洗室自动门控设备
274	LvADN	盥洗室自动门 NFB
275	LvDCS1，2	盥洗室自动门关闭开关 1，2
276	LvDOS1，2	盥洗室自动门开启开关 1，2
277	LVHe1~4	调整加热器等级 1~4
278	LvLp	盥洗室灯
279	LvLpN	盥洗室灯 NFB
280	LvLpS1，2	盥洗室灯开关 1，2
281	MaRConR1	设备室接触器插座 1
282	MaRLp1，2	设备室内照明 1，2
283	MaRLpN1，2	设备室室内照明 NFB 1，2
284	MC	主控制器
285	MCN1~3	主控制器 NFB 1~3
286	MCPR	主控制器接通继电器
287	MCR	主控制器继电器
288	MCRR	主控制器预留继电器
289	MC 切 R	主控制器「切」定位继电器
290	MDLN	门保安断路器
291	MDLR	门保安继电器
292	MGFR1，2	APU 故障中间继电器
293	MLpN	标志灯 NFB
294	MLpR1，2	标志灯继电器 1，2
295	MLpS	标志灯开关
296	MMBM1，2	主电机风机电机 1，2
297	MMBMN1，2	主电机风机电机 NFB 1，2
298	MMCOR	主电机切断继电器
299	MMCOR-R	主电机切断继电器 - 重新设置
300	MONN1，2	监控器设备 NFB 1，2

续表

序号	符号	设备名称
301	MOTN1, 2	监控器终端设备 NFB 1, 2
302	MRHPS	主风缸高压开关
303	MRLPS	主风缸低压开关
304	MRPSR	主风缸空压开关选择继电器
305	MRrAPSR	主风缸空压开关继电器
306	MSP1, 2	扬声器监控器 1, 2
307	MTBM	主变压器风机电机
308	MTBMN	主变压器风机电机 NFB
309	MTCOR	主变压器切断继电器
310	MTCOR-R	主变压器切断继电器-重新设置
311	MTCORR	主变压器切断预留继电器
312	MTOFR	主变压器油流量继电器
313	MTOFRR	主变压器油流量预留继电器
314	MTOPM	主变压器油泵电机
315	MTOPMN	主变压器油泵电机 NFB
316	MTr	主变压器
317	MTThR	主变压器热动继电器
318	MTThRR	主变压器热动预留继电器
319	MXR	混合继电器
320	MXRN1, 2	混合继电器 NFB 1, 2
321	NBR	正常制动继电器
322	NBTR	正常制动限时继电器
323	NRLpR	一定数量照明继电器
324	NVR	无电压继电器
325	NVR1N	无电压继电器 1 NFB
326	NVR1 VD	无电压继电器 1 电压检测仪
327	OCTN	过流变压器 NFB
328	PaConR1～4N	PC 接触器 NFB
329	PaIvN	PC 逆变器 NFB
330	Pan	受电弓

续表

序 号	符 号	设备名称
331	PanCGS	受电弓转换开关
332	PanCOR	受电弓切断继电器
333	PanCOR-R	受电弓切断继电器-重新设置
334	PanDAR	受电弓降弓命令辅助继电器
335	PanDRN	受电弓降弓命令继电器 NFB
336	PanDS	受电弓降弓开关
337	PanDWR	受电弓降弓继电器
338	PanIR	受电弓互锁继电器
339	PanN	受电弓 NFB
340	PanUCK	受电弓升弓保持阀
341	PanUR	受电弓升弓继电器
342	PanUS	受电弓升弓开关
343	PanUV	受电弓升弓阀
344	PanUVN	受电弓升弓阀 NFB
345	PCON	压力切断 NFB
346	PCOR	ATP 供电切断继电器
347	PCOV	压力切断阀
348	PDN1	目的地显示器断路器
349	PG1～4	脉冲发生器 1～4
350	PLpCOS1，2	主照明切断开关 1，2
351	PLpN1，2	主照明 NFB 1，2
352	PR	供电继电器
353	PS1～4	压力开关 1～4
354	RCAR	牵引命令辅助继电器
355	RConN	室内接触器 NFB
356	RConR1，2	室内接触器插座 1，2
357	RCS	锁闭气缸关闭检测开关
358	RLp	室内照明
359	RLpCAR	室内照明控制辅助继电器
360	RLpConR	室内照明接触器插座

续表

序号	符号	设备名称
361	RLpK	室内照明接触器
362	RLpN1~3	室内照明 NFB 1~3
363	ROR	头罩锁开、锁指令继电器
364	ROS	头罩锁开
365	ROV	头罩锁开、锁指令电磁阀
366	RrLp	预留灯
367	RrLpCgK	预留灯转换接触器
368	RrLpCgN	预留灯转换 NFB
369	RrLpCgN2	预留灯转换 NFB 2
370	RrLpCgR	预留灯转换继电器
371	RrLpCgS	预留灯转换开关
372	RrLpN	预留灯 NFB
373	RS	重启开关
374	RSR1	重启开关继电器
375	SBN1,2	子制动 NFB 1,2
376	SBNR	子制动继电器
377	SBN1R	子制动继电器 1
378	SBN1 补接	子制动 NFB 1 补接
379	SCNCRN1,2	部分控制 MCR NFB 1,2
380	SCN1~3	部分控制 NFB 1~3
381	SCK	部分控制接触器
382	SCR	部分控制继电器
383	SCTR1,2	部分控制限时继电器 1,2
384	SGZR1,2	部分故障继电器 1,2
385	SMCR1,2	部分 MCR1,2
386	SVCBCR	部分 VCB 关闭继电器
387	SVCBOR	部分 VCB 开启继电器
388	SConN1~4	运行接触器 NFB 1~5
389	SePR	传感器电源继电器
390	SePN	传感器电源 NFB

续表

序 号	符 号	设备名称
391	SG	速度发生器
392	SIV	静态逆变器
393	SKG1~4	防滑发生器1~4
394	SKN	防滑NFB
395	SKVR	防滑阀继电器
396	SKVRR	防滑阀预留继电器
397	SLR	防滑检测继电器
398	SLRR	防滑检测预留继电器
399	SP	扬声器
400	SPCOS	扬声器切断开关
401	SqS	顺序开关
402	SRLpN1	座位指定显示器断路器
403	SRLpN2	
404	SS1~4	速度传感器1~4
405	SVCBCR	部分真空电路断路器关闭继电器
406	SVCBOR	部分真空电路断路器开启继电器
407	SVCN	紧急制动切换控制断路器
408	TAX2N	TAX2 NFB
409	TAX2PK	TAX2电源接触器
410	TeLp	测试灯
412	TInFN	列车信息设备NFB
413	ToBz	卫生间蜂鸣器
414	ToBzR	卫生间蜂鸣器继电器
415	ToBzS1~3	卫生间蜂鸣器开关1~3
416	ToConN	卫生间连接器插座NFB
417	ToConR1,2	卫生间连接器插座1,2
418	ToFM1,2	卫生间风扇电机1,2
419	ToFMN1,2	卫生间风扇电机NFB 1,2
420	TSC1N	TSC1 NFB
421	TSC1PK	TSC1电源接触器

续表

序号	符号	设备名称
422	TSHeN	卫生间座位加热器 NFB
423	TThRN	车辆（轮胎）热动继电器 NFB
424	TThRR	车辆（轮胎）热动预留继电器
425	TWBat	列车无线广播蓄电池
426	TWBatN	列车无线广播蓄电池 NFB
427	TWCN	列车无线广播充电器控制 NFB
428	TWEmCgK	列车无线广播紧急转换接触器
429	TWEmCgS	列车无线广播紧急充电器开关
430	TWN	列车无线广播装置控制 NFB
431	TyClV	轮胎清洁阀
432	TyClVN	轮胎清洁阀 NFB
433	UBR	紧急制动继电器
434	UBRS	紧急制动重启开关
435	UBRSR	紧急制动重启开关继电器
436	UBRSWR	紧急制动重启开关继电器
437	UBS1，2	紧急制动开关 1，2
438	UBTR1，2	紧急制动限时继电器 1，2
439	UN1	配电盘内空调单元 1 电源（AC 400 V）NFB
440	UN2	配电盘内空调单元 2 电源 NFB
441	UN12	空调单元 1 控制电源（AC 100 V）NFB
442	UN22	空调单元 2 控制电源（AC 100 V）NFB
443	UCN3	空调显示设定器电源 NFB
444	UCN11	空调装置 1 内部接触器盘电源
445	UCN21	空调装置 2 内部接触器盘电源
446	UR0	设备命令继电器
447	UVN	紧急磁阀 NFB
448	UVR	紧急磁阀继电器
449	UVR1，2，3	紧急磁阀继电器 1，2，3
450	UVRS	紧急磁阀继电器短路开关
451	V1	电压计 1

续表

序号	符号	设备名称
452	V3	电压计 3
453	V4	电压计 4
454	VCB	真空断路器
455	VCBARN	真空电路断路器辅助继电器 NFB
456	VCBA1R	真空电路断路器辅助继电器
457	VCBCOR	真空电路断路器切断继电器
458	VCBCOR-R	真空电路断路器切断继电器-重启
459	VCBCR1，2	真空电路断路器关闭继电器 1，2
460	VCBCS	真空电路断路器关闭开关
461	VCBHe	真空电路断路器加热器
462	VCBN	真空电路断路器 NFB
463	VCBOAR	真空电路断路器开启辅助继电器
464	VCBOR1，2	真空电路断路器开启继电器 1，2
465	VCBOS	真空电路断路器开启开关
466	VCBRR	真空电路断路器预留继电器
467	VCgS	电压计转换开关
468	VDTN	电压检测变压器 NFB
469	VeFM	通风风扇电机
470	VeFMCN1，2	通风风扇电机控制 NFB 1，2
471	VeFMN	通风风扇电机 NFB
472	VN1	电压计 NFB 1
473	VN3	电压计 NFB 3
474	VN4	电压计 NFB 4
475	WaPFS	水泵浮动开关
476	WaPHe	水泵加热器
477	WaPHm	水泵小时计
478	WaPMV1	水泵磁阀 1
479	WaPMV2	水泵磁阀 2
480	WaP	水泵
481	WaPN	水泵 NFB
482	WaPR	水泵控制继电器

续表

序 号	符 号	设备名称
483	WaPTh	水泵加热器恒温器
484	WhDR	鸣笛声下降继电器
485	WhDV	鸣笛声下降阀
486	WHeN1,2	水加热器 NFB 1,2
487	WLMN	水位计 NFB
488	WLMR	水位计继电器
489	WPN	雨刮器 NFB
490	WVCN	水泵加压留置断路器
491	24 V 电源 N	24 V 电源 N
492	前进 R	换向开关「前进」定位继电器
493	后进 R	换向开关「后进」定位继电器
494	牵引指令 R	牵引指令继电器
495	恒速 SW	恒速开关
496	恒速切 SW	恒速切开关
497	复位 SW	复位开关
498	启动试验 SW	启动试验开关
499	车上试验 SW	车上试验开关
500	耐雪 SW	耐雪开关

任务二　动车组控制系统概述

【任务描述】

本任务主要介绍动车组控制系统的构成、控制电路的概念及控制系统的工作原理。学习完本任务，学生应对动车组牵引、制动工况等知识有初步的了解。

【背景知识】

一、电力牵引控制技术特点

电力牵引控制系统是以牵引电动机为研究对象，由于牵引功率等级要求较高，因此一般牵引电机的电压等级和电流等级很大，无法直接进行控制，所以目前基本都采用电力电子变流装置来实现对牵引电机的控制。图 1-2-1 为一般电力牵引控制系统组成图。

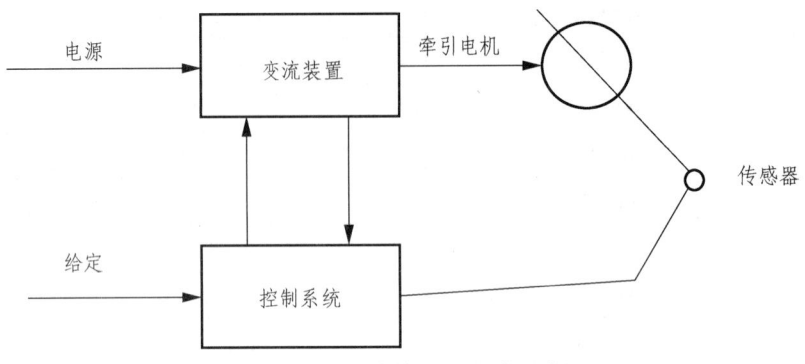

图 1-2-1　电力牵引控制系统组成图

将司机的给定量和检测到的被控量进行比较，形成偏差控制信号，经过控制系统去控制电力电子变流装置的输出信号，即控制牵引电机的输入信号，从而达到控制被控量的目的。为达到调速和提高牵引性能的目的，其中牵引电机的被控量主要是电机转速、电机电压、电机电流、电机功率及电机励磁电流等。

在电力牵引系统中，牵引电动机通过变流装置进行供电，变流装置实际上是整个系统的电能变换电路。电力牵引控制系统经历了 3 个阶段的发展历史。早期的电力牵引控制系统为继电器控制系统，主要借助继电器和接触器等开关电器实现机车的起动、停车及调速。随着电力电子技术的发展，出现了集成电路特别是的运算放大器组成的模拟控制系统。但是由模拟电路组成的调节器，其校正参数不易调节，一经确定就不易改变，所以模拟控制系统对不同类型的机车适用性较差，更换机车型号必须重新设计控制系统。近代电子技术趋于成熟，特别是微处理器的出现，计算机逐渐应用于机车控制系统。目前，随着高速铁路的发展，在高速动车组中，机车中微处理器越来越多，用来实现机车运行中牵引制动特性的控制、故障检测、保护、记录与显示等功能，分别完成不同层次的控制功能，构成列车控制网络。

二、动车组控制系统的基本原理

动车组控制电路将控制牵引变流器、牵引变压器、制动装置及辅助装置的控制电器、信号装置和控制电源连成一个电气控制系统，并接收和传递列车网络信息控制装置的指令和状态信息，实现对动车组的操纵和控制。

CRH380A 型动车组为 6M2T 编组，时速 300 km。每辆动车有 1 台牵引变流器和 4 台牵引电机，由一个计算机控制器进行控制。每辆车的制动装置由一个制动控制单元（BCU）进行控制，为了相互传递信息，完成协调统一的控制，构成一种基于列车信息网络的分布式控制系统。

来自司机室的牵引指令、制动指令及其他指令通过列车信息网络传送给各车的计算机控制器或者BCU，以实现对列车牵引与制动的运行控制。同时对各设备的状态进行检测，一旦发生故障立即进行保护和记录，并通过列车信息网络将故障信息及时反馈到司机室，为司机提供故障处理的措施。

三、动车组牵引与制动的控制过程

1. 牵引指令

由司机操作司机主控制器发出，牵引指令主要包括：

（1）方向指令：前进/后进，控制牵引电机的转动方向。

（2）牵引工况指令：牵引电机工作于电动机工况。

（3）牵引级位指令：1~10级位，对应不同功率等级的牵引特性。

（4）恒速指令：控制列车恒速运行。

2. 制动指令

由司机操作司机制动控制器，制动指令主要包括：

（1）再生制动指令：优先再生制动，牵引电机工作于发电机工况。

（2）常用制动级位指令：1~7级位，对应不同减速度等级的制动特性。

（3）快速制动指令：通过贯通线发出，可操作，或保护时动作。

（4）紧急制动指令：通过贯通线发出，可操作，或保护时动作。

3. 车辆信息终端装置的相关链接及指令的传递

整个列车的牵引与制动是通过每个车辆单元来实现的，以1辆动车为例，如图1-2-2所示。

由司机室发出牵引指令（方向、牵引工况、牵引级位）通过中央装置传送至列车级网络，车辆终端装置接收来自列车网络的指令，然后传递给本车的牵引变流器的计算机控制器，实现对牵引变流器、牵引电机的控制。

由司机室发出的制动指令（再生制动工况、制动级位）通过中央装置传送至终端装置，终端装置将制动指令传送到本车的制动控制单元（BCU），BCU向牵引变流器发出再生制动模式指令，优先实施再生制动，此时牵引电机工作于发电机状态，在制动列车的同时将制动能量回馈至电网。同时，牵引变流器将再生信息反馈到BCU，当BCU检测到再生制动力不足时，向空气制动系统发出指令，补充空气制动。

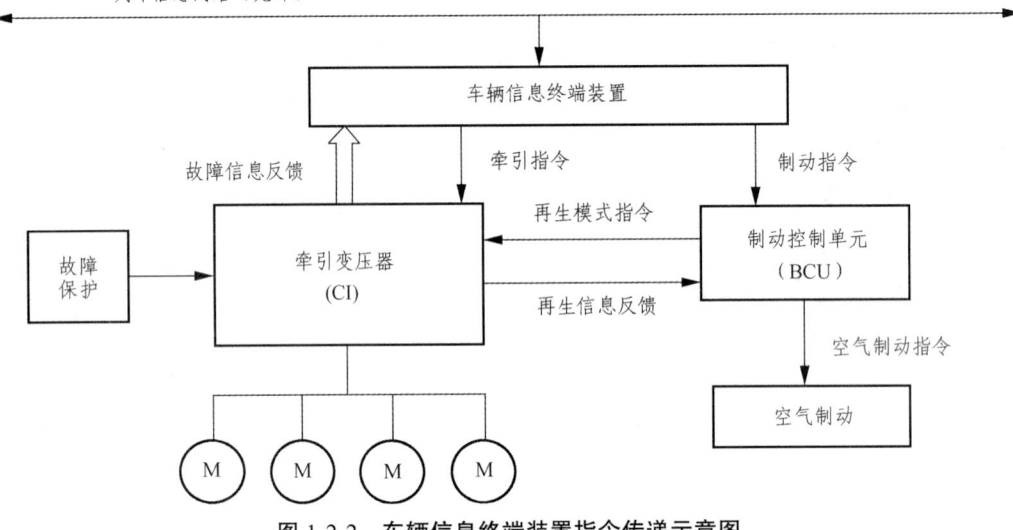

图 1-2-2　车辆信息终端装置指令传递示意图

同时，还要检测故障并进行故障保护，将故障信息反馈终端，再通过列车级网络反馈到司机室中央装置，在显示屏上显示并指导处理故障。

四、列车信息网络系统的构成

1. 列车级网络结构

列车级网络由中央装置、终端装置、列车信息显示器、显示控制装置、IC 卡读写装置及乘客信息显示器等设备构成，其网络设备在列车上的配置如表 1-2-1 所示。动车组列车级网络一般有两种类型。其一为光纤环网，连接所有中央装置与终端装置，采用 ANSI/ATA-878.1（ARCNET）协议；其二为自我诊断传输网，以总线方式连接中央装置与终端装置，采用 HDLC 作为数据交换协议。列车信息网络结构如图 1-2-3 所示。

表 1-2-1　列车级网络设备配置

车辆编号	T1c-1	M2-2	M1-3	T2-4	T1K-5	M2-6	M1S-7	T2C-8
中央装置	1							1
终端装置	1	1	1	1	1	1	1	1
列车信息显示器	2						1	2
显示控制装置	2						1	2
IC 卡读写装置	2							2

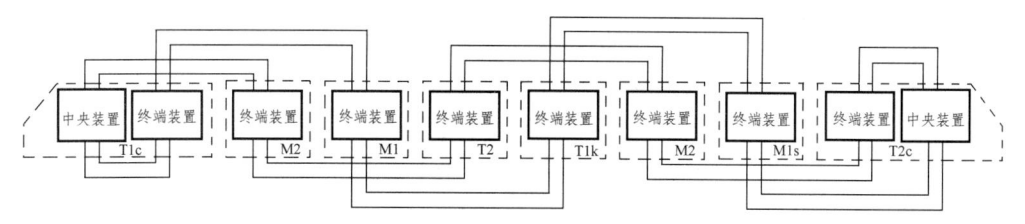

图 1-2-3　列车信息网络结构图

2. 车辆级网络结构

车辆级网络指中央装置/终端装置与车厢内设备之间信息交换的通道。中央装置/终端装置与设备之间采用点对点通信方式，牵引变流器（CI）、制动控制单元（BCU）与终端装置采用光纤连接，其他设备与中央装置、终端装置采用电流环方式连接。BCU/CI 装置配置如表 1-2-2 所示。

表 1-2-2　BCU/CI 装置配置

	T1c-1	M2-2	M1-3	T2-4	T1K-5	M2-6	M1S-7	T2C-8
	中央装置	终端装置	终端装置	终端装置	终端装置	终端装置	终端装置	中央装置
BCU	○	○	○	○	○	○	○	○
CI		○	○			○	○	

五、牵引变流器的控制

CRH380A 型动车组每辆车的一台牵引变流器由一台计算机控制器进行控制，如图 1-2-4 所示。

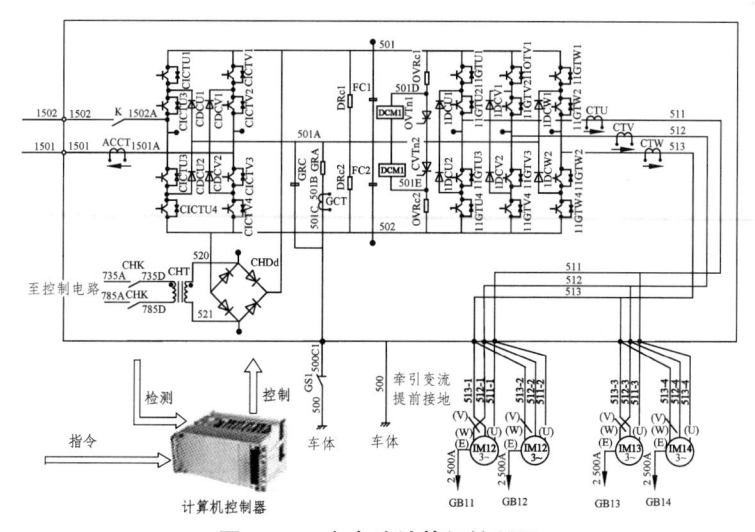

图 1-2-4　主电路计算机控制图

控制计算机除了具有通用计算机所具有的 CPU、存储器等部件外，重要的是要通过相关接口来解决信号的输入与输出问题，实现目标控制。

1. 检　测

计算机控制器要进行控制就必须通过各种传感器进行检测，形成闭环控制，达到最佳的控制精度；同时进行监测与保护。

检测环节主要包括：

（1）单相交流电流检测：电流传感器 ACCT。

（2）中间直流电压检测：DCPT1、DCPT2。

（3）接地故障电流检测：GCT。

（4）三相电流检测：CTU、CTV、CTW。

（5）牵引电机转速检测：各台牵引电机轴上的转速传感器。

2. 控　制

计算机控制器对牵引变流器的脉冲整流器和牵引逆变器进行控制，当出现故障时迅速进行保护。

控制环节主要包括：

（1）脉冲整流器控制：完成整流/再生的四象限变流控制。

（2）牵引逆变器控制：完成变频变压的控制。

（3）过压保护控制：直流电压过压时，触发晶闸管进行放电。

（4）过流、超压/欠压、接地保护控制：过电流、超电压/欠电压、接地时，进行封锁脉冲、停机保护。

【项目检测】

1. 请阐述 CRH380A 型动车组线号的分类。
2. 试述设备记号命名方法。
3. 分析动车组控制电路的概念。
4. 绘制车辆信息终端装置相关指令传递示意图并分析牵引、制动控制的工作原理。
5. 分析 CRH380A 型动车组控制系统的基本组成。

项目二　动车组牵引控制电路分析与检查

【项目描述】

本项目是对动车组牵引控制系统的整体认识。主要介绍 CRH$_2$/CRH380A、CRH$_3$/CRH380B 型动车组主电路、逻辑运行控制电路、受电弓、真空断路器等控制电路。通过对牵引控制原理的学习，要求学生会分析主电路和逻辑运行电路图，能按照动车组检修作业标准，根据常见故障处理办法，排除故障。

【项目任务】

（1）动车组主电路分析；
（2）逻辑运行控制电路；
（3）受电弓、真空断路器控制；
（4）牵引变流器控制；
（5）CRH380B 型动车组牵引控制。

任务一　动车组主电路分析

【任务描述】

本任务主要分析 CRH380A 型动车组主电路，使学生掌握 CRH$_2$/CRH380A 型动车组牵引传动系统的组成、工作原理。学习完本任务，学生应会分析主电路工作过程。

【背景知识】

一、主电路系统组成

牵引电路系统以 M1 车、M2 车为 1 个单元。电源由接触网通过受电弓从单相交流 25 kV、50 Hz 的接触网电压来获得，通过 VCB 与牵引变压器的一次绕组连接。牵引电路开闭由 VCB 来实施。牵引变压器 2 次绕组侧设有 2 个线圈，分别接入 1 台牵引变流器，一次侧的电压为 25 kV 时，二次侧绕组电压则为 1 500 V。牵引变压器 3 次绕组和辅助变流器连接，给辅助设备提供电源。

主电路的基本单元装置由 1 台牵引变压器、2 台主变流装置、8 台牵引电机构成。1 台主变流装置控制 4 台牵引电机，在牵引时向牵引电机提供电力，在制动时进行再生控制。此外，还具有保护功能。一个动力单元牵引系统的组成如图 2-1-1 所示。

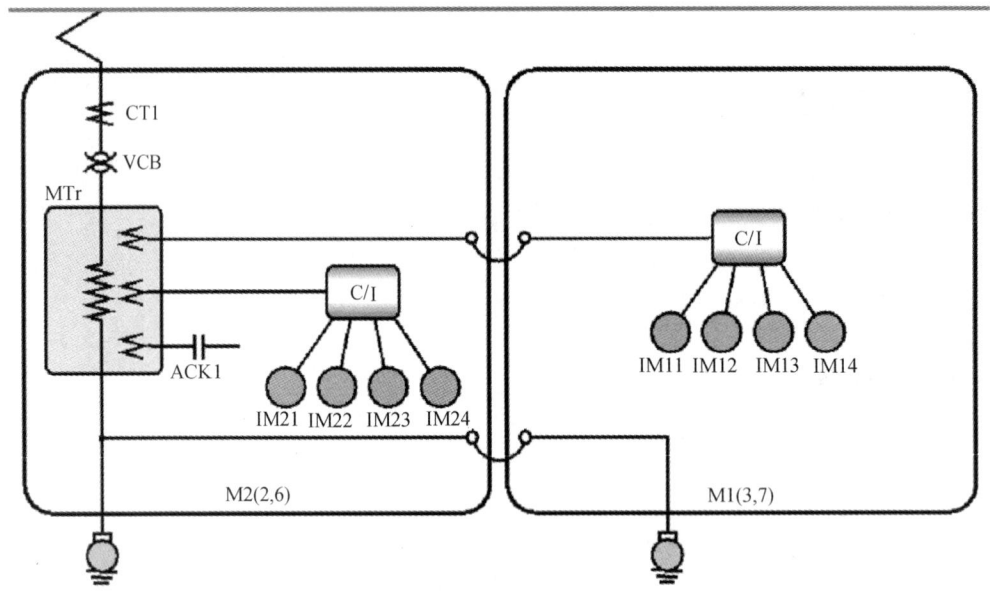

图 2-1-1　牵引传动系统组成框图

二、牵引传动系统原理

牵引传动系统原理如图 2-1-2 所示。

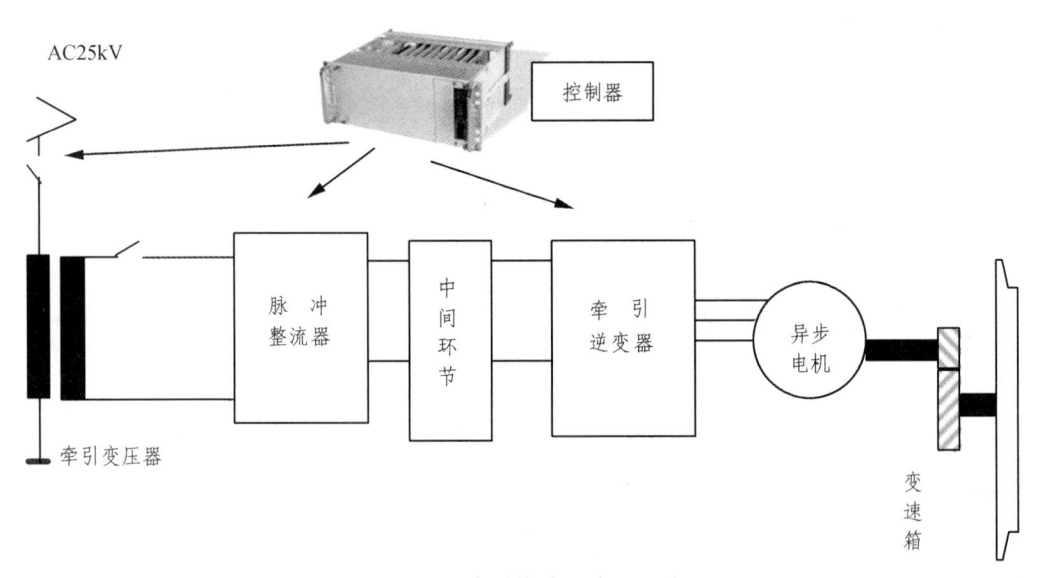

图 2-1-2　牵引传动系统原理图

牵引工况：受电弓将接触网 AC 25 kV 单相工频交流电，经过相关的高压电气设备传输给牵引变压器，牵引变压器降压输出 1 500 V 单相交流电供给牵引变流器，脉冲整流器将单相交流电变换成直流电，经中间直流电路将 DC 2 600 ~ 3 000 V 的直流电输出给牵引逆变器，牵引逆变器输出电压/频率可调的三相交流电源（电压：0 ~ 2 300 V；频率：0 ~ 220 Hz）驱动牵引电机，牵引电机的转矩和转速通过齿轮变速箱传递给轮对驱动列车运行。

再生制动：电制动在电制动时，一方面，通过控制牵引逆变器使牵引电机处于发电状态，牵引逆变器工作于整流状态，牵引电机发出的三相交流电被整流为直流电并对中间直流环节进行充电，使中间直流环节电压上升；另一方面，脉冲整流器工作于逆变状态，中间直流回路直流电源被逆变为单相交流电，该交流电通过真空断路器、受电弓等高压设备反馈给接触网，从而实现能量再生。

三、牵引传动系统主电路

1. 25 kV 特高压电路

牵引传动系统主电路简图如图 2-1-3 所示。

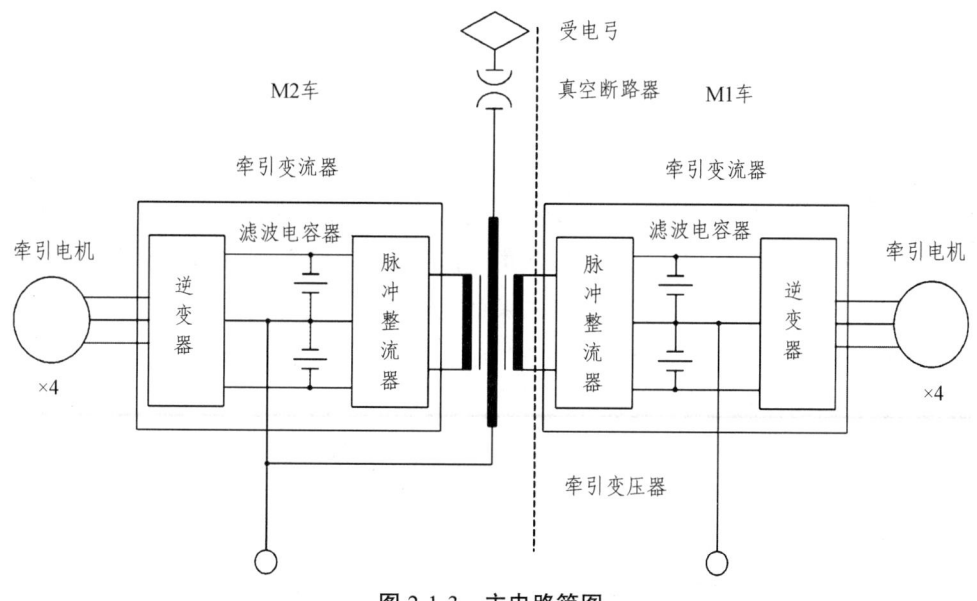

图 2-1-3 主电路简图

电源是 25 kV、50 Hz 单相交流电，使用安装在 4 号车、6 号车的受电弓的其中一个（2 个受电弓中的 1 个通常处在降弓折叠状态）从接触网上受电，2 号车与 6 号车之间用 25 kV

177

特高压电缆贯通连接。M1/M3/M5 车上装有牵引变压器，通过特高压电缆而贯通连接在各车的 25 kV 特高压电源，经由各车的特高压接头、主断路器 VCB，连接到牵引变压器原边绕组上。

2. 牵引变压器 2 次电路

牵引变压器（MTr）的低压侧由 3 个绕组构成，其中 2 个绕组是向列车驱动电路（牵引变流器）提供电力的 2 次绕组，剩下的是向动车组的照明、空调等辅助电路，控制电路，通信电路等提供电力的 3 次绕组。

3. 牵引变流器

2 次绕组中的 1 个绕组与 M1/M3/M5 车的牵引变流器连接，另 1 个绕组经由 M1/M3/M5 车与 M2/M4/M6 车之间的连接器连接到 M2/M4/M6 车的牵引变流器。牵引变流器除了向动力运行时的牵引电机提供电力、从制动时的电动机向接触网进行再生电力反馈之外，还具有保护机能。牵引变流器由把单相交流电变换成直流中间电的脉冲整流器部分和把变换的直流中间电变换成可变电压可变频率的 3 相交流电的逆变器部分、及获得直流恒压的直流平滑电路（滤波电容器）部分构成。此外在中间直流电路上设置由电阻和半导体开关构成的过电压保护电路，如图 2-1-4，2-1-5 所示。脉冲整流器通过 PWM 控制把电源输入侧的基本波功率因数控制到接近 1。由此可以降低接触网电压的变动，使设备小型化、降低电力消耗。逆变器在动力运行时，把输入的直流中间电压变换成根据控制指令可变电压可变频率的 3 相交流电，然后向并联的 4 台感应电动机统一供电，对感应电动机的速度·转矩进行控制。再生制动时，逆变器机能性地成为功率换向整流器，由感应电动机将感应的 3 相交流电输入给逆变器，然后由逆变器向直流中间电路侧输出直流电力。为了控制感应电动机的速度及扭矩，逆变器采用矢量控制方式进行控制。通过矢量控制，与电动机的扭矩有关的电流成分（转矩电流）及与电动机的磁场有关的电流成分（励磁电流）被分别独立控制。通过逆变器的矢量控制，高精度的扭矩控制、高速扭矩的控制指日可待。

4. 牵引电机

牵引电机在 M1、M2、M3、M4、M5、M6 各车的各转向架上各安装 2 台。电动机使用 3 相鼠笼式感应电动机，在反驱动一侧安装有速度传感器。速度传感器检测牵引电机的速度（旋转数）即列车速度，把速度信息送到上述逆变器。此速度信息（速度的反馈信号）是为电动机的速度控制、扭矩控制及制动控制所用。

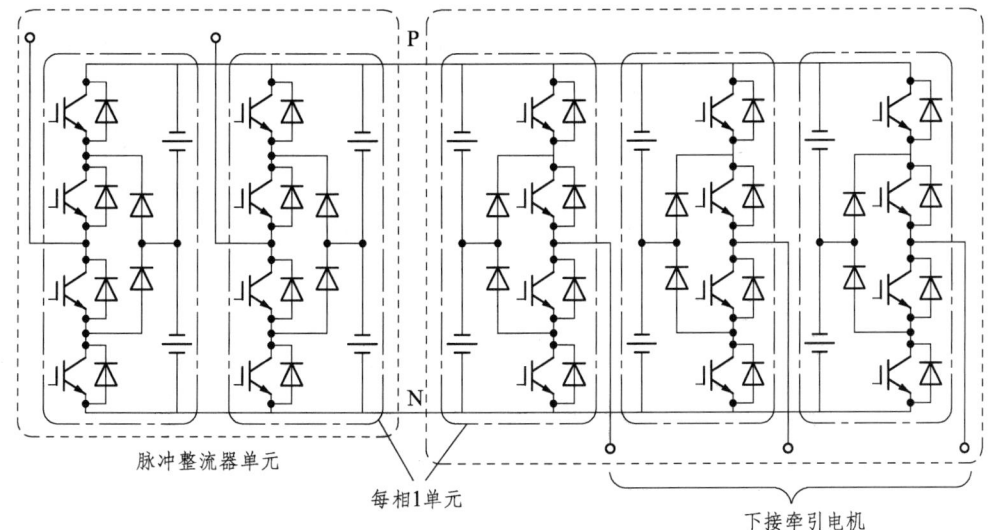

图 2-1-4　功率模块连接图

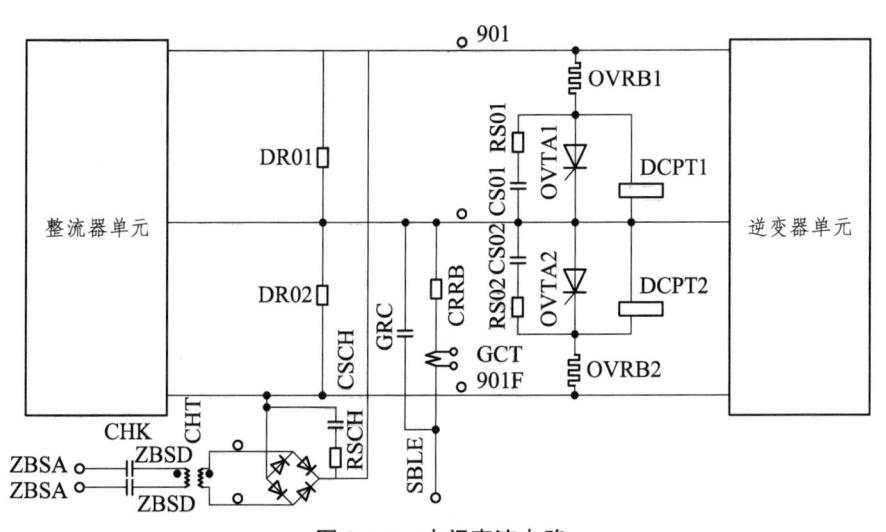

图 2-1-5　中间直流电路

5. 保护电路

（1）保护接地开关。受电弓和保护接地开关安装在同一车辆上。保护接地开关通过把特高压电源接地，来防止对车体施加特高电压。由于主断路器 VCB 的原因引起不能阻断主电路的事故电流时，或在接触网电压异常时，强制性地操作保护接地开关（EGS），把接触网接地，把接地电流流向接触网，让变电所的隔离开关跳闸，能使接触网处于无电压的状态。此外，在对高压设备箱内部进行检查时，为确保维修人员的安全，通过保护接地开关和高压设备箱间联动的锁定装置，预先把受电弓接地，即使受电弓上升，也能防止触电事故的发生。

（2）主断路器。安装主断路器 VCB 的目的是：在牵引变压器二次侧以后的电路发生故障时，能够迅速、安全、可靠地阻断过电流。在正常时，主断路器 VCB 也是对主电路的开闭进行操作的一种开关，它兼有断路器和开关的两种作用。

（3）交流避雷器。由于来自接触网的雷冲击（surge）及因负荷断路引起的开关（时）冲击（surge／浪涌）可以由与牵引变压器并联的交流避雷器（Arr）进行分路，并限制到由交流避雷器的电压限制特性决定的电压值。因此，交流避雷器的使用可以防止把高电压加在各设备上。

（4）变流器及过电流继电器变流器（CT1）接在 25 kV（特高压）的输入侧。交流过电流继电器（ACOCR1 和 ACOCR2）连接到变流器二次侧，经由变流器监视 25 kV 电路的电流，当变流器电流超过交流过电流继电器的设定值时，能够发出让 VCB 跳闸的跳闸信号。

6. 接地装置

主回路接地装置安装在 M1、M2、M3、M4、M5、M6 车的驱动轴齿轮装置的非车轮一侧。经由接地装置，把牵引变压器的回流线电流直接流到车轴，以防因回流线电流流到转向架轴承而引起的轴承损伤。牵引变压器接地线被连接到 M1/M3/M5 车与各驱动轴相对应的中转端子板上，此外，M2/M4/M6 车经由 M1/M3/M5 车与 M2/M4/M6 车之间的连接器（与 M1/M3/M5 车相同），连接到与各驱动轴对应的中转端子板，从那里连接到各轴的接地刷上。

任务二　逻辑运行控制

【任务描述】

通过对本任务的学习，学生应掌握主控制器的功能、牵引指令传递原理，会分析逻辑运行控制电路，并按照检修作业标准，检查与维护主控制器，会对主回路及主回路接触器动作进行测试。

【背景知识】

一、概　述

司机控制器在司机室内，T1c-1 或 T2c-8 内各有一套。司机控制器由方向控制器、牵引控制器和司机制动控制器组成，完成动车组牵引方向、牵引控制指令、制动指令设定，如图 2-2-1 所示。司机控制器在司机室内同时配合恒速开关和启动试验开关，实现恒速控制指令和变流器故障后的试验。

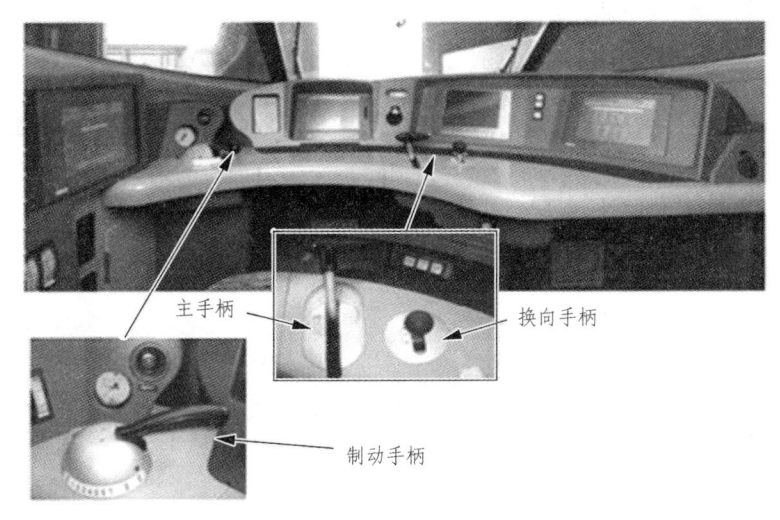

图 2-2-1　司机控制器在司机室的布置

动车组牵引控制的指令主要包括：前进、后进、牵引、级位等指令，司机通过主控制器（主手柄和换向手柄）进行操作。牵引控制指令的传递原理框图如图 2-2-2 所示。

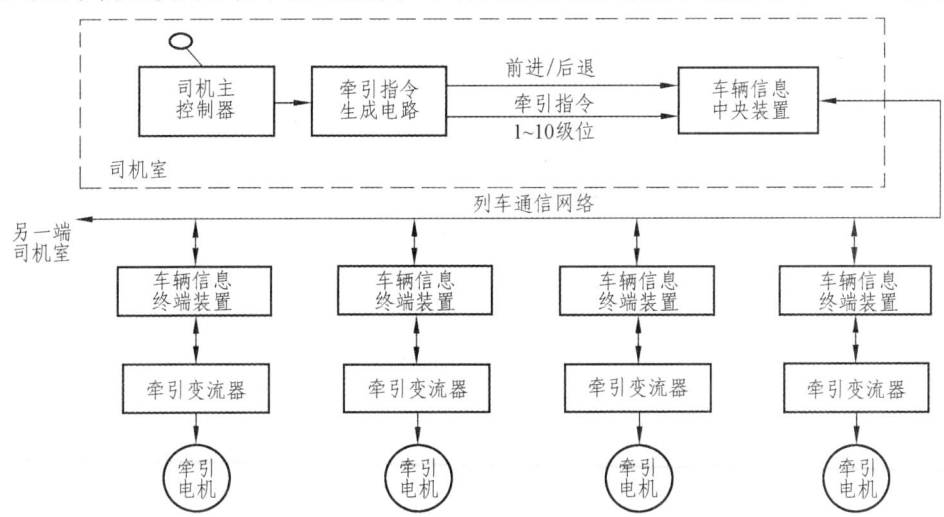

图 2-2-2　牵引控制器指令传递示意图

主控制器的前进（4 线）或后进（5 线）、牵引指令（9 线）及 1~10 级位指令（11、12、13、15、17、19 线）的各指令线被输入到车辆信息控制的中央装置，通过控制传送向牵引变流器传输指令，进行牵引运行控制。为保证控制电路按照指令正确动作，控制过程中必须满足一定的逻辑条件。

181

二、牵引控制器原理

1. 方向控制器

方向控制器又称方向手柄。如图2-2-3所示，方向手柄有3个位置："前"位、"切"位、"后"位。"前"位时，向前继电器得电动作；"后"位时，向后继电器得电动作；"切"位时，两个继电器均不动作。方向控制器控制生成牵引方向（向前或向后）指令条件和牵引指令继电器条件。

说明：所有的控制电源来自DC 100 V辅助电源103线，本节图中103-1,103-2,103-3分别表示与103线关联的第1~3个支路。

换向开关前位置时，换向开关前R就励磁（前进模式）。

换向开关后位置时，换向开关后R就励磁（后进模式）。

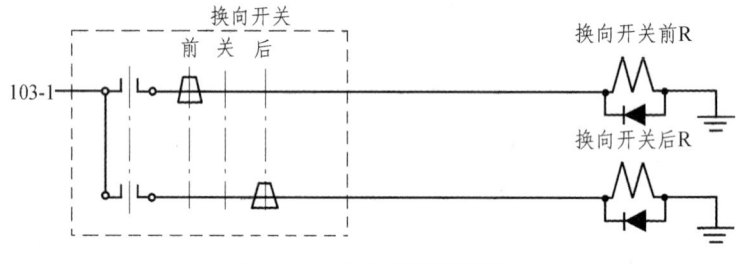

图2-2-3 方向控制器控制

1）方向指令生成条件

如图2-2-4和图2-2-5所示，在主控制继电器MCR励磁时，方向手柄在"前"位时，线4加压，向监控器传递向前指令；方向手柄在"后"位时，线5加压，向监控中央装置传递向后指令。

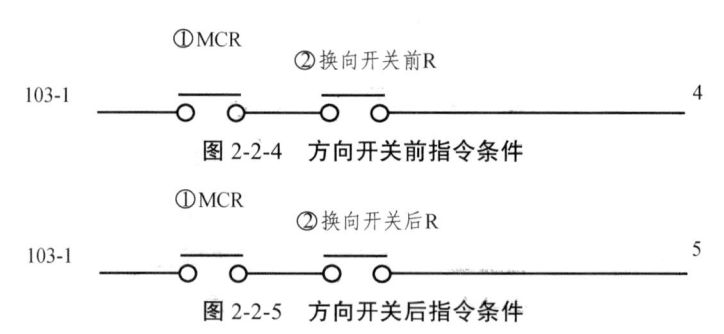

图2-2-4 方向开关前指令条件

图2-2-5 方向开关后指令条件

2）牵引指令R生成条件

如图2-2-6所示，在其他条件满足时，方向控制手柄离开"切"位。

①MCR　②换向开关前R　④JTR　⑤DIR　牵引指令R

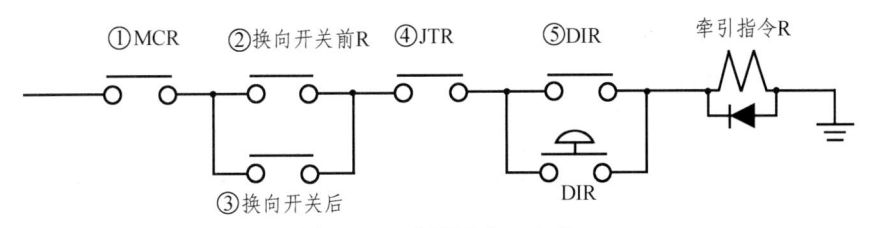

③换向开关后　　　　　　　DIR

图 2-2-6　牵引指令 R 条件

在"前"位或"后"位时，换向开关前 R 或后 R 得电，对应的常开解点闭合，牵引指令 R 得电动作。牵引指令 R 动作后，牵引指令才能发出。由此可见，方向手柄在"关"位时，是发不出牵引指令的。牵引指令 R 得电条件还有：

① 操作端：MCR 励磁；
② 换向手柄离开"切"位：换向开关前 R 或换向开关后 R 进行励磁；
③ 没有快速制动和紧急制动：JTR 励磁；
④ 侧拉门在关闭状态或关门联锁开关为 ON：DIR 励磁或 DIRS ON。

上述条件同时满足时，牵引指令继电器才能得电。这些条件说明，只有在安全条件下，方向控制器的操作才能生成牵引指令 R 动作条件。

2. 牵引控制器

牵引控制器又称主控制器（MC），主要功能是生成牵引指令的 10 个级位指令，同时生成牵引指令条件和恒速运行指令条件。

1）牵引指令级位

如图 2-2-7 所示，牵引方向手柄在"前"位或"后"位时，牵引指令继电器 R 得电动作。操作牵引控制器时，11 线、12 线、13 线、15 线、17 线、19 线被分别加压，各线输入至监控中央装置，通过网络向牵引变流器传输牵引指令。各线输入监控器中央装置，进行动力运行控制。

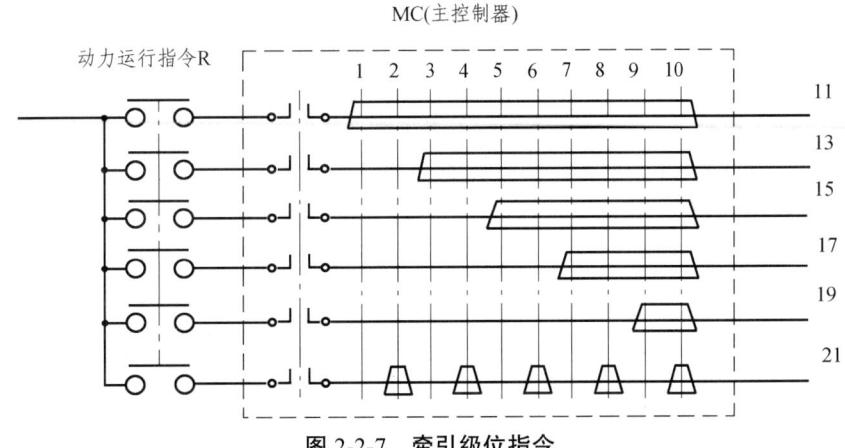

图 2-2-7　牵引级位指令

根据牵引控制器手柄的位置不同，不同的线加压，形成了10级的牵引指令，级位与各线加压的对应关系如表2-2-1所示。

表2-2-1 牵引控制器级位与指令线对应

		主控制器级位指令									
		1	2	3	4	5	6	7	8	9	10
加压线	11	○	○	○	○	○	○	○	○	○	○
	13		○		○	○	○	○	○	○	○
	15					○	○	○	○	○	○
	17							○	○	○	○
	19									○	
	12		○		○		○		○		○

○=「加压」、空白处=「无加压」

2）牵引指令条件

牵引指令条件是要通知监控中央装置，发出牵引控制指令。

把MC处在「切」位置、MC切R进行励磁。由此MCPR可以励磁，能使牵引指令条件（9线）有效。逻辑关系如图2-2-8所示。

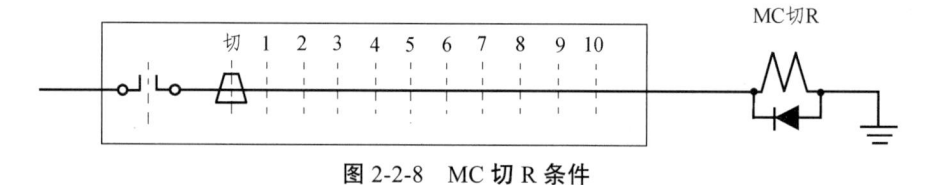

图2-2-8 MC切R条件

MCPR条件如下，逻辑关系图如图2-2-9所示。

满足以下条件，MCPR励磁。

＜条件＞①∩②（∩表示and，∪表示or）：

① 牵引指令R励磁：参照图2-2-6。

② MC断开R励磁：（MC空挡状态）参见图2-2-8。

※MCPR一旦励磁，动力运行指令R直到非励磁为止，一直自我保持。

MCPR得到励磁后，主控制器指令通过9线，可以输入到监控器。

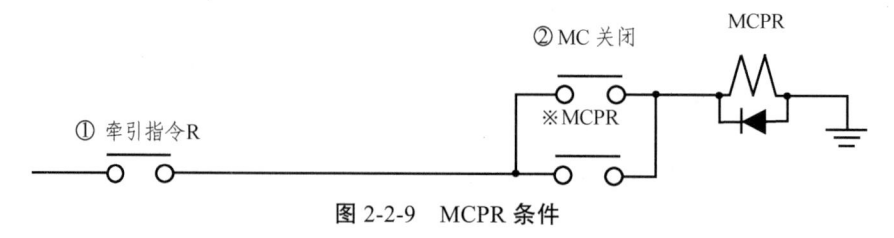

图2-2-9 MCPR条件

图 2-2-8 中 MC 处在「切」(空挡)位置，MC 切 R 进行励磁。MC 切 R 常开触点闭合，在方向手柄不在"关"位时，主控手柄接通继电器 MCPR 得电，并且在主控制器其他级位运行时通过辅助触点保持状态不变。图 2-2-9 中 MCPR 常开触点闭合，在其他条件满足时，9 线得电，同时继电器 PR 的触点闭合。9 线连向监控中央装置，表示牵引指令有效，PR 通过触点信号连至制动控制器表明牵引指令有效。

在①~⑩项中如果满足以下条件，牵引指令线（9 线）进行加压及 PR 励磁。PR 的触点信号输入到制动装置，使制动装置识别牵引运行模式，如图 2-2-10 所示。

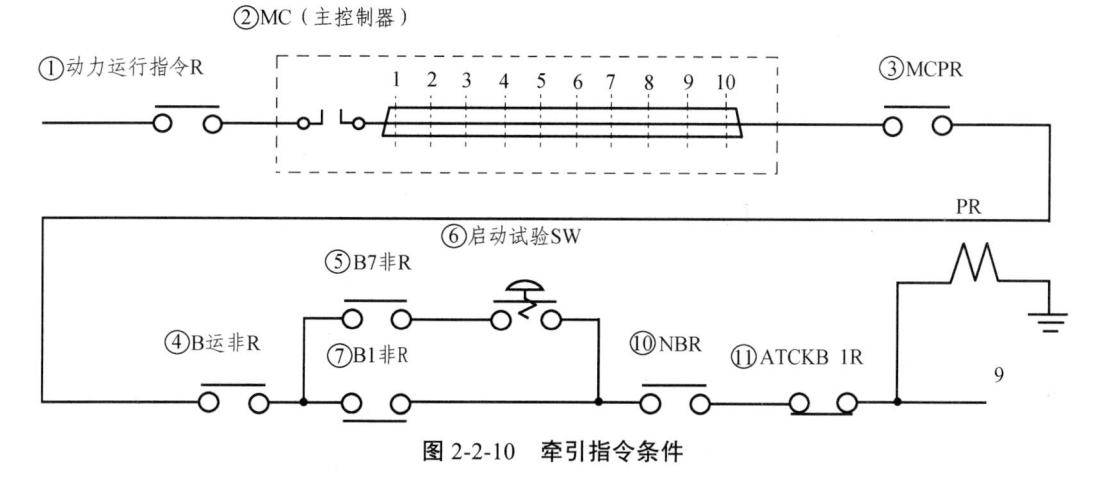

图 2-2-10 牵引指令条件

（条件）①∩②∩③∩④∩{（⑤∩⑥）∪⑦}∩⑧∩⑨：

① 牵引指令 R 励磁：参照图 2-2-7。

② MC 级位为 1~10。

③ MCPR 励磁：参照图 2-2-9。

④ B 运非 R 励磁。

⑤ B7 非 R 励磁。

⑥ 起动试验 SW 为 ON。

⑦ B1 非 R 为非励磁。

⑧ NBR 励磁：缓解 ATP 常用制动。

⑨ ATCKB1R 为非励磁：ATP 缓和制动 B1。

上述条件同时满足时，牵引指令有效。上述条件说明，一旦有制动指令，不管来自制动手柄还是 ATP，牵引指令条件不能生成。因此制动比牵引有更高的优先级，从而保证行车的安全。

3）定速开关电路（定速行驶）

定速控制指令的输出条件是：在 ATPCOS 正常位置 [ATP 有效、没有 Cut out（切断）]、

LKJCOS 正常位置［已有信号设备有效、没有 Cut out（切断）］、动力运行在 2 挡位以上的基本条件下，通过操作司机台的定速开关（定速 SW），定速继电器（CSR）得到励磁（见图 2-2-11）、CSR 的 NO 触点处在关闭状态，输入到车辆信息控制的中央装置（23 线）。

在①~⑪的项目中，如果满足以下条件，CSR 励磁。

（条件）①∩②∩③∩④∩⑤∩⑥∩⑦∩⑧∩⑨∩⑩∩⑪：

① 牵引指令 R 励磁。

② ATPCOR 为励磁：ATP 正常。

③ LKJCOR 为励磁：LKJ 正常。

④ B 运非 R 励磁。

⑤ B1 非 R 为非励磁。

⑥ NBR 励磁：缓解 ATP 常用制动。

⑦ ATCKB1R 为非励磁。

⑧ EBR 励磁：缓解 ATP 非常制动。

⑨ 定速关闭 SW 为 OFF。

⑩ MC 挡固定在 5~10 中的任意一个。

⑪ 定速 SW 为 ON。

※定速 SW 变为 ON，当 CSR 被励磁后，即使定速 SW 被开放也进行自我保持。

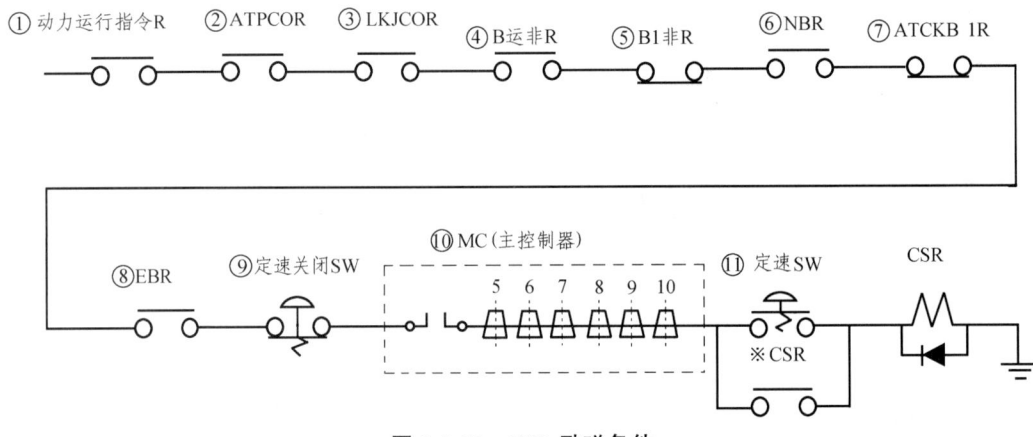

图 2-2-11 CSR 励磁条件

4）定速控制条件（23 线）

在①、②的项目中，如果满足以下条件，定速控制条件（见图 2-2-12）（23 线）被加压（定速控制指令）。

（条件）①∩②：

① 牵引动力运行指令 R 励磁。

② CSR 励磁。

```
① 动力运行指令R    ② CSR
───o  o────────o  o──────────────── 23
```

图 2-2-12　定速控制条件

3. 与控制相关的其他电路

前面介绍了司机控制器操作及直接相关牵引控制电路，为了便于理解该系统，与司机控制器相关的一些控制电路也在此予以说明。

1）主控制继电器 MCR

主控制继电器决定司机的操作是否有效，每端司机室内有一个主控制继电器，只有在主控制继电器闭合时，司机操作有效。当在动车组其中一端司机室进行主控操作时，通过联锁控制，另一端司机室的操作无效。主控制器继电器的操作和联锁如图 2-2-13 和图 2-2-14 所示。

以下是主控制继电器的控制条件，在如下条件下，主控制继电器 MCR 闭合：

① 制动控制器不在拔取位：B 运非 R 励磁。
② MCRR 非励磁：相反侧的先头车的 MCR 非励磁。
③ MXR 非励磁：与其他编组没有连挂。

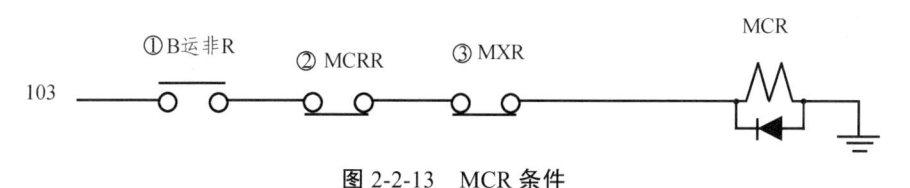

```
         ①B运非R    ② MCRR     ③ MXR              MCR
103 ─────o    o────o    o────o    o─────────⎍⎍⎍───┤
```

图 2-2-13　MCR 条件

T1c-1 车主控制器继电器 MCR 以 3 线（103 线）作为电源，在制动设定器手柄位置（运转~快速）位（制动设定器手柄没有拔下、有效）使 "B 运非 R" 触点闭合及主控制器辅助继电器 MCRR 常闭触点 NC 闭合（另一侧司机台的主控制器非有效）的条件下动作。

为了保证只能在一侧的司机室驾驶，即在 T1c-1 车驾驶时，T2c-8 车操作无效（反之亦然），MCR 和 MCRR 进行联锁控制。

主控制器辅助继电器 MCRR 受控于另一端司机室的主控制继电器的状态，另一侧主控制继电器合上时，MCRR 励磁，该侧主控制继电器 MCR 不能得电。T1c-1 和 T2c-8 车的主控制继电器联锁关系如图 2-2-14 所示，联锁信号由贯通线 3X（3Z）和 3Y（3W）传递。这种联锁关系使司机只能在一端驾驶有效。

如果与其他编组有连挂关系时，连挂处的主控制继电器不能得电动作，也就是中间司机不能是操作端。

图 2-2-14　MCR 和 MCRR 的联锁

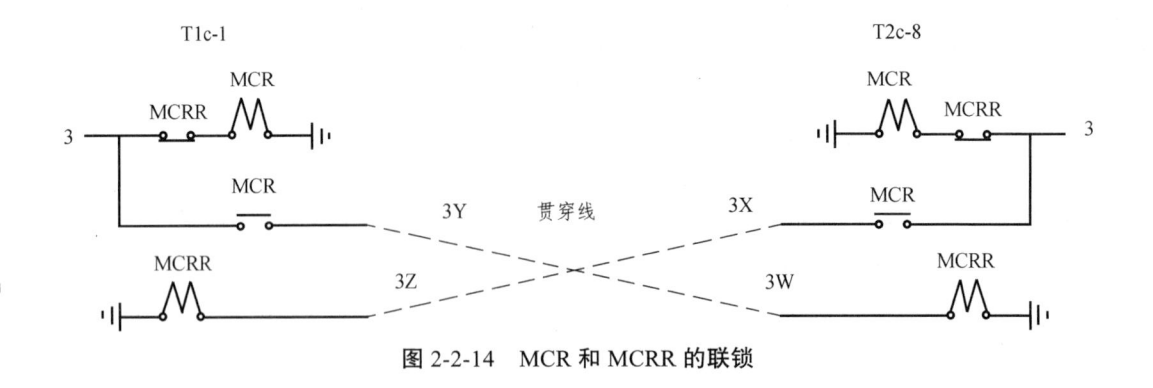

任务三　受电弓、真空断路器控制

【任务描述】

本任务主要介绍受电弓、真空断路器控制电路的工作原理。通过本任务的学习，学生应会分析受电弓联锁控制、升降弓及真空断路器的工作过程。

【背景知识】

一、受电弓的管理

CRH2 型动车组受电弓设置在 T2-4 车、M2-6 车上，CRH380A 型动车组受电弓设置在 M3-4 车、M5-6 车上。正常情况下，只能单弓升起。因此当受电弓上升联锁装置继电器（PanIR）选择一侧的受电弓时，将不能输入另一侧受电弓的上升指令。受电弓的升降指令能够通过设置在司机台的操作开关或者监控器的显示器发出。

1. MCR 和 MCRR 的联锁装置

T1c-1 车、T2c-8 车的主控制器继电器 MCR 与主控制器辅助继电器 MCRR 的联锁关系参照运行指令逻辑部分。

若对 T2c-8 车 MCRR 进行了励磁，贯穿线 110 线（紧急接地开关 EGS 条件），111 线（VCB 条件）从 T2c-8 车 MCRR 触点被加压（DC 100 V），VCB 辅助继电器（VCBRR）、接地保护开关继电器（EGSR）各线圈被励磁，各继电器的触点是关闭的状态。

2. T2-4 车和 M2-6 车或者 M3-4 车、M5-6 上的联锁装置

M3-4 车、M5-6 车的 PanIR、受电弓上升指令继电器（PanUR）如图 2-3-1 所示。对 M3-4 车输入受电弓的上升指令后，通过 106G 线 M5-6 车的 PanIR 被励磁。由于 M5-6 车的 PanIR 被励磁，M5-6 车的 PanIR 的常闭触点是打开的状态，因此 PanUR 没有被励磁。M5-6 车被输入受电弓上升指令的情况下，按照同样的逻辑，M3-4 车的 PanUR 不能励磁。这样来保证单弓升起。

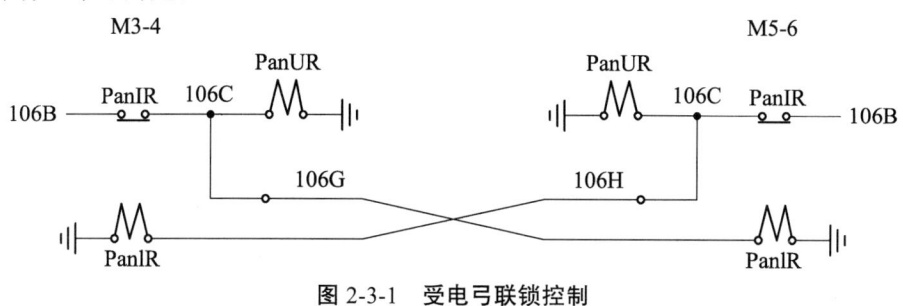

图 2-3-1 受电弓联锁控制

3. 升起受电弓的指令

在 EGSR、VCBRR 没被励磁的状态下，操作升起受电弓开关（PanUS）后，升起受电弓的指令通过切换开关（PanCGS）选择 106X 线（M2-6 车）或者 106Y 线（T2-4 车）被加压（注意：CRH380A 是 M5-6 车或者 M3-4 车）。106 线被加压后，受电弓上升指令继电器 PanUR 被励磁，PanUR 的 a 触点闭合，如果没有输入降下受电弓的指令（PanDWR 非励磁），受电弓上升电磁阀 PanUV 被励磁，受电弓上升，如图 2-3-2 所示。

由监控器显示器输入升起受电弓的指令，单元指令继电器（URO1）或（URO4）切换到监控器终端装置一侧，对该单元的 PanUR 进行励磁。

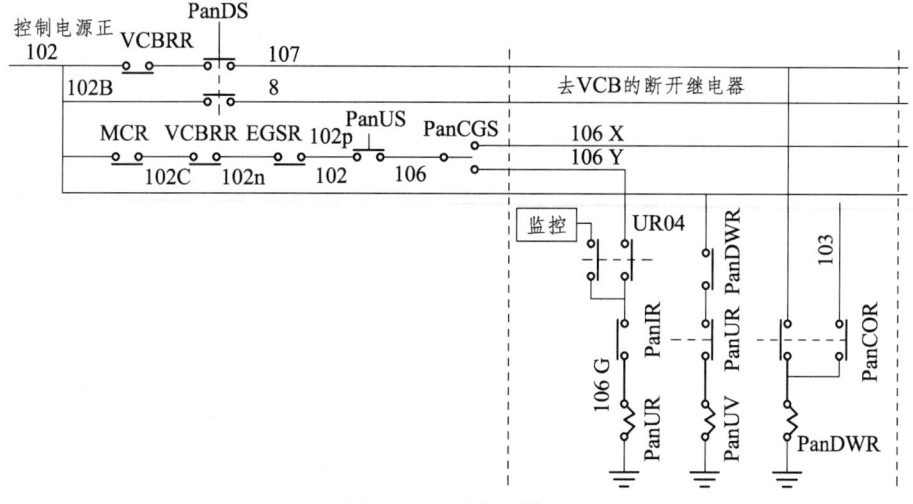

图 2-3-2 受电弓控制

4. 降下受电弓的指令

按下降下受电弓开关（PanDS），受电弓下降指令 107 线被加压，同时 VCB 断开指令 8 线被加压（参照辅助回路连接）。107 线被加压，降下受电弓继电器（PanDWR）被励磁，其常闭接点断开 PanUV 的励磁；同时并联的降弓辅助继电器（PanDWAR）也被励磁，其常闭接点断开 PanUR 的励磁，保证受电弓可靠降下。

由监控器显示器输入降下受电弓的指令，切断受电弓指令继电器（PanCOR）被励磁，由此 PanDWR 工作。

二、真空断路器控制电路

正常工作时，真空断路器 VCB 接通或断开 25 kV 高压电路与牵引变压器的连接；故障时通过 VCB 能够快速、安全、可靠地切断电流，保护电路和保证列车安全。它兼有断路器和开关的两种作用。

1. VCB 投入控制

VCB 投入是在确认 4 或 6 号车的受电弓升起后操作 VCB 投入开关（VCBCS），VCB 投入指令的 7 线得电，VCBCR1 励磁。各车的 VCB 投入条件，其保护装置都没有动作，此时 VCBOR2 得电励磁。在 VCBCR1 和 VCBOR2 都励磁后，在 M1/M3/M5 车和 M2/M4/M6 车的牵引变流器的接触器处在开放（KRR 消磁）状态和主变压器的油泵用 NFB（MTOPMN）投入为条件，VCB-M 进行励磁，VCB 投入。

1）VCB 投入控制命令

如图 2-3-3 所示，在主控继电器 MCR 得电励磁时，VCB 投入开关（VCBCS）闭合，或者由信息控制终端装置发出的自动过分相合 VCB 指令，SVCBCR 闭合，VCB 的投入指令线 7 得电加压。

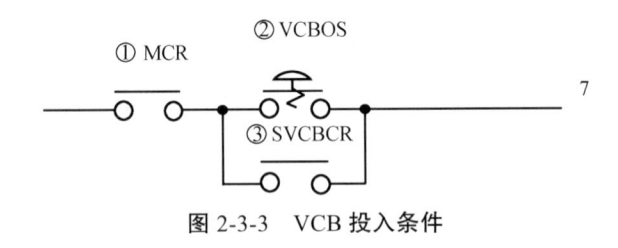

图 2-3-3 VCB 投入条件

2）VCBCR1 条件

如图 2-3-4 所示，在 MCR 励磁，VCBCS 闭合，同时信息显示器没有发出单元选择指令，UR0* 非励磁时，VCBCR1 励磁。

①MCR　②VCBCS　③UR0*　　　　　VCBCR1

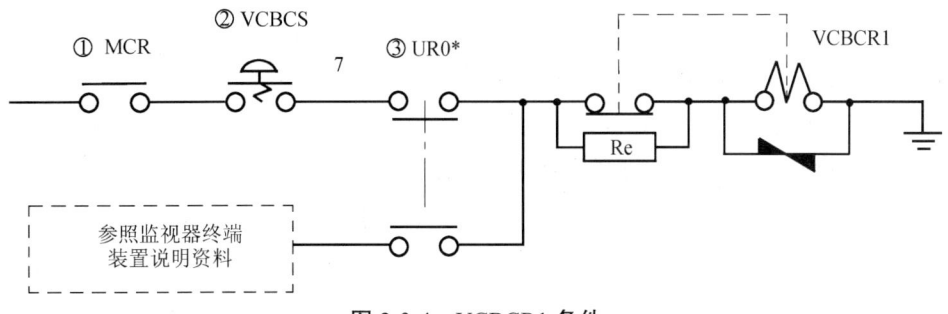

参照监视器终端
装置说明资料

图 2-3-4　VCBCR1 条件

3）VCBOR2 条件

如图 2-3-5 所示，VCBOR2 得电有联锁条件和系统正常条件两类，所有条件满足时 VCBOR2 得电励磁。即下列条件中①∩②∩③∩④∩⑤∩⑥∩（⑦∪⑧）∩⑨∩（⑩∪⑪）∩⑫有效时，VCBOR2 闭合。

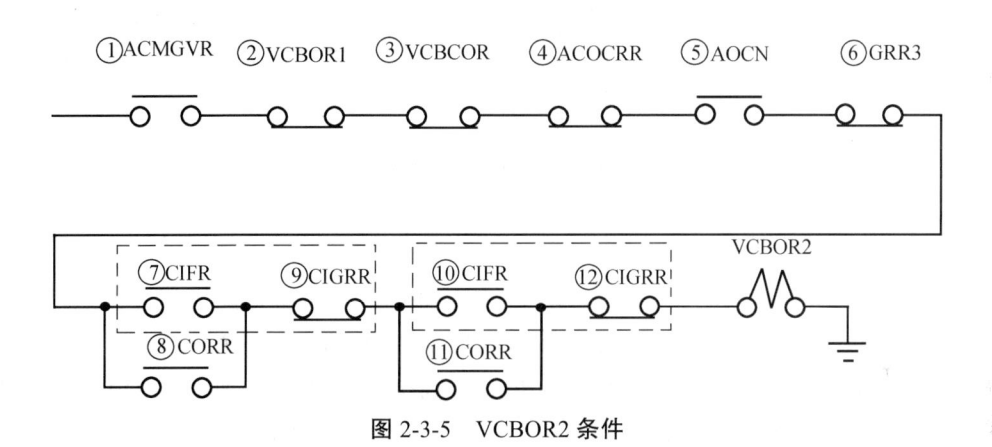

①ACMGVR　②VCBOR1　③VCBCOR　④ACOCRR　⑤AOCN　⑥GRR3

⑦CIFR　⑨CIGRR　⑩CIFR　⑫CIGRR　VCBOR2

⑧CORR　⑪CORR

图 2-3-5　VCBOR2 条件

（1）ACMGVR 励磁：辅助气压正常。

（2）VCBOR1 非励磁：无 VCB 断开指令。

（3）VCBCOR 非励磁：监视器显示器没有发出断开 VCB 的指令。

（4）ACOCRR 非励磁：不是 1 次（原边）过电流。

（5）AOCN 励磁：不是 3 次过电流。

（6）GRR3 非励磁：3 次电路没有接地。

（7）CIFR 励磁：牵引变流器装置正常。

（8）CORR 励磁：牵引电机切除。

（9）CIGRR 非励磁：牵引变流器装置接地正常。

4）VCB-M 条件

如图 2-3-6 所示，VCB-M 得电后，VCB 闭合动作。VCB-M 在条件：
①∩{（②∩③∩④∩⑤）∪⑦}∩⑥有效时闭合。

① OCTN（变压器过电流 NFB）非励磁。

② MTOPMN 励磁：牵引变压器油泵断路器投入。

③ KRR 非励磁：牵引变流器装置接触器断开（M1/M3 车）。

④ KRR 非励磁：牵引变流器装置接触器断开（M2/M4 车）。

⑤ VCBCR1 励磁。

⑥ VCBOR2 励磁。

⑦ VCB 处于 ON 的位置。

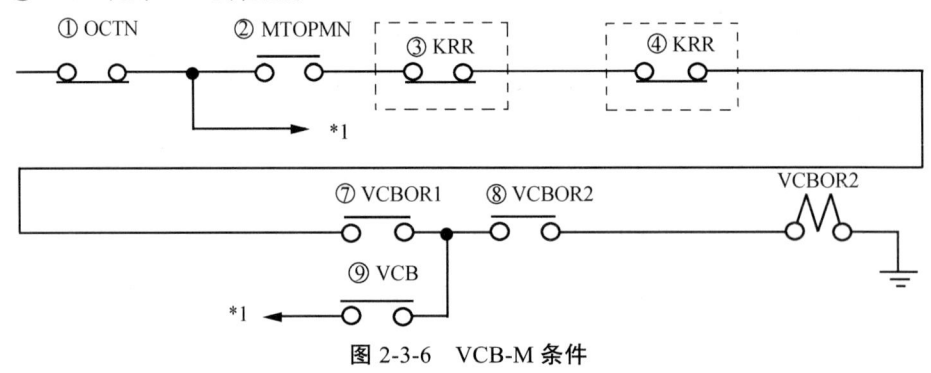

图 2-3-6　VCB-M 条件

2. VCB 断开控制

通常的 VCB 断路是操作 VCB 开放开关（VCBOS），VCB 断路指令的 8 线被加压，VCBOR1 工作，VCB-M 成为无加压，编组的所有 VCB 都开放。另外，操作降下受电弓开关（PanDS）的时候，为防止由受电弓造成的电流断路，对 8 线加压，使用 VCB 将电流断路。作为异常时的断路，由以下的任一动作造成 VCBOR2 的无加压，该单元的 VCB 都断开。

1）VCB 断开指令条件

如图 2-3-7 所示，在断路器分断开关 VCBOS 或者过电分相装置发出的断开 VCB 命令后，SVCBOR 闭合，VCB 断开指令（8 线）被加压，VCBOR1 被励磁。

图 2-3-7　VCB 的断开命令

2）异常时 VCB 断开

作为异常时的断路，由以下的任一动作造成 VCBOR2 的无电压，该单元的 VCB 断开。

① ACMGVR（小型空气压缩机调压器用继电器）：OFF（辅助气压的低下）；
② VCBCOR（VCB 开放继电器）：ON（由设备远程控制的断开）；
③ ACOCCR（交流电流辅助继电器）：ON［1 次（原边）过电流检测］；
④ AOCN（辅助电路过电流 NFB）：OFF（3 次过电流检测）；
⑤ GRR3（第 3 级电路接地继电器）：ON（3 次电路接地检测）；
⑥ CIFR（牵引变流器故障检测继电器）：OFF（牵引变流电路故障检测）；
⑦ GRR（初级电路接地继电器）：ON（初级电路接地检测）。

任务四　牵引变流器控制

【任务描述】

本任务主要介绍有关有关牵引变流器设备间的控制、状态信息等的接口。牵引控制器除完成牵引控制外，还与监控装置终端交换信息，与主断路器控制接口交换信息，控制滤波电容的预充电。

【背景知识】

一、牵引变流器和车辆信息控制终端装置间的接口

牵引变流器和终端装置间的数据传送通过光缆进行，传送和接收控制指令信息及故障信号等。除了使用光缆传送的控制指令信息之外，作为备份，使用硬导线把下述信号输入到牵引变流器：

- 前进（4 线）；
- 后退（5 线）；
- 复位（6 线）；
- 牵引级位 A（9A 线）；
- 牵引级位 B（9B 线）。

另外，使用硬导线，把下列故障、状态信号等从牵引变流器输入到终端装置：

- 控制装置正常诊断用继电器（WDTR）；
- 牵引变流器故障检测用继电器（CIFR2）；
- 牵引变流器接地检测用继电器（CIGRR2）；

- 牵引变流器控制电源用继电器（DCR）；
- 主电路电流检测装置用继电器（CDR2）。

二、牵引变流器和制动控制装置间的接口

从牵引变流器向制动控制装置传送的信号：再生反馈；再生有效信号。

从制动控制装置向牵引变流器传送的信号：再生制动模式。

牵引变流器根据从来自制动控制装置的再生制动模式信号，控制电气制动。牵引变流器根据逆变器的输出电流和牵引电机的转速，计算制动转矩，作为再生反馈信号向制动控制装置传送。制动控制装置操作必要的制动力，当电气制动的制动力不足时，用空气制动加以补足。

通过牵引变流器对电制动力的不足进行检测，如检测出电制动力不足时，则 UBCDR（再生有效信号）接点处在打开的状态，向空气制动转移。UBCDR 接点处在打开状态，在制动控制装置侧，速度在 160 km/h 以上时，制动控制用压力开关 BCS2（检测压力、低压）为 OFF，或是速度在 160 km/h 以下时，制动控制用压力开关 BCS1（检测压力、高压）为 OFF 时，如果制动不足检测用定时继电器 UBTR 处在 OFF 的话，UV（紧急制动阀）的励磁断开，紧急制动动作。

三、有关牵引变流器和真空断路器 VCB 电路间的接口

1. VCB 投入的条件

为防止 VCB 投入时对牵引变流器产生冲击电流，牵引变流器一次侧电源接触器（K）先不投入，投入继电器（KRR）处于消磁状态。VCB 投入状态输入到牵引变流器后，能够先进行滤波电容器预备充电（CHK），牵引变流器一次侧电源接触器（K）再投入。

2. VCB 断开的条件

当 VCB 处在投入的状态时，若牵引变流器发生故障，故障检测用继电器（CIFR1）消磁；若牵引变流器接地发生异常，接地检测用继电器（CIGRR1）励磁时，就会断开 VCB。

四、滤波电容器预备充电

为防止牵引变流器一次侧电源投入用接触器（K）投入时产生过大冲击电流，在 K 投入前对滤波电容器进行充电。充电的时间从终端装置输入换向器（reverser）投入信号开始。以下表示从充电开始到 K 投入为止的流程。预充电电路如图 2-4-1，2-4-2 所示。

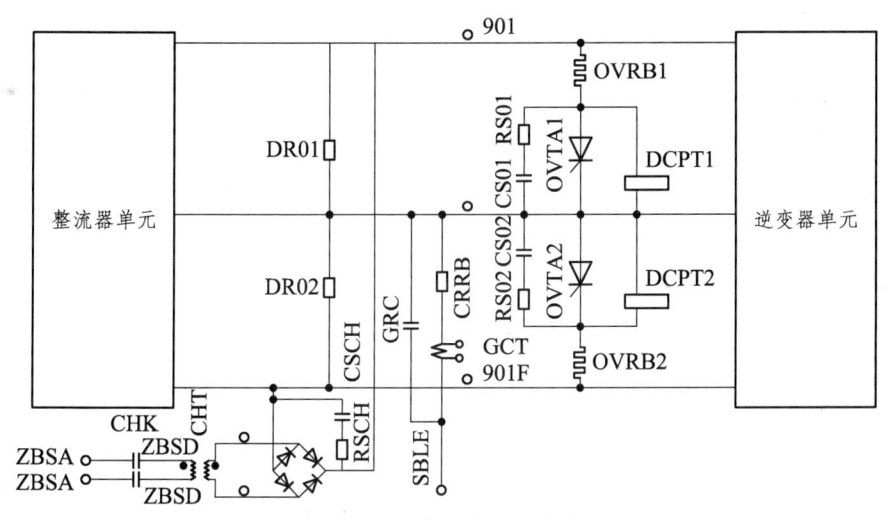

图 2-4-1　牵引变流器电路

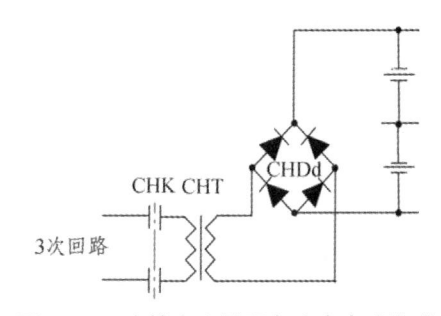

图 2-4-2　支撑电容器预备充电电路构成

- 换向器（reverser）投入
- 输出充电用接触器（CHK）投入
- 滤波电容器充电
- 充电用接触器（CHK）断开
- K 投入

五、故障保护动作

（1）1 次电路交流过电流，3 次电路接地异常。

当检测到 1 次电路交流过电流（ACOCR）、3 次电路接地异常（GR3）时，VCB 跳闸，牵引变流器一次侧电源接触器（K）断开。此外，此信息（ACOCRR1、GRR3-1）还会输入终端装置。

195

（2）牵引变压器异常，通风机停止。

当检测到牵引变压器温度异常（MTThRR）、牵引变压器油压泵异常（MTOFRR）时，牵引变压器异常信息输入到牵引变流器。此外，当牵引变流器送风机（CIBM）、牵引电机送风机（MMBM）及送风机的电源切断（BMK）时，通风机停止的信息输入到牵引变流器。当输入牵引变压器异常、通风机停止的信息时，断开脉冲整流器-逆变器门极封锁（gate-off）及牵引变流器一次侧电源接触器（K）。这些信息也输入到终端装置。

（3）ACCT。

通过ACCT检测出牵引变压器2次电流。当检测到牵引变压器2次过电流时，通过电流值把脉冲整流器-逆变器门极封锁（gate-off），同时牵引变流器一次侧电源接触器（K）断开。

（4）CTU、CTV、CTW。

检测牵引电机的U、V、W三相电流。一旦检测到过电流或电流不平衡时，就会把脉冲整流器-逆变器的门极封锁（gate-off），同时牵引变流器一次侧电源接触器（K）断开。

非过电流的情况则是：当电流值为设定值以下时，脉冲整流器-逆变器的门极开通（gate-on）。

（5）GCT。

检测牵引变压器二次侧接地电流。根据设定值，OVTH on，脉冲整流器-逆变器门极封锁（gate-off），同时牵引变流器一次侧电源接触器（K）断开。

（6）过电压抑制可控硅单元（OVTH单元）。

OVTH单元如图2-4-1所示，该单元由可控硅、缓冲器（snubber）电阻器（OVRe1、OVRe2）、缓冲器电容（FC）、栅极驱动基板、直流电压检测器（DCPT1、DCPT2）等构成。

当检测到滤波电容器产生过电压时，控制电源关断（Off），可控硅为导通（ON），让滤波电容器具有放电的机能。

DCPT组装在OVTH单元内，对直流电压进行检测。当检测到OVTH误点弧（false firing）、直流过电压、直流低电压、电压异常等时，根据条件，脉冲整流器-逆变器门极封锁（gate-off）、牵引变流器一次侧电源接触器（K）等断开。

（7）冷却单元、机械室内过温度。

分别检测脉冲整流器U、V相温度（THCU、THCV），逆变器U、V、W相温度（THIU、THIV、THIW），机械室内温度（CITHR1~5）。当检测到过温度时，采取脉冲整流器-逆变器门极封锁（gate-off）、牵引变流器一次侧电源接触器（K）断开的保护措施。

任务五　CRH380B型动车组牵引控制

【任务描述】

本任务是对CRH380B型动车组牵引系统的整体认识。通过对本任务的学习，学习者掌握其工作原理，会分析主电路工作过程。

【背景知识】

一、高压供电

1. 受电弓

接触网提供AC 25 kV电压的交流电，由受电弓受流。CRH380B型动车组每列车配备2台受电弓，通过车顶高压电缆连接一个高压系统的两个牵引单元，正常运行过程中每个高压系统只需要升起一个受电弓受流即可。

2. 真空断路器（图2-5-1）

每个独立的高压系统配置了两个主断路器，分别安装在02、07车顶端部位置。主断路器不但用来开关牵引单元的运行电流，也可以用来中断故障情况下的过流以及短路电流。为了维护和检修高压设备，主断路器安装了双极接地开关，接地开关将主断路器两端与工作接地连接。接地开关具有防止短路的功能。

图2-5-1　真空断路器

3. 接地开关（图2-5-2）

一旦接地开关接通，就可以通过闸刀将牵引装置和接地电路连接在一起实现接地。接地开关由上部外壳和下部外壳组成。上部外壳通过4个M10螺栓安装在牵引车辆车顶上，其中包含一根轴，两把可移动闸刀安装在轴的末端。下部外壳安装在车顶下方，其中包含一根控制杆，用于手动操作接地开关，将两把闸刀从平衡位置移动到主断路器的相关接地触点处。

图 2-5-2 接地开关结构

4. 避雷器（图 2-5-3）

动车组每个变压器车设置有 2 个避雷器：一个避雷器安装在每个受电弓的右后方用于保护列车以及后段的电气系统，防止过压通过接触线进入列车（如，闪电过压）；另一个避雷器位于变压器原边的前端，用于防止主变压器中开关产生的不能承受的电压。

图 2-5-3 避雷器

5. 电压、电流互感器（图 2-5-4、2-5-5）

网端检测装置由电流互感器、电压互感器构成。电压互感器用于测量和监视电网接触线的电压。电流互感器被接到每一个主断路器下口，用于测量动车组的电流。另外两个互感器用于监测主变压器。这两个互感器用来测量牵引单元的线电流以及回流电流。

图 2-5-4　电压互感器　　　　　　图 2-5-5　电流互感器

6. 高压隔离开关

动车组全列共 2 个车顶隔离开关，位于变压器车顶，在正常情况下处于闭合状态，当发生故障时隔离开关断开将车顶电缆隔离。如果一个牵引单元的主电路系统出现故障，列车控制系统可隔离车顶线路，从而使另一个牵引单元可操作。

7. 高压跳线（图 2-5-6）

车顶高压线必须越过车之间的连接部分。这由车端的支持绝缘子及支持绝缘子跨接电缆实现。跨接电缆的设计适用于车体之间的最大相对运动。复绕设计能够满足车体间的最大相对运动。每单个绕组的尺寸能够满足最大运行电流要求。如果一个绕组断了，电流会被另一个绕组保持，而且通过目测就很容易检查。

图 2-5-6　高压跳线

8. 牵引变压器

CRH380B 型动车组牵引变压器位于动车组 TC02/TC07 车下设备舱中，变压器及冷却单元集成在一个框架内。变压器为单相变压器，主变压器将 25 kV/50 Hz 的一次电压降至供 4 个牵引绕组使用的 1 850 V/50 Hz 的二次电压，它的次级绕组为牵引变流器提供电能。

三、牵引系统

牵引系统主要为动车组提供牵引动力，主要设备包括牵引变流器、过压限制电阻器、牵引电机、牵引电机冷却风机。牵引系统原理图如图 2-5-7 所示。

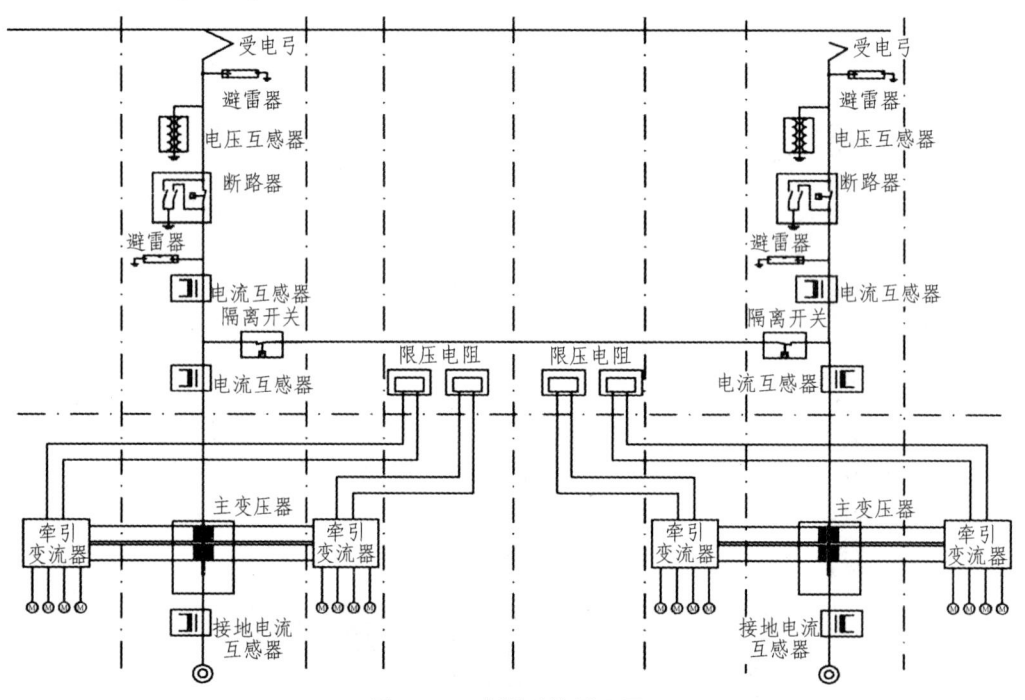

图 2-5-7 牵引系统原理图

CRH380B 型动车组中装有 4 个完全相同且互相独立的动力单元。每一个动力单元有一个带牵引控制单元的牵引变流器，以及 4 个并联的牵引电动机。每一个牵引变流器基本上由 2 个四象限斩波器（4QC），带谐振电路的中间电压电路，1 个制动斩波器 BC 以及 1 个脉冲宽度调制逆变（PWMI）牵引变流器的输入线路接触器，由列车控制单元 TCU 控制两组四象限斩波器（4QC）、一组逆变器、一组牵引控制装置、冷却系统及中间直流环节，每一组逆变器控制 4 台牵引电机。变流器的主要功能是将牵引变压器输出的 1AC1 850 V/50 Hz 交流电，经四象限整流得到 3 200～3 600 V 的中间直流电压，再经逆变器输出电压、频率可调的三相交流电为牵引电机供电。

动车组设 4 个电压限制器。每个一个动力单元含一个电压限制器。电压限制器位于 04/05 中间车的端部。车顶上限压电阻器是用来防止牵引变流器过电压。在变流器发生故障的情况下，限压电阻器能确保限定的、安全放电的中间电路。当电制动所产生的能量不能被弓网吸收时，过压限制电阻器会及时地将这些能量转换成热能。

动车组有 16 个牵引电机，这些电机被安装在下列动力转向架上：01 车、03 车、06 车、08 车，为四极三相异步牵引电机。该电机采用强迫风冷却，采用温度监测方式以防止牵引电机过热，采用机械力传递系统将牵引电机的驱动力矩传递到轮对。这套系统主要由轴向、径向都具有柔性的联轴节以及轮对上的齿轮传动装置组成。联轴节的设计可以补偿在驱动过程中电机与车轮间的相对运动。

任务六　故障案例分析

【任务描述】

本任务主要介绍主回路故障保护和故障案例。通过本任务学习，学习者会分析故障原因并掌握故障处理办法。

【背景知识】

一、主回路故障

主回路故障保护如表 2-6-1 所示。

表 2-6-1　主回路故障处理

故障种类	保护动作 VCB 跳闸	保护动作 K 断开	保护动作 变流器不输出	显示 故障指示灯	显示 故障代码	显示 其他显示画面	复位方法及步骤
变压器一次过电流	√	√	√	VCB	162	配电盘信息	先按复位开关；然后合 OCTN；再次合 VCB
变压器油泵停止运行	√	√	√	—	165	配电盘信息	合上油泵断路器
变压器绝缘油循环停止	—	√	√	电气设备	132	配电盘信息	状态解除后自动复位
变压器温度上升	—	√	√	电气设备	133	配电盘信息	状态解除后自动复位

续表

故障种类	保护动作 VCB跳闸	保护动作 K断开	保护动作 变流器不输出	显示 故障指示灯	显示 显示器画面 故障代码	显示 显示器画面 其他显示画面	复位方法及步骤
变压器三次过电流	√	√	√	VCB	163	配电盘信息	再次接通ACON；接通VCB
变压器三次侧接地	√	√	√	VCB	164	配电盘信息	按下复位开关；再次合上VCB
同步电源异常（过电压）	—	—	√	—	—	变流器（各车）	故障1 s且状态解除后自动复位
同步电源异常（欠电压）	—	—	√	—	—	变流器（各车）	故障1 s且状态解除后自动复位
同步电源异常（频率）	—	—	√	—	—	—	故障1 s且状态解除后自动复位
变压器二次过电流1	—	—	√	—	—	变流器（各车）	故障1 s且状态解除后自动复位
变压器二次过电流2	√	√	√	电气设备VCB	141 005	变流器（各车）配电盘信息	运转配电盘牵引变流器1断路器重新投入
直流过电压1	—	—	√	—	—	变流器（各车）	故障1 s且状态解除后自动复位
直流过电压2	—	—	√	—	—	变流器（各车）	故障1 s且状态解除后自动复位
直流过电压3	—	√	√	—	004	变流器（各车）	操作复位开关
直流欠电压1	—	—	√	—	—	—	故障1 s且状态解除后自动复位
直流欠电压2	—	√	√	—	—	变流器（各车）	故障1 s且状态解除后自动复位
直流电压异常	—	—	√	—	—	—	故障1 s且状态解除后自动复位
主电路器件异常	√	√	√	电气设备VCB	141 005	变流器（各车）配电盘信息	运转配电盘牵引变流器1断路器重新投入
直流100 V异常	—	√	√	—	004	变流器（各车）	操作复位开关
控制电源异常	—	√	√	—	004	变流器（各车）	操作复位开关
闸控电源异常	—	√	√	—	004	变流器（各车）	操作复位开关

续表

故障种类	保护动作 VCB跳闸	保护动作 K断开	保护动作 变流器不输出	故障指示灯	显示 故障代码	显示 其他显示画面	复位方法及步骤
微机异常	—	√	√	电气设备	139	配电盘信息	操作复位开关
牵引电机过电流1	—	—	√	—	004	变流器（各车）	故障1s且状态解除后自动复位；在间隔10s以内两次检测时，操作复位开关
牵引电机过电流2	—	√	√	—	004	变流器（各车）	操作复位开关
牵引电机电流不平衡	—	√	√	—	004	变流器（各车）	操作复位开关，维持3s
脉冲发生器异常	—	√	√	—	004	变流器（各车）	操作复位开关
制动力过大	—	—	√	—	—	变流器（各车）	制动断开后复位
冷却装置温度过高	—	√	—	—	—	变流器（各车）	状态解除后自动复位
设备室内温度过高	—	√	—	—	—	变流器（各车）	状态解除后自动复位
MM、CI风机停止运行	—	√	√	电气设备	137 138 134	变流器（各车）配电盘信息	状态解除后自动复位（各风机断路器再次接通）
OVTh误点弧	—	√	√	—	004	变流器（各车）	故障发生后5s且待故障解除后自动复位；在间隔30s以内三次检测时，K断开、操作复位开关
充电不良	—	—	—	—	005	变流器（各车）	重新合上牵引变流器1
主变压器二次侧接地1	—	√	√	—	004	变流器（各车）	操作复位开关
主变压器二次侧接地2	√	—	—	电气设备VCB	142 004	变流器（各车）配电盘信息	再次接通VCB操作复位开关
再生制动失效	—	—	—	—	—	—	制动解除
牵引电机不工作	—	—	—	—	—	变流器（各车）	故障1s且状态解除后自动复位

二、故障处理过程举例

1. 受电弓无法升起

受电弓无法升起的故障处理过程如表 2-6-2 所示。

表 2-6-2　受电弓无法升起的故障处理过程

现象	MON 显示受电弓未升起，网压表无显示。
车种	CRH380A、CRH380AL
原因	① 两端司机室配电盘中的【受电弓·VCB】断路器处于断开位。 ② 辅助风缸压力过低。 ③ EGS 处于闭合状态。 ④ VCB 处于闭合状态。 ⑤ 【04、06 车（CRH380A）】/【05、13 车（CRH380AL）】组合配电盘中的【升弓】断路器处于断开位。 ⑥ CRH380AL 型动车组 05、13 车组合配电盘中的【阀板电源 1、2】断路器处于断开位。
行车	故障处理后正常运行
步骤	处理过程
1	1.1 确认主控端司机室配电盘【受电弓·VCB】断路器是否处于闭合状态，若断开，则闭合。 1.2 确认"准备未完"显示灯是否熄灭，若灯亮，则右旋【辅助空气压缩机控制】旋钮保持 3 s，启动辅助空气压缩机打风，直到"准备未完"显示灯灭。 1.3 确认 EGS 是否处于断开状态，若闭合，则闭合主控端司机室【保护接地】断路器，右旋【保护接地切除】旋钮开关保持 3 s，断开 EGS 后，再将【保护接地】断路器断开。 1.4 确认 VCB 是否处于断开状态，若闭合，则按压【VCB 断】按钮，断开 VCB。 1.5 若受电弓仍无法升起，通知随车机械师。

续表

步骤	处理过程
2	2.1 立即确认另一司机室配电盘中的【受电弓·VCB】断路器是否处于闭合状态，若断开，则闭合。 2.2 确认〖04、06车（CRH380A）〗/〖05、13车（CRH380AL）〗组合配电盘中的【升弓】断路器是否处于闭合状态，若断开，则闭合。 2.3 确认〖05、13车（CRH380AL）〗组合配电中的【阀板电源1、2】断路器是否处于闭合状态，若断开，则闭合。 2.4 确认完毕，通知司机。
3	3.1 再次进行升弓操作，若受电弓仍不能升起，则进行换弓操作。 3.2 若换弓后受电弓也不能升起，则远程切除所有受电弓，逐一远程操作升弓，但不能升两近弓（重联、CRH380AL）。 3.3 若动车组所有受电弓均无法升起，则机械师通知司机申请救援。

2. 全列 VCB 不能闭合

全列 VCB 不能闭合故障处理过程如表 2-6-3 所示。

表 2-6-3　全列 VCB 不能闭合故障处理过程

现象	按压【VCB合】按钮或过分相后，全列 VCB 不能闭合。
车种	CRH380A、CRH380AL
原因	① VCBOR3 继电器常开触电粘连，导致 8 号线有电。 ② EXR1 继电器常开触点粘连，导致 8 号线有电。
行车	先应急处理，无效后停车处理
步骤	处理过程
1	1.1 不停车，按压【VCB合】按钮，若闭合，则继续运行。 1.2 若不闭合，确认主控端司机室配电盘【受电弓·VCB】断路器是否处于闭合状态，若断开，则闭合。

续表

步骤	处理过程	
1		1.3 确认"准备未完"显示灯是否熄灭,若灯亮,则右旋【辅助空气压缩机控制】旋钮保持3 s,启动辅助空气压缩机打风,直到"准备未完"显示灯灭。 1.4 将方向手柄置于"关"位。 1.5 按压【VCB合】按钮,若全列VCB仍不能闭合,通知随车机械师。
2		2.1 立即断开〚2、6车(CRH380A)〛/〚02、08、10、14车(CRH380AL)〛组合配电盘中的【受电弓断路器】断路器。 2.2 处理完毕,通知司机。 2.3 司机再次按压【VCB合】按钮,若全列VCB仍不能闭合,通知随车机械师。
3		3.1 随车机械师断开〚02、04、06车(CRH380A)〛/〚02、04、06、08、10、12、14车(CRH380AL)〛组合配电盘中的【真空断路器】断路器。 3.2 断开完毕,通知司机。
	3.3 随车机械师逐个闭合【真空断路器】断路器,通知司机依次进行RS复位并按压【VCB合】按钮,通过此操作判断导致全列VCB不能闭合的故障单元。 3.4 找到故障单元后,随车机械师断开该单元对应组合配电盘中的【真空断路器】断路器。 3.5 司机远程切除故障VCB单元,并闭合ACK2进行扩展供电。	
4		若动车组过分相区后,全列VCB不能自动闭合,按如下程序处理: 4.1 司机发现过分相区后,全列VCB不能自动闭合,通知随车机械师。 4.2 随车机械师立即确认受电弓升起车厢对应组合配电盘中的【过分相VCB控制1】、【过分相VCB控制2】、【过分相装置电源】、【过分相控制1】、【过分相控制2】断路器是否处于闭合状态,若断开,则闭合。 4.3 确认完毕,通知司机。 4.4 若动车组过分相区后,全列VCB仍不能自动闭合,司机采取手动过分相。

3. 保护接地开关合上后无法断开

保护接地开关合上后无法断开的故障处理过程如表 2-6-4 所示。

表 2-6-4　保护接地开关合上后无法断开的故障处理过程

现象	EGS 处于闭合状态，且无法断开。
车种	CRH380A、CRH380AL
原因	1. 司机室配电盘中的【保护接地】断路器处于断开位。 2. 司机室的【保护接地合】按钮或旋钮处于闭合位。 3. 辅助风缸风压过低。 4. 组合配电盘中的【保护接地断】断路器处于断位。
行车	停车处理
步骤	处理过程
1	1.1 确认主控端司机室配电盘中的【保护接地】断路器是否处于闭合状态，若断开，则闭合。 1.2 确认司机室的【保护接地开关】旋钮是否处于"合"位，若在"合"位，则旋至"断"位。 1.3 确认"准备未完"显示灯是否熄灭，若灯亮，则右旋【辅助空气压缩机控制】旋钮保持 3 s，启动辅助空气压缩机打风，直到"准备未完"显示灯灭。 1.4 右旋司机室配电盘中的【保护接地切除】旋钮开关 3 s，若保护接地开关仍不能切除，通知随车机械师。
2	2.1 立即确认〖04、06 车（CRH380A）〗/〖05、13 车（CRH380AL）〗配电盘中的【保护接地断】断路器是否处于闭合状态，若断开，则闭合。 2.2 确认完毕，通知司机。

207

续表

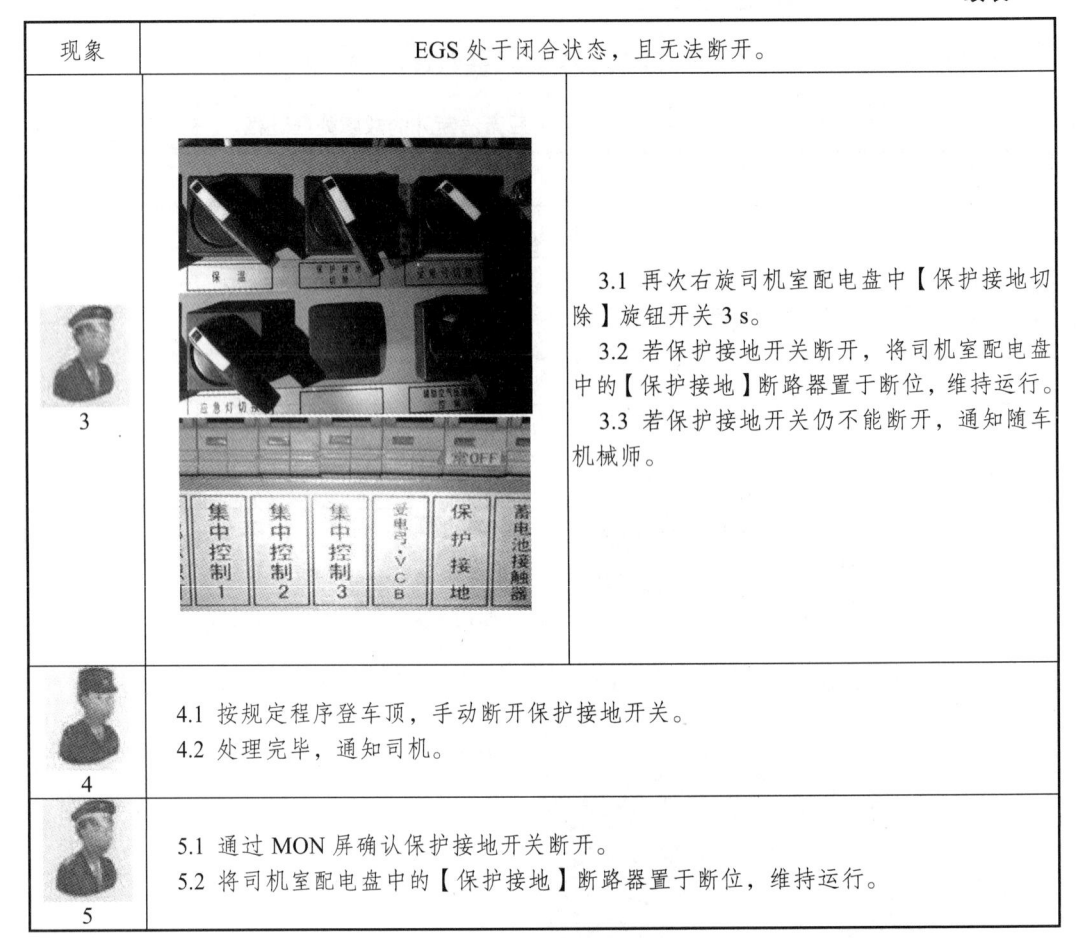

现象		EGS处于闭合状态,且无法断开。
3		3.1 再次右旋司机室配电盘中【保护接地切除】旋钮开关3 s。 3.2 若保护接地开关断开,将司机室配电盘中的【保护接地】断路器置于断位,维持运行。 3.3 若保护接地开关仍不能断开,通知随车机械师。
4		4.1 按规定程序登车顶,手动断开保护接地开关。 4.2 处理完毕,通知司机。
5		5.1 通过MON屏确认保护接地开关断开。 5.2 将司机室配电盘中的【保护接地】断路器置于断位,维持运行。

4. 牵引变流器故障(004)

牵引变流器故障(004)的处理过程如表2-6-5所示。

表 2-6-5　牵引变流器故障（004）的处理过程

现象	K 断开，此动车无法牵引和再生制动。
车种	CRH380A、CRH380AL
原因	① 直流过电压。 ② 控制电源异常。 ③ 牵引电机过电流。 ④ 牵引电机电流不平衡。 ⑤ PG 异常。 ⑥ 主变压器二次侧接地。
行车	继续运行
步骤	处理过程
1	当 MON 屏主菜单页面闪现"故障发生信息"提示，并伴有声音报警时，司机触按左下方【故障详情】键，确认故障情况，并通知随车机械师。
2	MON 屏切换至"牵引变流器故障（1 004）"故障信息页面。
3	3.1 通过 MON 屏"牵引变流器信息（编）"页面，确认故障详情。 3.2 通过 MON 屏"牵引变流器信息（车）"页面，查看故障原因。
4	4.1 RS 复位。 4.2 若故障消除，正常运行。 4.3 若复位 3 次（每次间隔不少于 3 s）故障仍未消除，远程切除相应 M 车，维持运行。

5. 牵引变流器故障2（005）

牵引变流器故障2（005）的处理过程如表2-6-6所示。

表2-6-6 牵引变流器故障2（005）的处理过程

名称	2.3 牵引变流器 故障2（005）
现象	① VCB 或 K 断开。 ② VCB 断开时，司机操纵台故障显示灯"VCB"灯点亮，且故障未处理前不允许再次闭合 VCB（若故障仅为二次侧过电流2时，可远程切除故障 M 车后，投入 VCB）。 ③ 牵引和再生制动力降低。
车种	CRH380A、CRH380AL
原因	① 牵引变压器二次侧过电流2。 ② 主电路器件异常。 ③ 牵引变流器中间电路充电不良。
行车	继续运行
步骤	处理过程
1	当 MON 屏主菜单页面闪现"故障发生信息"提示，并伴有声音报警时，司机触按左下方【故障详情】键，确认故障情况，并通知随车机械师。
2	MON 屏切换至"牵引变流器故障2（005）"故障信息页面。
3	3.1 通过 MON 屏"牵引变流器（车）"页面，确认原因。 3.2 远程切除故障 M 车，并通知随车机械师。

续表

步骤	处理过程
4	4.1 立即将相应车配电盘中的【牵引变流器1】断路器断开15 s再投入。 4.2 处理完毕，通知司机。
5	5.1 若故障消除，远程复位M车，正常运行。 5.2 若故障未消除，远程切除该M车，维持运行。

【项目检测】

1. 分析牵引传动系统的组成。
2. 分析CRH380A型动车组主电路结构。
3. 试画图分析牵引控制的工作过程。
4. 分析方向控制器的逻辑运行指令电路的工作原理。
5. 分析牵引控制器逻辑运行指令电路的工作原理。
6. 请绘出主控制器继电器联锁控制电路并分析其工作过程。
7. 试分析真空断路器VCB控制电路的工作原理。
8. 分析牵引变流器与再生制动的控制过程。
9. 试分析升降弓工作过程。

项目三　复兴号动车组牵引控制电路分析

【项目描述】

本项目是对复兴号动车组 CR400AF、CR400BF 牵引控制系统的整体认识。通过本项目的学习,学生应掌握复兴号动车组牵引系统的组成、工作原理,能分析主电路、控制电路的工作过程及故障保护。

【项目任务】

(1)能进行 CR400AF 动车组高压、牵引控制电路分析。
(2)能进行 CR400BF 动车组牵引系统分析。

任务一　CR400AF 动车组高压、牵引控制电路分析

【任务描述】

本任务主要介绍 CR400AF 动车组高压、牵引控制系统。学习完本任务,学生应掌握整个系统的组成、功能,并会分析电路。

【背景知识】

一、高压系统

1. 高压系统性能

高压系统具有为全车供电、电气保护、监测网压及提供工作电流的作用。3、6 车各设置 1 个基本高压单元,由受电弓、高压隔离开关、真空断路器、避雷器、电压互感器、电流互感器、高压接头、高压电缆及接地装置等部件组成。

2. 技术特点

(1)低阻力。集成式高压设备箱不突出车体外轮廓,有利于降低车辆运行阻力。

（2）小型化。高压系统采用高压部件集成在高压箱体里的设计方式，节省了安装空间，如图 3-1-1 所示。

（3）节能环保，维护量减少。高压部件集成在高压箱里，受环境污染影响小，可减少对高压部件的擦拭次数，节约人工和水资源。

（4）主动受电弓可根据速度、受电弓位置、不同线路信息等，控制气路控制单元，实现主动控制，如图 3-1-2 所示。

图 3-1-1　集成高压设备箱

图 3-1-2　主动控制受电弓

3. 高压系统原理

TP03 车和 TP06 车各设置 1 个基本高压单元，每个高压单元的设置相同；隔离开关可隔离对应的高压单元；通过真空断路器可对故障受电弓、电压互感器、电流互感器等进行隔离；每个高压单元通过电流、电压互感器进行检测，实施过压、过流保护；每个高压单元设置 2 个避雷器，实现高压回路过电压两级保护。高压系统如图 3-1-3 所示。

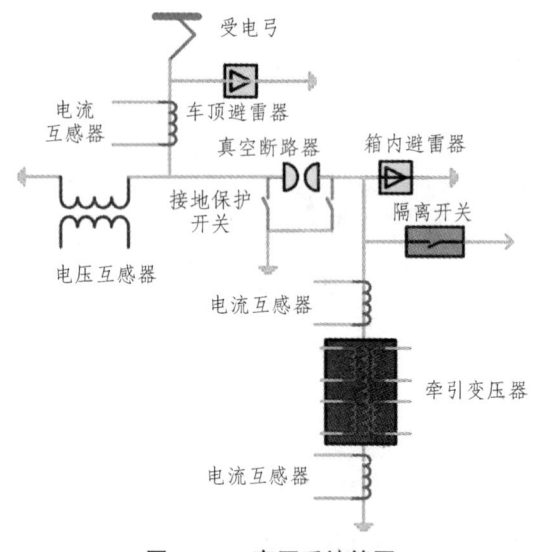

图 3-1-3　高压系统简图

4. 受电弓控制

受电弓升起和降下控制分 TCMS 控制和硬线控制，有正常升降弓和紧急牵引模式下升降弓。如图 3-1-4 所示。

5. VCB 控制

VCB 闭合和断开控制分 TCMS 控制和硬线控制，有正常控制 VCB 和紧急牵引模式下控制 VCB 两种情况，如图 3-1-5 所示。

6. 紧急断电控制

正常运行过程中，在没有触发紧急断电环路断开条件发生情况下，紧急断电环路建立，当环路失电后，将触发紧急断电，动车组将通过硬线指令触发 VCB 断开，受电弓降下。

当运行中由于某联锁条件故障导致紧急断电环路断开无法恢复时，可通过操作升起受电弓单元司机室的紧急断电旁路开关实现环路的旁路功能，避免单点故障造成受电弓无法升起，如图 3-1-6 所示。

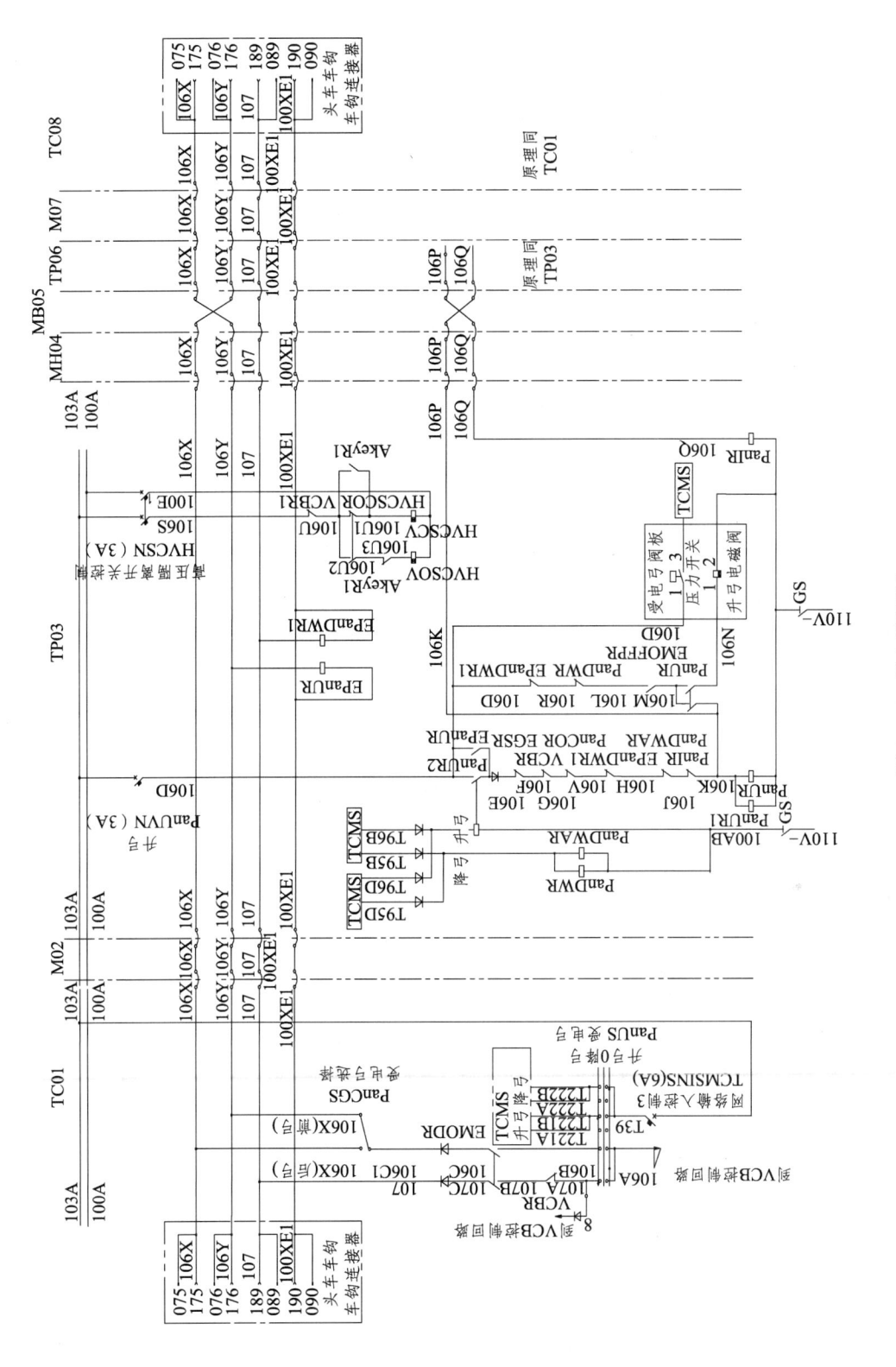

图 3-1-4 受电弓控制

图 3-1-5 VCB 控制

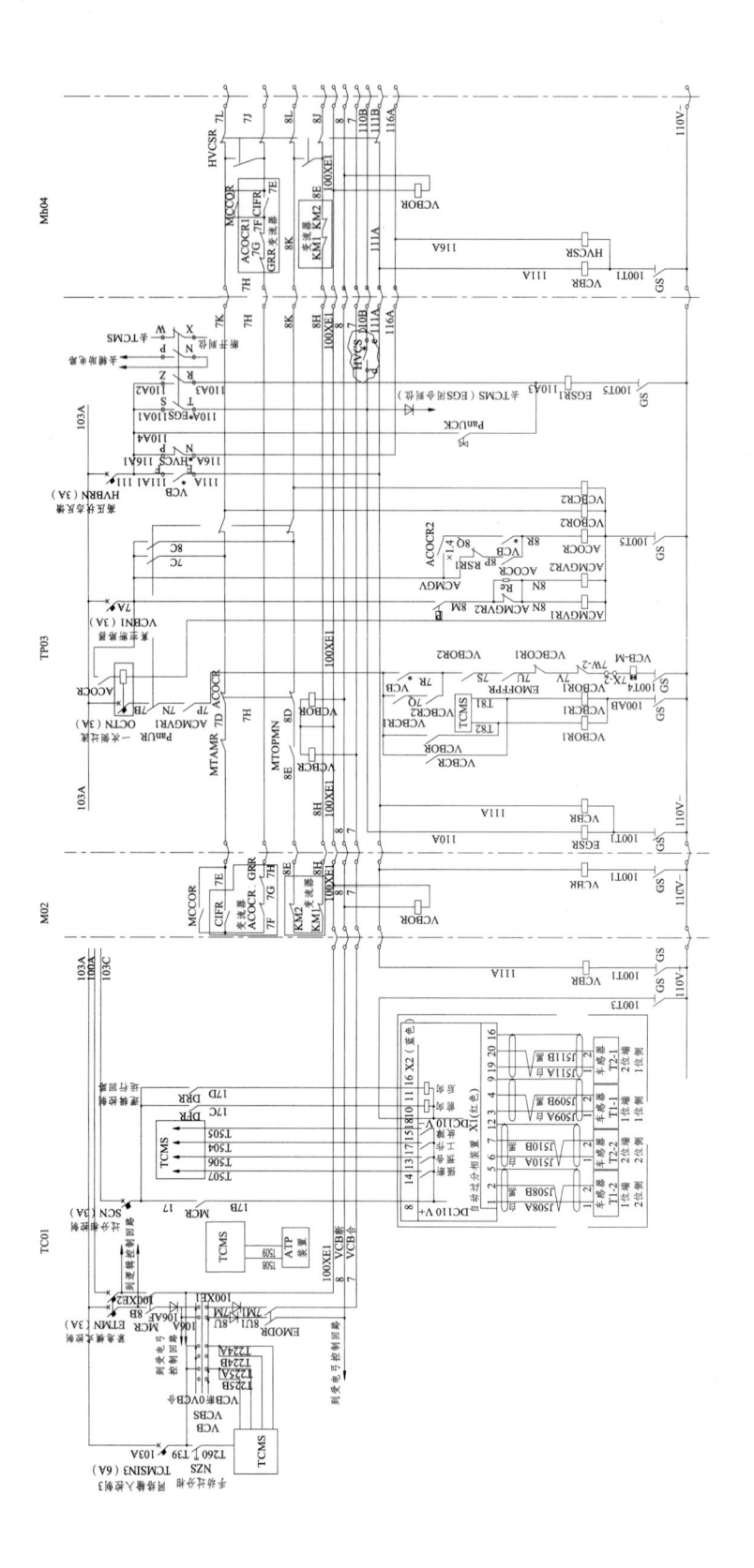

图 3-1-6 紧急断电控制

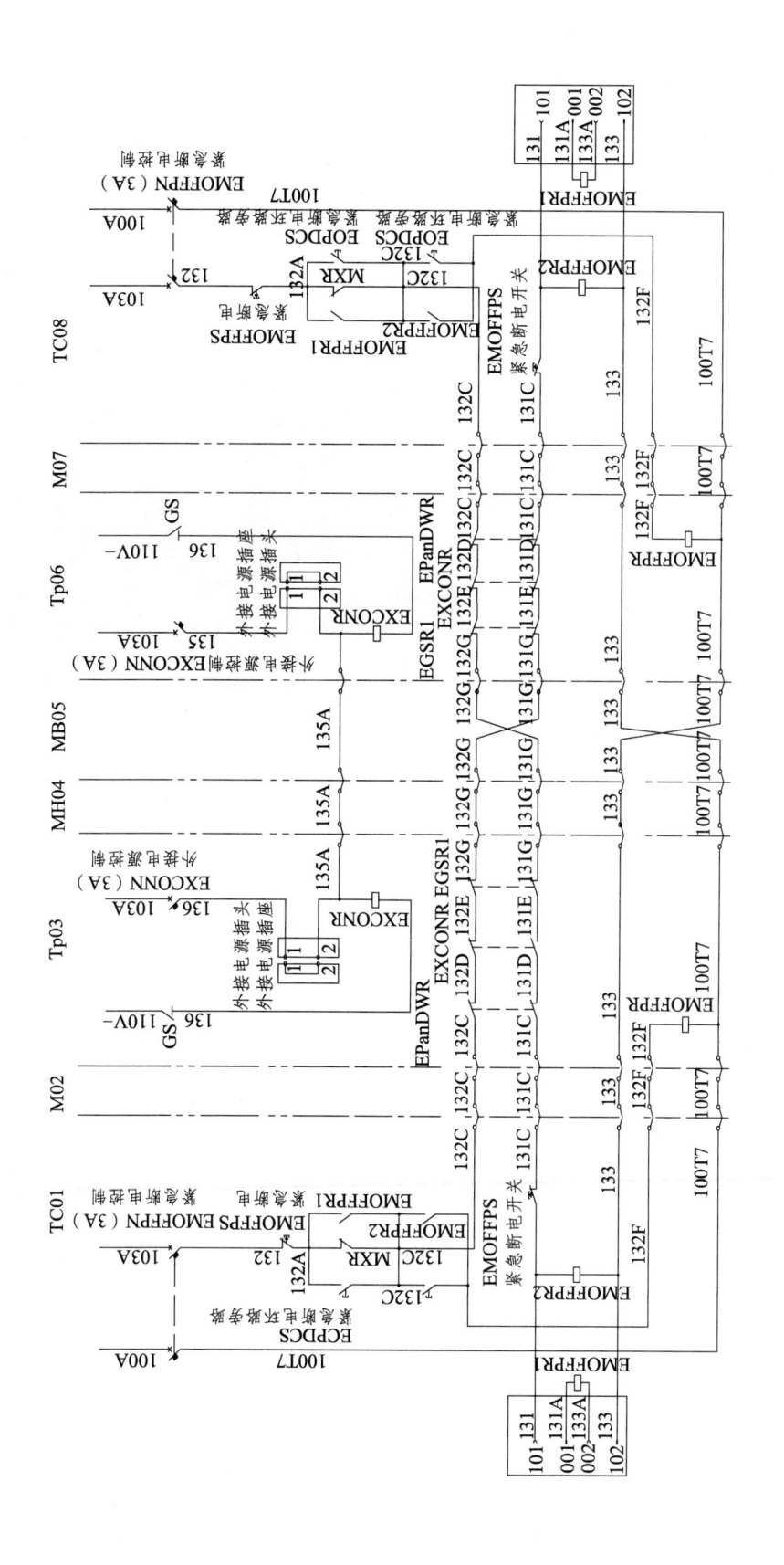

7. 高压隔离开关控制电路

动车组正常运行时，高压隔离开关是闭合的，当单元发生接地或过流故障需要切除高压母线时，通过操作 HMI 显示屏上的远程切除按键，可以选择性地断开 TP03 或 TP06 车的高压隔离开关，如图 3-1-7 所示。当切除指令有效时，HVCSCOR 继电器得电，使得 HVCSOV 阀得电，带动高压隔离开关打开。需要再次复位时，只能在 HMI 显示屏上通过远程复位来完成，如图 3-1-8 所示。

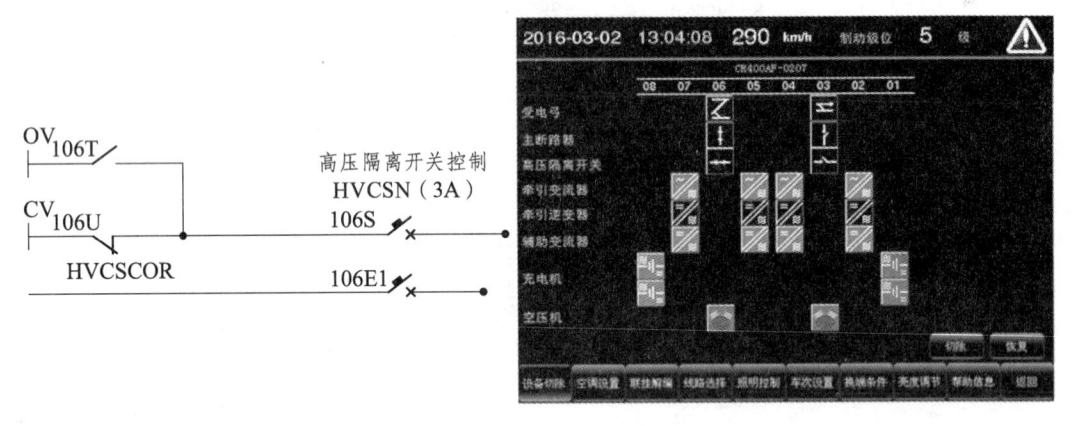

图 3-1-7 隔离开关控制

图 3-1-8 HMI 显示屏

8. 网侧过流控制电路

当网侧电流传感器检测到网侧电流大于 1 200 A 时，升弓单元的过流继电器动作，故障组 VCB 跳开，【一次侧过流】断路器跳开，且无法闭合；可以通过操作 RS 复位，TCMS 输出 RSR1 继电器得电，RSR1 常闭触点断开，使得 ACOCR 继电器失电，一次侧过流断路器可以投入，如图 3-1-9 所示。

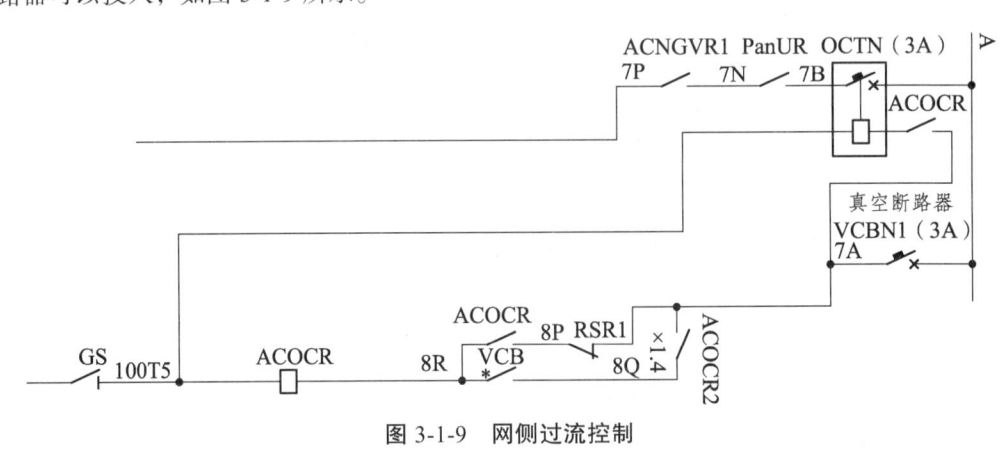

图 3-1-9 网侧过流控制

9. 高压联锁控制（EGS 控制）

CR400AF 动车组保护接地开关(EGS)动作气路中增加了气路控制联锁盒，如图 3-1-10 所示。

EGS 闭合条件：EGCV 电磁阀得电动作，控制 EGS 闭合。

EGS 断开条件：EGOV 电磁阀得电动作，控制 EGS 断开。

EGS 闭合气路　　　　EGS 断开气路

图 3-1-10　高压联锁控制

高压联锁控制操作方法如下。

维护时：

（1）投入主控，在司机室操作保护接地控制开关至红点位。

（2）将 3、6 车辅助空压机钥匙箱内的 EGOGK 和 PanUCK 手柄置于水平位置，拉开外箱，按下取钥匙【黑色（开锁）】按钮，可取出打开气路联锁盒的钥匙（蓝色）。

（3）分别将 3、6 车蓝色钥匙插入本车的气路联锁盒逆时针旋转 60°，确认 EGS 闭合到位。

（4）分别按下 3、6 车气路联锁盒蓝色按钮并保持，将黄色钥匙顺时针旋转 60°后取出。

（5）将取出的 3、6 号车黄色钥匙插入 4 车的安全联锁盒内，按照操作说明可取出 3、6 车高压设备箱绿色钥匙和外接电源连接器箱绿色钥匙，分别可以打开 3、6 车高压设备箱和 3、6 车的外接电源连接器箱。

维护后：

（1）将 3、6 车高压设备箱绿色钥匙和外接电源连接器箱绿色钥匙全部放回 4 车安全联锁盒，取出 3、6 车的气路联锁盒的黄色钥匙。

（2）分别在 3、6 车气路联锁盒处下蓝色按钮并保持，同时插入本车对应的黄色钥匙逆时针旋转 60°，松开按钮，将蓝色钥匙顺时针旋转 60°后取出。

（3）分别在 3、6 车辅助空压机钥匙箱处，按下取钥匙【黑色（开锁）】按钮并保持，将蓝色钥匙归还至钥匙箱后松开取钥匙【黑色（开锁）】按钮。

（4）将 3、6 车辅助空压机钥匙箱内的 EGOGK 和 PanUCK 手柄置于垂直位置。

（5）在司机室操作保护接地控制开关至非红点位，通过 HMI 屏确认全列 EGS 已断开到位。

二、牵引系统

1. 牵引系统构架

牵引系统构架如图 3-1-11 所示。全列为两个对称的动力单元（4M4T），每个动力单元通过 1 台主变压器将 25 kV 网压降压后输送给 2 个牵引变流器，变流器经交-直-交变换，为本车 4 台三相异步牵引电机供电，辅助变流器为车辆提供 AC 380 V 辅助用电。牵引系统结构特点如下：

（1）主辅一体化结构，集成度高。

（2）架控模式——动力冗余度高。

（3）直接转矩控制——优良的控制性能。

（4）二重四象限及载波移相控制——有效抑制网侧谐波。

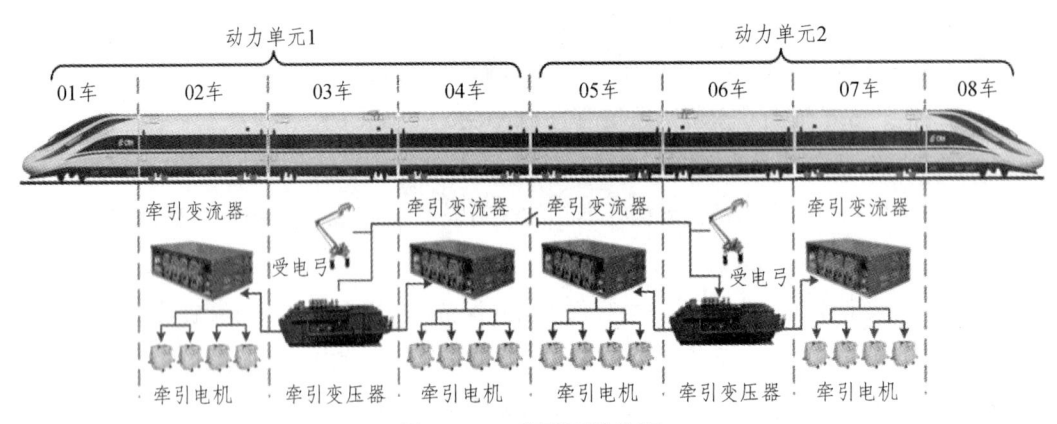

图 3-1-11 牵引系统构架

2. 主要功能与特点

主要功能：牵引、再生制动、辅助发电、过分相不断电、无火回送发电等。

主要特点：主辅一体化可实现过分相及回送发电功能，集成度高；架控模式，动力冗余度高；二重四象限可有效抑制网侧谐波。

牵引系统的其他控制功能还包括：

（1）执行 TCMS 故障降级模式和限速指令。

（2）执行 TCMS 关于辅助变流器供电相关指令。

（3）牵引系统内部限速管理。

（4）紧急牵引。

（5）中间直流回路充电。

（6）变流器的启动。

（7）中间直流回路电压监控。

（8）四象限移相控制。

（9）接地故障监控。

（10）牵引安全联锁。

（11）轮径校正。

（12）变流器冷却监控。

（13）牵引电机冷却监控。

（14）防空转/电制滑行控制。

（15）网压/功率限制。

3. 牵引制动特性

车辆牵引三种运行模式：级位模式、速度模式、紧急牵引模式。

（1）级位模式：由网络系统根据级位信息生成牵引力百分比，发送给各车牵引变流器实现牵引控制。牵引级位共设置8级。

（2）速度模式：由网络系统根据目标速度生成牵引力百分比或再生制动力百分比，发送给各车牵引变流器实现恒速控制。

（3）紧急牵引模式：在紧急牵引模式下工作时，牵引手柄置于牵引区，各车牵引变流器接收牵引指令信号，发挥50%的功率。

4.牵引系统性能

（1）额定牵引功率10 000 kW，再生制动功率不小于牵引功率的1.3倍。

（2）具备过分相发电（>78 km/h 发电，<55 km/h 退出；CR300AF 为 >70 km/h 发电，<55 km/h 退出）功能。

（3）系统具有牵引、再生制动、辅助发电等齐备的系统功能。

（4）系统对过压、过载、超温、超速、空转及各部件具有完备的保护方案。

（5）救援回送（>55 km/h 发电，<35 km/h 退出；CR300AF 为 >50 km/h 发电，<30 km/h 退出）自发电功能。

牵引变流器增设 DC/DC 模块，转入回送模式时，DC 110 V 电压逆变后输出电压给中间直流电压充电，建立牵引电机所需的励磁电流，电机转为发电工况，通过中间直流环节为辅助变流器提供工作电源，如图 3-1-12 所示。

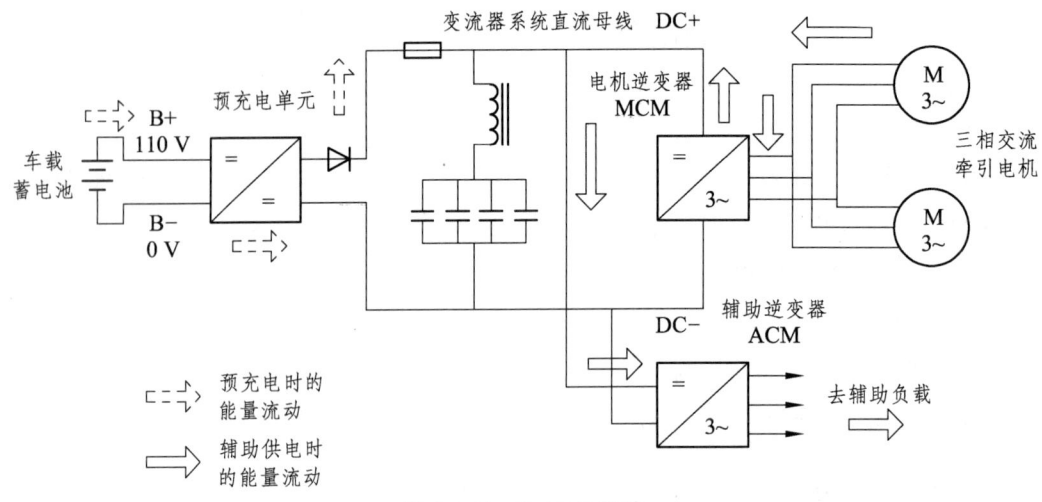

图 3-1-12　DC/DC 模块

三、控制电路

牵引控制单元（TCU）是电传动系统核心控制部分，由外部 DC 110 V 供电，通过检测电压、电流、速度、温度、压力等量，完成对牵引变流器的闭环实时控制，实现列车所需要的牵引功能。TCU 具有符合列车通信网络标准的 MVB 通信接口和以太网车辆级通信协议，与中央控制单元等形成控制与通信系统；同时，TCU 还具备当列架控制与诊断系统出现故障时，可用硬线实现紧急牵引的功能。

1. 过分相控制功能

牵引变流器根据网络发送的过分相指令进行过分相控制。收到过分相指令时，列车速度 > 80 km/h 则进行微制动发电，列车速度 < 55 km/h 时则退出微制动发电。

紧急工况下，过分相区时牵引变流器停机。

进分相区控制过程如下：

（1）收到过分相指令后，在 0.8 s 时间内卸载牵引力矩或者制动力矩，并控制牵引逆变器转为微制动发电状态，然后封锁四象限。

（2）VCB 断开后，断开短接接触器。

出分相区控制过程如下：

（1）过分相指令撤销且 VCB 闭合后，变流器进行充电短接动作。

（2）短接闭合后，延时 1 s 再闭合短接接触器，然后再延时 1 s 启动四象限。

（3）牵引逆变器退出微制动发电状态，进入正常的牵引、制动响应状态。

2. 救援回送发电控制功能

牵引变流器根据网络发送的救援回送指令进行救援回送控制。救援回送发电要求列车速度 > 55 km/h，当列车速度 < 35 km/h 时退出救援回送发电。

进入救援回送发电控制过程如下：

（1）列车启动前（列车速度 = 0），方向指令有效，救援回送指令有效，DC 110 V 电源输入有效。

（2）牵引变流器无故障。

（3）列车速度 > 55 km/h 后，启动斩波升压模块给中间回路充电，完成充电工作后，斩波升压模块退出工作，然后启动牵引逆变器建立中间电压（3 000 V）。

（4）中间电压建立后启动辅助逆变器。

（5）列车速度 < 35 km/h 时退出救援回送发电。

3. 紧急牵引控制功能

硬线紧急牵引指令有效时，认为列车处于紧急牵引工况。紧急牵引工况时，只信任硬线指令。当满足下述所有条件时，启动牵引变流器输出 50%牵引力：

（1）紧急牵引模式有效。

（2）紧急牵引指令有效。

（3）牵引手柄状态位信号有效。

（4）方向指令有效。

4. 牵引使能和零位加载功能

（1）牵引使能电路。

通过确认主控信号有效、方向信号有效（前向或后向），车辆无紧急制动，车辆无常用制动，牵引手柄牵引扇区，全列车门关闭，ATP 未输出紧急制动、常用制动、牵引切除信号后，牵引使能继电器 PCR 动作，PCR 通过 TCMS 进行采集，并将使能信号转发给 TCU，如图 3-1-13 所示。

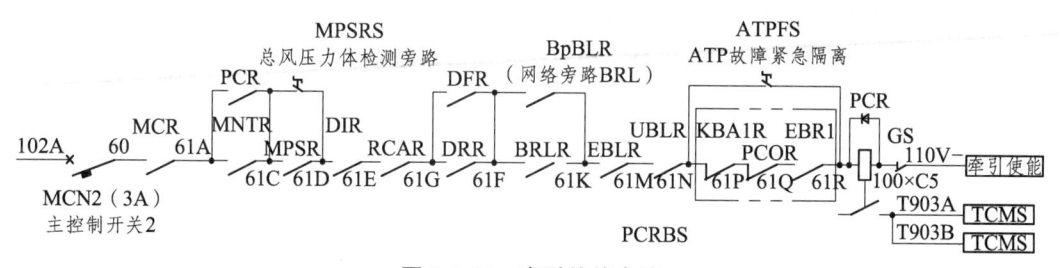

图 3-1-13 牵引使能电路

（2）司控器手柄零位加载电路。

为保证行车安全，在发生紧急制动等情况导致牵引丢失后，牵引再次施加时必须先要让牵引手柄回到"关"位，再打到一定牵引挡位，有效防止问题消除后牵引异常施加，如图3-1-14所示。

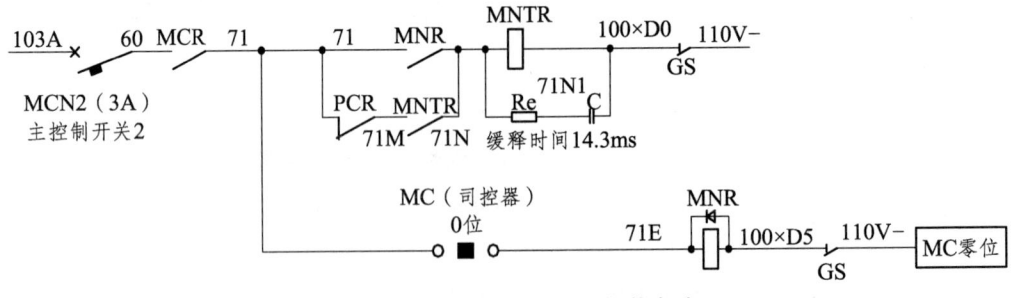

图 3-1-14 司控器手柄零位加载电路

任务二 CR400BF 动车组牵引系统分析

【任务描述】

本任务是对 CR400BF 动车组牵引系统的整体认识。学习完本任务，学生应掌握系统的组成、主电路的结构及故障保护。

【背景知识】

一、系统架构

1. 系统组成

牵引系统由两个对称的牵引单元组成，每个牵引单元由两个动车和两个拖车构成。牵引变压器通过4个次级绕组将25 kV接触网电压降压后分别输送给2个牵引变流器，牵引变流器经交-直-交变换，为本车4台三相异步牵引电机供电，同时通过中间直流环节为辅助变流器提供电能，如图3-2-1所示。

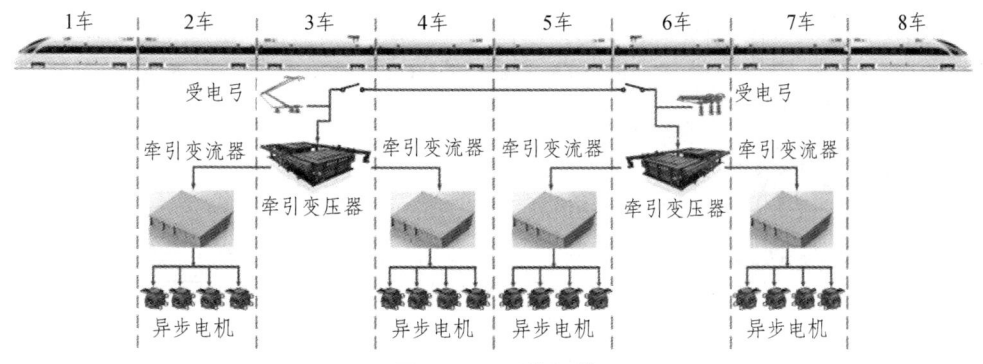

图 3-2-1　系统组成

2. 主电路

主电路分为两种，一种是辅助分离牵引系统主电路，另一种是辅助一体牵引系统主电路，如图 3-2-2 和图 3-2-3 所示。

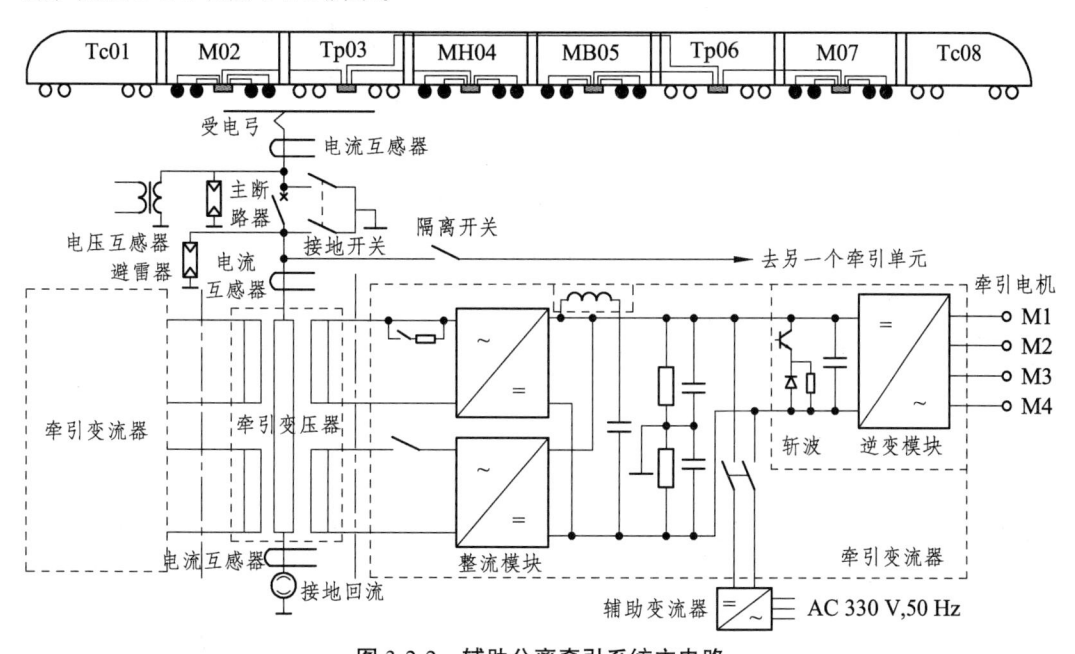

图 3-2-2　辅助分离牵引系统主电路

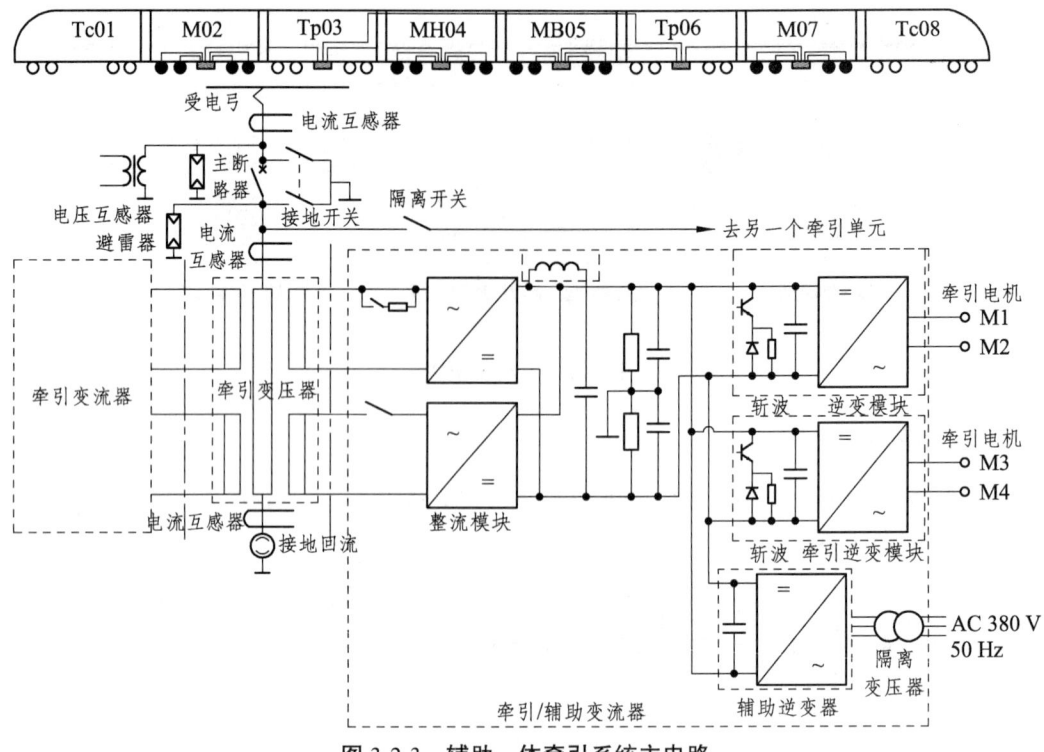

图 3-2-3 辅助一体牵引系统主电路

牵引变流器安装在动车组动力车车下的牵引设备箱中。每一个牵引变流器基本上由 2 个四象限斩波器（4QC）、带谐振电路的中间电压电路、1 个制动斩波器 BC 以及 2 个脉冲宽度调制逆变（PWMI）牵引变流器的输入线路接触器组成，由列车控制单元（TCU）控制。

二、牵引性能

牵引传动技术的发展目的在于改善轨道车辆的牵引和制动性能，提高整个车辆系统的可靠性和能源使用效率，降低能耗，尽量避免对电网的污染，有效地降低运行成本，满足运营需求。

动车组牵引系统的主要作用是在牵引运行时将电能转换成机械能（能量变换与传递的路径如图 3-2-4 中蓝色箭头所示），再生制动运行时将机械能转换成电能（能量变换与传递的路径如图 3-2-4 中白色箭头所示）。

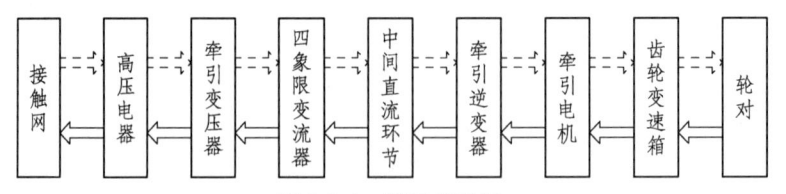

图 3-2-4 能量传递图

三、系统功能

1. 运行方向选择

司机室激活后，升起受电弓，闭合 VCB，将方向开关置于前向位，车门环路闭合，制动缓解后即可操作牵引手柄施加牵引使车辆运行。

2. 操纵模式选择

司控器手柄配套一个操纵模式选择按钮，可选择当前牵引模式为级位模式或速度模式，如图 3-2-5 所示。

操作模式切换需在手柄零位时进行。从级位模式转为速度模式时，设定的起始速度值为当前列车实际速度；由速度模式转为级位模式时，设定的起始级位值为 0。

图 3-2-5　司控器手柄

3. 自发电功能

动车组具备自动过分相功能。当速度大于 78 km/h 过分相时，牵引变流器中间直流环节电压可维持，辅助系统通过牵引电机再生制动产生的电能维持正常工作，如图 3-2-6 所示。

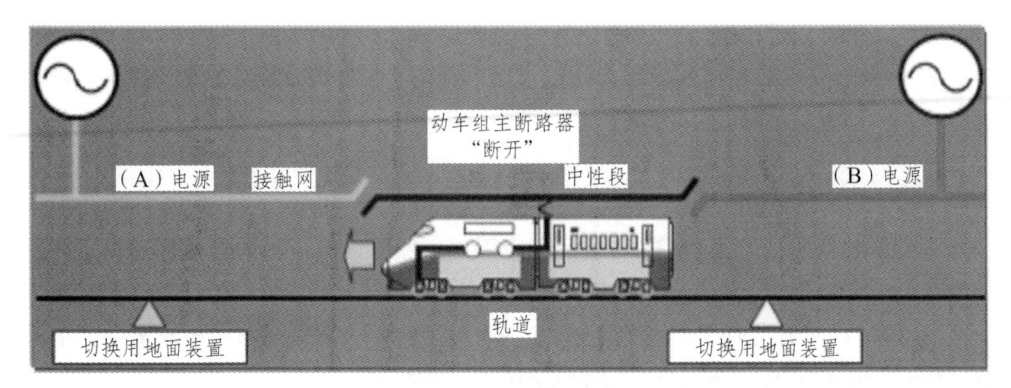

图 3-2-6　自动过分相

速度大于 55 km/h 时启动无火回送模式，牵引变流器增设逆变模块，转入回送模式后，若速度小于 35 km/h 则退出回送模式。DC 110 V 电压逆变后输出电压给中间直流电压充电，建立牵引电机所需的励磁电流，电机转为发电工况，通过中间直流环节持续为辅助变流器提供工作电源，如图 3-2-7 所示。

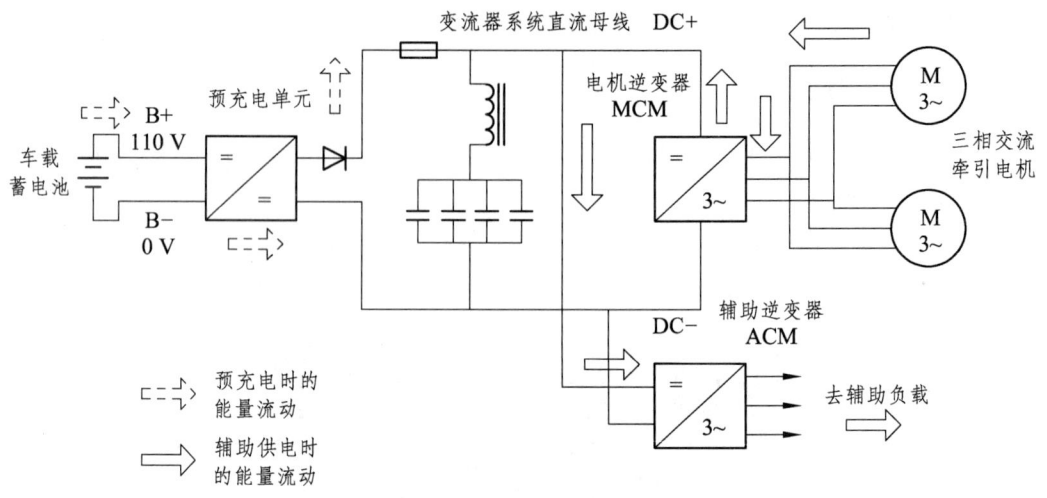

图 3-2-7 中间直流电路

四、故障保护

1. 网压限制

当 TCU 检测到网压过低或过高时，TCU 立即封锁四象限及逆变器脉冲，自动跳开主断或主接触器，待网压恢复正常后再重新投入。

2. 变流器冷却单元超温或压力异常

TCU 检测到变流器冷却水温超过设定阈值时，封锁全部变流器脉冲，待冷却水温恢复正常值后，自动复位故障。

TCU 检测到变流器冷却系统压力超过设定阈值时，会封锁变流器脉冲，待压力恢复正常值以后，自动复位故障。

3. 牵引变压器保护

牵引变压器原边过流保护：TCU 检测到牵引变压器原边电流瞬时峰值超过设定阈值或有效值超过设定阈值时，TCU 封锁脉冲，跳开 VCB。

牵引变压器原边接地保护：TCU 检测到牵引变压器原边高压侧及回流侧电流差值超过设定阈值时，TCU 封锁所有脉冲，跳开 VCB。

油流保护：当油流速度过低时，油流继电器会动作，车载电气检测到油流过低持续10 s，封锁脉冲，断开 VCB。

油温保护：通过 PT100 温度传感器检测变压器入口/出口油温。报警分为三级，达到第一、二级温度保护时仅限制牵引功率，达到第三级温度保护时将封锁 TCU 脉冲并自动跳开主断。

油压保护：当变压器内部压力过大时，其压力释放阀会动作，车载电气检测到此动作后，封锁脉冲，断开 VCB。

油位保护：当油位较低时，变压器低液位报警继电器会动作，车载电器检测到此动作后，进行报警提示；当油位更低时，变压器低液位切除继电器会动作，车载电气检测到此动作后，封锁脉冲，断开 VCB。

当 TCMS 检测到电机温度超过设定阈值时，封锁相应逆变器脉冲。当电机温度恢复正常值后，软件自动复位故障。

4. 牵引电机保护

检测装置将电机温度告知 TCMS，TCMS 会将电机温度与环境温度进行比较，产生两级过温保护。定子温度超温不限制列车速度，驱动端和非驱动端超温时将限值列车速度，同时通知 TCU 封锁相应逆变器脉冲。当电机温度恢复正常值后，软件自动复位故障。

5. 其他保护

直流回路过压：中间直流回路电压超过设定阈值时，TCU 封锁所有脉冲，并断开短接接触器。当中间直流电压恢复正常值后，软件自动复位故障。

直流回路充电异常：充电在预定时间内达不到指定电压设定阈值时，封锁全部变流器脉冲，分断主断。

牵引系统接地保护：通过牵引变流器中间回路接地电压，可对牵引变压器二次侧、中间直流环节、牵引逆变器交流侧、辅助变流器高压侧进行接地检测，当牵引变流器中间直流接地检测电压异常时报接地故障，并进行断主断或封锁牵引保护。

牵引系统短路及过流保护：通过牵引变压器原边电流、四象限输入电流、逆变器输出电流、中间直流环节电流、中间直流环节电压传感器，可检测牵引系统各部件的输入/输出短路、过流故障。当变流器输出电流发生过流故障时，会封锁 IGBT 脉冲；当变压器输入发生过流时，会分断主断；当发生短路故障时，会分断主断或封锁故障牵引单元。

高压系统差动保护：通过牵引变压器原边电流和接地回流互感器，当二者差值超过阈值时，TCMS 自动跳开主断，进行高压牵引系统保护。

【项目检测】

1. 分析 CR400AF 动车组网侧过电流控制电路。
2. 简述 CR400AF 动车组高压联锁控制的操作方法。
3. 分析 CR400AF 动车组救援回送功能。
4. 分析 CR400BF 动车组主电路工作原理。
5. 简述 CR400BF 动车组牵引系统故障保护。

项目四　动车组制动控制电路分析

【项目描述】

本项目是对动车组制动控制系统的整体认识学习。通过学习制动控制系统的组成、制动方式的分类、制动控制原理等相关知识，学生应会分析制动控制逻辑运行电路图，能按照动车组检修作业标准查除故障。

【项目任务】

（1）认识动车组制动控制系统组成。
（2）进行制动控制电路分析。

任务一　认识动车组制动控制系统组成

【任务描述】

本任务介绍动车组制动控制系统的基本组成、制动方式及功能。学习完本任务，学生应掌握制动控制装置在列车上的布置，并会绘制和分析制动指令传递原理图。

【背景知识】

一、动车组制动控制系统的组成

CRH_2型动车组制动系统采用复合制动模式，即再生制动+电气指令式空气制动。电气指令式空气制动是微机控制的直通式电空制动。制动控制系统包括：制动信号发生装置、制动信号传输装置、制动控制装置。制动信号发生装置即司机制动控制器，位于1、8号（T1c、T2c）车司机室操纵控制台。制动信号传输装置包括中央装置、车辆终端装置，借助于列车信息控制系统采集与传输制动指令，同时接收制动状态指令。制动控制装置作为接收制动指令、实现制动力控制的集中控制设备吊装在每辆车的地板下，内部集成了制动控制单元（BCU）、空气阀类组件、风缸等。

制动控制设备主要构成及分布情况见表 4-1-1。

表 4-1-1　制动控制设备主要构成及分布情况

编组情况		1	2	3	4	5	6	7	8
设备分布		T1c	M2	M1	T2	T1k	M2	M1s	T2c
司机制动控制器		√							√
制动指令传输装置	指令传输中央处理装置	√							√
	指令传输网络	列车信息控制网络							
	传输终端装置	√	√	√	√	√	√	√	√
制动控制装置		√	√	√	√	√	√	√	√
基础制动装置		√	√	√	√	√	√	√	√

再生制动和空气制动转换动作的发生，是由微机根据所产生的制动力的多少决定的。如果再生制动力不足，便以空气制动来补充。

同时，两个头车司机室内各安装一台制动指令转换装置，该装置可将连挂机车的列车管空气压力变化信号转换成电信号，用于在被救援时实施制动。

二、动车组制动控制系统的功能

动车组制动指令方式采用手动制动方式及由 ATP/LKJ 控制的自动制动方式并用，动作方式采用电气再生制动方式与电气指令式空气制动方式并用的电-空协调制动的控制模式，对应速度-黏着曲线模式进行制动力控制，还具有滑行检测机能及应载荷机能。优先采用电制动，当电制动力不足时，补充空气制动。根据指令类型的不同，制动控制可分为常用制动、快速制动、紧急制动、辅助制动和耐雪制动 5 种模式。对应的控制线如下：

（1）常用制动（61～67 线、10 线加压）。

（2）快速制动（152 线不加压、10 线加压）。

（3）紧急制动（153 线、154 线不加压）。

（4）辅助制动（411、461 线之间加压）。

（5）耐雪制动（157 线加压）。

CRH_2 制动系统具有常用制动、快速制动、紧急制动、辅助制动及耐雪制动功能。

1. 常用制动

常用制动级位设 1~7 级（记以 1N~7N），以 1M1T 为单元对动车再生制动力和空气制动力（包括动车和拖车的）进行协调控制，拖车空气制动延迟投入。

CRH_2 制动系统采用数字指令式，由 61~67 号线共 7 根制动指令线组成，共可形成 7 级常用制动。制动系统会自动进行延迟充气控制。延迟时，将 M 车上产生的再生制动力多余的部分转移到 T 车上去，维持编组列车上所需要的制动力。常用制动还具有空重车载荷调整功能，可按需要改变制动力，使动车组能够保持一定的减速度。

2. 快速制动

快速制动采用与常用制动相同的复合制动模式，并具有常用最大制动（7级）1.5 倍的制动力，操作制动手柄或未能减速到在闭塞区间设定的速度时，由 ATP 或 LKJ2000 发出的指令起作用。

3. 紧急制动

紧急制动按安全回路失电而启动的制动模式进行设置。下列任何一种情况均可导致全回路失电而引起紧急制动指令的产生：

① 总风压力下降到规定值以下。
② 列车分离。
③ 检测到制动力不足。
④ 操作紧急制动按钮，使紧急电磁阀失电。
⑤ 换端操纵，手柄置于（钥匙）拔取位。

以上的紧急制动使各车按不同速度范围产生纯空气制动作用，在列车速度处于 160~200 km/h 范围内采用相对较低的减速度；在 160 km/h 以下速度范围内采用相对较高的减速度；紧急制动不具有空重车载荷调整功能。

4. 辅助制动

在制动装置异常、制动指令线路断线及传输异常时可启用电气指令式的辅助制动，能产生相当于 3 级、5 级、7 级常用制动及快速制动的空气制动。

操作司机控制台上的辅助制动模式发生器（SBT）开关和头车配电盘内辅助制动模式发生器（ASBT）开关可以产生辅助制动。但辅助制动与列车速度的快慢无关，即所发出的制动力的大小也不随列车速度和列车重量的改变而改变，只发出预定的制动力。这一点与常用制动、快速制动不同。

除此以外应注意，制动控制装置还进行主空气压缩机与开闭车门的速度控制，因此，使用辅助制动时不应断开制动控制装置的电源。

5. 耐雪制动

设置耐雪制动的目的是防止降雪时雪块进入制动盘和闸片之间。耐雪制动动作时，制动油缸会轻轻地推出闸片堵塞闸片和制动盘面之间的空隙，防止雪的进入。耐雪制动于行驶速度 110 km/h 以下，在耐雪制动开关置于作用位并且操纵制动手柄时动作。耐雪制动对应的制动缸（BC）压力设定值为（60±20）kPa，这是制动缸在满足制动条件时的预充压力，在 BCU 输出实际空气制动控制信号时，制动缸依然按照所需的空气制动力的大小充气到相应的压力。耐雪制动对应的制动缸（BC）压力设定值可通过调整 BCU 面板上的开关来改变。

任务二　制动控制电路分析

【任务描述】

本任务介绍动车组制动控制器的功能、工作原理以及制动控制电路。学习完本任务，学生应会分析制动控制电路，并根据检修作业标准排查处理故障。

【背景知识】

一、制动控制概述

1. 制动控制原理

动车组制动控制系统能够实现制动指令的发出及传输、常用制动及快速制动的控制、紧急制动的控制、辅助制动的控制、耐雪制动的控制、空气制动与再生制动的协调控制等。动车组的制动指令由司机制动控制器发出电气指令，经列车信息控制系统传送到每辆车的制动控制装置，由制动控制装置的 BCU 运算，按制动控制规律（减速度随速度的变化）实施再生制动和空气制动。其中空气制动通过控制电空转换阀（EP 阀）的电流，送出与电流对应的空气压力信号到中继阀，控制中继阀送出压缩空气到转向架基础制动装置，由增压气缸经空-油变换作用将气压转变成油压，最后经制动盘液压卡钳的液压缸推动闸片压制动盘面，完成制动作用。为保证控制电路按照指令正确动作，控制过程中必须满足一定的逻辑条件。一个动力单元制动控制指令传递原理如图 4-2-1 所示。

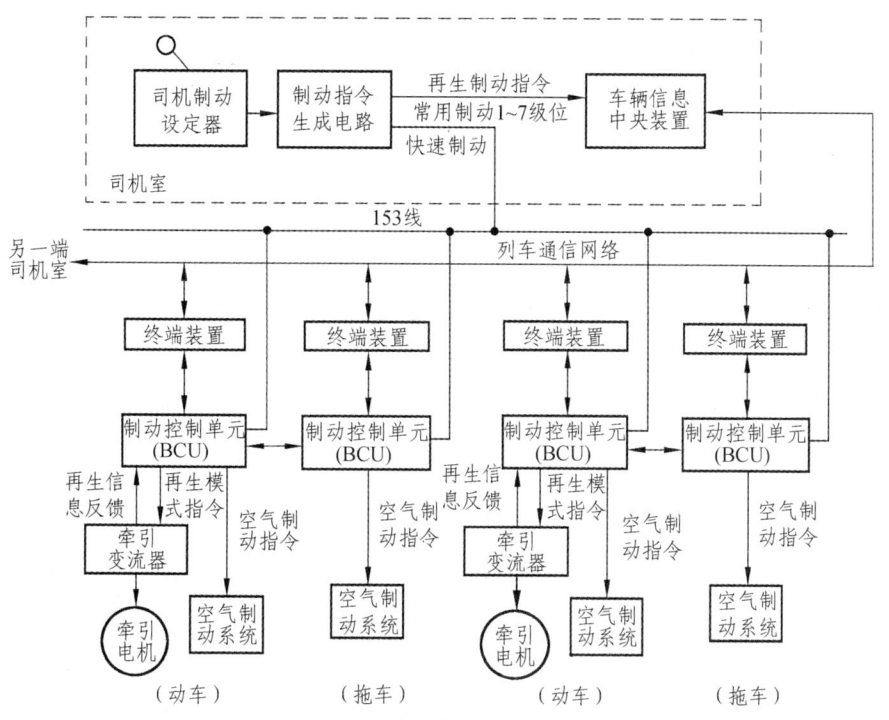

图 4-2-1 动车组制动控制原理

2. 制动控制器的功能

CRH$_2$型动车组 CMC100 司机制动控制器(简称司控制动器)操作面板外形如图 4-2-2 所示,有"运行""1~7级""快速"及"拔取"等 10 个位置。司控制动器有 4 种功能:其一,在"运行"位,与牵引控制信号联锁,生成牵引指令条件,牵引指令有效;其二,在制动级位,发出 1~7 级常用制动;其三,在"快速"位时,发出快速制动级位指令;其四,在"拔取"位,在紧急情况下激发快速制动。此外,还要生成再生电气制动指令。

图 4-2-2 制动手柄

二、制动控制器电气指令电路

图 4-2-3 是制动器级位开关及继电器逻辑控制原理图,对应有 9 对触点开关和 9 个继电器。各个位置与继电器对应关系如表 4-2-1 所示。

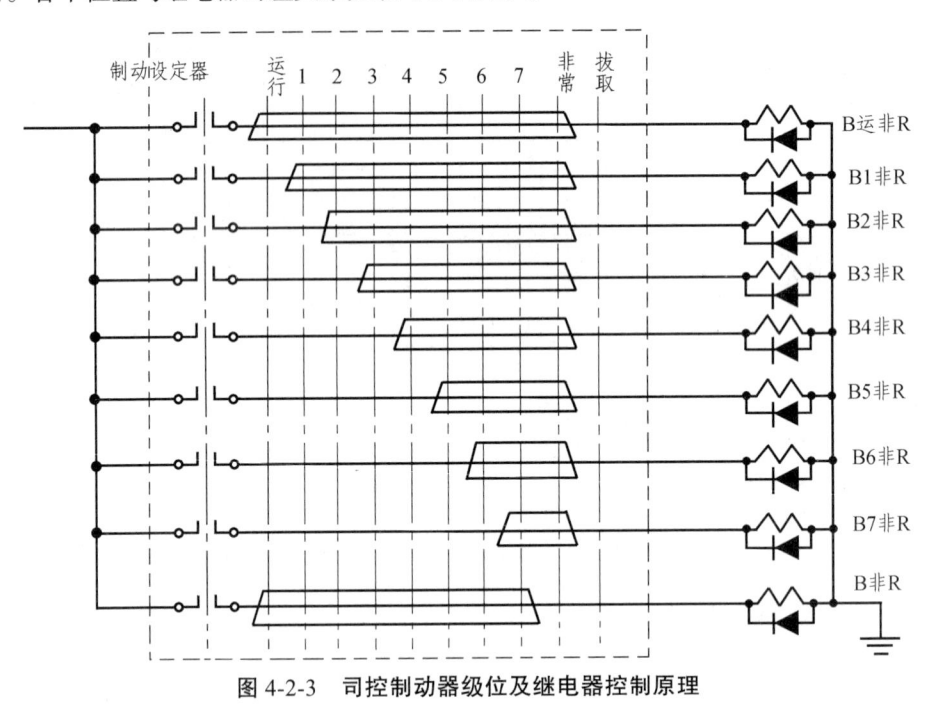

图 4-2-3 司控制动器级位及继电器控制原理

表 4-2-1 制动设定器和励磁继电器的对应

继电器	制动设定器指令									
	运转	1	2	3	4	5	6	7	应急
B 运非 R	○	○	○	○	○	○	○	○	○
B1 非 R		○	○	○	○	○	○	○	○
B2 非 R			○	○	○	○	○	○	○
B3 非 R				○	○	○	○	○	○
B4 非 R					○	○	○	○	○
B5 非 R						○	○	○	○
B6 非 R							○	○	○
B7 非 R								○	○
B 非 R	○	○	○	○	○	○	○	○	

注:○ = 励磁,空白 = 非励磁。

1. 常用制动指令电路分析

常用制动的制动力指令是由制动指令线（61~67线）经由中央装置、终端装置送到BCU，并且通过10线发出指令决定再生制动是否可用。为提高制动指令的安全程度，还用硬线贯穿方式将67线（常用最大制动）连接到BCU。

常用制动指令的发生装置为司机制动控制器、ATP、制动指令转换器。根据司机制动控制器的操作位置，B1非R~B7非R励磁，通过其常开触点闭合使61~67线得电。在超过限制速度后，通过ATP实施常用制动，释放NBR，通过NBR的常闭触点来励磁ATCBR。由此，ATCBR的常开触点闭合，61、66、67线得电，发出最大常用制动指令。若通过ATP判断制动指令为B1或B4时制动力已经足够，单独励磁ATCKB1R或励磁ATCKB1R和ATCKB4R，使61线或64线得电，使B1或B4指令发出。

动车组救援与回送时，制动指令转换器与机车的BP管连接，将BP压力信号供给制动指令转换器。制动指令转换器将根据BP压力信号，使X61~X67线得电，励磁B1非R~B7非R。接受相同型号动车组救援时，直接使贯穿线（61~67线）得电。

有再生制动指令时，电-空协调控制将按以下步骤进行：各车的BCU识别制动指令，根据速度和车辆重量进行计算，输出所需的制动力。若再生制动指令线（10线）得电，则牵引控制单元将根据BCU的再生制动模式电压（制动力指令值）进行再生制动力控制，将所得到的再生制动力的结果反馈到BCU。BCU接受从牵引控制单元反馈（再生反馈电压和电流检测信号CDR）的再生制动力，将不足部分的制动力由空气制动补足。

10线在B1非R、ATCBR、ATCKB1R中的任意一个励磁时得电，送出再生制动条件有效的指令。但在车速<5 km/h、辅助制动选择、动力制动开放SW为打开的任意情况时，不会发送指令给10线。

2. 快速制动指令电气电路

通常快速制动贯穿线（152线）向BCU传输得电信号，保持快速制动为关闭状态，即在152线失电时，BCU启动快速制动。

快速制动作用在以下情况下发出：

① 司机制动控制器操作（置快速位）；
② ATP给出快速制动指令（EBR失电）；
③ JTR失电。

1）司机制动控制器操作

通过司机制动控制器置【快速】位，快速位继电器（B非R）失磁，其常开触点打开，152线失电。

2）通过 ATP 的快速制动（EBR 失电）

通过 ATP 的动作，总配电盘上用于 ATP 快速制动的继电器（EBR）失电，因此，其常开触点打开，使 152 线失电。但是，若 ATPCOS 处在断开的位置（ATPCOR 励磁），则 ATP 快速制动继电器（EBR）不起作用。

3）通过 JTR 失电引起的快速制动

154D 线在失电时 JTRTD 落下，接着 JTR 失磁。

154D 线在以下情况下由常得电变为失电状态：

① MR 压力过低。

总风管压力开关（MRHPS）→总风管压力开关继电器关闭（MRrAPSR）→154B1～154B2 之间断开。

② 列车分离。

电气连接器断开→154 线失电。

③ 制动力不足的检测。

用于检测车辆制动力不足的时间继电器（UBTR）失磁→紧急制动继电器（UVR）失磁→154A-154K 间断→154 线失电。

④ 司机制动控制器置拔取位。

B 运非 R 常开触点断开→MCR 失磁→154M 线失电。

⑤ 乘务员操纵紧急制动开关。

⑥ 启动紧急制动开关（UBS1 或 UBS2）→154A 失电。

4）快速制动模式空气制动与再生制动的关系

若将司机制动控制器置于快速位置，由于 B1 非 R 处于励磁状态，因此 10 线也处于得电状态。当动车组处于由 ATP 引起的快速制动状态时，由于 EBR 失电的同时 NBR 也失电，所以 ATCBR 励磁。JTR 失电时 ATCBR 也会励磁。由于 ATCBR 励磁，ATCBR 的常开触点变为关闭状态，10 线得电。所以，在发出快速制动指令时，通向牵引变流器的再生制动指令线 10 线得电；与此同时，根据从 BCU 送来的再生制动模式电压，再生制动控制单元（由牵引变流器担任）按与常用制动时同样的方式产生制动作用。

3. 紧急制动指令电路

经由头车 153K 的常开触点，贯穿线（153 线）得电。从 153 线、经由后位司机台的 MCR 的常闭触点使贯穿线（154 线）得电。

紧急制动在以下情况下起作用：
① 列车分离。
② 总风管压力过低。
③ 检测到制动力不足。
④ 紧急电磁阀失电。
⑤ 司机制动控制器手柄置于拔取位。

1）列车分离时

列车分离处前一端的车辆只有 154 线失电，JTR 失磁，快速制动发挥作用。在列车分离处后一端的车辆，153 线、154 线系统一起变为失电状态，在紧急制动电磁阀（UV）失磁、紧急制动作用的同时，JTR 失磁导致 152 线失电，发出快速制动指令。制动缸 BC 压力将获得紧急制动和快速制动两者中产生的最高压力值。

2）总风管压力过低时

通过总风管压力开关（MRHPS）对两端头尾车机罩内的总风管压力进行检测，低于设定值（590±10）kPa 时，触点断开。由于 MRHPS 的触点断开，总风管压力开关继电器（MRrAPSR）变为失磁。由此，MRrAPSR 的常开触点变为断开状态，打开 153K 继电器，153 线失电，同时，其他触点使 154D 线失电，JTR 失磁。由此，UV 失磁，在紧急制动发挥作用的同时，也发出快速制动指令。

3）检测到制动力不足时

在检测到制动力不足时，UBTR 失磁。当 UBTR 失磁时，UV 和 UVR 的供电电路在 153B～153C 之间被断开。UV 失磁后，启动该车的紧急制动；与此同时，由于由 UVR 的常开触点，154A～154K 之间被断开，因此 JTR 失磁，152 线失电，快速制动起作用。

（1）制动力不足检测的条件。

用于检测各车制动力不足的继电器（UBR）在失磁状态时，检测制动力不足功能开始启动（见图 4-2-4）。155 线得电时，155R 的常开触点闭合，UBR 励磁，若以下的条件成立时变为失磁。

条件：①∩{②∪（③∩④）}∩⑤∩⑥
① B 运非 R 为失磁：司机制动控制器置于拔取位。
② B5 非 R 励磁：司机制动控制器置于 "B5-快速" 位。
③ 70SR 励磁：速度在 70 km/h 以下。
④ B7 非 R 磁：司机制动控制器置于 "B7-快速" 位。
⑤ NBR 为失磁：启动 ATP 制动（常用）。

⑥ JTR 为失磁：启动快速制动。

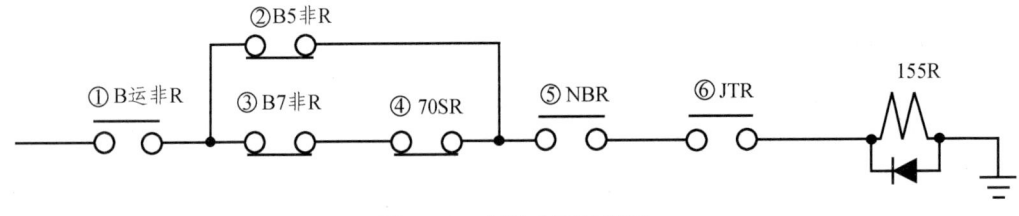

图 4-2-4　制动力不足检测

当 UBR 为失磁时，UBR 的常开触点打开，UBTR 在以下电路中呈自保状态。此状态时制动力不足检测功能启动（见图 4-2-5）。

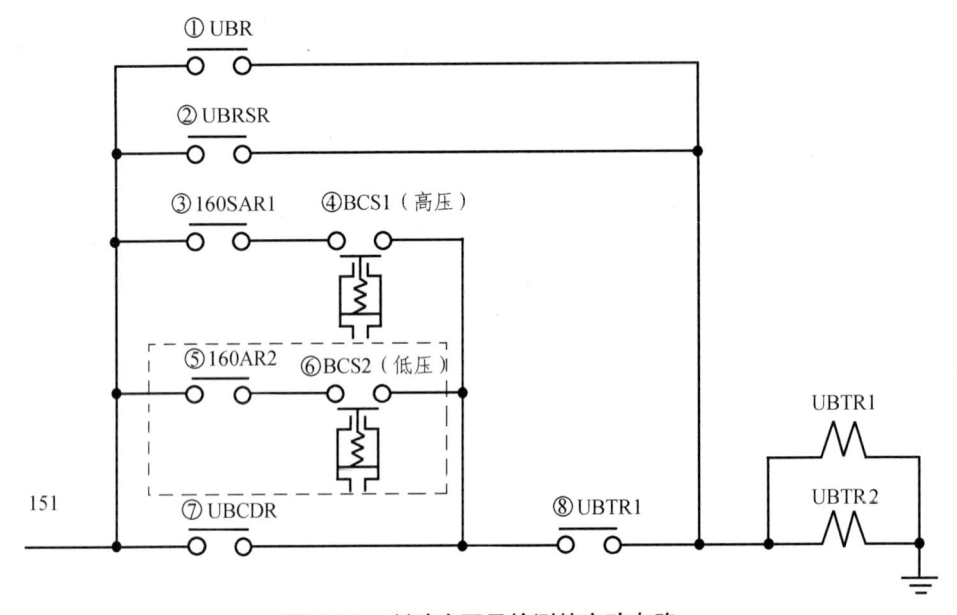

图 4-2-5　制动力不足检测的启动电路

当速度达到 160 km/h 时，BCS2（低压）变为 OFF，或者当速度在 160 km/h 以下时，将 BCS1（高压）变为 OFF；与此同时，若牵引变流器检测到再生制动力不足（UBCDR OFF）时，UBTR 将自保电路断开而失电。当 UBTR 为 OFF 后，UV（紧急制动阀）失磁，紧急制动起作用。在 UBR 为 OFF 期间，当 UBTR 失电后即使恢复了制动压力（制动力）检测，仍为失电状态。

制动力不足检测电路的复位：当制动力不足检测的功能未启动时，UBR 再次励磁，UBTR 励磁；若检测制动力不足的条件不成立，则 UBR、UBTR 也构成自保电路。URTR 在 UBRSR（用于紧急制动复位开关的继电器）励磁时也进行同样的复位。

（2）紧急制动的复位方法。

紧急制动启动后动车组将减速直至停车，中途无法缓解，必须进行复位操作。

继电器（156R）在以下的条件成立时励磁。

条件：①∩②∩③∩④

① B 非 R 为失磁：司机制动控制器置于"快速"位。

② B 7 非 R 励磁：司机制动控制器置于"7-快速"位。

③ UBRSWR 励磁：根据紧急制动复位开关（UBRS）处理复位。

④ MCR 励磁：操纵端司机制动控制器置于"运行-快速"位

继电器（156R）为 ON 后，156 线（紧急复位贯穿线）得电，各车的 UBRSR（用于紧急制动复位开关的继电器）励磁。在 UBSR 的常开触点闭合使 UBTR 励磁，只要当 153 线恢复得电、UV 和 UVR 重新励磁，紧急制动即可复位、解除（见图 4-2-6）。

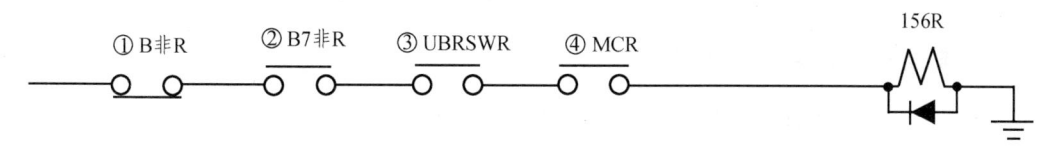

图 4-2-6 紧急制动的复位

4. 辅助制动指令电路

使用辅助制动时，平时被打开的辅助制动断路器 SBN1（司机台）和 SBN2（配电盘）关闭，辅助制动继电器（SBNR）励磁。在操纵端使用司机制动控制器时，根据手柄位置，B1-3K、B4-5K、B6-7K、B 非 K 之一得电，从辅助制动模式发生器（司机台用）向贯穿线（411 线、461 线）输出交流电压。辅助制动模式发生器（各车用）将 411 线、461 线的电压变压、整流后，供给 BCU，直接控制 EP 阀。由此构成不经由列车信息控制装置的制动控制通路。由于 SBNR 的常闭触点变为断开状态，指令线（10 线）变为失电状态，再生制动不会发挥作用。

5. 耐雪制动指令电路

装备耐雪制动的目的是：在下雪时为防止雪进入制动盘和闸片之间。为此，需将闸片推出，堵塞闸片和制动盘面之间的间隙。这个功能可通过操作司机控制台的耐雪制动开关（耐雪 SW）使 157 线得电，经由列车信息控制装置，将指令传送到各车的 BCU，BCU 通过识别速度（110 km/h 以下）来发出。

三、原理图连接条件说明

1. 制动指令条件（61 线）（1 挡）

如果满足以下条件，则制动指令（61 线）被加压。
（条件）：①∪②∪③

① B1 非 R 励磁（见图 4-2-7）。

② ATCBR 励磁（ATP 最大常用制动）。

③ ATCKB1R 励磁（ATP 缓和制动 1N）。

图 4-2-7　制动指令条件 1 挡

2. 制动指令的条件（62 线）（2 挡）

如果满足以下条件，则制动指令（62 线）被加压：

B2 非 R 励磁（见图 4-2-8）。

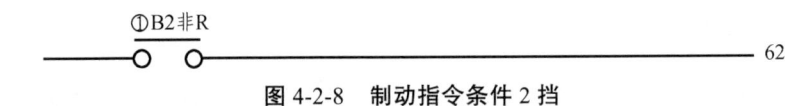

图 4-2-8　制动指令条件 2 挡

3. 制动指令的条件（63 线）（3 挡）

如果满足以下条件，则制动指令（63 线）被加压：

① B3 非 R 励磁（见图 4-2-9）。

图 4-2-9　制动指令条件 3 挡

4. 制动指令的条件（64 线）（4 挡）

在①、②的项目中，如果满足以下条件，则制动指令（64 线）被加压。

条件：①∪②

① B4 非 R 励磁（见图 4-2-10）。

② ATCKB4R 励磁（ATP 缓和制动 4N）。

图 4-2-10　制动指令条件 4 挡

5. 制动指令的条件（65 线）(5 挡)

如果满足以下条件，则制动指令（65 线）被加压：

B5 非 R 励磁（见图 4-2-11）。

图 4-2-11　制动指令条件 5 挡

6. 制动指令的条件（66 线）(6 挡)

在①~②的项目中，如果满足以下条件，则制动指令（66 线）被加压。

条件：①∪②

① B6 非 R 励磁（见图 4-2-12）。

② ATCBR 励磁（ATP 最大常用制动）。

图 4-2-12　制动指令条件 6 挡

7. 制动指令的条件（67 线）(7 挡)

在①~②的项目中，如果满足以下条件，则制动指令（67 线）被加压。

条件：①∪②

① B7 非 R 励磁（见图 4-2-13）。

② ATCBR 励磁。

图 4-2-13　制动指令条件 7 挡

8. 快速制动

向由快速制动贯穿线（152 线）组成的制动控制器输送加压信号，保持快速制动为关闭状态。

在①~③的项目中，若满足以下条件，则 152 线被加压。

条件：①∩②∩③（见图 4-2-14）

① JTR 励磁（不在紧急制动）。

② EBR 励磁（不在 ATP 非常制动）。

③ B 非 R 励磁（不在快速制动位）。

快速制动指令条件——当 152 线没有被加压（失电）时，制动控制器（BCU）识别快速制动指令，立即启动快速制动。

图 4-2-14 快速制动指令条件

快速制动于以下情况时起作用：

① 制动设定器操作（制动设定器手柄"快速"位置）。

② 根据 ATP 的快速制动（释放 EBR）。

③ 根据释放 JTR 的快速制动（受多种因素控制）。

1）制动设定器操作

将制动设定器置于"快速"位，"快速"位置继电器"B 非 R"变为非励磁，其 a 接点打开，关断输向 152 线的电压。

2）通过 ATP 的快速制动（释放 EBR）

通过 ATP 的动作，释放总配电盘上用于 ATP 快速制动的继电器（EBR），由此断开其 a 触点，关断输向 152 线的电压。但是，若 ATPCOS 处在断开的位置（ATPCOR 励磁），则用于 ATP 快速制动的继电器（EBR）不起作用。

3）通过释放 JTR 的快速制动

154D 线在失电时，JTRTD 断开，JTR 的励磁停止。154D 线在以下情况时变为失电：

① MR（主风缸）压力降低：总风管高气压开关关闭（MRHPS）→总风管气压开关继电器关闭（MRrAPSR）→153K 断电→154B1-154B2 间断。

② 列车分离：电气连接器断开→154 线没有电压。

③ 制动力不足的检测：车辆上用于检测制动力不足的时限继电器（UBTR）消磁→紧急制动阀继电器（UVR）消磁→154A-154K 间断→154 线没有电压。

④ 拔取制动设定器：B 运非 R 的 a 触点断开→MCR 消磁→154M 线消磁。

⑤ 乘务员开关处理：启动紧急制动开关（UBS1 或 UBS2）→154A 没有电压。

JTR 的条件：

如果满足以下条件，则通过 JTRTD、JTR（1P191608-14F）进行励磁，不实施快速制动。

条件：①∩②∩③∩④（见图 4-2-15）

从另外一侧先头车的
贯穿线（154线）

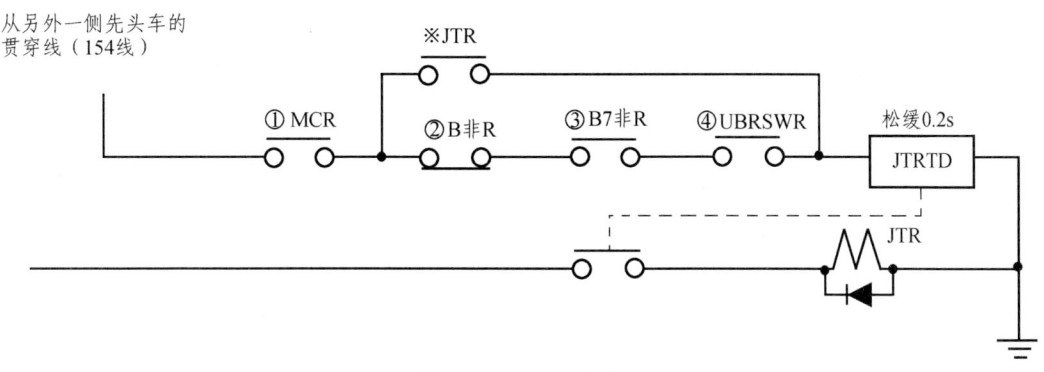

图 4-2-15　JTR 条件

① MCR 励磁。

② B 非 R 为非励磁。

③ B7 非 R 励磁。

④ UBRSWR（紧急制动重启）励磁。

※一旦 JTR 励磁，则进行自保持（自锁），直至 154 线变为无加压时，JTR 才非励磁。当 JTRTD 从励磁变为非励磁时，延时 0.2 s 后释放→JTR 无励磁→快速制动动作。

4）与再生制动的关联

① 若将制动设定器置于"快速"位置时，由于"B1 非 R"处于励磁状态，因此 10 线也处于被加压的状态。

② 由 ATP 引起的快速制动时，由于释放 EBR 的同时也释放 NBR，所以 ATCBR 被励磁，ATCBR 的 a 接点变为关闭状态，10 线被加压。

③ JTR 非励磁时 ATCBR 也会被励磁，10 线被加压。

所以在发出快速制动指令时，在牵引变流器输入 10 线加压的指令，与此同时，从制动控制装置（BCU）输入再生制动模式信号，再生制动控制如常用制动时一样起作用。

再生制动指令的条件（10 线）：

在①~⑦的项目中，如果满足以下条件，则再生制动指令线（10 线）被加压。

条件：（①∪②∪③）∩（④∪⑤）∩⑥∩⑦（见图 4-2-16）

① B1 非 R 励磁。

② ATCBR 励磁。

③ ATCKB1R 励磁。

④ 5SR 为非励磁：速度在 5 km/h 以上。

⑤ 空挡 R 励磁。

⑥ SBNR 为非励磁：（制动装置正常，不是辅助制动模式）。

⑦ 电气制动开放开关 SW 为 OFF（关闭）（再生制动没有被切断）。

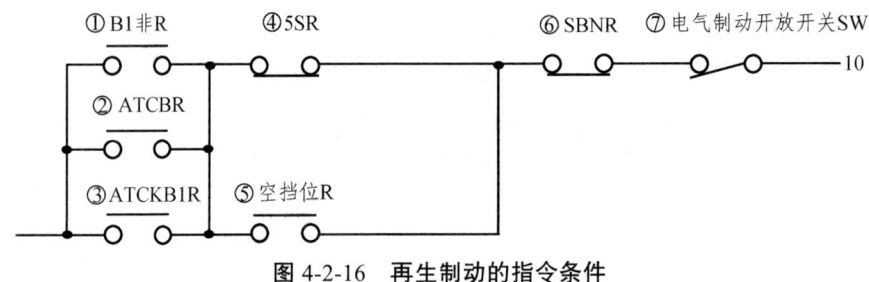

```
①B1非R    ④5SR           ⑥SBNR   ⑦电气制动开放开关SW
○—○  ┬  ○—○       ┬    ○—○     ○—○————10
②ATCBR  │                │
○—○  │                │
③ATCKB1R ⑤空挡位R
○—○     ○—○
```

图 4-2-16　再生制动的指令条件

9. 紧急制动

经由头车的 153K 的 a 接点、贯穿线（153 线）得到加压。从 153 线、经由后位司机台的 MCR 的 b 接点，对贯穿线（154 线）进行加压，不实施紧急制动。一旦 153 线失电，紧急制动。

紧急制动在以下场合发挥作用：

① 列车分离。

② 总风管压力降低。

③ 检测制动力不足。

④ 紧急电磁阀被关闭。

⑤ 制动设定器手柄被拔取。

153K 的条件：

在①~③的项目中，如果满足以下条件，则 153K 被励磁。当 153K 被励磁后，153 线（正常运行时加压的贯穿线）被加压，构成紧急制动电路。当此电路变为没有加压时，紧急制动及快速制动工作。

条件：①∩②∩③（见图 4-2-17）

① B 运非 R 励磁。

② MCR 励磁。

③ MRrAPSR 励磁：总风缸用气压开关为 ON（接通）。

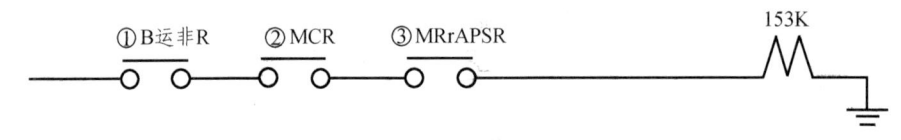

```
①B运非R   ②MCR    ③MRrAPSR              153K
——○—○————○—○————○—○——————〰〰——⏚
```

图 4-2-17　153K 的条件

1）列车分离时

列车分离处的前位一侧的车辆只有 154 线系统没有被加压，JTR 被消磁，快速制动发挥作用。

在列车分离的后位一侧的车辆，153 线、154 线系统均变为无电压，在紧急制动电磁

阀（UV）消磁、紧急制动作用的同时，JTR 消磁。由于 152 线没有加电压，快速制动也得到指令。BCU（制动控制单元）将以紧急制动和快速制动的高位优先得到处理。

2）总风管管压降低时

通过总风管用高压开关（MRHPS）对两头车机罩内的总风管压力进行检测，低于设定值（590±10）kPa 时，断开接点。由于 MRHPS 的接点被打开，总风管用气压开关继电器（MRrAPSR）变为非励磁，其 a 接点变为打开状态，断开 153K 继电器的励磁。在将 153 线为不加压的同时，别的接点将 154D 线为不加压，对 JTR 消磁。由此，UV（紧急电磁阀）消磁，在紧急制动发挥作用的同时，快速制动也得到指令。

3）制动力不足检测时

在检测到制动力不足时，UBTR（紧急制动限时继电器）进行消磁。当 UBTR 被关闭时，UV（紧急磁阀）和 UVR（紧急磁阀继电器）的加压电路在 153B～153C 之间被阻断。UV 被消磁后，启动该车辆的紧急制动。与此同时，由于由 UVR 的 a 接点，154A～154K 之间被阻断，因此 JTR 被消磁，失去了对 152 线的加压，快速制动动作。

4）156R 的条件（紧急复位）

在①～④的项目中，如果满足以下条件，则 156R 励磁。当 156R 被励磁时，贯穿线 156 被加压。当 156 线变为没有加压时，启动紧急制动。

条件：①∩②∩③∩④（见图 4-2-18）

① B 非 R 为非励磁。
② B7 非 R 励磁。
③ UBRSWR（紧急制动重启开关继电器）励磁。
④ MCR 励磁。

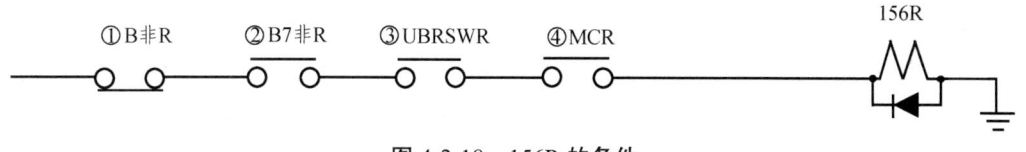

图 4-2-18　156R 的条件

5）UBRSWR 的条件（紧急制动复位）

如果满足以下条件，则 UBRSWR 励磁（见图 4-2-19）：

UBRS 为 ON：紧急制动复位开关为 ON（闭合）。

图 4-2-19　UBRSWR 的条件

继电器（156R）为 ON 后，156 线（紧急复位贯穿线）被加压，各个车辆的 UBRSR（用于紧急制动复位开关的继电器）被励磁。在 UBRSR 的 a 接点将 UBTR 投入励磁后，只要当 153 线的加压被恢复，就构成 UV 和 UVR 的励磁电路，紧急制动就被复位而解除。

10. 耐雪制动

装备耐雪制动的目的是：在下雪时，为防止雪进入制动盘和闸瓦之间，轻轻地将闸瓦压紧，关闭在闸片和制动盘之间的缝隙。操作司机台的耐雪制动开关（耐雪 SW），157 线被加压，经由车辆信息控制装置，操作人员将指令输送到各车辆的 BCU。BCU 通过识别速度（110 km/h 以下）来发挥作用。

耐雪制动指令条件（157 线）：

如果满足以下条件，则耐雪制动指令（157 线）被加压。

条件：①∩②（见图 4-2-20）

① 耐雪 SW 为 ON。

② MXR 为非励磁：没有和其他编组连挂。

图 4-2-20　耐雪制动指令条件

11. 辅助制动

使用辅助制动时，投入平时被断开的辅助制动断路器 SBN1（司机台）和 SBN2（配电盘），辅助制动继电器（SBNR）被励磁。在选择好的司机台使用制动设定器时，根据手柄位置，B 非 K、B1-3K、B4-5K、B6-7K 开始工作，从辅助制动模式产生器（司机台用）向贯穿线（411 线、461 线）输出交流电压。辅助制动模式产生器（各车辆用）将 411 线、461 线的电压变压、整流后，供给制动控制装置，直接控制 EP 阀。由此构成不经由车辆信息控制装置的制动控制路径。由于 SBNR 的 b 接点变为打开状态、指令线（10 线）变为非加压，再生制动不会发挥作用。

1）SBNR 的条件（辅助制动）

如果满足以下条件，则 SBNR 励磁：

SBN 1 辅助接点为 ON：辅助制动用断路器的辅助触点为 ON（见图 4-2-21）。

当 SBNR 励磁后，辅助制动的级位信号输出继电器，如 B6-7K、B4-5K、B1-3K、B 非 K 变为可以励磁，从辅助制动模式产生器发出辅助制动力指令变为可能。

①SBN1辅助接点　　　　　　　　　　　　　　　SBNR

图 4-2-21　SBNR 条件

2）B6～7K 的条件（辅助制动模式）

如果满足以下条件，则 B6～7K 励磁。

条件：①∩②∩③（见图 4-2-22）

① SBNR 励磁。

② B6 非 R 励磁。

③ B 非 R 励磁。

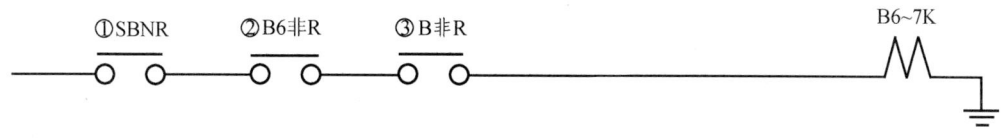

①SBNR　②B6非R　③B非R　　　　　　　B6~7K

图 4-2-22　B6～7K 的条件

3）B4～5K 的条件（辅助制动模式）

如果满足以下条件，则 B4～5K 励磁。

条件：①∩②∩③（见图 4-2-23）

① SBNR 励磁。

② B4 非 R 励磁。

③ B6 非 R 为非励磁。

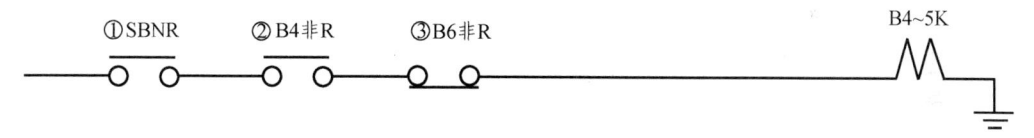

①SBNR　②B4非R　③B6非R　　　　　　　B4~5K

图 4-2-23　B4～5K 的条件

4）B1～3K 的条件（辅助制动模式）

如果满足以下条件，则 B1～3K 励磁。

条件：①∩②∩③（见图 4-2-24）

① SBNR 励磁。

② B1 非 R 励磁。

③ B4 非 R 为非励磁。

图 4-2-24　B1~3K 的条件

5）B 非 K 的条件（辅助制动模式）

如果满足以下条件，则 B 非 K 励磁。

条件：①∩②∩（③∪④）（见图 4-2-25）

① SBNR 励磁。

② MCR 励磁。

③ B 非 R 为非励磁。

④ JTR 为非励磁。

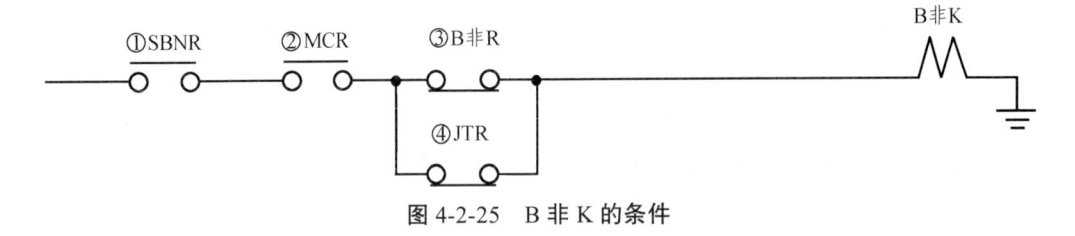

图 4-2-25　B 非 K 的条件

【项目检测】

1. 分析动车组制动控制系统的基本组成。
2. 简述 5 种制动模式及对应的指令线。
3. 分析什么情况下发生快速制动。
4. 分析 JTR 励磁的条件。
5. 简述制动控制器的功能。

项目五　动车组辅助供电系统电路分析

【项目描述】

本项目主要介绍辅助供电系统的构成、供电方式、交直流供电回路、扩展供电、开关门控制等方面。通过本项目的学习,学生应能分析辅助供电系统电路,能根据检修作业标准排查及处理故障。

【项目任务】

(1)浅析辅助变流器。
(2)进行辅助电源电路分析。
(3)能利用辅助电源及其他控制电路。
(4)进行开关门控制学习。
(5)进行故障案例分析。

任务一　浅析辅助变流器

【任务描述】

本任务是对动车组辅助变流器相关知识的学习,主要介绍交直交型和直交型辅助变流器主电路结构、工作原理以及典型动车组应用的辅助变流器。

【背景知识】

一、辅助变流器

为了保证列车正常运行,列车上设有三相交流辅助电路和辅助机械装置。由于主变压器、牵引变流装置、牵引电动机等在运行时发出大量的热量,需要通风机进行强迫风冷;列车的制动、受电弓以及车上各种气动机械要装置压缩机来提供风源等。所有这些辅助装置都要用三相鼠笼异步电动机来驱动。为此,需要在列车上设置三相交流电源,这是由辅助变流器完成的。列车的控制系统以及照明系统,需要直流电源,这是由辅助整流器完成的。在升弓前或高压设备、主变压器出现故障时,相关系统由蓄电池供电。因此,列车辅助供电系统的直流部分包括辅助整流装置和蓄电池。

列车辅助供电系统主要由辅助变流器、辅助整流器以及相关的组件构成。辅助变流器用来提供三相 AC 400 V 的电源，由静止变流器来实现；辅助整流器用来提供直流电源，由整流装置来实现。

为了防止因辅助供电设备故障而影响机车的正常运行，辅助供电系统要求具有很高的冗余度，因此，列车一般采用电源独立的多台辅助变流器同时供电，部分辅助变流器间还可以转换连接。

辅助变流器的输出端电压为 PWM 波，此电压具有很高的 du/dt 值。为了减小高的 du/dt 值对辅机造成的不利影响，一般要求在逆变器的输出端增设 EMC 滤波器，使输出电压的电压上升斜率（du/dt 值）$\leqslant$ 500 V/μs、最大尖峰电压 $U_{pk} \leqslant 1\,000$ V。

1. 辅助变流器的结构与特点

根据辅助变流器输入侧的不同，辅助变流器的主电路可以分为两种类型：一是输入侧为交流，称之为交直交型；一是输入侧为直流，称之为直交型。现在分别予以介绍。

1）交直交型辅助变流器

交直交型辅助变流器由机车牵引变压器辅助绕组供电，由脉冲整流器、中间直流回路、逆变器 3 部分组成，其结构如图 5-1-1 所示。采用交直交型辅助变流器的电路原理如图 5-1-2 所示。各部分的功能如下：

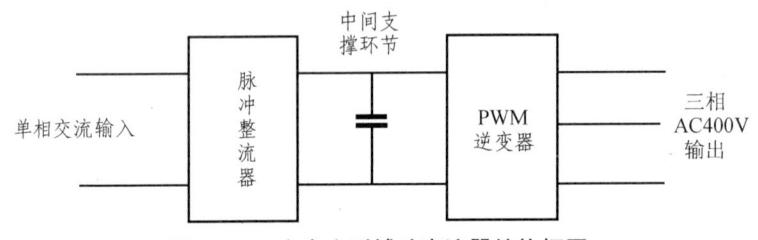

图 5-1-1　交直交型辅助变流器结构框图

① 脉冲整流器：脉冲整流器将牵引变压器输入的单相交流电压变换成恒定的直流电压，采用脉宽调制方式。

② 中间直流回路：滤波电容器将稳定的直流电压供给后段的逆变器。

③ 逆变器：逆变器将直流电压变换成为三相交流电压。

为了减少电网输入的高次谐波干扰，需要在牵引变压器和脉冲整流器之间增加滤波环节，以抑制谐波电流。

采用交直交型结构的辅助变流器具有以下特点：

① 牵引变压器需要提供辅助绕组为辅助变流器供电。

② 采用脉冲整流器能够保证输入侧较高的功率因数。

③ 变流器的启动方式为软启动，能够有效减小电机的启动电流。

④ 可以在较大的网压范围内工作。

⑤ 输出电压稳定，三相输出电压平衡。

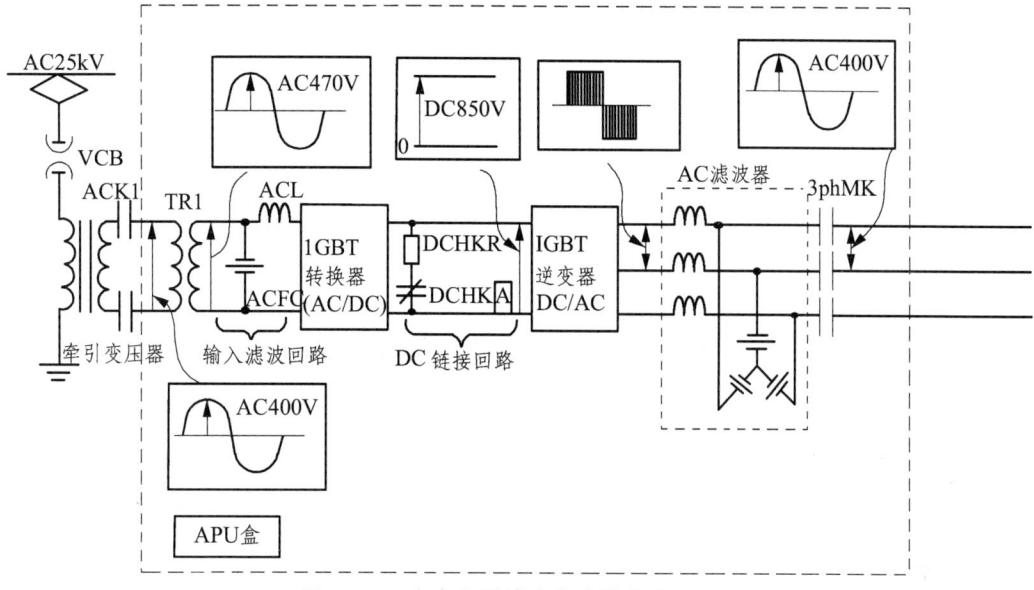

图 5-1-2　交直交型辅助变流器电路原理图

2）直交型辅助变流器

直交型辅助变流器直接从牵引变流器的中间直流环节取流，因此它只需要逆变器就可以实现直流电到三相交流电的变换。但是，为了保证输出电压的正弦度以及 400 V 的电压值，必须额外增加降压设备。一般有两种组合：一是斩波降压变换 + 逆变器，如图 5-1-3（a）所示，典型的电路原理如图 5-1-4 所示；一是逆变器 + 三相降压变压器，如图 5-1-3（b）所示，典型的电路原理如图 5-1-5 所示。为了保证输出电压波形的正弦度，必须保证逆变器的输出占空比，这就使得逆变器在输入直流电压较高时，输出的交流电压值也比较高，从而必须使用降压变压器降压。

① 斩波降压变换［对应于 5-1-3（a）的结构］：将牵引变流器的中间直流电压降到合适的值，保证逆变器的输出电压为 400 V。

② 三相降压变压器［对应于 5-1-3（b）的结构］：利用电磁感应原理，将逆变器输出的较高的交流电压降至 400 V。

③ 逆变器：逆变器将直流电压变换成三相交流电压。

与交直交型辅助变流器相比，直交型辅助变流器具两个显著特点：

① 无须牵引变压器提供辅助绕组，而是直接从牵引变流器的中间直流环节取流。

② 必须采取降压措施，确保输出电压的幅值。

（a）

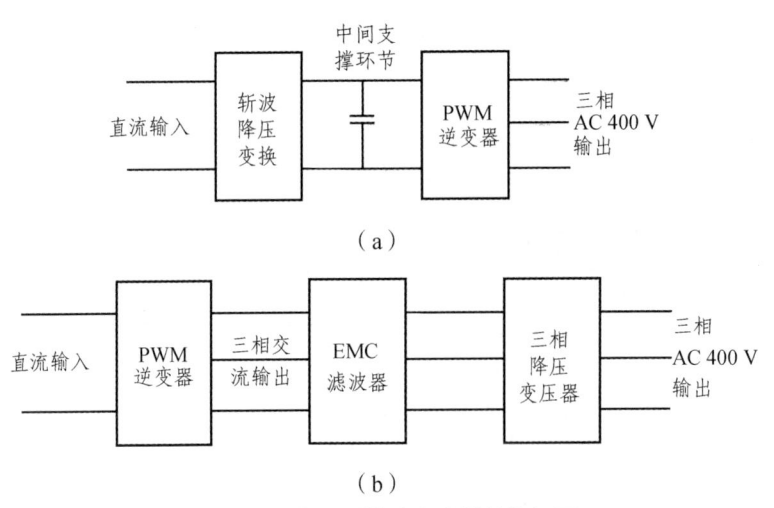

（b）

图 5-1-3 直交型辅助变流器结构框图

2. 辅助变流器的工作原理

辅助变流器会用到脉冲整流器、斩波器、降压逆变器、三相降压变压器。

1）脉冲整流器的工作原理

辅助变流器中用到的脉冲整流器的结构、作用及工作原理与列车牵引四象限脉冲整流器相同，因此不再赘述。而且，由于辅助变流器供电的设备不需要进行能量反馈，脉冲整流器也就不需要进行能量的逆向流动，因此，辅助变流器的脉冲整流器控制要比牵引脉冲整流器简单。

2）逆变器的工作原理

辅助变流器采用的逆变器与列车牵引传动系统采用的两电平 PWM 逆变器，在结构、作用及工作原理上是相同的，在此不再赘述。由于用电设备不需要转速的精确控制，也不需要进行能量反馈，因此其控制也比较简单。

3）三相降压变压器的工作原理

三相降压变压器和普通的电力变压器没有区别，在此不再赘述。

4）降压斩波器的工作原理

斩波器是利用自关断器件来实现通断控制，将直流电源电压断续加到负载上，通过通、断的时间变化来改变负载电压平均值，也称之为 DC-DC 变换器。它具有效率高、体积小、质量轻、成本低等优点。快速电力电子器件的出现，为斩波频率的提高创造了条件，提高斩波频率可以减少低频谐波分量，降低对滤波元器件的要求，减小了体积和质量。

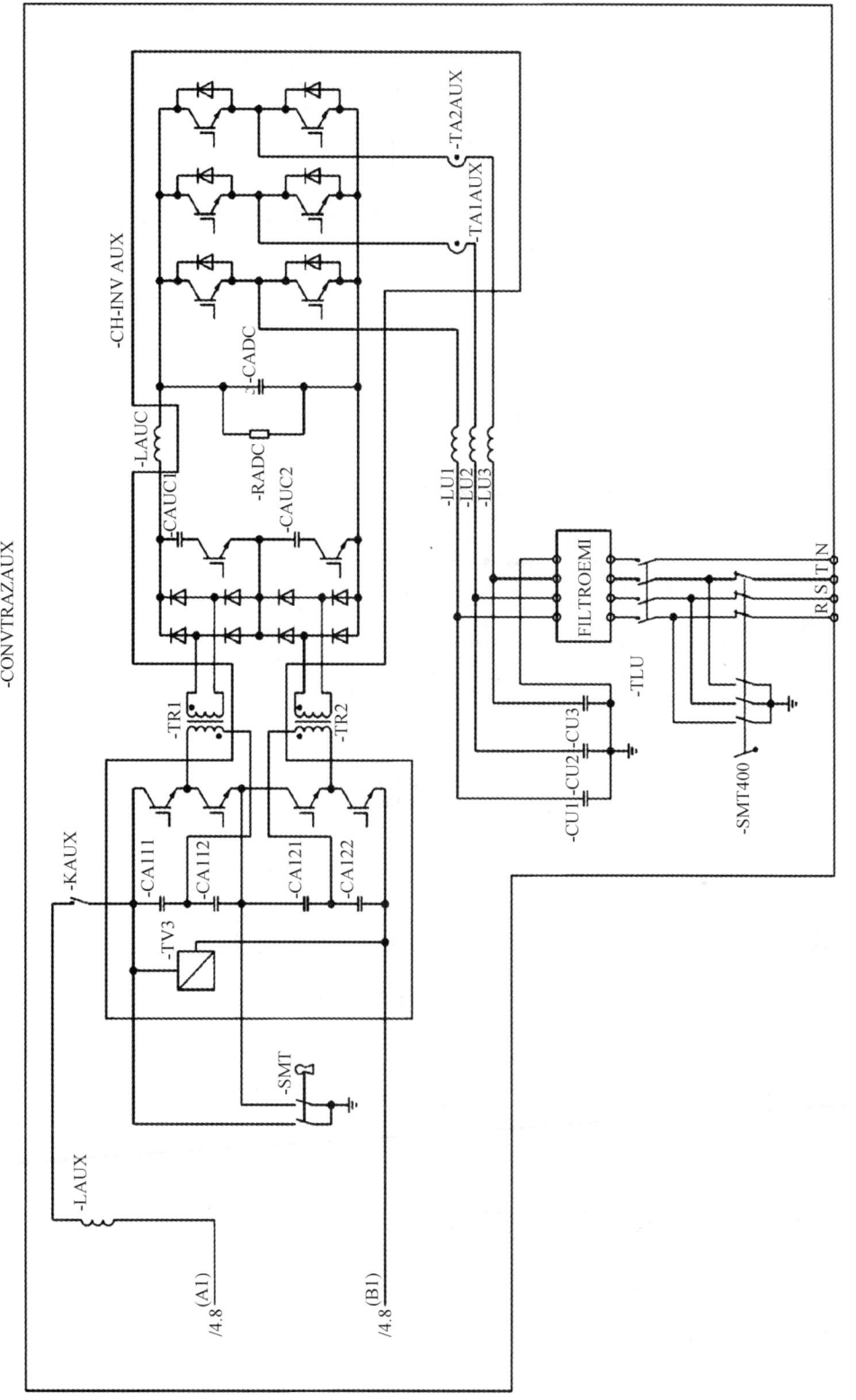

图 5-1-4 采用斩波降压变换的直交型辅助变流器电路原理图

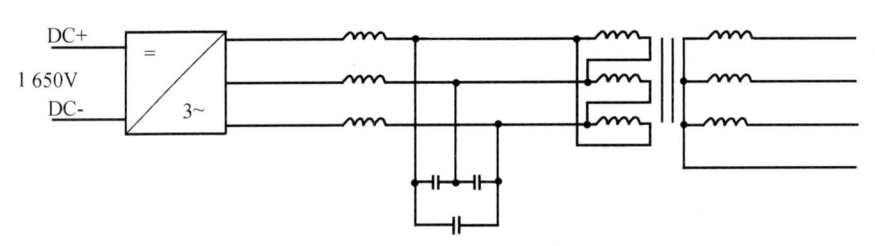

图 5-1-5　采用降压变压器的直交型辅助变流器电路原理图

二、直流供电系统

直流供电系统主要由整流装置和蓄电池组成。

列车整流装置的主要作用有：为列车的直流用电设备如控制系统、照明系统提供电源；为蓄电池充电。

整流装置一般采用脉冲整流器或者斩波器获得所需的直流电压。如图 5-1-6 所示为整流装置的电路原理图。

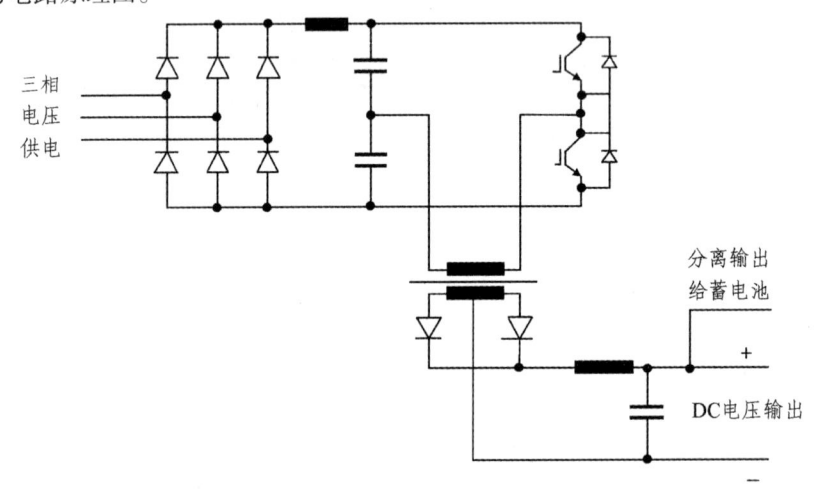

图 5-1-6　整流装置电路原理图

蓄电池是为了在整流装置无法提供直流电源时（如动车相关设备发生故障；或者动车没有升弓，整流装置无法供电）为相关的设备提供电源，同时还兼有为整流出来的直流电压滤波、稳压的作用。

三、典型动车组辅助供电系统简图

我国高速列车的辅助供电系统各有特点：如图 5-1-7 所示为 CRH_1 的辅助供电系统结构图，图 5-1-8 所示为 CRH_2 的辅助供电系统结构图，图 5-1-9 所示为 CRH_3 的辅助供电系统结构图。

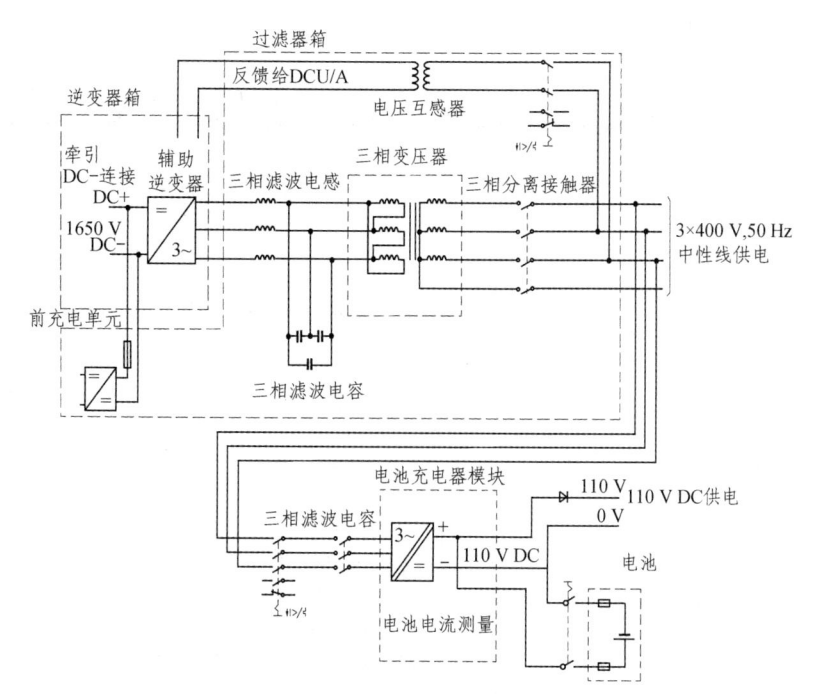

图 5-1-7　CRH₁ 的辅助供电系统结构

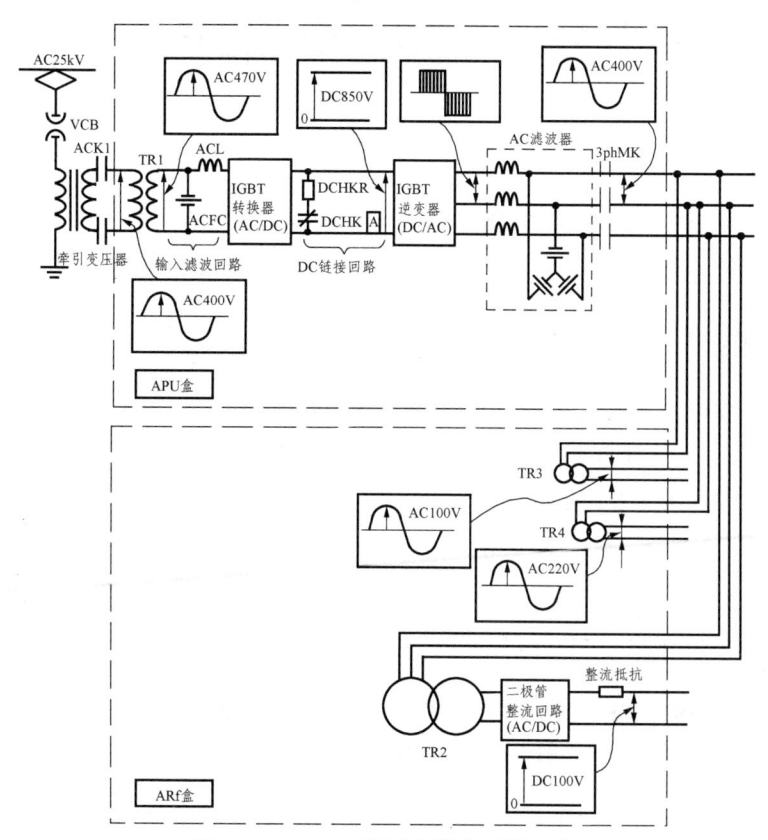

图 5-1-8　CRH₂ 的辅助供电系统结构

257

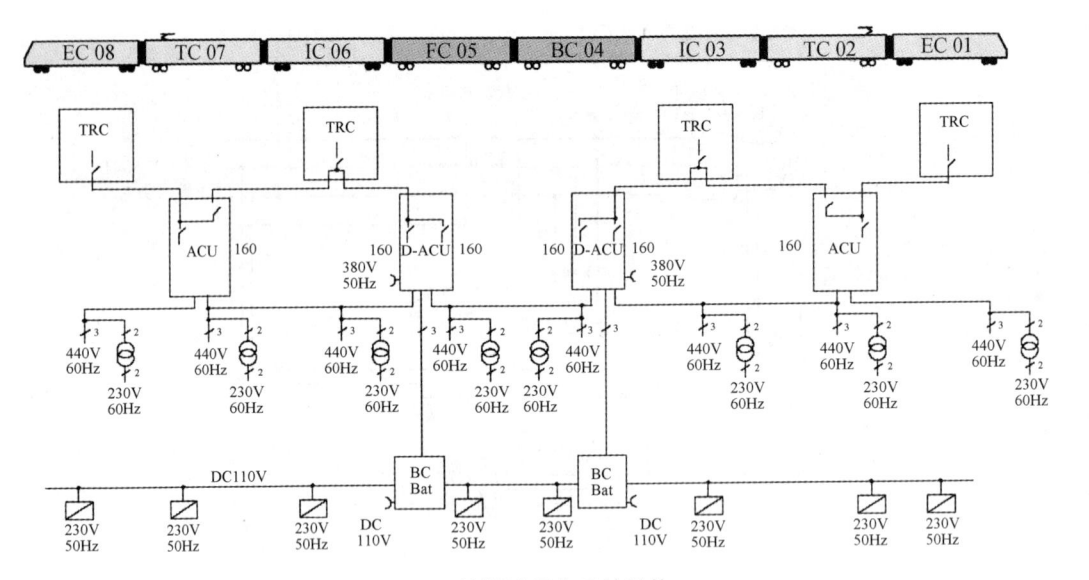

图 5-1-9　CRH$_3$ 的辅助供电系统结构

任务二　辅助电源电路分析

【任务描述】

本任务主要分析 CRH$_2$、CRH380A 型动车组辅助电源电路，通过学习，学生应掌握动车组辅助电源主电路结构，会分析交直流供电原理，为以后从事动车组检修工作打下基础。

【背景知识】

一、辅助供电系统概述

CRH$_2$ 动车组由 8 辆车组成，其中 4 辆动车 4 辆拖车，首尾车辆设有司机室，可双向驾驶，编组配置如图 5-2-1 所示。

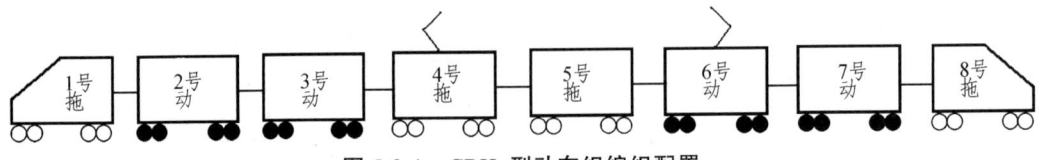

图 5-2-1　CRH$_2$ 型动车组编组配置

辅助供电系统由牵引变压器辅助绕组、辅助电源装置、蓄电池、辅助及控制用电设备、

地面电源等几部分组成。辅助电源装置由辅助电源箱（APU）和辅助整流器箱（ARF）两部分构成。其中辅助及控制用电设备包括各种交流及直流用电设备。

动车组的 M1-2、M3-4、M5-6 号车分别安装有 1 台牵引变压器 MTr；T1c-1、T2c-8 号车分别安装有 1 组辅助电源装置；2、4、6 号车分别安装有 1 组蓄电池组；M2-2、M2-6 号车车体侧面分别安装一个外部电源插座；所有车厢上安装有各种辅助及控制用电设备。

CRH_2 车组辅助供电系统由牵引变压器 3 次辅助绕组提供电源，采用干线供电方式，按各电源系统贯穿全列车。和牵引变压器 3 次线圈直接连接的系统有空调装置、换气装置以及 ATP 主控电源。辅助电源装置（APU）的输入为 AC 400 V，该设备作为电源向 5 个系统提供电源，分别为非稳定单相 AC 100 V 系统、稳定单相 AC 100 V 系统、稳定单相 AC220 V 系统、稳定三相 AC 400 V 系统、DC 100 V 系统。

辅助供电系统采用冗余设计，在动车组上安装 2 台牵引变压器，其辅助绕组输出至辅助电源装置（APU）的 AC 400 V 电压分别供电给 4 节车厢。当一台牵引变压器故障时，为了使另一台正常运转，牵引变压器能够通过辅助绕组向 8 节车厢供电，设置了用于切换的辅助绕组电源感应回路。当辅助绕组电源切换后，空调装置半功率运行。相邻单元具有相互支援功能，在动车组上安装 2 台辅助电源装置，一台辅助电源装置供给 4 节车厢所需辅助用电。当一台辅助电源装置发生故障时，为了使另一台正常运转的辅助电源装置能够向 8 节车厢供电，设置了用于切换的扩展供电回路。辅助电源装置输出容量的设计能够在故障时用一台正常运转的辅助电源装置向整列车供电。因此，当一台辅助电源装置故障时无须减少负荷。

辅助系统设有完善的安全接地措施以及自诊断功能和故障保护功能。在列车信息控制系统和辅助电源装置之间设置自诊断功能接口，由列车信息控制系统实施。

动车组车外车体侧面装有连接外部电源的插座（AC 400 V、单相、50 Hz），M2 车（2 号车及 6 号车）上各有一处。车辆检修基地设置有外部电源，可供辅助电路的工作。

二、辅助电源主电路结构

辅助电源由辅助电源装置（APU）和辅助整流器（ARF）两个装置组成，如图 5-2-2 所示，图中上方虚线框内是辅助电源装置的功能方块图，下方虚线框内是辅助整流器的功能方块图。

APU 各环节的主要作用：

① 输入滤波电路：输入滤波电路降低从电网输入到脉冲整流器及逆变器的高频电流分量。

② IGBT 脉冲整流器：脉冲整流器将牵引变压器输入的单相交流电压变换成稳压的直流电压，控制方式采用脉冲宽度调制方式。

③ DC 中间电路：滤波电容器将稳定的直流电压供给后端的逆变器，当 APU 停止时，滤波电容的放电由 DCHK 和 DCHKR（放电接触器和放电电阻）完成。

④ IGBT 逆变器：逆变器将直流电压变换成为恒压恒频（CVCF）的三相交流电压。

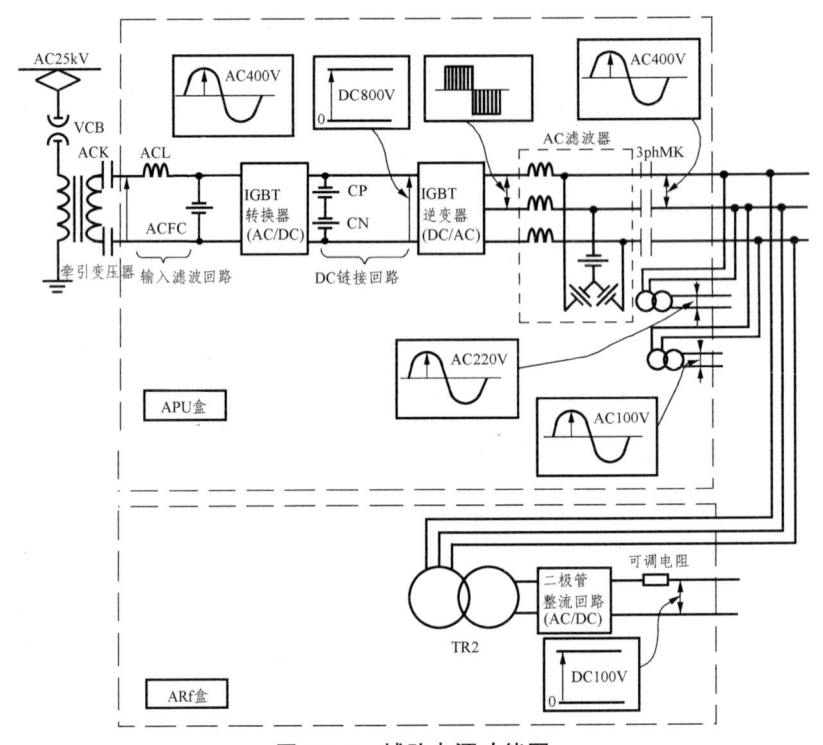

图 5-2-2 辅助电源功能图

⑤ 输出 LC 滤波电路：LC 滤波电路降低逆变器输出电压中由于功率器件的通断所产生的高频电压分量，使其输出畸变较小的正弦波电压。

输出接触器：输出接触器 3 phMK 起接通和切断负载的作用。

ARF 主要由三相变压器（TR2，400 V/78 V）和三相二极管整流桥模块、单相变压器（TR3）、单相变压器（TR4）组成。ARF 的输入电压由辅助电源 APU 输出的三相稳压电源提供。TR2 和三相二极管整流模块输出稳定的 DC 100 V 电压，TR3 输出稳压单相 AC 100 V/50 Hz 电源，TR4 输出稳压单相 AC 220 V/50 Hz 电源。

APU 由 APU 输入辅助整流器、PWM 三相输出逆变器、逆变器输出变压器、CVCF 输出变压器、辅助变压器等构成。辅助整流器柜由整流器变压器、辅助整流器构成。其内部电路结构如图 5-2-3 所示。

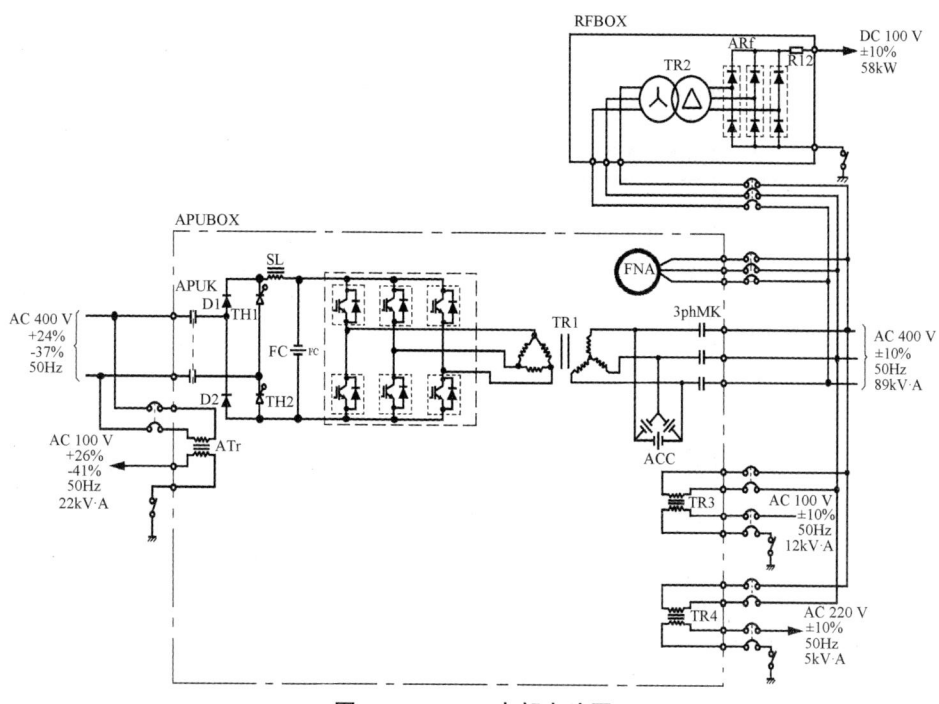

图 5-2-3　APU 内部电路图

三、交直流供电原理分析

1. 交直流供电原理分析概要

CRH380A 型动车组辅助电路电源从安装在 M1-2、M3-4、M5-6 车的牵引变压器 MTr 的 3 次绕组得到。M1-2、M3-4、M5-6 车的牵引变压器的 3 次绕组电源 AC400 V、50 Hz 分别通过电磁接触器 ACK1 被连接到贯穿线 704、754 线系统。设置在 M4-5 车的延长供电用的电磁接触器 ACK2 平时断开，以防止来自 M1-2 号车和 M5-6 号车两个系统的电源的混接触。在两辆先头车辆 T1-1、T2-8 上各设置辅助电源装置（APU）1 台，在 8 辆编组上共设置 2 台，从上述贯穿线 704、754 线系统获得电源。M4-5 号车 APU3 的 772、782、792 在 M3-4、M4-5 号车内独立形成供电干线。

2. 交流电路

表 5-2-1 是按不同电源系统进行电源、电压、各车辆负荷的汇总。辅助电源装置（APU），有供给三相（400±10%）V、50 Hz 的稳定化电源的逆变器（SIV）及仅仅把牵引变压器三次绕组电压进行降压的辅助变压器（ATr）的两种电源。此外，整流器箱（ARF Box）

的内部设置有接受SIV的输出电力，向302线及202线提供单相AC 220 V及AC 100 V(1±10%)、50 Hz 的稳定化电源的恒压变压器（CVT）。辅助电源装置（APU3），仅有供给三相（400±10%）V、50 Hz的稳定化电源的逆变器（SIV）。

表5-2-1　交流电源系统各种电源、车辆各用电设备汇总

电源系统	电源	电压	车辆	负荷
704、754线	牵引变压器辅助绕组	单相400 V，50 Hz	各车	空调装置、换气装置
			T1-1、T2-8 M4-5	辅助电源装置（APU）辅助电源（APU3）
			T1-1、M1-2、M2-3、M3-4、M4-5、M5-6、M6-7、T2-8	电茶炉
771、781、791线	T1c-1、T2c-8 APU-SIV	三相400 V ±10%、50 Hz	M1-2、M5-6 M1-2、M2-3 M5-6、M6-7	变压器油循环泵（MTOPM）变压器电动送风机（MTrBM）牵引变流器电动送风机牵引电动机电动送风机
			M2-3、M6-7	空气压缩机
			T1-1、T2-8	辅助整流器（ARF）
302线	T1-1、T2-8 APU-CVT	单相220 V ±10%、50 Hz	M4-5（餐车）	厨房设备
			各车	插座
202线	T1-1、T2c-8 APU-Arf-CVT	单相100 V ±10%、50 Hz	各车	空调控制、显示设定器
			T1-1、M1-2、M2-3、M3-4、M4-5、M5-6、M6-7、T2-8	给水装置
			T1-1、T2-8	辅助制动
251线	T1-1、T2-8 APU-Atr	单相100 V +26%，−41%、50 Hz	各车	电加热

上述内容中，704、754线系统，771、781、791线三相电源系统及302线系统，在一侧电源发生故障时，为了能够实现扩展供电，在M4-5车设置电磁接触器ACK2，在M3-4车设置BKK。为了避免与来自M1-2车及M5-6车的电源发生混接，正常时这些电磁接触器均处于断开位。

2. 直流供电回路

表5-2-2是直流电源系统中各种电源、各车辆用电设备的汇总。

表 5-2-2 直流电源系统各种电源、车辆用电设备汇总

电源系统	电 源	电 压	车 辆	负 荷
102 线	M1-2、M4-5、M6-7 蓄电池（Bat）、103 线（BatK1，ON 时）	DC 100 V +10%、-10%	T1-1、T2-8	运转控制（含受电弓升弓、VCB 控制）
			M3-4、M5-6	辅助空气压缩机 蓄电池
103 线	T1-1、T2-8 ARF	DC 100（1±10%）V	各 车	辅助电路、监控装置、制动装置、关车门装置
			M1-2、M2-3、M3-4、M4-5、M5-6、M6-7	牵引变流器控制
			T1c-1、T2c-8	ATP
			T2c-8	列车无线用 专用蓄电池
103B 线	102 线（RrLpCgK，ON 时）、103 线（RrLpCgK，OFF 时）	DC 100（1±10%）V	各 车	广播、应急灯
			T1-1、M1-2、M2-3、M3-4、M5-6、M6-7、T2-8	污物处理装置
			M4-5	自动广播
			T1-1、T2-8	标志灯、摘挂装置、刮雨器装置
115 线	103 线（BatK2 ON 时）	DC 100（1±10%）V	各 车	空调控制、自动门装置、客室照明、客室（空调）电动送风机

1）102 线系统

102 线系统从蓄电池直接供电，平时被加压，在 BatK1 ON 与 103 线连接时，蓄电池从辅助整流器 ARF 得到浮动充电。当蓄电池电压异常下降时，由电压检测电路检测，BatN2 变为 OFF 状态，阻止蓄电池的过放电。以[T1-1、M1-2]、[M2-3、M3-4]、[M4-5、M5-6]、[M6-7、T2-8] 为单位进行贯穿，没有编组贯穿。

2）103 线系统

103 线整个编组贯穿。动车组最初上电时，没有升起受电弓，APU 没有启动而输出 DC 100 V 电压时，通过蓄电池供电接触器 BatK1 将 102 线与 103 线连接，103 线由蓄电池通过 102 线提供 DC 90 V 的蓄电池电压。当完成升起受电弓、闭合 VCB 及启动 APU 等工作后，辅助整流器（ARF）通过接触器 ArfK 向 103 线提供 DC 100 V 的电压。

3）103B 线系统

平时从 103 线供电，应急灯切换接触器 RrLpCgK 平时非励磁，经由它的常闭接点由

103给103B供电,当接触网停电时与应急灯切换联动,经由RrLpCgK的常开接点,由102线供电。103B以各车为单位,没有编组贯穿。

4）115线系统

蓄电池的充电电路确立后,经由ArfK,103线被加压;进而经由BatK2,115线被加压。115线与102线相同没有编组贯穿,而是以蓄电池为单位贯穿。

任务三　辅助电源其他控制电路

【任务描述】

本任务主要介绍直流电源系统、三次电源扩展供电控制、BKK接通控制、APU装置控制。

【背景知识】

一、直流电源系统

1. 蓄电池接触器（BatK1、BatK2）

制动设定器BV（运行—快速）投入,对控制BatK1的105线进行加压。随后制动设定器投入,对继电器（BVR1）加压,由于BVR1的接点关闭,102线对蓄电池用接触器（BatK1）线圈加压。和BVR1的接点并联的有VCB的辅助接点,VCB如果处于投入的状态,即使制动设定器手柄被拔掉,BatK1线圈也会继续加压。

由于BatK1接点的关闭,蓄电池Bat与103线连接,蓄电池通过与103线连接的辅助整流器ARF进行浮动充电。

在蓄电池和102线间插入有蓄电器用辅助接触器BatN2的常闭接点。另与蓄电池并联,连接有蓄电池电压监视用电压表V_1和电压检测电路。当蓄电池电压低于规定值时,电压检测器把内部接点关闭,对蓄电池用辅助接触器继电器BatVDR线圈进行加压;通过关闭BatVDR接点,对蓄电池用辅助接触器BatN2线圈进行加压;通过BatN2接点断开,把蓄电池Bat分开,阻止过放电。确立辅助整流器输出后,114线被加压,蓄电池用接触器BatK2R线圈被加压。由于BatK2R接点的关闭,从102线对BatK2线圈加压,BatK2接点的关闭,使103线和115线连接。

如果和其他编组联挂,按照下图的连接,使联挂编组方的蓄电池控制分并用继电器

JBVR 动作。关闭 JBVR 的常开接点，由 102 线对 BatK1 控制的 105 线加压，对联挂编组方也可以发出 BatK1 投入的指令。

2. 应急灯切换电路

按下应急灯切换开关 RrLpCgS，发出应急灯投入指令，170 线被加压，同时应急灯切换接触器 RrLpCgK 线圈被加压。RrLpCgK 投入后，连接在 103B 线的负荷的供电从 102 线切换到 103 线。

3. 辅助电源装置

电压确立（101 线加压）后，辅助整流器整流装置直流电源接触器用继电器 ARfKR、辅助整流器整流装置直流电源接触器 ARfK 动作，对 103 线加压 DC（1±10%）V。而且，ARfKR 常开接点经由停放用继电器 MLpR1 的常闭接点对 BatK2 控制指令 114 线进行加压。

二、三次电源扩展供电控制

1. 三次电源扩展供电控制概要

M1-2、M5-6 车牵引变压器辅助绕组电源 AC400V、50Hz 通过交流电路用接触器 1（ACK1），连接 704、754 线。M3-4 车上设置的交流电路用接触器 2（ACK2）为防止来自 M1-2 车、M5-6 车两系统的电源的混乱接触，保持不间断打开。当停止使用一方的牵引变压器时，通过监控器的显示器输入 3 次电源感应指令，将 704、754 线在编组中贯穿，可以通过另一方的变压器 3 次绕组来供给电源。M3-4 车牵引变压器辅助绕组电源 AC 400 V、50 Hz 通过交流电路用接触器 1（ACK1），连接 704Z、754Z 线，仅给 5 号车的 APU3 提供电源。

2. 辅助绕组电源感应断开指令

辅助绕组电源感应断开指令从监控器传送到终端装置，通过终端装置、M2 车的辅助绕组扩展供电复位指令继电器（MTCOR-R）被励磁。MTCOR-R 被励磁后，交流电路用接触器投入继电器（ACK2R）被消磁，因此 ACK2 消磁，辅助绕组电源感应电路断开。由于辅助绕组电源感应电路断开，交流电路用接触器投入继电器 1（ACK1R）被励磁，因此 ACK1 投入。但当由外部电源供给电源时，EXR2 的常闭接点处于打开状态，则 ACK1 不能投入。

感应电源断开指令（监控器显示器）→MTCOR-R 励磁→ACK2R 消磁→ACK2 开放（辅助电源感应解除）→ACK1R 励磁→ACK1 投入。

3. 辅助绕组电源感应指令

辅助绕组电源感应指令由监控器传送到终端装置，由终端装置对 M2 车的辅助绕组扩展供电指令继电器（MTCOR）励磁。该 MTCOR 和 ACK1，外部电源用继电器（EXR）以及 VCB 的动作信息被输入到终端装置后，根据逻辑构成，4 号车的 ACK2R 励磁，ACK2 投入。

感应电源指令（监控器显示器）→MTCOR 励磁→ACK1R 消磁→ACK1 断开→ACK2R 励磁→ACK2 投入→辅助电源感应完成。

三、BKK 接通控制

1. BKK 接通控制概要

设置在两辆头车的辅助电源装置（APU）中，当 1 台发生故障时，设在 M3-4 车的 BKK 投入，由此将 771、781、791 线从正常单元感应为异常单元的电路。设置在 M4-5 号车的辅助电源装置（APU3）发生故障时，设置在 APU3 内部的 BKK2 投入，由 T2-8 车的 APU 给 APU3 实施扩展供电。

2. BKK 投入指令

设置在两辆先头车上的 APU 中的任一个输出 BKK 投入信号后，MGFR1 或 MGFR2 消磁，MGFR1 或 MGFR2 的常闭接点处于关闭状态。在这种状态下，BKK 投入指令传送到终端装置上后，由终端装置对 M3-4 车的 BKK 投入继电器（BKKR）励磁，BKKR 的常开接点处于关闭状态，BKK 被投入。设置在 M4-5 号车的辅助电源装置（APU3）发生故障时，输出 BKK2 投入信号，BKK2AR 失电，BKK2AR 的常闭接点处于关闭状态。在这种状态下，BKK2 投入指令传送到终端装置上后，由终端装置对 M4-5 车的 BKK2R 投入继电器（BKK2RR）供电，然后 BKK2R 得电。此时如果两辆头车的 APU 都正常工作，则 MGFR3、MGFR4 的常开接点都处于闭合状态，这样，BKK2 被投入。

四、APU 装置控制

1. APU 装置控制概要

辅助电源装置（APU）的基本单元是由逆变器箱及辅助整流器箱构成。该装置安装在 T1-1 及 T2-8 车体的底下。APU 是给牵引变流器通风机、牵引电机通风机、牵引变压器通风机、压缩机等提供电力的三相交流输出，给辅助电路、监视装置、制动装置、关门装置、牵引变流器控制等提供电力的单相直流输出，给空调控制、显示器、水泵装置、辅助制动等提供电力的单相交流输出的电源装置。

2. 逆变器箱

逆变器由以下几部分构成：将由牵引变流器的辅助（三次）绕组提供的单相交流电力转换成中间直流电力的变频器部分和对被转换后的中间直流电力进行波形整形后形成的三相交流电力的变频器，以及吸收中间直流电力的电压涟波、得到恒压的直流平滑电路（滤波电容器）部分。为了在牵引变流器的辅助（三次）侧与逆变器部分实现绝缘，把变压器（TR1）放入变频器部分的投入侧。另外，在逆变器箱中设置了辅助变压器（ATr），由牵引变流器的辅助（三次）绕组提供的单相交流电力在 ATr 中降压到 AC 100 V，通过 251 线提供给各车。

3. 辅助整流器箱

辅助整流器箱由将逆变器箱供给的三相交流电力转换成单相直流电力的变频器部分和吸收转换后的直流电力的涟波电压，由直流平滑电路部分形成的辅助整流装置和为提供降压后的单相交流电力的变压器构成。由辅助整流装置通过 103 线向各车提供 DC 100 V，TR3、TR4 则分别通过 202 线、302 线向各车提供单相 AC 100 V、AC 220 V。

任务四　开关门控制

【任务描述】

本任务主要分析侧拉门电路、内端拉门电路及残疾人用厕所自动门电路的 3 种门的电路。通过学习，学生应会分析电路的工作过程。

【背景知识】

一、侧拉门电路

1. 关动作

根据乘务员开关的关门指令，通过 103 线，使 142Z 线（一位侧）或 143Z 线（二位侧）被加压，由此，用于关门电磁阀的关门指令继电器（DVCR1：一位侧，DVCR2：二位侧）被励磁。DVCR 被励磁后，用于关门电磁阀的继电器（DVR11、12、13：一位侧，DVR21、22、23：二位侧）为非励磁。由此，DVR11、31（一位侧）或 DVR21、41 的接点被打开，关门电磁阀 DV11、31（一位侧）或 DV21、41（二位侧）变为非励磁，门被关上。在关门状态下（DIRR 励磁），速度达到 30 km/h 时，压紧电磁阀 DV12、32（一位侧）或 DV22、42（二位侧）被励磁，按压气缸把门压紧保持气密。

2. 开动作

根据乘务员开关的关门指令，142 线（一位侧）或 143 线（二位侧）被加压，由此，用于关门电磁阀的打开指令继电器（DVOR1：一位侧，DVOR2：二位侧）被励磁。DVOR被励磁后，用于关门电磁阀的继电器（DVR11、12、13：一位侧，DVR2122、23：二位侧）被励磁。关门压紧检测继电器（DPSR1、3：一位侧，DPSR2、4：一位侧）变为非励磁，当速度在 30km/h 以下（30DLR 励磁）时，压紧电磁阀变为非励磁，油压被释放，通过内部装有的弹簧，按压气缸得到松缓。由于压紧装置的油压降低，压力开关 PS1、3（一位侧）或 PS3、4（二位侧）的接点被连接，关门电磁阀变为 ON，完成开门动作。并且，以速度 5km/h 作为安全关门的条件，以速度 30km/h 作为按压动作的条件。

3. 车侧灯

根据关门开关（DS1、3：一位侧，DS2、4：二位侧）来检测门的开关状态，由于关门开关的接点为关（关门状态），关门连动辅助继电器（DIRR11、12、31、32：一位侧，DIRR21、22、41、42：二位侧）被励磁。关门连动辅助继电器被励磁后，作为车侧灯亮灯条件的 DIRR 接点变为打开，车侧灯灭灯。

4. 上下车门语音控制装置

伴随关门电磁阀继电器的动作，侧拉门开关时，从扬声器发出声音。在一位侧、二位侧分别设有扬声器，进行开关一侧能够自动识别。

5. 内端拉门电路

通过设在客室侧、台侧的光线感应开关，把信号输入自动门开关装置（ADCD）后，内端拉门进行开和关的动作。

二、残疾人用厕所自动门的电路

残疾人用厕所自动门装置设置在 M3-4，通过操作厕所自动门的开关（LvDOS/LvDCS），进行厕所自动门的开关动作。

三、连接图各个条件的说明（侧拉门电路）

1. DVOR、DVCR 条件

在 DVS＊开关"开"的位置，若满足以下的条件，各个继电器将励磁（见图 5-4-1）：
若将 DVS＊的打开开关变为 ON，则 DVOR＊将励磁；

若将DVS＊的关闭开关变为ON，则DVCR＊将励磁。

（＊=1：一位侧，＊=2：二位侧）

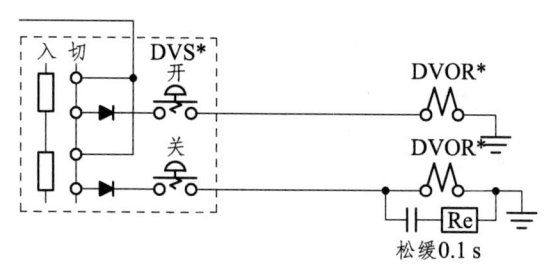

图5-4-1　DVOR、DVCR条件

2. DVR条件

若满足以下的条件，则DVR的各个继电器将励磁（见图5-4-2）。

条件：①∩②∩③∩④

① DVCR＊为非励磁：参照1 OVOR、OCVR条件。

② DVOR＊励磁：参照1 OVOR、OCVR条件。

③ 5DLR 为非励磁：速度在5 km/h以下。

④ DICOS＊为OFF。

（＊=1：一位侧，＊=2：二位侧）

※DVR＊1 被励磁后，①、③、④将进行自保直至其中的任意一个打开为止。

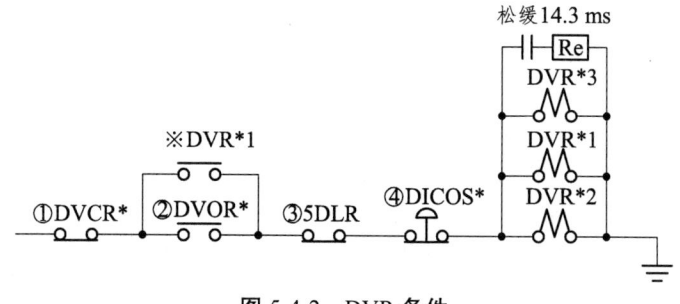

图5-4-2　DVR条件

3. DPSR条件

若满足以下条件，则DPSR#将励磁（见图5-4-3）。

条件：①∩②

① DVR＊2 为非励磁：参照2 DVR条件。

② PS#的常闭接点在接通的位置。

（＊=1：一位侧，＊=2：二位侧。#=1~4：门1~4）

①DVR*2　②PS#　　　　　　　DPSR*

图 5-4-3　DPSR 条件

4. DV#1 条件（关门用电磁阀）

若满足以下条件，则 DV#1 将动作（励磁）（图 5-4-4）。

条件：①∩②

① DVR*1 励磁：参照（2）。

② PS# 的常开接点在接通的位置。

（*=1：一位侧，*=2：二位侧，#=1~4：门 1~4）

①DVR*1　②PS#　　　　　　　DV#1

图 5-4-4　DV#1 条件

5. DV#2 条件（门压紧电磁阀）

若满足以下条件，则 DV#2 将动作（励磁）（见图 5-4-5）。

条件：①∪（②∩③）

① DPSR# 励磁：参照（3）。

② 30DLR 为非励磁：速度在 30 km/h 以上。

③ DIRR#1 励磁：参照（6）。

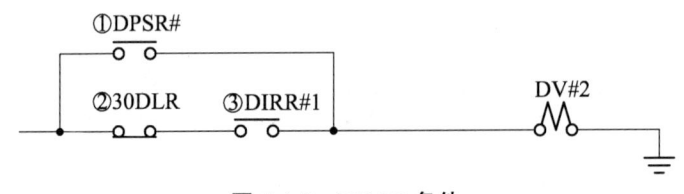

（#=1~4：门 1~4）

①DPSR#
②30DLR　③DIRR#1　　DV#2

图 5-4-5　DV#2 条件

6. DIRR 条件

若满足以下条件，DIRR 将励磁（见图 5-4-6）。

DS# 为 ON：门#为关闭状态。

（#=1~4：门 1~4）

图 5-4-6　DIRR 条件

7. 车侧灯条件

若满足以下条件，则车侧灯＊将亮灯（图 5-4-7）。

条件：①∪②

① DIRR＊2 为非励磁：参照 6 DIRR 条件。

② DIRR&2 为非励磁：参照 6 DIRR 条件。

图 5-4-7　车侧灯条件

8. 33COR 条件

若满足以下条件，则 33X 线将加压，33COR 进行励磁（图 5-4-8）：
DLS 为 ON。

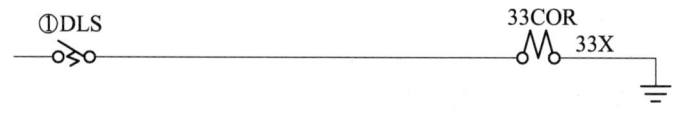

图 5-4-8　33COR 条件

9. 30DLR 条件

若满足以下条件，则 33 线加压，且 30DLR 将励磁（图 5-4-9）。

条件：①∩②

① 30SR 励磁：速度为 30 km/h 以下。

② 33COR 为非励磁：参照 8 SSCOR 条件。

图 5-4-9　30DLR 条件

10. 5DLR 条件

若满足以下条件，则 146 线加压，5DLR 进行励磁（图 5-4-10）：

5SR 为非励磁：速度为 5 km/h 以上。

图 5-4-10　5DLR 条件

11. DIR 条件

若满足以下条件，则 144 线加压，DIR 将励磁（图 5-4-11）。

※电源将从 MCR 为非励磁的头车侧开始被贯穿。

条件：{①∪（②∩③）}∩{④∪（⑤∩⑥）}∩⑦　（中间车没有⑦）

① DICOS2 为 ON

② DIRR41 励磁：参照 6 DIRR 条件。

③ DIRR21 励磁：参照 6 DIRR 条件。

④ DICOS2 为 ON。

⑤ DIRR31 励磁：参照 6 DIRR 条件。

⑥ DIRR11 励磁：参照 6 DIRR 条件。

⑦ MCR 励磁：参照运行指令逻辑部分。

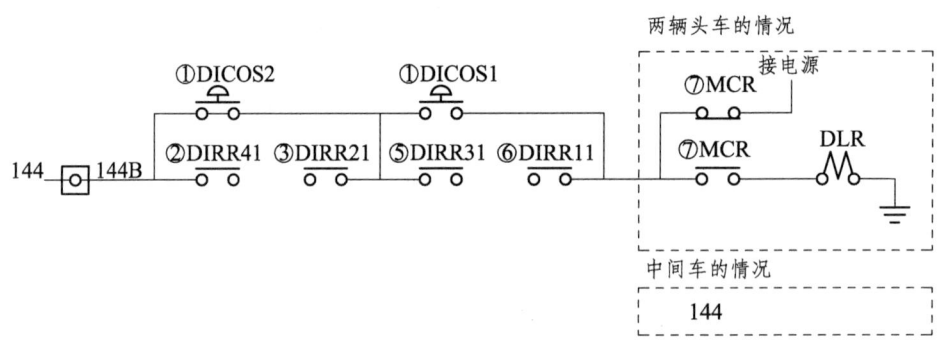

图 5-4-11　DIR 条件

任务五　故障案例分析

【任务描述】

通过对本任务的学习，根据前面已学理论知识积累，学生应能分析故障案例产生原因及处理过程，为从事动车组检修工作、排查电路故障打下基础。

【背景知识】

一、辅助电源装置故障（135）

辅助电源装置故障（135）及其处理过程如表 5-5-1 所示。

表 5-5-1　辅助电源装置故障（135）及其处理过程

现象	本单元 APU 停机，本动力单元所有的辅助电源失电。
车种	CRH380A、CRH380AL
原因	① 负载设备故障导致 APU 输出电压。 ② 负载设备漏电流故障引起 APU 三相输出不平衡。 ③ APU 三相电压 AC 400 V 输出接地。 ④ APU 自身故障。
行车	继续运行
步骤	处理过程
1	当 MON 屏主菜单页面闪现"故障发生信息"提示，并伴有声音报警时，司机触按左下方【故障详情】键，确认故障情况，并通知随车机械师。
2	MON 屏切换至"辅助电源装置 故障（135）"故障信息页面。 2.1 进行 RS 复位。 2.2 若故障消除，正常运行。 2.3 若故障未消除，通知随车机械师。
3	3.1 立即将故障车相应配电盘中的【辅助电源装置控制】断路器断开，15 s 后再投入。 3.2 处理完毕，通知司机。

二、辅助电源装置通风机停止（143）

辅助电源装置通风机停止（143）及其处理过程如表 5-5-2 所示。

表 5-5-2　辅助电源装置通风机停止（143）及其处理过程

现象	此 APU 停机，此动力单元所有的辅助电源失电。
车种	CRH380A、CRH380AL
原因	① 电源线故障、通风机内部故障。 ② 【辅助电源装置】断路器故障。
行车步骤	继续运行
	处理过程
1	当 MON 屏主菜单页面闪现"故障发生信息"提示，并伴有声音报警时，触按左下方【故障详情】键，确认故障情况，并通知随车机械师。
2	MON 屏切换至"辅助电源装置通风机停止（143）"故障信息页面。
3	3.1 立即将故障车相应配电盘中的【辅助电源装置】断路器断开 15 s，再投入。 3.2 处理完毕，通知司机。

续表

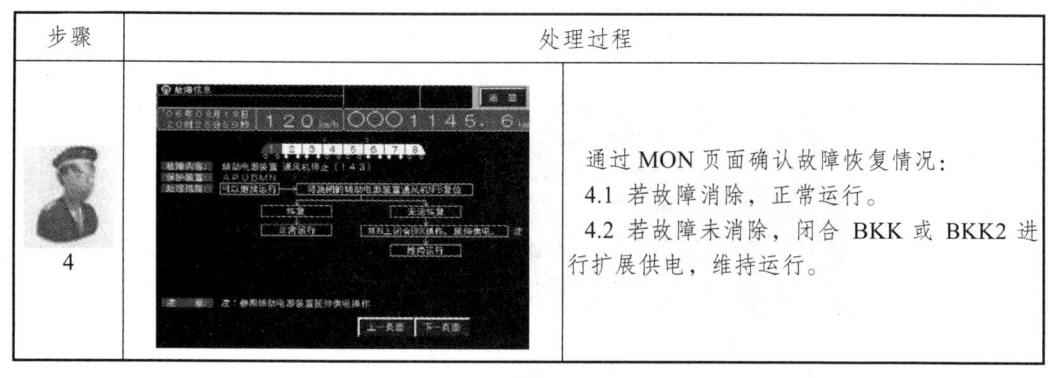

步骤	处理过程
4	通过 MON 页面确认故障恢复情况： 4.1 若故障消除，正常运行。 4.2 若故障未消除，闭合 BKK 或 BKK2 进行扩展供电，维持运行。

三、辅助电源装置 ACVN1 跳闸（146）

辅助电源装置 ACVN1 跳闸（146）及其处理过程如表 5-5-3 所示。

表 5-5-3　辅助电源装置 ACVN1 跳闸（146）及其处理过程

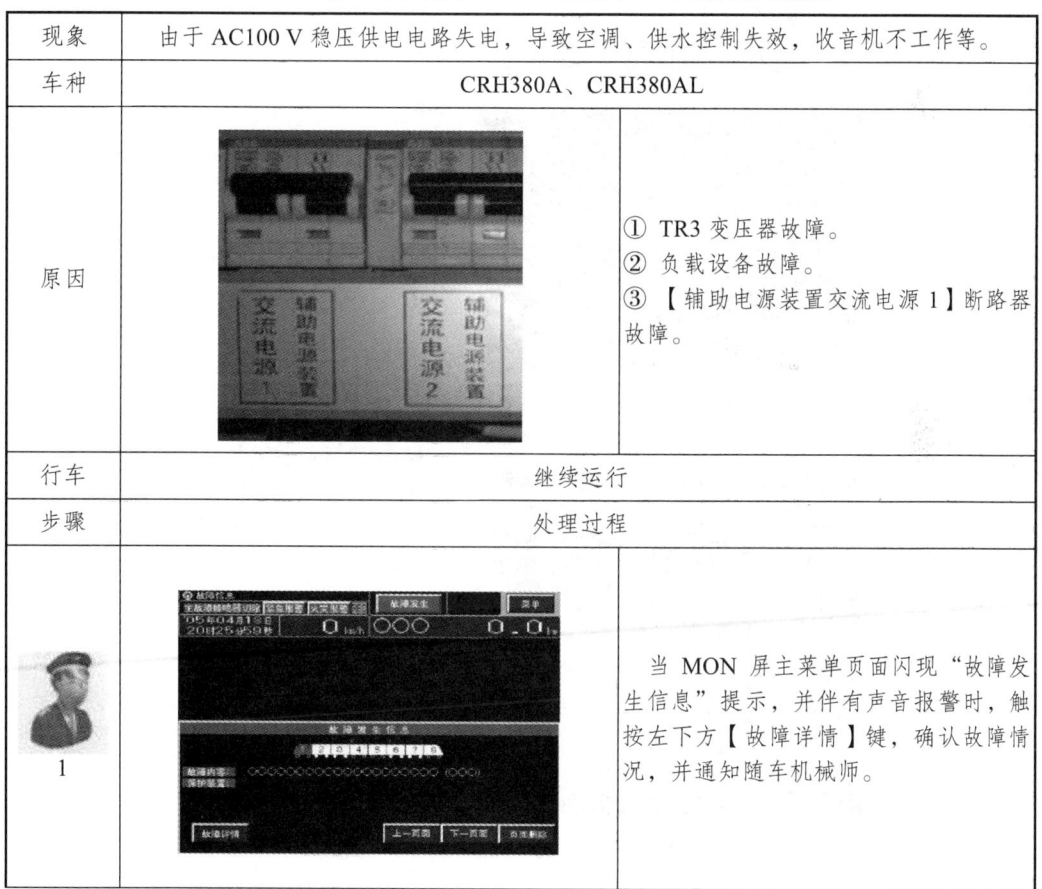

现象	由于 AC100 V 稳压供电电路失电，导致空调、供水控制失效，收音机不工作等。
车种	CRH380A、CRH380AL
原因	① TR3 变压器故障。 ② 负载设备故障。 ③【辅助电源装置交流电源1】断路器故障。
行车	继续运行
步骤	处理过程
1	当 MON 屏主菜单页面闪现"故障发生信息"提示，并伴有声音报警时，触按左下方【故障详情】键，确认故障情况，并通知随车机械师。

275

续表

步骤	处理过程	
2		MON 屏切换至"辅助电源装置 ACVN1 跳闸 146"故障信息页面。
3		3.1 立即将故障相应配电盘中的【辅助电源装置交流电源 1】断路器断开 15 s 再投入。 3.2 处理完毕,通知司机确认。
4		通过 MON 屏确认故障恢复情况: 4.1 若故障消除,正常运行。 4.2 若故障未消除,维持运行,并通知随车机械师。
5		5.1 断开控制单元内各车如下用电设备断路器:空调控制、信息显示设定、给水装置、收音机、辅助制动等。 5.2 先闭合【辅助电源装置交流电源 1】断路器,然后逐一闭合用电设备断路器。 5.3 闭合用电设备断路器过程中,若"辅助电源装置 ACVN1 跳闸"故障再次出现,则断开故障设备断路器。 5.4 重复 5.2、5.3 步操作,直到所有用电设备断路器闭合完毕。 5.5 切除故障设备断路器,闭合【辅助电源装置交流电源 1】断路器,维持运行。

四、辅助电源装置 ACVN2 跳闸（147）

辅助电源装置 ACVN2 跳闸（147）及其处理过程如表 5-5-4 所示。

表 5-5-4　辅助电源装置 ACVN2 跳闸（147）及其处理过程

现象	由于 AC 220 V 供电电路的失电，导致厨房设备、电源插座等失电。
车种	CRH380A、CRH380AL
原因	① TR4 变压器故障； ② 负载设备故障； ③ 断路器故障。
行车	继续运行
步骤	处理过程
1	当 MON 屏主菜单页面闪现"故障发生信息"提示，并伴有声音报警时，司机触按左下方【故障详情】键，确认故障情况，并通知随车机械师。
2	MON 屏切换至"辅助电源装置 ACVN2 跳闸 147"故障信息页面。
3	3.1 随车机械师确认断路器状态，若处于断开位执行第 5 步；若处于闭合位，立即将故障车配电盘中的【辅助电源装置交流电源 2】断路器断开 15 s 再投入。 3.2 处理完毕，通知司机确认。

 4	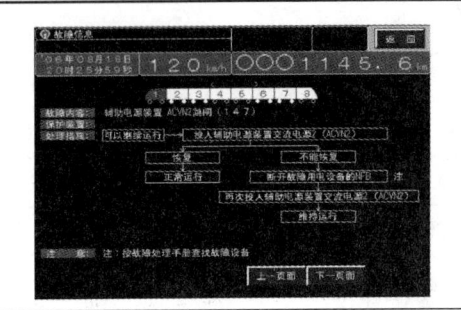	通过 MON 屏确认故障恢复情况： 4.1 若故障消除，正常运行。 4.2 若故障未消除，维持运行，并通知随车机械师。
 5	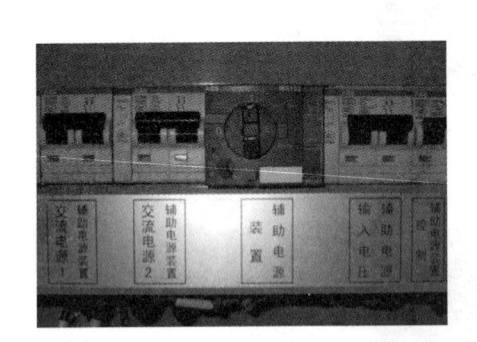	5.1 断开控制单元内各车如下用电设备断路器：05 车（CRH380A）/09 车（CRH380AL）单门展示柜、消毒柜、散热风机、单门冷冻箱以及微波炉插座；01、03、00 车（CRH380AL）微波炉插座等。 5.2 先闭合【辅助电源装置交流电源 2】断路器，然后逐一闭合用电设备断路器。 5.3 在闭合用电设备断路器过程中，若"辅助电源装置 ACVN2 跳闸"故障再次出现，则断开故障用电设备断路器。 5.4 重复 5.2、5.3 步操作，直到所有用电设备断路器闭合完毕。 5.5 切除故障设备断路器，闭合【辅助电源装置交流电源 2】断路器，维持运行。

【项目检测】

1. 简述动车组辅助供电系统的构成。
2. 分析 CRH$_2$ 型动车组牵引变压器和辅助电源的冗余特性。
3. 分析 CRH$_2$/CRH380A 型动车组各路电源系统及对应的负载。
4. 分析 CRH380A 型动车组交直流供电原理。
5. 简述 BKK 扩展供电的工作原理。
6. 试述 CRH380A 型动车组五路电源是怎么变换过来的。
7. 试述 CRH380B 型动车组交流供电回路的工作原理。

参考文献

[1] 中国铁路总公司劳动和卫生部，中国铁路总公司运输局. CRH_{2C} 二阶段、CRH380A（L）动车组机械师[M]. 北京：中国铁道出版社，2015.

[2] 中国铁路总公司高速动车组技术[M]. 北京：中国铁道出版社，2016.

[3] 宋文胜，冯晓云. 电力牵引交流传动控制与调制技术[M]. 北京：科学出版社，2014.

[4] 邱成. 动车辅助电气系统与设备[M]. 北京：北京交通大学出版社，2012.

[5] 冯晓云. 电力牵引交流传动及其控制系统[M]. 北京：高等教育出版社，2009.

[6] 陈坚. 电力电子学——电力电子变换和控制技术[M]. 北京：高等教育出版社，2009.

[7] 李益民，张维. 动车组制动系统[M]. 成都：西南交通大学出版社，2009.

[8] 王月明. 动车组制动技术[M]. 北京：中国铁道出版社，2010.

[9] 郑华熙，高吉磊，郑琼林. 我国高速动车组辅助供电系统的比较与分析[J]. 电气传动，2010（3）.

[10] 李国平. 国内外高速列车辅助供电系统[J]. 机车电传动，2003（5）.

[11] 刘志明，史红梅. 动车组装备[M]. 北京：中国铁道出版社，2007.

[12] 董锡明. 高速动车组工作原理与结构特点[M]. 北京：中国铁道出版社，2007.

[13] 胡学永，邓学寿. CRH_2型 200 km/h 动车组辅助供电系统[J]. 机车电传动，2008（5）.